AA *pocket* World Atlas

GW00356847

AA *pocket*
World
Atlas

Published by arrangement with De Agostini – Rand McNally Limited, Griffin House, 161 Hammersmith Road, London W6 8SD.

A CIP Catalogue record for this book is available from the British Library.

ISBN 0 7495 1982 7

© Instituto Geografico De Agostini 1998

© This edition first published by The Automobile Association 1998

All rights reserved

No part of this publication may be reproduced, stored in a retrieval system, or transmitted in any form or by any means, electronic, electrical, chemical, mechanical, optical, photocopying, recording, or otherwise, without prior written permission.

This book may not be lent, resold, hired out or otherwise disposed of by way of trade in any form of binding or cover other than that in which it is published without the prior consent of the publisher.

The contents of the atlas are believed correct at the time of printing. Nevertheless the publishers cannot accept responsibility for errors or omissions or for changes in details given in this book or for the consequences of any reliance on the information provided by the same.

Published by AA Publishing (a trading name of AA Developments Limited, whose registered office is Norfolk House, Priestley Road, Basingstoke, Hampshire, RG24 9NY. Registered number 1878835).

Printed in the EU, Officine Grafiche De Agostini – Novara 1998

Front cover globe: Mountain High Maps™ Copyright © 1993 Digital Wisdom, Inc.

CONTENTS

WORLD: Key to map pages

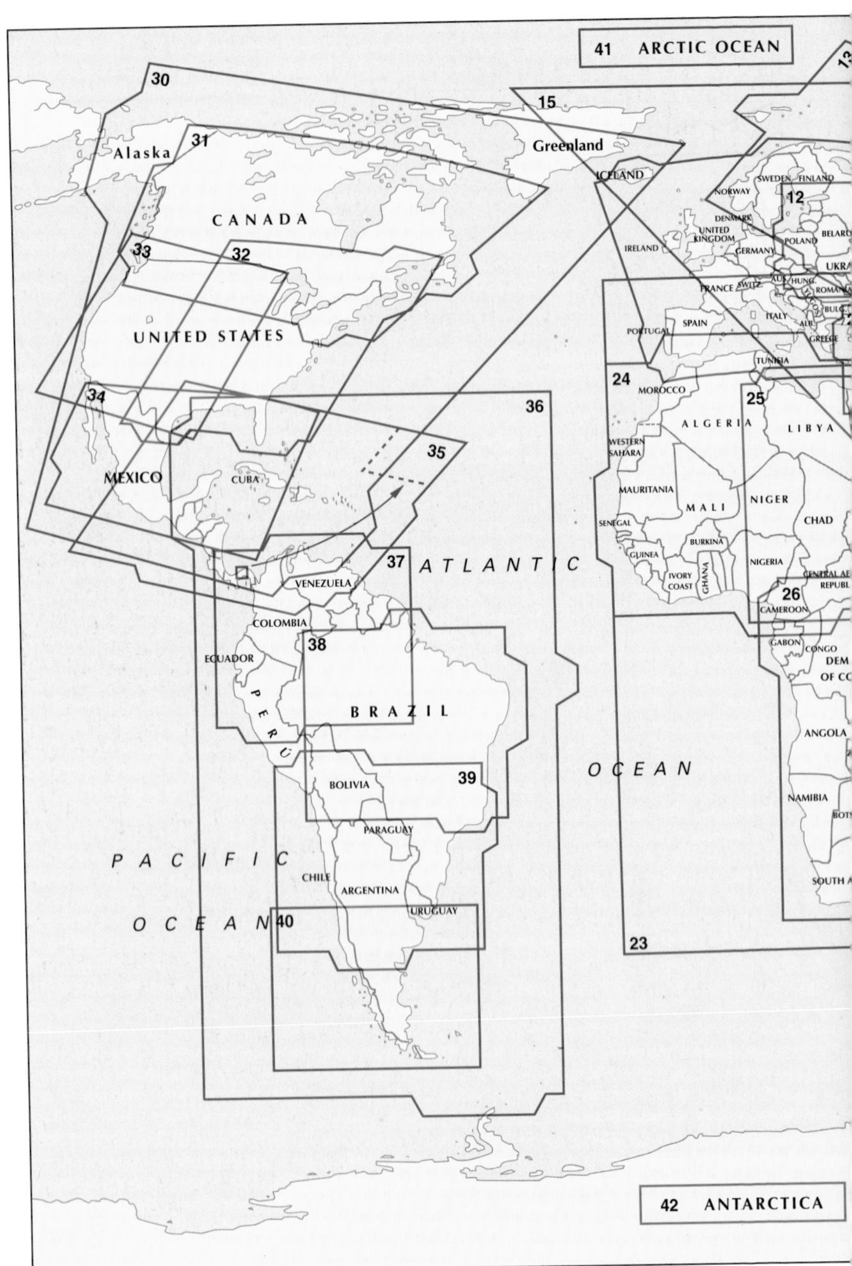

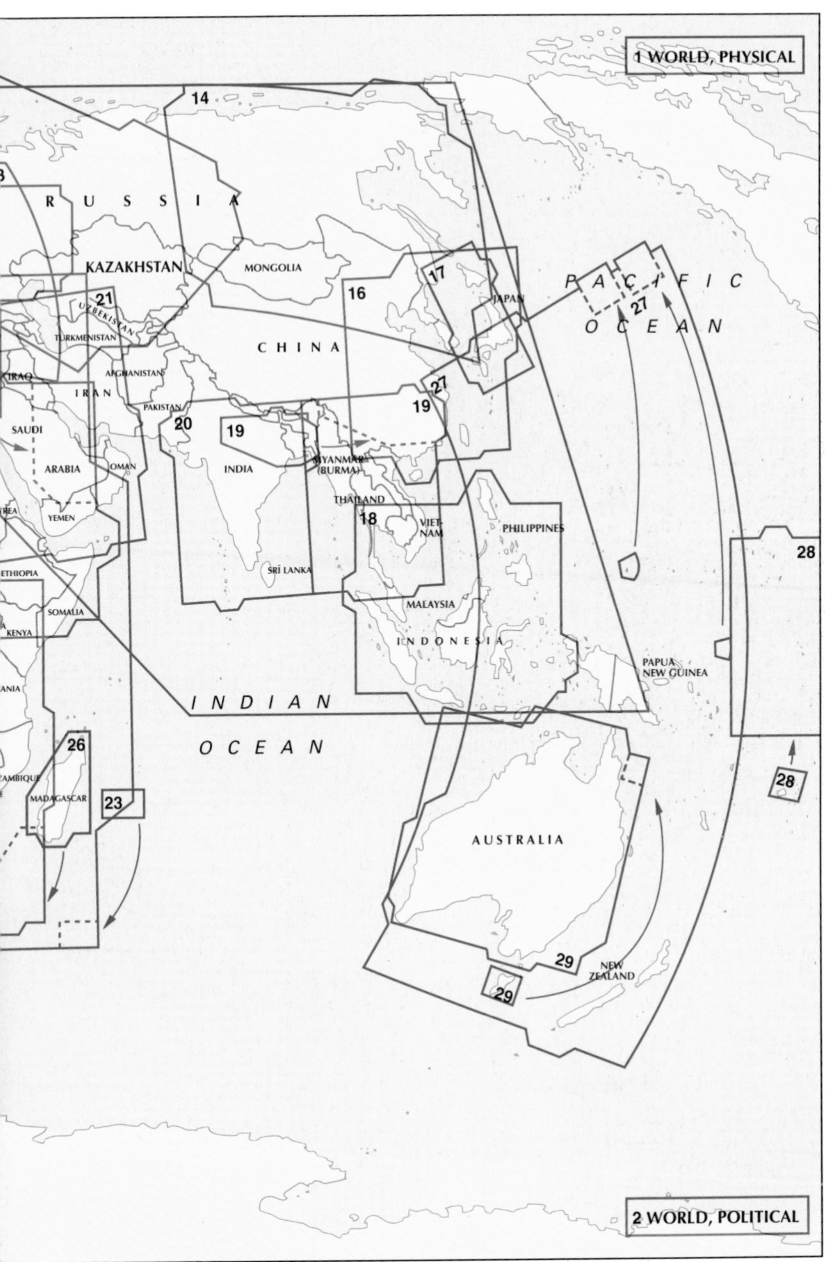
1 WORLD, PHYSICAL
14
RUSSIA
KAZAKHSTAN
MONGOLIA
21
UZBEKISTAN
TURKMENISTAN
16
17
JAPAN
PACIFIC
OCEAN
27
CHINA
AFGHANISTAN
IRAQ
IRAN
PAKISTAN
27
19
20
19
SAUDI
ARABIA
INDIA
OMAN
MYANMAR (BURMA)
THAILAND
YEMEN
18
VIET-NAM
PHILIPPINES
28
ETHIOPIA
SRĪ LANKA
SOMALIA
MALAYSIA
KENYA
INDONESIA
PAPUA NEW GUINEA
INDIAN
OCEAN
26
MADAGASCAR
23
28
AUSTRALIA
29
NEW ZEALAND
29
2 WORLD, POLITICAL

EUROPE: Key to map pages

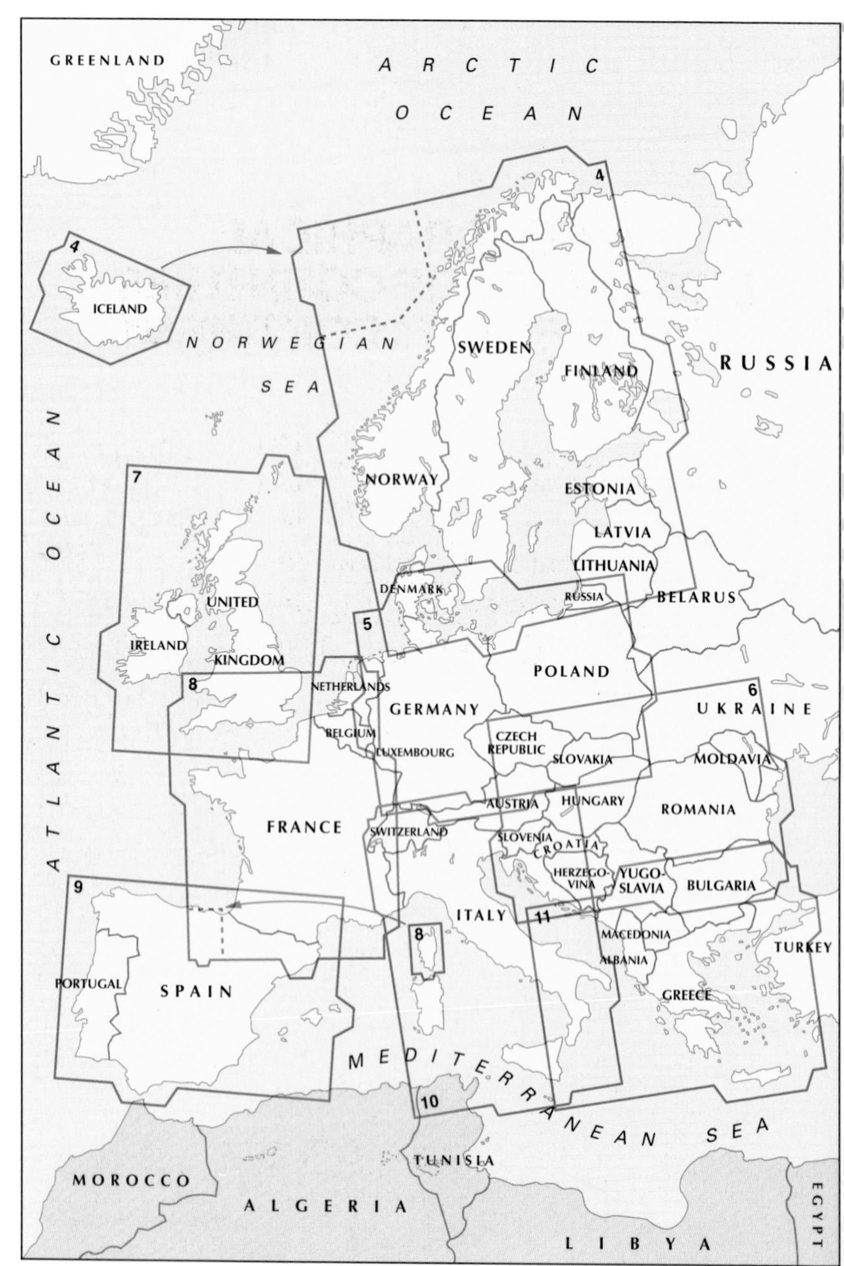

A GEOGRAPHICAL DICTIONARY OF COUNTRIES, CONTINENT BY CONTINENT

STATE (official name/ English translation)	CAPITAL ① inhabitants	AREA (sq km) POPULATION DENSITY (inhab/sq km)			LIFE EXPEC ANCY (in yea M
ALBANIA (Republika e Shqipërisë/ Republic of Albania)	Tirana (Tiranë) 243 000	28 748	3 256 000	113	69.6 7
ANDORRA (Principat d'Andorra/ Principauté d'Andorre/ Principality of Andorra)	Andorra la Vella (Andorre-la-Vieille) 15 600	453	52 000	115	74.0 8
AUSTRIA (Republik Österreich/ Republic of Austria)	Vienna (Wien) 1 533 000	83 859	7 712 000	92	72.1 7
BELGIUM (Koninkrijk België/ Royaume de Belgique/ Kingdom of Belgium)	Brussels (Brussel/Bruxelles) 960 000	30 518	9 950 000	326	70.0
BOSNIA-HERZEGOVINA (Republika Bosnia i Hercegovina)	Sarajevo 526 000	51 129	4 350 000	85	68.0
BULGARIA (Republika Bulgarija/ Republic of Bulgaria)	Sofia (Sofiya) 1 221 000	110 994	8 990 000	81	68.3
CROATIA (Republika Hrvatska/ Republic of Croatia)	Zagreb 763 000	56 538	4 750 000	84	67.0
CZECH REPUBLIC (Ceská Republika)	Prague (Praha) 1 212 000	78 864	10 365 000	131	68.1
DENMARK (Kongeriget Danmark/ Kingdom of Denmark)	Copenhagen (København) 467 000	43 093	5 140 000	119	71.9
ESTONIA (Eesti Vabariik/ Republic of Estonia)	Tallinn 484 000	45 100	1 578 000	35	65.8
FINLAND (Suomen Tasavalta/ Republiken Finland/ Republic of Finland)	Helsinki (Helsingfors) 491 000	338 145	4 986 000	15	70.7
FRANCE (République Française/ French Republic)	Paris 2 152 000	543 965	56 600 000	104	72.7
GERMANY (Bundesrepublik Deutschland/Federal Republic of Germany)	Berlin 3 410 000	356 957	79 479 000	223	72.2

© ISTITUTO GEOGRAFICO DE AGOSTINI S.p.A. · NOVARA

⸱SS ⸱NAL ⸱UCT ⸱	LANGUAGES	RELIGIONS	ECONOMY
740	Albanian (Gheg and Tosc [off.])	Muslim 70%; Orthodox 20%	**Economy** Mainly agriculture (cereals, potatoes, sugar beet, olives, fruit), animal farming and industry (food processing, textile and tobacco production, building materials). **Mineral resources** Substantial reserves of chromite and petroleum.
600	Catalan (off.); Spanish; French	Catholic	**Economy** As a free-trade (duty-free) zone, considerable income is generated by tourism, trade and banking. **Agriculture** Another main economic activity. Cattle and pigs are the chief livestock, cereals, potatoes and tobacco the principal crops.
360	German	Catholic 84%; Protestant 6%	**Industry** Dominates the economy (mechanical, chemical, wood, paper, textile and food production). Tourism is thriving. **Mineral resources** Iron, magnesite, petroleum, lignite, lead. **Agriculture** Almost self-sufficient (cereals, sugar beet).
390	Flemish; French	Catholic	**Economy** Relies mainly on manufacturing. Brussels profits from being the HQ of the EC. **Agriculture** Main crops: cereals, potatoes, beet. Dairy farming is thriving. **Industry** Coal mining and the production of machinery, textiles, chemicals, food, diamonds.
741	Serbo-Croat	Muslim; Christian	**Economy** Based on agriculture (cereals, tobacco, fruit) and animal farming. **Mineral resources** Copper, lead, zinc, gold and iron. **Industry** Mechanical, electronics, chemical, textile and food industries.
320	Bulgarian	Orthodox 80%; Muslim 13%	**Economy** Essentially agricultural (cereals, potatoes, beet, vines, tobacco). Roses are traditionally grown too. **Mineral resources** Coal, iron, copper, lead and zinc. **Industry** The food, mechanical and electronic sectors are well established.
226	Croat	Catholic 76%; Orthodox 11%	**Agriculture** Principal crops: cereals, potatoes, beet, vines, olives. Animal farming is productive. **Principal resources** Timber from the large forests, coal, bauxite, hydrocarbons. **Industry** Mechanical, chemical, food, textiles and wood.
200	Czech	Catholic	**Economy** Dominated by heavy industry, although the country has profited from its considerable timber and coal reserves. **Agriculture** Cereals, hops and beet are cultivated widely. **Industry** Food, textile, mechanical and chemicals.
510	Danish	Protestant	**Agriculture** Animal farming (dairy products, meat) is important to domestic and export markets. Also fishing and arable farming (cereals, potatoes, sugar beet). **Industry** Primarily food, mechanical, chemical and ceramic production.
349	Estonian	Lutheran	**Economy** Dominated by agriculture (cereals, potatoes, animal fodder crops), animal farming (pigs, cattle), forestry and mineral resources (bituminous shale, phosphorites, peat). **Industry** Food processing, wood- and metalworking.
060	Finnish; Swedish	Protestant	**Economy** Dense forestation provides great quantities of timber, much for export, the rest for wood and paper factories. **Agriculture** Dairy farming and fishing are significant. **Industry** Metalworking, shipbuilding and food processing.
830	French	Catholic	**Agriculture** Extensive fishing, arable (cereals, potatoes, beet, grapes for wine) and animal farming. **Principal resources** Coal, petrol, natural gas, timber. **Industry** Food, machinery, vehicles, chemicals, electronics, textiles, fashion, rubber.
750	German	Protestant 41%; Catholic 41%	**Economy** Very strong, notably industry (metals, mechanical, chemicals, electronics) and services. **Agriculture** Main crops: potatoes, cereals, beet, hops for brewing. Animal farming. **Mineral resources** Coal, lignite, potassium salts.

STATE (official name/ English translation)	CAPITAL ① inhabitants	AREA (sq km) POPULATION		DENSITY (inhab/sq km)	L EXF AN (in y M
GREECE (Elliniki Dimokratía/ Hellenic Republic)	**Athens** (Athínai) 885 000	131 957	10 123 000	77	72.2
HUNGARY (Magyar Köztársaság/ Hungarian Republic)	**Budapest** 2 016 000	93 033	10 364 000	111	65.4
ICELAND (Lyðveldið Ísland/ Republic of Iceland)	**Reykjavík** 96 700	102 819	255 000	2	75.7
IRELAND (Poblacht na h'Éireann/ Republic of Ireland)	**Dublin** (Baile Átha Cliath) 503 000	70 283	3 503 000	50	71.0
ITALY (Repubblica Italiana/ Republic of Italy)	**Rome** (Roma) 2 693 000	301 302	56 800 000	187	73.2
LATVIA (Latvija)	**Rīga** 916 000	64 500	2 683 000	41	64.2
LIECHTENSTEIN (Fürstentum Liechtenstein/ Principality of Liechtenstein)	**Vaduz** 4 900	160	29 000	181	66.1
LITHUANIA (Lietuva)	**Vilnius** 582 000	65 200	3 725 000	57	66.9
LUXEMBOURG (Grand-Duché de Luxembourg/Grand Duchy of Luxembourg)	**Luxembourg** 76 000	2 586	381 000	147	70.6
MACEDONIA (Republika Makedonija)	**Skopje** 406 000	25 713	2 030 000	79	68.0
MALTA (Republic of Malta/ Repubblika ta' Malta)	**Valletta** 9 200	316	354 000	1120	73.8
MONACO (Principauté de Monaco/ Principality of Monaco)	**Monaco** 1 234	1.9	30 000	15 789	-
THE NETHERLANDS (Koninkrijk der Nederlanden/Kingdom of the Netherlands)	**Amsterdam** 695 000	41 574	14 893 000	358	73.7

© ISTITUTO GEOGRAFICO DE AGOSTINI S.p.A - NOVARA

GROSS NATIONAL PRODUCT (2)	LANGUAGES	RELIGIONS	ECONOMY
340	Greek	Orthodox	**Agriculture** Important economically. Main crops: cereals, olives, vines, citrus fruits, cotton, tobacco. Livestock and fishing also important. **Industry** Tourism highly profitable; also food processing, petrochemicals, textiles, metals and chemicals.
560	Hungarian	Catholic 64%; Protestant 23%	**Agriculture** Among the major crops are cereals, potatoes, sugar beet and grapes. Animal farming is significant. **Mineral resources** Bauxite, petroleum and coal. **Industry** Machinery, textiles, chemicals and food.
240	Icelandic	Protestant	**Economy** Fishing (cod, herrings) is vital. **Agriculture** Small-scale: the inhospitable climate is most suitable for grazing and sheep rearing. **Industry** Mainly fish storage and processing; hydroelectricity fuels the profitable aluminium-smelting plants.
500	Irish (off.); English	Catholic 93%; Anglican 3%	**Economy** Essentially agricultural, with livestock (sheep and cattle) of primary importance. Main crops: cereals, potatoes and sugar beet. **Principal resources** Peat, zinc and natural gas. **Industry** Food processing, machinery and brewing.
150	Italian	Catholic	**Agriculture** Important to the domestic economy (cereals, olives, vines, citrus fruits, tomatoes, beet). Also animal farming (cattle, pigs) and fishing. **Industry** Cars, machinery, chemicals, food, textiles, clothing and tourism.
176	Lettish	Lutheran; Orthodox	**Economy** Heavily industrialized, specializing in metals, food, electronics, textiles, chemicals and wood. **Agriculture** Of secondary importance. Cereals, potatoes, flax, beet and fodder are the main crops. Also dairy farming and fishing.
000	German	Catholic	**Economy** Dominated by tourism and industry (particularly precision instruments, chemicals, pharmaceutics, food, textiles, ceramics). **Agriculture** Relatively modest. Main crops: cereals, potatoes, vegetables. Main livestock: cattle, pigs, sheep.
796	Lithuanian	Catholic	**Agriculture** Dominates the economy (cereals, potatoes, flax, beet, vegetables). Animal farming and forestry are also important activities. **Industry** Major industries are food, machinery, textiles, wood and chemicals.
860	Letzeburgish; French; German	Catholic	**Agriculture** The leading products are cereals, potatoes and grapes. Animal farming is widespread. **Industry** The most developed sector of the economy, particularly iron and steel, machinery, chemicals, rubber and plastics.
697	Macedonian	Orthodox	**Economy** Industry and mining (of iron, chromite, copper and lignite) predominate. **Agriculture** Main crops: cereals, tobacco, cotton, fruit. Also sheep breeding and forestry. **Industry** Chiefly food, metals, chemicals and textiles.
820	Maltese; English	Catholic	**Agriculture** Cereals, potatoes, vegetables, fruit and flowers. Animal farming and fishing are important. **Industry** Main sectors: clothing, food, electronics, shipbuilding, publishing and tobacco. Tourism is a major source of foreign revenue.
636	French; Monegasque	Catholic	**Economy** Light industry, banking, casinos and tourism are the main sources of revenue. **Industry** Textiles, clothing, electronics, chemicals, pharmaceutics and paper are among the chief manufactured goods.
010	Dutch	Catholic 36%; Protestant 26%	**Agriculture** Main crops: cereals, potatoes, fruit, beet, flowers (tulips, hyacinths). Animal farming and fishing are important. **Mineral resources** Natural gas, petrol. **Industry** Food, chemicals, electronics and rubber are manufactured.

© ISTITUTO GEOGRAFICO DE AGOSTINI S.p.A. - NOVARA

	STATE (official name/ English translation)	CAPITAL ① inhabitants	AREA (sq km)	POPULATION	DENSITY (inhab/sq km)	LIFE EXPECTANCY (in years) M
	NORWAY (Kongeriket Norge/ Kingdom of Norway)	Oslo 461 000	323 878	4 242 000	13	73.3 79
	POLAND (Polska Rzeczpospolita/ Republic of Poland)	Warsaw (Warszawa) 1 656 000	312 683	38 180 000	122	66.8 7
	PORTUGAL (República Portuguesa/ Portuguese Republic)	Lisbon (Lisboa) 830 000	91 191	10 251 000	112	70.6 7
	ROMANIA (România)	Bucharest (Bucureşti) 2 127 000	237 500	23 207 000	98	66.5 7
	SAN MARINO (Serenissima Repubblica di San Marino/Most Serene Republic of San Marino)	San Marino 2 300	60.6	23 000	379	73.2 7
	SLOVAKIA (Slovenská Republika Republic of Slovakia)	Bratislava 441 000	49 036	5 297 000	108	66.9 7
	SLOVENIA (Republika Slovenija Republic of Slovenia)	Ljubljana 267 000	20 251	1 950 000	96	67.0 7
	SPAIN (Reino de España/ Kingdom of Spain)	Madrid 3 121 000	498 507	36 950 000	74	73.6 7
	SWEDEN (Konungariket Sverige/ Kingdom of Sweden)	Stockholm 674 000	449 964	8 559 000	19	74.2 8
	SWITZERLAND (Schweizerische Eidgenossenschaft; Confédération Suisse)	Berne (Bern) 134 000	41 285	6 712 000	162	74.0 8
	UNITED KINGDOM (United Kingdom of Great Britain and Northern Ireland)	London 6 378 000	244 100	55 487 000	227	72.2
	VATICAN CITY (Stato della Città del Vaticano/ State of the Vatican City)		0.44	1 000	—	—
	YUGOSLAVIA (Federativna Republika Jugoslavija/Federal Republic of Yugoslavia)	Belgrade (Beograd) 1 554 000	102 173	10 300 000	101	68.1

© ISTITUTO GEOGRAFICO DE AGOSTINI S.p.A. - NOVARA

SS ONAL UCT)	LANGUAGES	RELIGIONS	ECONOMY
350	Bokmaal; Nynorsk	Protestant	**Agriculture** Main crops: cereals, potatoes. Animals are profitably reared for dairy products (sheep), meat (reindeer), fur. Fishing is a major industry. **Principal resources** Timber, petrol, natural gas. **Industry** Mechanical, chemical and wood-processing.
760	Polish	Catholic	**Agriculture** Main crops: cereals, potatoes, beet, tobacco, flax, hops, hemp. Animal farming and fishing are practiced. **Mineral resources** Coal, lignite, copper, silver, sulphur. **Industry** Iron, steel, machinery, food and textiles are important.
260	Portuguese	Catholic	**Agriculture** Cereals, potatoes, tomatoes and grapes (for prosperous wine industry) are the chief crops. Fishing (sardines). **Principal resources** Cork, pyrethrum and tungsten. **Industry** Textiles, clothes, chemicals and ceramics.
540	Romanian	Orthodox	**Agriculture** Cereals, potatoes, beet, fruit and grapes are the main crops. Animal farming and forestry are important. **Mineral resources** Petroleum, natural gas, lignite, coal, iron. **Industry** Metallurgy, food and chemical production.
590	Italian	Catholic	**Economy** Tourism and the sale of postage stamps are the backbone of the economy. **Agriculture** Principal crops: cereals, grapes and olives. **Industry** Principal products: food, textiles, leather goods, ceramics and other local crafts.
960	Slovak	Catholic	**Agriculture** An important sector of the economy (cereals, potatoes, sugar beet, vines, tobacco). Cattle, pigs and sheep are reared. **Mineral resources** Copper, iron, lead and zinc. **Industry** Food, textile and metal industries.
307	Slovene	Catholic	**Agriculture** Dairy and arable farming (cereals, potatoes, beet, vegetables, fruit). **Principal resources** Timber, iron, lead, zinc, copper, lignite, mercury. **Industry** Iron, steel and textile production, mechanical and chemical engineering.
150	Spanish (Castilian); Catalan; Basque; Galician	Catholic	**Agriculture** Dairy farming and fishing are widespread. Main crops: cereals, grapes, citrus fruits, olives. **Principal resources** Cork, coal. **Industry** Main products: consumer goods, chemicals, food, textiles. Tourism is also important.
710	Swedish	Protestant	**Agriculture** Limited (cereals, potatoes, beet). Animal farming and fishing at a modest level. **Principal resources** Plentiful timber, iron, lead, zinc, copper and hydroelectricity. **Industry** Motor vehicles, machinery, food, paper and wood.
270	German; French; Italian; Romansch	Catholic 48%; Protestant 44%	**Economy** Rich, as a result of its status as an international financial centre and its plentiful hydroelectricity. **Agriculture** Mainly dairy farming. **Industry** Main products: food, textiles, chemicals, pharmaceutics, precision instruments. Tourism.
570	English	Protestant; Catholic 9%	**Agriculture** Mainly dairy farming (sheep, cattle) and fishing. **Mineral resources** Rich reserves of petrol, natural gas, coal. **Industry** Services, banking, tourism and manufacturing (metals, chemicals, food, textiles and bricks).
—	Italian and Latin (both off.)	Catholic	**Economy** The City attracts pilgrims and tourists from all over the world. Its revenue derives from charitable donations and income from investments.
490	Serbo-Croat	Orthodox	**Economy** Agriculture-based, with cereals, tobacco, fruit and grapes among the main crops. Animal farming and forestry are profitable. **Industry** Major concerns are machinery, textiles, food and paper.

© ISTITUTO GEOGRAFICO DE AGOSTINI S.p.A. - NOVARA

STATE (official name/ English translation)	CAPITAL ① inhabitants	AREA (sq km)	POPULATION	DENSITY (inhab/sq km)	L EXP AN (in y M
ARMENIA (Haikakan Hanrapetoutioun)	**Jerevan** 1 199 000	29 800	3 335 000	112	69.0
AZERBAIJAN (Republik Azarbaijchan)	**Baku** 1 150 000	86 600	7 134 000	82	66.6
BELARUS (BYELORUSSIA) (Respublika Belarus)	**Minsk** (Mensk) 1 589 000	207 600	10 260 000	49	66.8
GEORGIA (Sakartvelos Respublika/ Republic of Georgia)	**Tbilisi** 1 260 000	69 700	5 460 000	78	63.9
KAZAKHSTAN (Kazak Respublikasy)	**Akmola** 280 200	2 717 300	16 740 000	6	63.9
KYRGYZSTAN (Kyrgyz Respublikasy)	**Bishkek** (Biškek) 616 000	198 500	4 394 000	22	64.3
MOLDOVA (Republika Moldovenească)	**Chişinău** 665 000	33 700	4 362 000	129	65.5
RUSSIA (Rossiya/Rossiyskaya Federativnaya Respublika)	**Moscow** (Moskva) 8 769 000	17 075 400	148 288 000	8	64.2
TAJIKISTAN (Respublika i Tojikiston)	**Dušhanbe** (Dušanbe) 595 000	143 100	5 303 000	37	66.8
TURKMENISTAN (Türkmenostan)	**Ašgabat** 398 000	488 100	3 668 000	7	61.8
UKRAINE (Ukraïna)	**Kiev** (Kyiv) 2 587 000	603 700	51 889 000	86	66.1
UZBEKISTAN (Ozbekiston Respublikasy)	**Taškent** 2 073 000	447 400	20 514 000	46	66.0
CIS (Commonwealth of Independent States)		22 100 900	281 347 000	13	

EUROPE Total   Ⓐ   10 396 569   709 019 000   68

© ISTITUTO GEOGRAFICO DE AGOSTINI S.p.A. - NOVARA

OSS ONAL DUCT ②	LANGUAGES	RELIGIONS	ECONOMY
710	Armenian	Orthodox	**Agriculture** Chief crops are wheat, potatoes, vegetables, fruit, grapes, cotton and tobacco. Livestock includes cattle, sheep and goats. **Industry** Metalwork, machinery, chemicals, food and bricks.
750	Azerbaijani	Muslim (Shiite 75%; Sunni 25%)	**Economy** Depends mainly on its reserves of oil (plus natural gas) and manufacturing (machinery, chemicals, petrochemicals). **Agriculture** Arable (cereals, cotton, tobacco, tea, grapes, fruit) and animal farming are significant.
960	Belarussian	Orthodox; Catholic	**Economy** Based on agriculture (cereals, potatoes, sugar beet, vegetables, fruit, flax), animal farming (cattle, pigs) and industry (metals, electronics, chemicals, food, textiles).
410	Georgian	Orthodox	**Agriculture** Cereals, citrus fruits, grapes, tea, flowers and tobacco. Animals are kept for meat and wool. **Principal resources** Manganese ore, hydroelectricity. **Industry** Developing rapidly. Main products: metals, chemicals and bricks.
720	Kazakh	Muslim (Sunni); Orthodox	**Economy** Plentiful resources (coal, petrol, iron, natural gas, tungsten, copper, lead, zinc) aid industrial growth (metals, chemicals, textiles). **Agriculture** Animal farming; much of the population grows crops (cereals, cotton, sugar beet).
030	Kyrgyz	Muslim (Sunni); Orthodox	**Agriculture** Cereals, potatoes, sugar beet and fruit are the principal crops, with sheep, goats and cattle the main livestock. **Industry** Textiles, tanning, metallurgy, machinery, electronics, mining (coal, uranium).
830	Romanian	Orthodox	**Agriculture** Arable farming – cereals, potatoes, beet, fruit, grapes (for wine), vegetables, sunflower seeds – and animal herding are vital to the economy. **Industry** The major products are machinery, textiles, chemicals and processed food.
310	Russian	Orthodox	**Economy** Owing to abundant resources (hydrocarbons, combustibles, timber, minerals) all industrial sectors are highly developed. **Agriculture** Large-scale. Main crops: cereals, potatoes. Animal farming and fishing are also practiced.
340	Tajik	Muslim (Sunni)	**Agriculture** The main products are cotton, vegetables, fruit and seeds. Sheep, goats and cattle are raised. **Mineral resources** Uranium, gold, iron and lead. **Industry** Concentrates on food and textiles (carpets).
370	Turkmen	Muslim (Sunni)	**Agriculture** Cotton is one of the chief exports; animal breeding (especially karakul sheep) is also important. **Principal resources** Plentiful petroleum and natural gas. **Industry** Machinery, textiles (especially carpets) and petrochemicals.
700	Ukrainian	Christian	**Agriculture** Animal and arable farming (cereals, potatoes, sunflower seeds, beet) are widespread. **Economy** Rich deposits of minerals (coal, iron) have helped the development of the iron and steel, mechanical and chemical industries.
750	Uzbek	Muslim (Sunni)	**Agriculture** Cotton, cereals, vegetables and fruit are the main crops, sheep and goats the main livestock. **Mineral resources** Large reserves of natural gas, petrol, coal, lead, zinc and gold. **Industry** Machinery-building and chemicals.

ludes the Azores Is (Portugal), Asian Greek Islands, e European parts of Turkey and the CIS; excludes Canary Is (Spain) and Madeira (Portugal).

① The local form is given in brackets only when it differs from the English form

② Per inhabitant, in US$.

© ISTITUTO GEOGRAFICO DE AGOSTINI S.p.A. - NOVARA

STATE (official name/ English translation)	CAPITAL ① inhabitants	AREA (sq km)	POPULATION	DENSITY (inhab/sq km)	LIFE EXPECT ANI (in yei M
AFGHANISTAN (Da Afghānistān Jamhuriat Republic of Afghanistan)	Kābul 1 424 000	652 225	16 922 000	26	41.0
BAHRAIN (Dawlat al-Baḥrain)	Manama (Al Manāmah) 151 500	678	516 000	761	71.0
BANGLADESH (Gana Praja Tantri Bangladesh/People's Republic of Bangladesh)	Dhaka 6 105 000	143 998	105 000 000	729	56.9
BHUTAN (Druk-Yul/ Realm of the Dragon)	Thimphu 30 000	47 000	1 476 000	31	49.2
BRUNEI (Negara Brunei Darussalam/Sultanate of Brunei)	Bandar Seri Begawan 55 100	5 765	264 000	46	72.6
CAMBODIA (Roat Kâmpŭchéa/ State of Cambodia)	Phnom Penh 564 000	181 035	8 781 000	48	47.0
CHINA (Zhonghua Renmin Gongheguo/People's Republic of China)	Peking (Beijing) 5 770 000	9 536 499	1155 790 000	121	68.4
CYPRUS (Kypriakí Dimokratía/ Kibris Cumhuriyeti/ Republic of Cyprus)	Nicosia 187 000	9 251	710 000	77	73.9
INDIA (Bhārat Juktarashtra/ Republic of India)	Delhi 294 000	3 287 782	849 638 000	258	58.1
INDONESIA (Republik Indonesia/ Republic of Indonesia)	Jakarta 7 829 000	1 529 072	180 910 000	118	58.5
IRAN (Jomhurī-e- Islāmī-e-Irān/ Islamic Republic of Iran)	Tehrān 6 620 000	1 648 196	56 250 000	34	64.0
IRAQ (Al Jumhūrīya al-'Irāqīya/ Republic of Iraq)	Baghdād 3 844 600	434 128	17 903 000	41	63.0
ISRAEL (Medinat Yisra'el/ State of Israel)	Jerusalem 524 000	20 700	4 975 000	240	74.5
JAPAN (Nihon or Nippon/ Land of the Rising Sun)	Tōkyō 8 163 000	372 819	123 921 000	332	75.9

© ISTITUTO GEOGRAFICO DE AGOSTINI S.p.A. - NOVARA

GROSS NATIONAL PRODUCT ②	LANGUAGES	RELIGIONS	ECONOMY
160	Dari; Pushto	Muslim (Sunni) 80%	**Economy** Mainly agricultural (cereal crops); cotton is widely cultivated for the textile industry. Animal farming is the basic livelihood of nomads. **Mineral resources** Rich, under-exploited reserves of natural gas and iron ore.
6910	Arabic	Muslim 85%	**Economy** Relies on petroleum, refined locally for export. An important financial centre. **Industry** Booming, particularly food, cement, chemicals, aluminium. **Agriculture** Fishing (fish, pearls) and agriculture are the traditional activities.
220	Bengali (off.); English	Muslim 86.6%; Hindu 12.1%	**Economy** Agriculture-based. Rice is the main crop, followed by jute, tea, sugar-cane, cotton and tobacco. Animal farming is widespread and fishing is important. **Industry** Food processing and textile manufacturing are developing.
180	Dzongkha	Buddhist; Hindu	**Economy** Extremely poor. Agriculture (cereals, potatoes, fruit), stock-raising (mainly cattle, then pigs, sheep and goats) and lumbering (firewood) employ virtually the whole population of this rural country. Local crafts are exported.
7 860	Malay; English; Chinese	Muslim 63%; Buddhist 14%	**Economy** Rich reserves of petroleum and natural gas make Brunei one of the wealthiest countries in Asia. **Agriculture** Rice, bananas and citrus fruits; forestry and fishing. **Industry** Chiefly petrochemicals, food, wood and rubber.
200	Khmer (off.); French	Buddhist	**Agriculture** Dominates the economy, especially rice. Fishing and animal farming are traditional livelihoods. Forests are particularly rich (rubber and timber). **Industry** Primarily food processing, textiles, tobacco and mechanical industries.
370	Chinese; Uighur; Tibetan; Mongol	Confucian 19%; Budd. 14%; Mus. 5%; Christ.	**Economy** Essentially agricultural. The largest rice producer in the world. Pig farming, fishing and silk-worm breeding are important. **Principal resources** China is rich in minerals and fuel. **Industry** All sectors are developing rapidly.
8640	Greek; Turkish	Christian; Cypriot 81%; Mus. 19%	**Economy** Based on agriculture (wine, olives, citrus fruits and potatoes). Sheep and goat farming are practiced on a modest scale, as is fishing. **Industry** Principally mineral extraction (of pyrite, chromite, asbestos) and tourism.
330	Hindi (off.); English; Telugu; Bengali; Marathi; Urdu	Hindu 80%; Muslim 11%	**Economy** Agriculture-based. Cereals and rice are the most profitable crops. Livestock are reared extensively, although mainly to meet subsistence needs. Some income raised through fishing and forestry. **Industry** Growing rapidly.
610	Bahasa Indonesia (off.); Javanese	Muslim 87%; Christian 9.6%	**Economy** Almost half the population is involved in agriculture (rice, tea, coffee, sugar-cane, palm-oil, coconuts, tobacco). Second largest rubber producer. **Principal resources** Rich mineral reserves (oil) contribute to developing industry.
2320	Persian (Farsi)	Muslim (Shia)	**Principal resources** Profits from international sales of oil and natural gas are being used to enhance all sectors of the economy. **Industry** The mining, petrochemical, mechanical and textile (carpet) industries are flourishing.
650	Arabic; Kurdish	Muslim (Sunni, Shia)	**Economy** Petroleum is a major source of foreign revenue. **Agriculture** Employs a third of the population, thanks to fertile river basins. Cereals grown for domestic market; dates for export. **Industry** Textiles, chemicals, cement, food, paper.
8330	Hebrew (off.); Arabic	Jewish; Muslim	**Economy** Structurally modern and well organized. All sectors are flourishing, especially agriculture. **Industry** Manufacturing (chemical, mechanical, textiles), mining (diamonds) and tourism are particularly lucrative.
320	Japanese	Shintoist; Buddhist	**Economy** Most industrialized in Asia, third world-wide. All manufacturing sectors well developed (mechanics, electronics, chemicals, textiles and paper). **Agriculture** Mainly rice; fishing is important to domestic and export markets.

© ISTITUTO GEOGRAFICO DE AGOSTINI S.p.A. · NOVARA

STATE (official name/ English translation)	CAPITAL ① inhabitants	AREA (sq km)	POPULATION	DENSITY (inhab/sq km)	LIFE EXPECT-ANCY (in years) M	F
JORDAN (Al Mamlaka al Urdunīyah al Hāshemīyah/Hashemite Kingdom of Jordan)	**Ammān** 936 000	97 740	3 285 000	34	64.2	67
KUWAIT (Dawlat al-Kuwait/ State of Kuwait)	**Kuwait City** 44 400	17 818	2 241 000	126	71.2	75
LAOS (Satharanarath Pasathipatai Pasason Lao/Lao People's Democratic Republic)	**Vientiane** (Viengchane) 377 400	236 800	4 262 000	18	47.8	50
LEBANON (Al-Jumhūrīya al-Lubnānīya)	**Beirut** (Bayrūt) 474 900	10 400	2 965 000	285	65.1	69
MALAYSIA (Persekutuan Tanah Malaysia/ Federation of Malaysia)	**Kuala Lumpur** 1 103 000	329 758	18 239 000	55	68.8	73
THE MALDIVES (Dīvehi Jumhuriya/ Republic of Maldives)	**Malé** 55 100	298	222 000	745	62.2	5
MONGOLIA (Mongol Uls/ Mongolian Republic)	**Ulan Bator** (Ulaanbaatar) 548 000	1 566 500	2 140 000	1	61.2	6
MYANMAR (BURMA) (Pyidaungsu Myanma Naingngandaw/ Union of Myanmar)	**Yangon** (Rangoon) 2 459 000	678 033	42 561 000	63	60.0	6
NEPAL (Nepāl Adhirājya/ Kingdom of Nepal)	**Kathmandu** 393 500	147 181	19 379 000	131	55.4	5
NORTH KOREA (Chosun Minchu-chui Inmin Konghwa-Guk/Democratic People's Republic of Korea)	**P'yŏngyang** 2 639 000	120 538	22 937 000	190	66.2	7
OMAN (Sulṭanat 'Umān/ Sultanate of Oman)	**Muscat** 50 000	212 457	1 559 000	7	62.2	6
PAKISTAN (Islāmi Jamhūrīya e-Pakistān/ Islamic Republic of Pakistan)	**Islāmābād** 204 400	796 095	115 520 000	145	59.3	
PHILIPPINES (Republika ñg Pilipinas/ Republic of the Philippines)	**Manila** 1 599 000	300 000	62 000 000	207	62.5	
QATAR (Dawlat al-Qaṭar/ State of Qatar)	**Doha** (Ad Dawhah) 217 000	11 437	455 000	39	66.9	

© ISTITUTO GEOGRAFICO DE AGOSTINI S.p.A. - NOVARA

GROSS NATIONAL PRODUCT	LANGUAGES	RELIGIONS	ECONOMY
20	Arabic	Muslim	**Economy** Quite poor; the arid soil yields only vegetables, citrus fruits and cereals. **Principal resources** Phosphates and potash (the main export). **Industry** Food processing, chemical, cement and tobacco manufacture.
60	Arabic	Muslim	**Economy** Rich oil reserves make Kuwait one of the world's wealthiest countries. **Agriculture** Fishing is traditionally strong; irrigation is used to expand arable land. **Industry** Chemical, mechanical and cement plants supplied by natural gas.
30	Lao (off.); French	Buddhist	**Economy** The least developed in Indochina. Agriculture, forestry and fresh-water fishing are almost the only economic activities. **Agriculture** Rice is the principal crop. **Industry** Largely limited to the production of local crafts.
50	Arabic (off.); French	Christian 42%; Muslim 29%	**Agriculture** Olives, citrus fruits, grapes, fruit and vegetables are the main yields. Minimal animal farming and fishing. **Industry** The principal employers in this sector are the oil-refineries, cotton-mills, and cigarette and cement factories.
90	Malay (off.); English; Chinese	Mus. 53%; Buddhist; Taoist; Christian	**Agriculture** Mainly rice, coconuts, palm-oil, coffee, tea, pineapples and rubber (of which Malaysia is the world's largest exporter). **Mineral resources** Abundant tin, petrol, bauxite, copper. **Industry** Tourism is being promoted.
60	Dhivehi	Muslim	**Agriculture** The majority of the population is involved in fishing or cultivating coconuts (fish and coconut fibre being the principal exports). Most staple foods have to be imported. **Industry** Tourism is growing rapidly.
73	Mongolian	Buddhist	**Economy** Depends mainly on animal herding (sheep, goats, cattle, horses, camels). Some cereals are cultivated. **Industry** Centres on food processing. **Principal resources** The country has deposits of copper and coal.
00	Birmano (off.); English	Buddhist 88%	**Agriculture** Dominates. Teak and forestry products have replaced rice as the principal export. Crops for industrial use include sugar-cane, tobacco, jute and cotton. **Mineral resources** The country has considerable reserves of oil.
80	Nepali (off.); Bihari	Hindu 89%; Buddhist 5%	**Economy** Dominated by cultivation (cereals, potatoes, jute, sugar-cane, tobacco) and animal farming (yak, cattle, buffalo, goats). **Industry** Small-scale, mainly processing industries. Tourism is flourishing and brings in foreign revenue.
40	Korean	Buddhist; Confucian; Shintoist	**Economy** Dominated by mining (coal, iron, copper, lead). **Industry** Iron and steel production, mechanical and chemical engineering and textile manufacture all well established. **Agriculture** Principal crops are rice, maize and potatoes.
50	Arabic (off.); English	Muslim (Sunni)	**Economy** Depends on the export of petrol and natural gas. Of lesser importance: agriculture (vegetables, fruit, dates), animal farming (goats, sheep), and fishing. **Industry** Metallurgical (copper), petrochemical and cement production.
00	Urdu (nat.); English	Muslim	**Economy** Expanding. **Agriculture** Flourishing, the main crops being cereals, sugar-cane and cotton. Cotton is the principal export, and also supplies a productive textile industry. **Mineral resources** Petroleum, natural gas and coal.
40	Tagalog (Filipino); English	Catholic 84%	**Agriculture** Fundamental to the economy (rice, maize, coconuts, sugar-cane, bananas). Fishing is also important. **Industry** Mining growing rapidly (gold, copper) along with food processing, electronics, chemicals and textiles.
370	Arabic	Muslim (Sunni)	**Economy** Relies on its plentiful reserves of petroleum and natural gas. **Industry** Petrochemicals and cement are the chief industrial products. **Agriculture** Fishing and nomadic animal herding are traditional livelihoods.

© ISTITUTO GEOGRAFICO DE AGOSTINI S.p.A. - NOVARA

STATE (official name/ English translation)	CAPITAL ① inhabitants	AREA (sq km)	POPULATION	DENSITY (inhab/sq km)	LIFE EXPECT ANCY (in year M
SAUDI ARABIA (Al Mamlaka al'Arabīya as-Sa'ūdīya/Kingdom of Saudi Arabia)	Riyadh (Ar Riyād) 1 308 000	2 153 168	15 267 000	7	61.7
SINGAPORE (Republik Singapura/ Republic of Singapore)	Singapore	639	2 763 000	4324	70.3
SOUTH KOREA (Daehan-Minkuk/ Republic of South Korea)	Seoul (Sŏul) 10 628 000	99 237	43 530 000	438	66.9
SRĪ LANKA (Srī Lanka Prajatantrika Samajawadi Janarajaya)	Colombo 615 000	65 610	17 247 000	263	69.1
SYRIA (Al Jumhūrīya al 'Arabīya as Sūrīya)	Damascus (Dimashq) 1 326 000	185 180	12 524 000	67	65.2
TAIWAN (REPUBLIC OF CHINA) (Chung-hua Min Kuo)	Taipei 2 718 000	36 202	20 489 000	566	71.3
THAILAND (Prathet Thai/ Kingdom of Thailand)	Bangkok 5 876 000	513 115	55 884 000	109	63.8
TURKEY (Türkiye Cumhuriyeti/ Republic of Turkey)	Ankara 2 553 000	755 688	51 277 000	69	68.0
UNITED ARAB EMIRATES (Al Imārāt al 'Arabīya al-Muttahida)	Abu Dhabi 243 000	83 600	1 945 000	23	68.6
VIETNAM (Công Hòa Xã Hôi Chu' Nghiã Viêt Nam/Socialist Republic of Vietnam)	Hanoi 1 089 000	329 566	67 589 000	205	63.7
YEMEN (Al-Jumhūrīya al-Yamanīyah/ Republic of Yemen)	San'a 427 000	524 342	11 843 000	22	49.0

ASIA   27 140 550 3 121 179 000 115

ASIA   Total ⒶⒶ   44 032 038 3 210 194 000 73

© ISTITUTO GEOGRAFICO DE AGOSTINI S.p.A. · NOVARA

SS NAL UCT)	LANGUAGES	RELIGIONS	ECONOMY
070	Arabic	Muslim (Sunni)	**Economy** Petroleum is the most valuable resource (Saudi Arabia is the world's third biggest producer of crude oil). **Industry** Mainly petrochemical. Tourism is also flourishing (many pilgrims visit the sacred cities of Mecca and Medina).
390	Chinese; Malay; Tamil; English	Tao. 29%; Bud. 27%; Mus. 16%; Christ. 10%	**Economy** Dominated by industrial sector (electronics, ship-yards, textiles, chemicals, rubber, metallurgical and petro-chemical plants). A major international financial and com-mercial centre, the island also has a thriving fishing industry.
340	Korean (off.)	Budd.40%; Christ. 28%; Conf. 17%	**Agriculture** Mainly rice, potatoes, cotton and tobacco. Also fishing. **Mineral resources** Rich in coal, iron, gold and tungsten. **Industry** Well developed mechanical, electronic, textile and petrochemical sectors .
600	Sinhalese; Tamil (off.); English	Bud. 69%; Hindu 15%; Christ. 7%; Mus. 8%	**Economy** Essentially agricultural (rice, coconuts, tea, cinnamon, coffee). The forests yield caoutchouc. **Industry** Precious stones are mined; textiles, cement, rubber and chemicals are manufactured. Tourism is increasing.
10	Arabic	Muslim (Sunni) 75%; Christ. 10%	**Economy** Based on agriculture (wheat, cotton, grapes, olives, vegetables and fruit). Sheep farming is widespread. **Industry** Mining (petroleum, phosphates), textiles, food, leather, cement and glass industries are all developing.
810	Chinese	Confucian; Buddist	**Agriculture** Well-organized; rice, sugar-cane, tea and sweet potatoes are the main crops. Little animal farming, but fishing is profitable. **Industry** Textiles are the primary pro-duct, plus electronics, machinery, petrochemicals and toys.
580	Thai	Buddist	**Economy** Still fundamentally agricultural: rice, maize, cas-sava and sugar-cane are the chief products. Fishing, forestry (timber, caoutchouc) and mining (tin) are important. Tourism is now the primary foreign exchange earner.
320	Turkish (off.); Kurdish	Muslim	**Agriculture** Employs almost half the population (cereals, cotton, vine, olive, fruit, sugar beet, tobacco). Animal farming is widespread. **Industry** The food, textile, chemical and machinery sectors are expanding; tourism is flourishing.
370	Arabic (off.); English	Muslim 95%	**Economy** One of the wealthiest countries in the world due to extensive on- and off-shore reserves of petroleum and natural gas. Fishing and pearl cultivation are traditional livelihoods. **Industry** Petrochemical, metallurgical and cement.
10	Vietnamese	Buddist; Taoist	**Economy** Much of the work force is employed in cultivating rice. Cassava, sweet potatoes, coconuts, tea and tobacco are also grown. Fishing is important. **Industry** Mining (coal, petrol), metal, food and chemical sectors are well developed.
540	Arabic	Muslim	**Economy** Agriculture (cereals, dates, vegetables, fruit, cot-ton, coffee) and fishing employ most of the population, while sheep, goats and cattle are herded. **Industry** Oil is mined; chemical, textile and cement production is increasing.

cludes Christmas and Cocos Is, Hong Kong, Macao, Sinai
ninsula, Gaza Strip and the Asian parts of the CIS, but
cludes Irian Jaya and Socotra.

① The local form is given in brackets only when it differs from the English form

② Per inhabitant, in US$

© ISTITUTO GEOGRAFICO DE AGOSTINI S.p.A. - NOVARA

AFRICA

STATE (official name/ English translation)	CAPITAL ① inhabitants	AREA (sq km)	POPULATION	DENSITY (inhab/sq km)	LIFE EXPECTANCY (in years) M
ALGERIA (Al Jumhūrīya al Jazā'iriya ad Dīmūqrātīya ash-Sha'bīya)	**Algiers** (Al Jazair) 1 687 600	2 381 741	25 660 000	11	65.0 6:
ANGOLA (República de Angola/ Republic of Angola)	**Luanda** 1 136 000	1 246 700	10 303 000	8	44.9 4:
BENIN (République du Bénin/ Republic of Benin)	**Porto-Novo** 164 000	112 622	4 889 000	43	49.0 5
BOTSWANA (Republic of Botswana)	**Gaborone** 134 000	600 372	1 320 000	2	52.7 5
BURKINA FASO (République de Burkina Faso/ Republic of Burkina Faso)	**Ouagadougou** 442 200	274 200	9 242 000	34	47.6 5
BURUNDI (République du Burundi/ Republika y'Uburundi/ Republic of Burundi)	**Bujumbura** 235 400	27 834	5 600 000	201	50.0 5
CAMEROON (République du Cameroun/ Republic of Cameroon)	**Yaoundé** 653 700	475 442	11 932 000	25	53.5 5
CAPE VERDE (República de Cabo Verde/ Republic of Cape Verde)	**Praia** 61 700	4 033	341 000	84	63.0 6
CENTRAL AFRICAN REPUBLIC (République Centrafricaine)	**Bangui** 597 000	622 436	3 015 000	5	48.0 5
CHAD (République du Tchad/ Republic of Chad)	**N'djamena** 594 000	1 284 000	5 819 000	4	45.9
COMOROS (République Fédérale Islamique des Comores)	**Moroni** 22 000	1 862	481 000	258	54.0
CONGO (République Populaire du Congo/People's Republic of the Congo)	**Brazzaville** 760 000	342 000	2 346 000	7	52.1
DEMOCRATIC REPUBLIC OF CONGO (République Démocratique du Congo)	**Kinshasa** 3 741 000	2 344 885	36 672 000	15	50.3
DJIBOUTI (République de Djibouti/ Jumhūrīya Jībutī/ Republic of Djibouti)	**Djibouti** 220 000	23 200	541 000	23	47.4

GROSS NATIONAL PRODUCT ②	LANGUAGES	RELIGIONS	ECONOMY
2020	Arabic (off.); French; Berber	Muslim	**Agriculture** Supplies processing industry (vines, vegetables, olives, citrus fruit) and satisfies subsistence needs. **Mineral resources** Hydrocarbons. **Industry** Developing gradually; traditional crafts bring in foreign revenue.
620	Portuguese (off.); Bantu languages	Cath. 65%; Animist; Protestant	**Agriculture** One of the country's main economic activities; coffee, cotton, tobacco, palm-oil, sugar-cane and sisal are the principal crops. **Mineral resources** Mining (petroleum, diamonds and iron) generates considerable income.
380	French (off.); Fon; Yoruba; Adja	Animist 63%; Cath. 18%; Mus. 15%	**Agriculture** Dominates the economy. Cereals, cassava, cotton and palm-oil are the main products. Animal farming and fishing are widely practiced. **Industry** Limited to the processing of agricultural goods.
2590	English (off.); Setswana	Animist; Christian 30%	**Economy** Traditionally based on animal farming (especially cattle) and subsistence agriculture (cereals, legumes, groundnuts, citrus fruit). **Principal resources** Diamonds, coal, copper and nickel are the main mineral exports.
350	French (off.); Mossi; Fulani	Animist; Mus. 30%; Christ. 10%	**Economy** Very poor and with few natural resources. **Agriculture** Cereals, sugar-cane and cotton are the only crops of any importance. Cattle rearing is becoming more widespread.
210	French and Kirundi (both off.); Swahili	Cath. 65%; Animist; Protestant	**Economy** Principally agrarian. **Agriculture** The main source of employment. The most important subsistence crops are sweet potatoes and cassava; coffee, tea and cotton are exported.
940	French and English (both off.); Fulani; Sao; Bamileke	Animist 40%; Mus. 22%; Cath. 21%	**Agriculture** A major sector of the domestic economy. Crops include cereals, cocoa, coffee, sugar-cane, palm-oil, cotton and bananas. Forests provide timber and caoutchouc. **Industry** The oil industry is of growing importance.
750	Portuguese (off.); Crioulu	Catholic	**Agriculture** Yields a variety of products, but in quantities insufficient to sustain the local population. **Economy** Export trade is boosted by the production of sea salt and fishing (tuna, lobster).
390	French (off.); Sangho (nat.); Sudanese dialects	Animist 57%; Prot. 15%; Mus. 8%	**Agriculture** Cereals, cassava and bananas are cultivated for domestic consumption; cotton, groundnuts, palm-oil and coffee for export. **Principal resources** Diamonds and gold are sold internationally. **Industry** Largely food processing.
220	French and Arabic (off.); other local languages	Muslim 50%; Animist 44%	**Agriculture** Cotton plantations are a highly profitable part of the economy. Cereal crops are also significant, as is fishing (on Chad's internal rivers and lakes). Animal farming is quite advanced. **Industry** Very limited.
500	French and Arabic (both off.); other local languages	Muslim	**Agriculture** The main economic activity, producing vanilla, cloves, ylang-ylang, copra, coffee, cocoa and bananas for export. Some fishing. **Industry** Generally quite undeveloped although the islands are beginning to attract tourists.
120	French (off.); local languages	Animist 47%; Catholic 38%	**Economy** Oil is a major source of foreign revenue, thanks to reserves of petroleum and natural gas. **Agriculture** Well organized (mainly sugar-cane, coffee, cocoa, palm-oil and cassava); the forests provide timber for export.
220	French (off.); other local dialects	Cath. 48%; Prot. 29%; Animist	**Agriculture** Cassava, rice, maize and bananas are the chief subsistence crops; coffee, cotton, cocoa, tea, caoutchouc and palm-oil are exported. **Mineral resources** Tin, copper, diamonds, petroleum and zinc are mined for export.
600	Arabic and French (both off.); other local languages	Muslim	**Economy** Impoverished, largely as the land is so arid and infertile. Relies mainly on service industries, particularly the capital's port and airport. **Agriculture** Low rainfall restricts agriculture to nomadic animal grazing (sheep, goats, camels).

© ISTITUTO GEOGRAFICO DE AGOSTINI S.p.A. · NOVARA

STATE (official name/ English translation)	CAPITAL ① inhabitants	AREA (sq km)	POPULATION	DENSITY (inhab/sq km)	LIFE EXPE AN (in ye M
EGYPT (Jumhūrīyat Miṣr al 'Arabīya/ Arab Republic of Egypt)	**Cairo** (Al Qāhirah) 6 069 000	942 247	54 688 000	58	59.0
EQUATORIAL GUINEA (República de Guinea Ecuatorial/Republic of Equatorial Guinea)	**Malabo** 30 700	28 051	356 000	13	44.4
ERITREA (Eritrea)	**Asmara** (Āsmera) 331 000	121 143	3 325 000	27	–
ETHIOPIA (Ityopya)	**Addis Ababa** 1 673 000	1 130 139	50 058 000	44	42.4
GABON (République Gabonaise/ Gabonese Republic)	**Libreville** 352 000	267 667	1 350 000	5	49.9
GAMBIA (Republic of the Gambia)	**Banjul** 44 500	11 295	884 000	78	41.4
GHANA (Republic of Ghana)	**Accra** 949 000	238 538	15 509 000	65	52.2
GUINEA (République de Guinée/ Republic of Guinea)	**Conakry** 705 000	245 857	7 052 000	28	42.0
GUINEA-BISSAU (República da Guiné-Bissau/ Republic of Guinea-Bissau)	**Bissau** 125 000	36 125	984 000	27	41.9
IVORY COAST (République de la Côte d'Ivoire/ Republic of the Ivory Coast)	**Yamoussoukro** 120 000	322 463	10 820 000	33	52.8
KENYA (Jamhuri ya Kenya/ Republic of Kenya)	**Nairobi** 1 429 000	582 646	23 183 000	40	56.5
LESOTHO (Muso oa Lesotho/ Kingdom of Lesotho)	**Maseru** 109 400	30 355	1 806 000	59	51.5
LIBERIA (Republic of Liberia)	**Monrovia** 465 000	111 369	2 520 000	23	53.9
LIBYA (Al Jamāhīrīya al 'Arabīya al-Lībīya ash Sha'bīya al-Ishtir ākīya)	**Tripoli** (Tarābulus) 591 000	1 775 500	4 325 000	2	59.1

© ISTITUTO GEOGRAFICO DE AGOSTINI S.p.A. - NOVARA

OSS IONAL DUCT ②	LANGUAGES	RELIGIONS	ECONOMY
620	Arabic (off.); French and English used commercially	Muslim 90%; Christian 7%	**Agriculture** Concentrated along the banks of the Nile. Main crops: cereals, cotton and sugar-cane. **Mineral resources** Petrol, natural gas, iron, phosphates. **Economy** Tourism and tolls on the Suez Canal bring in foreign currency.
330	Spanish (off.); Bubi; Fang; Pidgin English	Catholic 80%	**Agriculture** Cocoa and coffee are the most common plantation crops, followed by sugar-cane, bananas, palm-oil and coconuts. The country's main resource is its valuable timber (rosewood, ebony). **Industry** Almost none.
–	Tigrinya and Arabic (both off.); Italian	Coptic; Muslim	**Economy** Based on agriculture (cereals, citrus fruits, oilseed, cotton, tobacco, coffee), animal farming (sheep and goats), fishing and extracting sea salt. **Industry** Undergoing reconstruction.
120	Amharic (off.); Arabic; Oromo; other local languages	Coptic 55%; Muslim 35%	**Agriculture** The most profitable sector of the economy (coffee, tobacco, cotton, bananas and sugar-cane). Animals are reared extensively for their skins and leather. **Industry** Food processing and textile manufacture predominate.
780	French (off.); Bantu (Fang)	Christian	**Economy** Depends on the forests, which provide valuable timber. **Agriculture** Practiced only at subsistence level. **Principal resources** Petroleum, natural gas, uranium, manganese and gold are lucratively mined and exported.
360	English (off.); Wolof; Mandinka; Fula	Muslim 95%; Christ. 4%	**Economy** Depends on the cultivation of groundnuts. Other crops include cotton, cereals and palm nuts. **Industry** Manufacturing centres on processing groundnuts. Tourism is a rapidly growing industry.
400	English (off.); Asante; Ewe; Ga	Christ. 52%; Animist 35%; Mus. 13%	**Economy** Ghana is the third leading producer of cocoa, which it exports worldwide. Fishing, forestry and mining (diamonds, gold, bauxite, petroleum and manganese) are also important.
450	French (off.); Sudanese languages	Muslim 85%; Animist 5%	**Economy** Most of the workforce is employed in agriculture. Groundnuts, citrus fruits, bananas, pineapple, coffee and palm-oil are exported. **Mineral resources** Guinea has large reserves of bauxite, which is exported in considerable bulk.
190	Portuguese (off.); Creole; Sudanese languages	Animist 65%; Muslim 30%	**Economy** Agricultural: the main products are groundnuts, palm-nuts, cashew nuts and cotton, which are processed locally and then exported. Cereals are widely cultivated. Many inhabitants engage in fishing and lumbering.
690	French (off.); local languages	Animist 37%; Mus. 34%; Cath. 22%	**Economy** Most revenue comes from agriculture (especially from coffee and cocoa, followed by oil and palm-nuts), lumbering (valuable wood and caoutchouc) and mining (petroleum, diamonds). **Industry** Expanding.
340	Swahili (off.); Kikuyu; Kamba; English	Animist; Cath. 21%; Prot. 15%	**Agriculture** Flourishing: the broad range of crops include cereals, coffee, tea, sugar-cane, pyrethrum, cotton and sisal. Animal farming is widespread. **Industry** Productive, especially food processing. Tourism brings in substantial revenue.
580	English; Sesotho	Christian 90%; Animist 6%	**Economy** Very impoverished. **Agriculture** Barely above subsistence level (cereals, legumes, fruit). Animal farming is widespread; wool and mohair are exported. **Industry** Some mining (precious stones). Tourism is profitable.
400	English (off.); Sudanese languages	Christian; Animist 20%; Mus. 15%	**Agriculture** Coffee, cocoa, rice, citrus fruits and cassava; plantation crops such as palm-oil and caoutchouc are significant. **Mineral resources** Iron ore, diamonds and gold are mined. **Industry** Manufacturing industries are developing.
310	Arabic; other local languages	Muslim	**Economy** Depends on reserves of petroleum and natural gas. **Agriculture** Cereals, olives, grapes, citrus fruits and dates are among the main crops; animal farming is also practiced. **Industry** Centres on oil production.

© ISTITUTO GEOGRAFICO DE AGOSTINI S.p.A. - NOVARA

STATE (official name/ English translation)	CAPITAL ① inhabitants	AREA (sq km) POPULATION		DENSITY (inhab/sq km)	LIFE EXPECT ANCY (in year M
MADAGASCAR (Repoblika demokratika n'i Madagaskar/République démocratique de Madagascar)	Antananarivo (Tananarive) 1 050 000	587 041	11 493 000	19	54.0 5
MALAWI (Mfuko la Malaŵi/ Republic of Malawi)	Lilongwe 220 000	118 484	8 556 000	72	48.4 49
MALI (République du Mali/ Republic of Mali)	Bamako 646 200	1 240 142	8 299 000	6	45.0 47
MAURITANIA (Jumhūrīyat Mūrītānīya al-Islāmīya/Islamic Republic of Mauritania)	Nouakchott 393 000	1 030 700	2 036 000	2	45.0 48
MAURITIUS (Republic of Mauritius)	Port Louis 143 000	2 045	1 069 000	523	65.0 7
MOROCCO (Al Mamlakah al Maghribīya/ Kingdom of Morocco)	Rabat 556 000	458 730	25 698 000	56	61.6 6
MOZAMBIQUE (República de Moçambique/ Republic of Mozambique)	Maputo 1 070 000	799 380	16 084 000	20	46.9 5
NAMIBIA (Republic of Namibia/ Republiek van Namibie)	Windhoek 115 000	824 292	1 400 000	2	55.0 5
NIGER (République du Niger/ Republic of Niger)	Niamey 399 000	1 186 408	7 984 000	6	42.9 4
NIGERIA (Federal Republic of Nigeria)	Abuja 379 000	923 768	88 500 000	96	50.8 5
RWANDA (Republika y'u Rwanda/ République Rwandaise)	Kigali 234 000	26 338	7 150 000	271	48.8 5
SAO TOME E PRINCIPE (República Democrática de São Tomé e Príncipe)	São Tomé 35 000	964	123 000	127	64.0 6
SENEGAL (République du Sénégal/ Republic of Senegal)	Dakar 1 490 000	196 722	7 433 000	38	54.0 5
SEYCHELLES (Republic of Seychelles)	Victoria 24 300	453	68 000	150	65.3 7

© ISTITUTO GEOGRAFICO DE AGOSTINI S.p.A. - NOVARA

SS NAL UCT	LANGUAGES	RELIGIONS	ECONOMY
10	Malagasy; French	Anim. 50%; Cath. 25%; Prot. 20%; Muslim 5%	**Economy** The island depends largely on agriculture; coffee, vanilla, cloves and pepper are the principal exports. Rice and cassava are cultivated for domestic consumption. **Industry** Mainly food processing.
30	English (off.); Chichewa (nat.); other local dialects	Animist; Catholic 19%	**Economy** Relatively poor. Tobacco, cotton, sugar-cane and tea are cultivated for export; maize is the principal subsistence crop. **Industry** Growing modestly, particularly the food processing, cement manufacture and tobacco sectors.
30	French (off.); Bambara; local languages	Muslim 90%; Animist 9%	**Economy** Extremely poor, and based almost entirely on agriculture. Cotton, rice, cassava and groundnuts are the main crops. Fishing is important, and sheep, goat and cattle farming is well developed (droughts notwithstanding).
10	Arabic (off.); French; Poular; Wolof; Soninke	Muslim	**Agriculture** Severe droughts have hampered arable farming: cereals and dates are almost the only crops. Deep-sea fishing and nomadic animal farming (cattle, sheep) are widespread. **Principal resources** Rich reserves of iron ore.
20	English (off.); French; Creole; Hindi	Christ. 30%; Hindu 52%; Mus. 13%	**Economy** Depends on the production and export of sugar-cane, although there are also large plantations of tea, coffee and coco-palm. Fishing is profitable. **Industry** Mainly manufacturing; tourism is a significant source of revenue.
30	Arabic (off.); Berber; French	Muslim	**Agriculture** Cereals, grapes, vegetables and fruit are cultivated. Animal farming is widespread (sheep, goats, cattle). **Principal resources** Phosphates. **Industry** Food manufacturing, textile and tanning industries. Tourism is important.
70	Portuguese (off.); other local languages	Animist 48%; Cath. 14%; Mus. 16%	**Agriculture** The main crops are cotton and sugar-cane; also tea, sisal, cassava, cashew nuts, cereals, bananas. **Mineral resources** Rich but under-exploited deposits of coal, diamonds and bauxite. **Industry** Largely food manufacturing.
20	Afrikaans (off.); English; other local languages	Christian	**Economy** Depends on rich deposits of diamonds and uranium (plus copper, lead, zinc, silver and tin) which are exported internationally. **Agriculture** Animal farming and fishing are practiced widely. **Industry** Mainly food processing.
00	French (off.); Hausa; Tamashek; Poular; Djerma; Kanuri	Muslim; Animist 15%	**Economy** Uranium, the main mineral resource, is mined in substantial quantities, but agriculture employs the bulk of the population. Millet, sorghum, rice and cassava are the chief crops. Animals are farmed for their skins and leather.
90	English (off.); Sudanese languages (Hausa, Ibo, Yoruba)	Muslim 45%; Christian 38%	**Economy** In the past, agriculture predominated (cocoa, palm-oil, coconuts, groundnuts, caoutchouc and bananas), but oil is now the main source of revenue. **Industry** Mining (tin as well as oil) and food processing.
60	French; Kinyarwanda	Catholic 56%; Anim. 17%; Prot. 13%	**Agriculture** Coffee, tobacco, tea, pyrethrum and groundnuts are grown for cash; maize, rice, sorghum, sweet potatoes, cassava and bananas for subsistence. Some animal herding. **Principal resources** Tin, gold and tungsten.
50	Portuguese (off.); Creole	Catholic	**Agriculture** The mainstay of the economy. Cocoa, coffee, walnuts, palm-oil, coconuts, copra and bananas are the most important crops. Fishing is another source of revenue. **Industry** Scarcely developed.
20	French (off.); Sudanese languages (Wolof, nat.)	Muslim 85%	**Economy** Largely agrarian (groundnuts, cotton, cereals). Senegal is a leading producer of groundnuts. Fishing is important. **Principal resources** Phosphates. **Industry** Mainly groundnuts processing, oil production and tourism.
10	Creole (off.); English; French	Catholic	**Agriculture** Coconut palms, cinnamon and vanilla are the principal crops. Fishing is also an important aspect of the economy. **Industry** About a third of the labour force is employed in the highly successful tourist industry.

© ISTITUTO GEOGRAFICO DE AGOSTINI S.p.A. - NOVARA

STATE (official name/ English translation)	CAPITAL ① inhabitants	AREA (sq km) POPULATION		DENSITY (inhab/sq km)	LIFE EXPECTANCY (in years) M
SIERRA LEONE (Republic of Sierra Leone)	Freetown 470 000	71 740	4 260 000	59	41.4
SOMALIA (Jamhuuriyadda Diimoqraadiga Soomaaliya/ Somali Democratic Republic)	Mogadishu (Muqdisho) 500 000	637 657	6 760 000	11	43.4
SOUTH AFRICA (Republic of South Africa/ Republiek van Suid-Afrika)	Pretoria/Cape Town (Kaapstad)* 443 000/777 000	1 224 641	38 191 000	31	57.5
SUDAN (Jamhūrÿat es Sūdān/ Republic of Sudan)	Khartoum (Al Kharṭūm) 557 000	2 505 813	25 941 000	10	52.0
SWAZILAND (Umbuso we Swatini/ Kingdom of Swaziland)	Mbabane 38 000	17 364	798 000	46	56.2
TANZANIA (Jamhuri ya Muungano wa Tanzania/United Republic of Tanzania)	Dodoma 204 000	939 470	26 353 000	28	51.3
TOGO (République Togolaise/ Togolese Republic)	Lomé 400 000	56 785	3 643 000	64	51.3
TUNISIA (Al Jumhūrīyah at Tūnisīyah/ Republic of Tunisia)	Tunis 626 000	163 610	8 293 000	51	64.9
UGANDA (Republic of Uganda)	Kampala 651 000	241 038	16 830 000	70	51.4
ZAMBIA (Republic of Zambia)	Lusaka 982 000	752 614	8 023 000	10	54.4
ZIMBABWE (Republic of Zimbabwe)	Harare 863 000	390 759	10 130 000	26	57.9

AFRICA	29 981 681	630 136 000	21
AFRICA Total Ⓐ	30 249 096	632 915 000	21

© ISTITUTO GEOGRAFICO DE AGOSTINI S.p.A. - NOVARA

SS NAL UCT	LANGUAGES	RELIGIONS	ECONOMY
10	English (off.); Krio; Sudanese languages	Animist 51%; Muslim 39%	**Mineral resources** The chief exports, particularly diamonds, rutile and bauxite. **Agriculture** Mainly at a subsistence level, the principal crops being cocoa, coffee and palm kernels. **Industry** Processing industries.
50	Somali (off.); Arabic; Italian; English (adm.)	Muslim (Sunni)	**Economy** Depends on animal farming (cattle, sheep, goats, camels) and agriculture (cereals, cotton, sugar-cane, bananas). Both are major sources of employment. Fishing is on the increase.
30	Afrikaans and English (both off.); other local languages	Protestant; Animist; Cath. 8%	**Economy** The most prosperous in Africa. The mining sector (gold, diamonds, uranium, platinum, coal, iron), industry (mechanical, chemical and textile) and agriculture (cereals, vegetables, fruit) are all flourishing.
00	Arabic (off.); other local dialects	Mus. 73%; Animist 17%; Cath. 6%	**Agriculture** Cotton is the most important crop; cereals, dates, sugar-cane and oilseed are also cultivated. Nomadic herding is widespread. Sudan is one of the world's largest producers of gum arabic. **Industry** Relatively undeveloped.
60	English and siSwati	Christian 47%; Animist 40%	**Economy** Arable and animal farming, timber felling and mining are the main activities. **Agriculture** Sugar-cane and citrus fruits are cultivated widely. **Mineral resources** The country is quite rich in asbestos, carbon, diamonds and iron.
00	Swahili; English	Muslim; Christ. 30%; Hindu; Animist	**Agriculture** Coffee, tea, cotton, tobacco, sugar, sisal and cloves are grown for export. Animal farming and fishing are common. **Mineral resources** Diamonds and gold. **Industry** Food processing and textile production.
10	French (off.); Ewe; Poular; Hausa; Gour; Assirelii	Animist; Muslim 17%; Cath. 26%	**Agriculture** The population largely comprises subsistence farmers; coffee, cocoa, cotton, groundnuts and palm-oil are grown for export. **Mineral resources** Phosphates are the main export; iron ore is also mined. **Industry** Modest.
10	Arabic (off.); French; Berber	Muslim	**Economy** Based on agriculture (cereals, olives, grapes, citrus fruits, dates) and mining; phosphates and petrol account for over a third of exports. Fishing is profitable. **Industry** Mainly food processing and metallurgy. Tourism is increasing.
60	English and Swahili (both off.); Luganda	Cath. 40%; Prot. 20%; Muslim 6%	**Agriculture** Coffee, tea, cotton, tobacco, cocoa and sugar-cane are cultivated for export, while maize, millet, sorghum and cassava are the main subsistence crops. **Industry** Well developed in the food and metallurgical fields.
20	English (off.); local languages include Lozi, Nyanja, Tonga	Prot. 34%; Cath. 26%; Animist 27%	**Economy** Depends on mining (copper, cobalt, manganese, lead, zinc, tin) and the related industries of metal and chemical processing. **Agriculture** Limited; maize, cassava, groundnuts and tobacco are the most common crops.
20	English (off.); local languages include Chishona and Sindebele	Animist; Prot. 17%; Cath. 12%	**Agriculture** Wheat, maize, cotton, sugar, coffee, soya and tobacco are the principal crops. **Mineral resources** Gold, asbestos, coal, iron, silver, tin, nickel, copper and cobalt are exported. **Industry** Manufacturing is developing slowly.

cludes Saint Helena, Comoros Is, Réunion I., Madeira, anary Is, Ceuta, Melilla, Socotra, Western Sahara.

etoria (administrative); Cape Town (legislative)

(1) The local form is given in brackets only when it differs from the English form

(2) Per inhabitant, in US$

© ISTITUTO GEOGRAFICO DE AGOSTINI S.p.A. - NOVARA

STATE (official name/ English translation)	CAPITAL inhabitants	AREA (sq km)	POPULATION	DENSITY (inhab/sq km)	LIFE EXPECTANCY (in years) M
AUSTRALIA (Commonwealth of Australia)	**Canberra** 302 500	7 682 300	17 086 000	2	73.3 7
FIJI (Matanitu Ko Viti/ Republic of Fiji)	**Suva** 70 000	18 272	736 000	40	68.3 7
KIRIBATI (Republic of Kiribati)	**Bairiki** 2 100	849	72 000	85	50.6 5
MARSHALL ISLANDS (Republic of the Marshall Islands)	**Dalap-Uliga-Darrit** 17 600	181	44 000	243	61.0 6
MICRONESIA (Federated States of Micronesia)	**Palikir** —	707	111 000	157	64.0 6
NAURU (Republic of Nauru)	**Yaren** —	21	9 000	428	64.0 6
NEW ZEALAND (New Zealand)	**Wellington** 147 800	270 534	3 390 000	12	72.0 7
PALAU	**Koror** 10 500	487	15 000	31	—
PAPUA NEW GUINEA (Papua New Guinea)	**Port Moresby** 152 100	462 840	3 600 000	8	54.0
SOLOMON ISLANDS (Solomon Islands)	**Honiara** 35 300	28 369	319 000	11	59.9
TONGA (Pule'anga Tonga/ Kingdom of Tonga)	**Nuku'alofa** 28 900	748	96 000	128	61.0
TUVALU (The Tuvalu Islands)	**Fongafale** —	24	9 000	375	60.0
VANUATU (Ripablik Blong Vanuatu/ Republic of Vanuatu)	**Port-Vila** 19 300	12 189	147 000	12	61.1
WESTERN SAMOA (Malo Tuto'atasi/ Independent State of Western Samoa)	**Apia** 33 200	2 831	164 000	58	64.0
AUSTRALIA AND OCEANIA		8 480 352	25 798 000	3	
AUSTRALIA AND OCEANIA Total Ⓐ		8 942 252	29 128 000	3	

© ISTITUTO GEOGRAFICO DE AGOSTINI S.p.A. - NOVARA

GROSS NATIONAL PRODUCT ①	LANGUAGES	RELIGIONS	ECONOMY
4 440	English	Protestant; Catholic 26%	**Economy** Based on agriculture (cereals, fruit, sugar-cane, cotton) and animal farming (sheep, cattle). **Mineral resources** Vast reserves of coal, natural gas, oil, nickel, gold, iron ore and bauxite. **Industry** All sectors expanding.
1 640	English, Fijian; Hindi	Methodist; Hindu 38%; Muslim	**Economy** Sustained by agriculture (sugar-cane, bananas, coconuts and potatoes) and fishing. Tourism also generates considerable revenue. **Mineral resources** Subsoil is rich in gold and silver. The island is heavily forested.
700	English (off.); I-Kiribati	Protestant; Catholic	**Agriculture** Most of the population is involved in agriculture and fishing. The principal crop is the coconut palm. **Industry** The tourist industry is expanding.
500	English (off.); Marshallese	Protestant; Catholic 8.5%	**Economy** Based on subsistence agriculture and fishing. Main crops are coconuts, copra, cassava and fruit. **Industry** Tourism is well developed.
500	English	Protestant; Catholic	**Economy** Most islanders are involved in fishing and cultivation (coconuts, copra, sweet potatoes, cassava, bananas). **Industry** The tourist industry is growing fast.
000	Nauruan (off.); English	Protestant; Catholic 24%	**Economy** Nauru is the wealthiest country in Oceania thanks to its rich phosphate deposits (which cover nearly 75% of the island). Phosphate mining accounts for three-quarters of the country's GDP.
800	English	Protestant; Catholic 15%	**Economy** Dominated by livestock farming, particularly sheep (for wool and meat) and cattle (dairy products and beef). **Agriculture** Well established. **Industry** Expanding, due in part to inexpensive hydroelectricity.
—	English; Palauan	Christian	**Economy** At subsistence level. The archipelago relies mainly on agriculture (potatoes, coconuts, cassava and bananas) and fishing. **Industry** Tourism is beginning to develop.
900	English (off.); Pidgin-English; Motu; other local dialects	Animist; Catholic 27%	**Economy** Essentially agricultural; sweet potatoes, cocoa, coffee and coconuts are the main crops. **Principal resources** Mining (especially gold, silver, copper) generates considerable revenue. The island is richly forested.
570	English (off.); Pidgin-English; Melanesian and Polynesian languages	Protestant; Catholic 18%	**Economy** The population is largely employed in cultivating coconut palms and sweet potatoes. Timber, fish and copra are the main exports. **Industry** Fishing is a major concern; a modest food processing industry has been established.
010	English; Tongan	Protestant; Catholic 13%	**Economy** Some 58% of the population is involved in agriculture (coconuts, potatoes, cassava and groundnuts). The chief exports are copra and coconuts. Fishing is also profitable. **Industry** Tourism is well established.
30	Tuvaluan; English	Protestant	**Economy** The two main sources of income are coconuts and fishing. The country relies on revenue from emigrants and foreign aid.
60	Bislama; English (off.); French (off.); other local dialects	Animist; Catholic 14%	**Economy** Based on subsistence agriculture and fishing. Main crops are coconut palm, cocoa, groundnuts and maize. The islands are densely forested. **Mineral resources** Primarily manganese.
20	Samoan (off.); English	Protestant; Catholic 22%	**Economy** Agriculture is the country's main resource, the principal crops being bananas, coconuts and cocoa. Fishing and pig farming are also well developed. **Industry** Confined to the manufacture of agricultural products.

© ISTITUTO GEOGRAFICO DE AGOSTINI S.p.A. - NOVARA

udes Norfolk I., Macquarie I., Cook Is, Niue I., Tokelau
Pitcairn Is, New Caledonia, Wallis and Futuna, Po-
sia, Clipperton, Guam, Hawaii, Midway Is, American
oa, Wake Is, Mariana Is, Irian Jaya, Chilean Is.

① Per inhabitant, in US$1million

ANTARCTICA has an area of 14 107 637 sq km, including the
islands and ice-shelf (13 176 727 sq km without the ice-shelf).

STATE (official name/ English translation)	CAPITAL ① inhabitants	AREA (sq km) POPULATION DENSITY (inhab/sq km)			LIFE EXPECTANCY (in years) M
ANTIGUA AND BARBUDA (Antigua and Barbuda)	Saint John's 36 000	442	64 000	145	70.0
BAHAMAS (The Commonwealth of the Bahamas)	Nassau 172 000	13 939	259 000	18	69.0
BARBADOS (Barbados)	Bridgetown 7 600	431	258 000	598	72.9
BELIZE (Belize)	Belmopan 3 700	22 965	189 000	8	67.0
CANADA (Canada)	Ottawa 300 800	9 970 610	27 300 000	3	73.3
COSTA RICA (República de Costa Rica/ Republic of Costa Rica)	San José 297 000	51 100	3 064 000	60	72.4
CUBA (República de Cuba/ Republic of Cuba)	Havana (La Habana) 2 119 000	110 922	10 736 000	97	73.0
DOMINICA (Commonwealth of Dominica)	Roseau 15 900	751	71 000	94	73.0
DOMINICAN REPUBLIC (República Dominicana)	Santo Domingo 1 600 000	48 442	7 313 000	151	63.9
EL SALVADOR (República de El Salvador/ Republic of El Salvador)	San Salvador 481 000	21 041	5 392 000	256	63.0
GRENADA (State of Grenada)	Saint George's 7 500	344	101 000	293	69.0
GUATEMALA (República de Guatemala/ Republic of Guatemala)	Guatemala City 1 114 000	108 889	9 197 000	84	59.7
HAITI (République d'Haïti/ Republic of Haiti)	Port-au-Prince 514 000	27 400	6 625 000	242	53.1
HONDURAS (República de Honduras/ Republic of Honduras)	Tegucigalpa 608 000	112 088	4 708 000	42	61.9

© ISTITUTO GEOGRAFICO DE AGOSTINI S.p.A. - NOVARA

SS NAL UCT)	LANGUAGES	RELIGIONS	ECONOMY
70	English (off.); Creole	Protestant	**Economy** Domestic economy relies primarily on tourism and secondarily on agriculture (cotton, sugar-cane, coconuts, vegetables and fruit). Fishing is well developed. **Industry** Limited to the manufacture of agricultural products and rum.
20	English (off.); Creole	Protestant; Catholic 22%	**Economy** The tourist industry is the main source of revenue. Agriculture (sugar-cane, tomatoes, pineapple), fishing (shellfish and turtles) and the production of sea-salt are also important.
30	English	Protestant; Catholic 5%	**Economy** The island's economy is based entirely on sugar-cane. Maize, potatoes and cassava are produced for domestic consumption. Fishing is profitable. **Industry** Expanding. The tourist industry is highly developed.
50	English (off.); Spanish; Creole	Catholic 58%; Protestant 28%	**Economy** Agriculture-based; citrus fruits, cereals (rice and maize), coconuts, bananas and sugar-cane are the main cash crops. Other activities include fishing, animal farming and lumbering (cedar, mahogany, pine and rosewood).
60	English; French	Catholic 46%; Protestant 41%	**Economy** Cereal crops dominate (wheat, oats, rye, barley, maize). Cattle and animal-fur farming are also widely practiced. **Principal resources** The vast forests are a rich asset. **Industry** All sectors are well established.
30	Spanish	Catholic	**Economy** Primarily plantation agriculture (coffee, bananas, cocoa, sugar-cane, cotton and tobacco). Tuna-fishing and animal farming also generate considerable revenue. **Industry** Food processing is a principal industry.
00	Spanish	Catholic	**Economy** The national wealth depends on sugar-cane (the main export), tobacco, coffee and fruit. Also, animal farming and fishing. **Industry** Nickel-mining, food processing, and the textile and tobacco industries are the chief industries.
40	English (off.); French patois	Catholic	**Economy** Based on agriculture (bananas, citrus fruits, coconuts) and fishing. **Industry** The processing of agricultural products is developing rapidly. Tourism is also growing.
50	Spanish	Catholic	**Agriculture** Based on plantation crops (cocoa, sugar-cane, coffee, tobacco, coconuts). Also animal farming and fishing. **Mineral resources** Gold, silver and nickel are major exports. **Industry** Tourism brings in foreign revenue.
70	Spanish; Nahua; Maya	Catholic	**Economy** The main resource of this agricultural country is maize, followed by rice, beans, coffee, sugar-cane, cotton and sesame. Forests yield cedar, mahogany and rosewood. **Industry** Modestly developed.
80	English (off.); Creole; French patois	Catholic; Protestant 34%	**Economy** Agriculturally based. Citrus fruits, bananas, cocoa, coconuts, cotton, sugar-cane and nutmeg are cultivated. Fishing is an important pursuit. **Industry** Tourism is developing.
30	Spanish (off.); Mayan languages	Catholic; Protestant 25%	**Economy** Depends on plantation agriculture (bananas, coffee, sugar-cane, cotton, tobacco, and cocoa). Forests provide valuable wood, in particular mahogany and cedar. Sheep and cattle farming are profitable.
70	French; Creole	Catholic	**Economy** Essentially agricultural. The main crops are coffee, bananas and sisal, followed by cotton, sugar-cane, cocoa, citrus fruits and tobacco. **Principal resources** Bauxite is the sole mining resource of any significance.
70	Spanish (off.); other local languages	Catholic	**Agriculture** Bananas, coconuts, coffee and tobacco. **Principal resources** Timber (mahogany, cedar and pine). Gold, silver, lead, zinc and antimony are mined on a large scale. **Industry** Processing yields a high income.

© ISTITUTO GEOGRAFICO DE AGOSTINI S.p.A - NOVARA

STATE (official name/ English translation)	CAPITAL ① inhabitants	AREA (sq km)	POPULATION	DENSITY (inhab/sq km)	·LIFE EXPECTANCY ANC (in ye M
JAMAICA (Jamaica)	**Kingston** 104 100	10 991	2 375 000	216	70.4
MEXICO (Estados Unidos Mexicanos/United Mexican States)	**Mexico City** (Ciudad de México) 8 237 000	1 972 547	82 151 000	41	66.5
NICARAGUA (República de Nicaragua/ Republic of Nicaragua)	**Managua** 682 000	130 682	3 999 000	31	64.8
PANAMA (República de Panamá/ Republic of Panama)	**Panama City** 411 000	77 082	2 466 000	32	70.1
SAINT CHRISTOPHER (KITTS) AND NEVIS (Federation of Saint Christopher and Nevis)	**Basseterre** 18 500	269	44 000	163	65.9
SAINT LUCIA (Saint Lucia)	**Castries** 51 200	616	153 000	248	68.0
SAINT VINCENT AND THE GRENADINES (Saint Vincent and the Grenadines)	**Kingstown** 26 500	389	108 000	277	68.0
UNITED STATES OF AMERICA (United States of America)	**Washington** 607 000	9 355 855	250 928 000	27	72.0

NORTH & CENTRAL AMERICA Ⓐ 22 037 795 417 501 000 19
NORTH & CENTRAL AMERICA Total Ⓐ 24 227 189 422 159 000 17

© ISTITUTO GEOGRAFICO DE AGOSTINI S.p.A. - NOVARA

SS NAL JCT	LANGUAGES	RELIGIONS	ECONOMY
30	English	Protestant	**Economy** A leading producer of bauxite. **Agriculture** Plantation agriculture (tobacco, coffee, cocoa, bananas, sugar-cane, spices) is well developed. **Industry** Expanding. Tourism generates substantial foreign currency.
70	Spanish (off.); Nahua; Maya	Catholic 90%	**Economy** Oil, silver, lead, gold and sulphur are the mainstays of the domestic economy. **Agriculture** A third of the population is in agriculture and animal farming. **Industry** Rapidly expanding. Tourism is well developed.
40	Spanish (off.); other local languages	Catholic	**Economy** Principally plantation agriculture (coffee, cotton, cocoa, sugar-cane, and bananas). The forests are rich in valuable wood (mahogany, cedar, rosewood). **Industry** Relatively undeveloped.
30	Spanish (off.)	Catholic	**Economy** Sustained mainly by revenue raised by granting access to the Panama Canal. **Agriculture** Subsistence agriculture is practiced; large plantations growing bananas, coffee and cocoa also exist.
60	English (off.); Creole	Protestant	**Agriculture** The economy's main source of revenue, with cotton and sugar-cane the chief crops. **Industry** Agricultural processing is developing modestly while the tourist industry is undergoing rapid expansion.
00	English (off.); French patois	Catholic	**Agriculture** Domestic economy dominated by agriculture (potatoes, bananas, cocoa, coconuts and copra). Animal farming and fishing are developed. **Industry** Principally food processing and the production of fertilizers.
30	English (off.); Creole	Protestant; Catholic 19%	**Agriculture** Plantation agriculture yields potatoes, bananas, coconuts, cotton and exotic fruit, largely for the overseas market. **Industry** Industry in general is developing; tourism is well established.
60	English	Protestant 53%; Catholic 26%	**Economy** The economy of the United States is the most developed in the world. It is founded on highly specialized agriculture, substantial mineral reserves and power resources, and impressive industrial organization.

les the Virgin Is, Puerto Rico, Anguilla, Cayman Is, Turks
aicos, Bermuda, Montserrat, Guadeloupe, Martinique,
rre and Miiquelon, North American Antilles, Greenland.
des the 16 759 sq km and 1 135 000 inhabitants of
ii, which is included in Oceania.

① The local form is given in brackets only when it differs from the English form

② Per inhabitant, in US$

© ISTITUTO GEOGRAFICO DE AGOSTINI S.p.A. - NOVARA

	STATE (official name/ English translation)	CAPITAL inhabitants	AREA (sq km) POPULATION DENSITY (inhab/sq km)		LIFE EXPEC ANC (in yea M
	ARGENTINA (República Argentina/ Argentine Republic)	**Buenos Aires** 2 961 000	2 780 092	32 713 000 12	68.0
	BOLIVIA (República de Bolivia/ Republic of Bolivia)	**Sucre (legal); La Paz (admin.)** 101 000/126 000	1 098 581	7 612 000 7	50.9
	BRAZIL (República Federativa do Brasil/Federative Republic of Brazil)	**Brasília** 1 596 000	8 511 996	146 000 000 17	63.5
	CHILE (República de Chile/Republic of Chile)	**Santiago** 5 134 000	756 626	13 386 000 18	68.1
	COLOMBIA (República de Colombia/ Republic of Colombia)	**Santa Fe de Bogotá** 4 922 000	1 141 748	33 613 000 29	66.4
	ECUADOR (República del Ecuador/ Republic of Ecuador)	**Quito** 1 094 000	283 561	9 819 000 34	63.4
	GUYANA (Cooperative Republic of Guyana)	**Georgetown** 200 000	214 970	760 000 3	61.0
	PARAGUAY (República del Paraguay/ Republic of Paraguay)	**Asunción** 608 000	406 752	4 004 000 10	64.4
	PERU (República del Perú/ Republic of Peru)	**Lima** 6 115 000	1 285 216	21 998 000 17	62.9
	SURINAME (Republiek van Suriname/ Republic of Suriname)	**Paramaribo** 67 900	163 820	417 000 2	66.4
	TRINIDAD AND TOBAGO (Republic of Trinidad and Tobago)	**Port of Spain** 50 900	5 123	1 253 000 244	69.7
	URUGUAY (República Oriental del Uruguay/Eastern Republic of Uruguay)	**Montevideo** 1 248 000	176 215	3 112 000 17	68.9
	VENEZUELA (República de Venezuela/ Republic of Venezuela)	**Caracas** 1 290 000	912 050	19 733 000 21	67.0
	SOUTH AMERICA **SOUTH AMERICA**	Total (A)	17 736 750 294 420 000 16 17 833 382 294 762 000 16		

© ISTITUTO GEOGRAFICO DE AGOSTINI S.p.A. - NOVARA

GROSS NATIONAL PRODUCT ①	LANGUAGES	RELIGIONS	ECONOMY
2780	Spanish (off.); Guarani; Quechua	Catholic 91%	**Economy** Traditionally farming (crops and animals) and the manufacture of pastoral and agricultural goods. **Industry** Petroleum output is rising; iron and steel, mechanical goods, textiles and food also of importance.
650	Spanish; Quechua; Aymará	Catholic 94%	**Principal resources** Minerals, including tin, gold, silver, bismuth, lead, zinc, tungsten, antimony and oil. **Agriculture** Currently at subsistence level, but animal husbandry (cattle, sheep) is developing rapidly.
2920	Portuguese (off.); Carib; Tupí	Catholic 88%	**Economy** Based on plantation crops (coffee, cocoa, sugar-cane, tobacco, cotton). **Industry** Food processing (by large, specialized companies) is the main activity. Industry is prosperous. The country is densely forested.
2160	Spanish (off.); Araucanian	Catholic 89%	**Economy** The most profitable sector is mining, particularly of copper, nitrates, oil, gold, silver, iron ore and coal. **Agriculture** Agronomy, animal farming and fishing are booming. **Industry** In a good position to grow.
1280	Spanish (off.); other local languages	Catholic 94%	**Economy** Principal export is coffee; other profitable cash crops include tobacco, cotton and sugar-cane. **Mineral resources** Gold, silver, platinum, emeralds and oil. **Industry** Relatively undeveloped.
1020	Spanish (off.); Quechua	Catholic 90%	**Economy** Relies on plantation crops: cocoa, coffee, sugar-cane, bananas, tobacco, cotton. **Mineral resources** Of considerable importance, principally oil, gold, silver and iron. **Industry** Developing modestly.
290	English (off.); Creole; Hindu; Urdu	Hindu 37%; Prot. 31%; Cath. 11%; Mus. 9%	**Agriculture** Mainly cane, rice, coffee, cassava and citrus fruits. **Mineral resources** Large quantities of bauxite (Guyana's main export), as well as gold and diamonds. **Industry** Limited to the production of agricultural goods.
1210	Spanish (off.); Guaraní	Catholic	**Economy** Essentially agricultural. Cotton, tobacco and fruit are the main exports, and timber. Cattle ranching also a major concern. **Industry** Growing as a result of inexpensive hydroelectric power.
1020	Spanish, Quechua, Aymará (all off.)	Catholic 92%	**Economy** Agriculture-based. Principal crops are cotton, sugar-cane, coffee and fruit. Animal farming is an important economic activity, and fishing even more so. **Mineral resources** Oil, copper and silver. **Industry** Prosperous.
1510	Dutch (off.); Carib; Creole	Hindu 26%; Cath. 22%; Mus. 19%; Prot. 18%	**Economy** Depends on agricultural products (especially rice, sugar-cane, coffee, citrus fruits, bananas and coconuts) and mining (bauxite, gold). **Industry** Limited to the production of agricultural goods.
3320	English (off.); Spanish; Hindu; Creole	Cath. 32%; Prot. 28%; Hindu 24%	**Economy** Industry has superseded agriculture as the main source of revenue due to rich deposits of oil, natural gas and asphalt. Other major industrial activities include refining and the production of petrochemicals and fertilizers.
2860	Spanish	Catholic	**Economy** Rearing livestock (sheep and cattle) and food processing are the chief economic activities in Uruguay, with wool, meat and hides the principal exports. **Agriculture** Also developing.
3510	Spanish (off.); Carib	Catholic 92%	**Economy** Previously relied on plantation crops, but petroleum production and the petrochemical industry now account for most export earnings. Fishing is also profitable. The country has considerable forest resources.

Includes the Falkland Is, South American Antilles, Aruba and French Guiana

① Per inhabitant, in US$

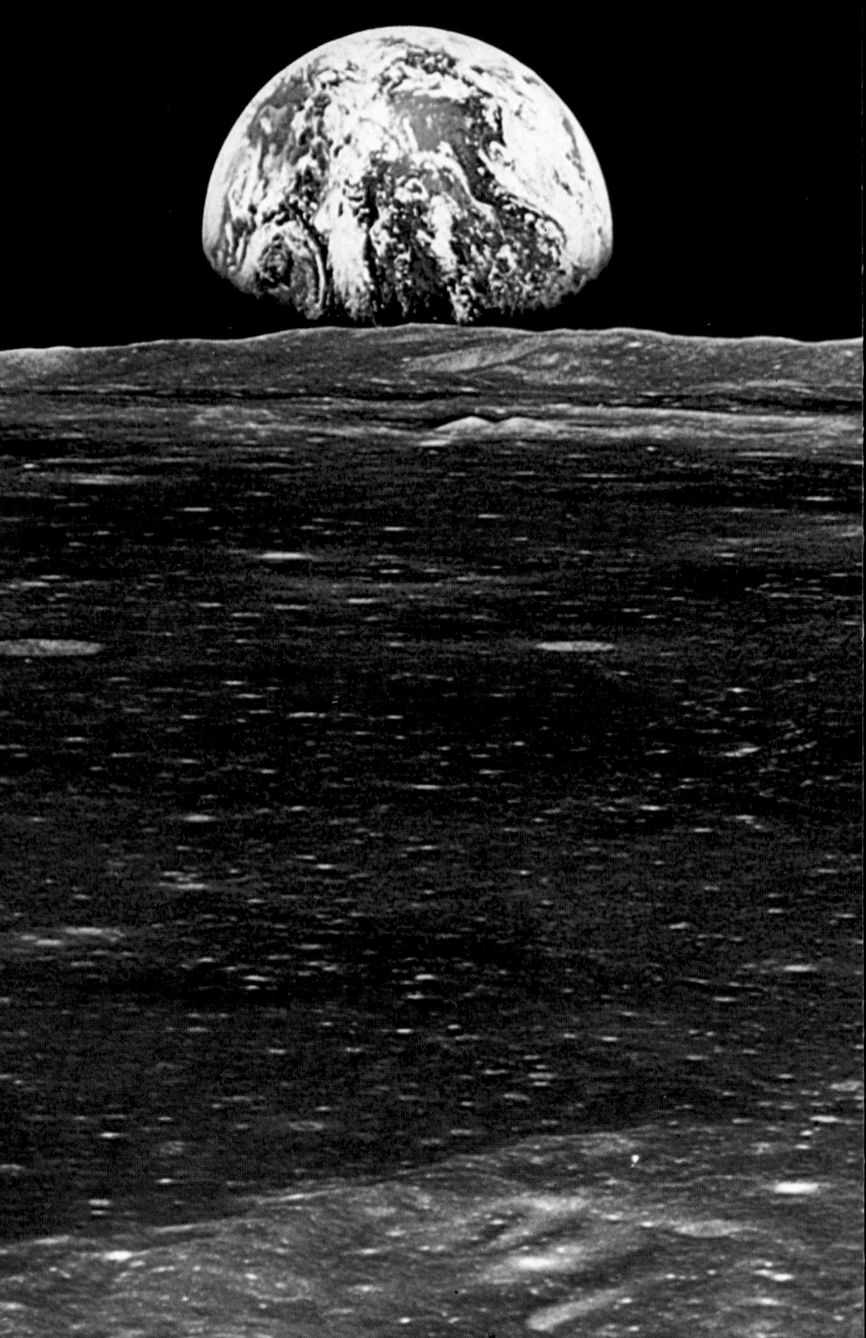

WORLD MAPS

Earth seen from the Moon
(image taken by astronauts aboard "Apollo 10" in May 1969)

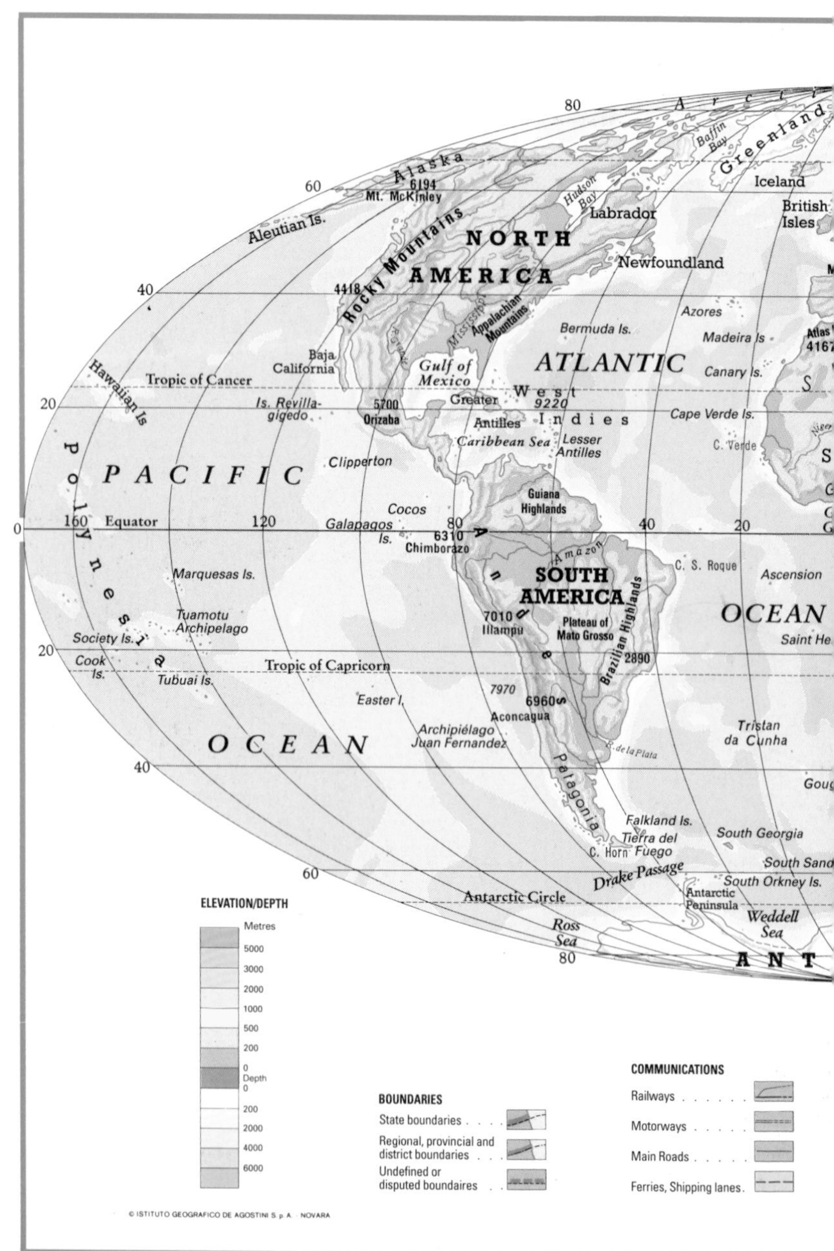

80

Arctic

Baffin
Bay

Greenland

Iceland

British
Isles

Alaska

60

6194
Mt. McKinley

Hudson
Bay

Labrador

Rocky Mountains

NORTH
AMERICA

Newfoundland

Aleutian Is.

40

4418

Appalachian Mountains

Bermuda Is.

Azores

Madeira Is.

Atlas
4167

Baja
California

Gulf of
Mexico

ATLANTIC

Canary Is.

S

Tropic of Cancer

West

Is. Revilla-
gigedo

20

5700
Orizaba

9220

Greater

Indies

Cape Verde Is.

Hawaiian Is

Antilles

Caribbean Sea

Lesser
Antilles

C. Verde

S

G

P A C I F I C

Clipperton

G

P
o
l
y
n
e
s
i
a

Cocos

Guiana
Highlands

0

160

Equator

120

Galapagos
Is.

80

6310
Chimborazo

Amazon

40

20

G

Marquesas Is.

SOUTH
AMERICA

C. S. Roque

Ascension

OCEAN

Tuamotu
Archipelago

Andes

Illampu

Plateau of
Mato Grosso

Brazilian Highlands

Society Is.

7010

Saint He.

20

Cook
Is.

Tropic of Capricorn

2890

Tubuai Is.

7970

Easter I.

6960

Archipiélago
Juan Fernandez

Aconcagua

Tristan
da Cunha

O C E A N

R. de la Plata

40

Patagonia

Goug

Falkland Is.

Tierra del
Fuego

South Georgia

C. Horn

South Sand

60

Drake Passage

South Orkney Is.

Antarctic Circle

Antarctic
Peninsula

Weddell
Sea

Ross
Sea

80

A N T

ELEVATION/DEPTH

Metres

5000
3000
2000
1000
500
200
0
Depth
0
200
2000
4000
6000

© ISTITUTO GEOGRAFICO DE AGOSTINI S.p.A. NOVARA

BOUNDARIES

State boundaries . . . .

Regional, provincial and
district boundaries . . .

Undefined or
disputed boundaires . . .

COMMUNICATIONS

Railways . . . . . .

Motorways . . . . .

Main Roads . . . . .

Ferries, Shipping lanes.

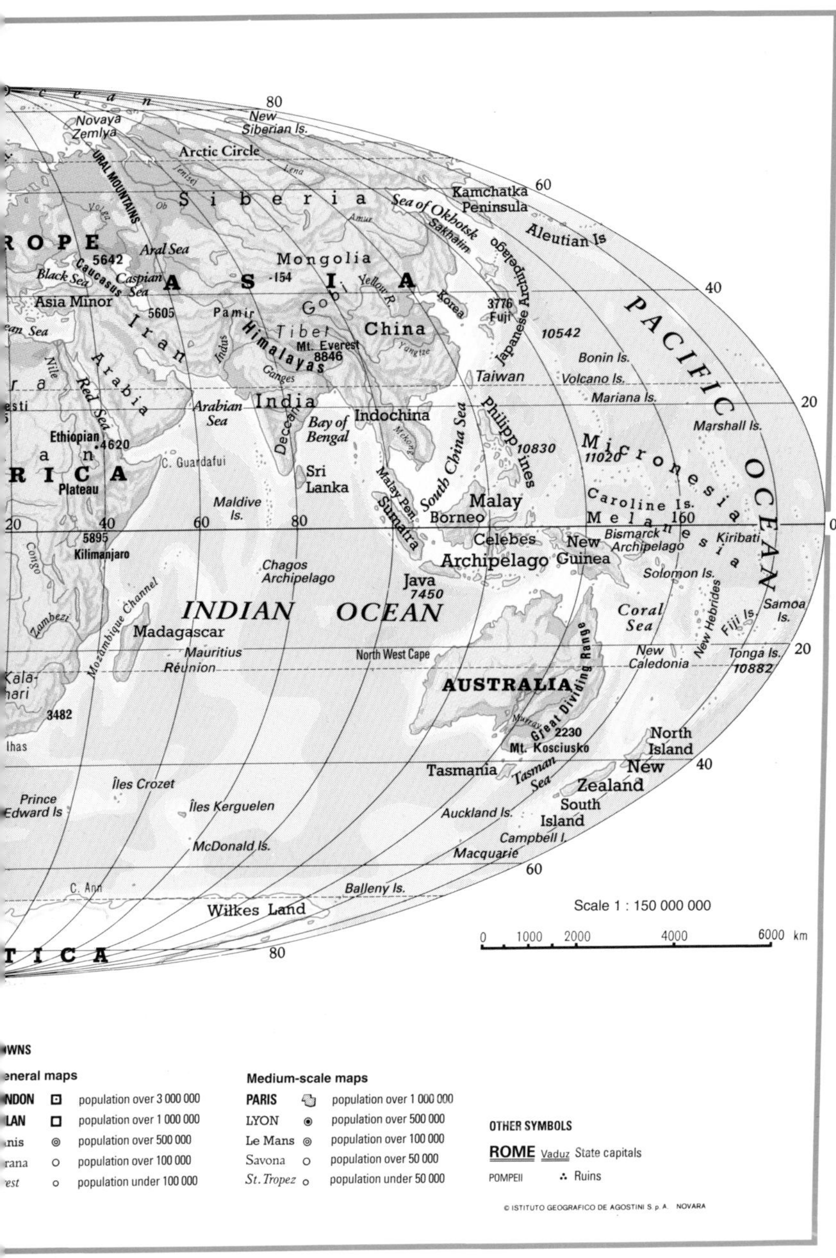

Scale 1 : 150 000 000

0   1000   2000   4000   6000 km

TOWNS

General maps

LONDON	⊡	population over 3 000 000
MILAN	☐	population over 1 000 000
Tunis	◉	population over 500 000
Parana	○	population over 100 000
Brest	○	population under 100 000

Medium-scale maps

PARIS		population over 1 000 000
LYON	◉	population over 500 000
Le Mans	◉	population over 100 000
Savona	○	population over 50 000
St. Tropez	○	population under 50 000

OTHER SYMBOLS

ROME Vaduz State capitals

POMPEII ∴ Ruins

© ISTITUTO GEOGRAFICO DE AGOSTINI S.p.A. NOVARA

43

1 GUYANA
2 SURINAME
3 French Guiana
4 UNITED KINGDOM
5 IRELAND
6 NETHERLANDS
7 BELGIUM
8 FRANCE
9 LUXEMBOURG
10 GERMANY
11 POLAND
12 ESTONIA
13 LATVIA
14 LITHUANIA
15 BELARUS
16 CZECH REPUBLIC
17 SLOVAKIA
18 AUSTRIA
19 HUNGARY
20 MOLDOVA
21 ROMANIA
22 SWITZERLAND
23 ITALY
24 SLOVENIA
25 CROATIA
26 BOSNIA-HERZEGOVINA
27 YUGOSLAVIA
28 MACEDONIA
29 ALBANIA
30 BULGARIA
31 GREECE
32 PORTUGAL
33 SPAIN
34 BURKINA
35 BENIN
36 CENTRAL AFRICAN REPUBLIC
37 CAMEROON
38 EQUATORIAL GUINEA
39 UGANDA
40 RWANDA
41 BURUNDI
42 MALAWI
43 ZIMBABWE
44 DJIBOUTI
45 ERITREA
46 OMAN
47 UNITED ARAB EMIRATES
48 QATAR
49 BAHRAIN
50 ARMENIA
51 GEORGIA
52 AZERBAIJAN
53 TURKMENISTAN
54 UZBEKISTAN
55 TAJIKISTAN
56 KYRGYZSTAN
57 BANGLADESH
58 CAMBODIA
59 British Indian Ocean Territory

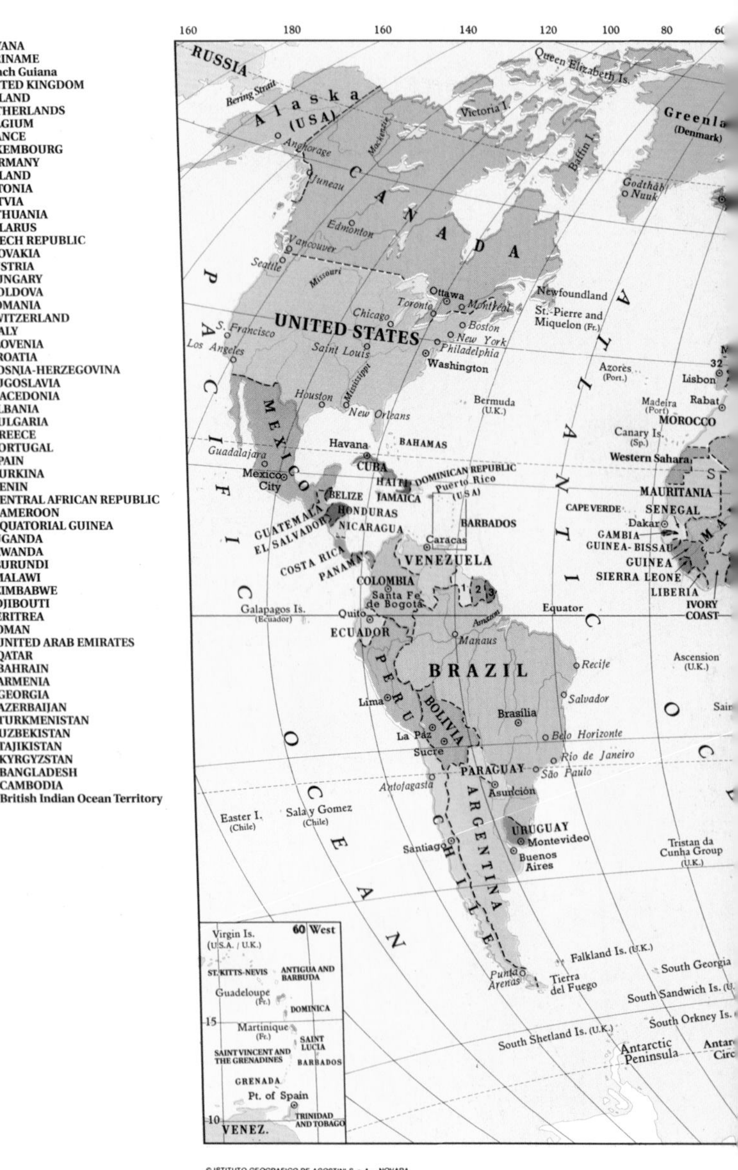

© ISTITUTO GEOGRAFICO DE AGOSTINI S.p.A. - NOVARA

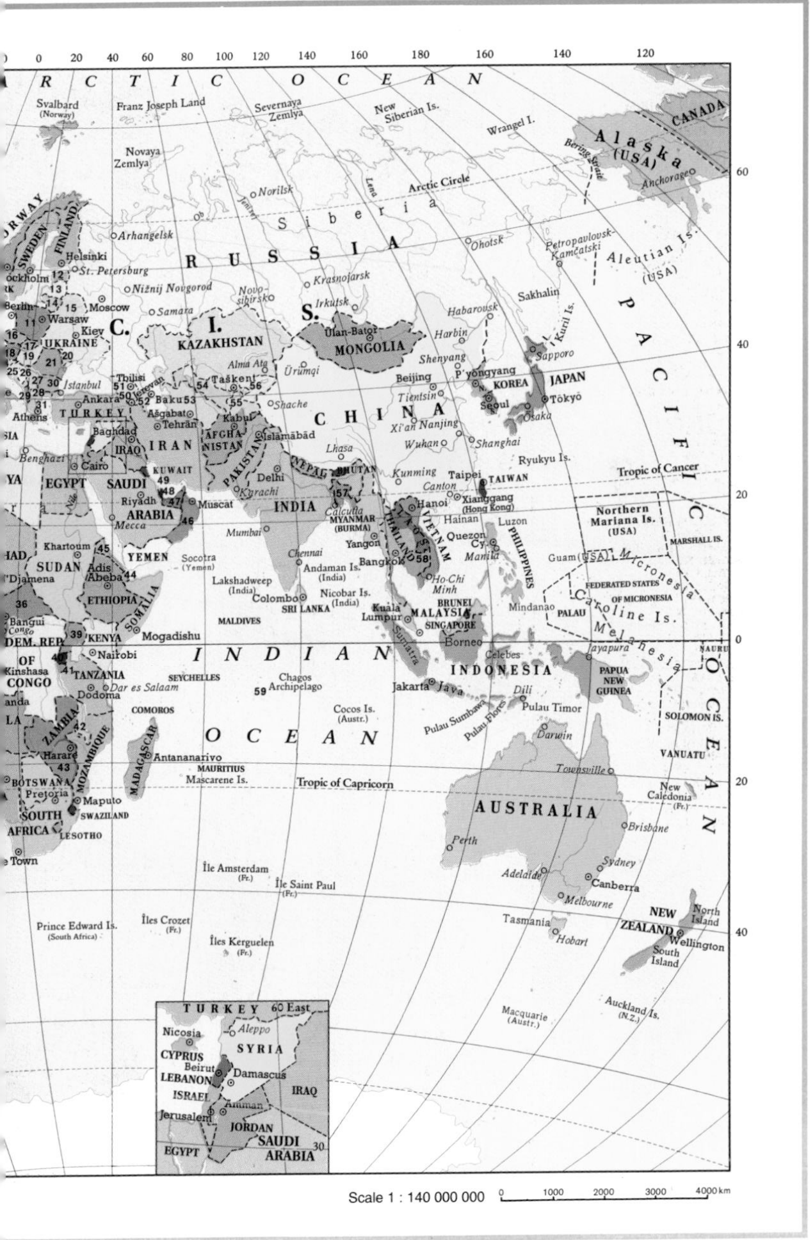
A R C T I C O C E A N
Svalbard (Norway)
Franz Joseph Land
Severnaya Zemlya
New Siberian Is.
Wrangel I.
Novaya Zemlya
Alaska (USA)
CANADA
Bering Strait
Anchorage
Arctic Circle
Norilsk
Lena
Siberia
NORWAY
SWEDEN
FINLAND
Arhangelsk
Helsinki
St. Petersburg
Stockholm
Nižnij Novgorod
Moscow
Samara
Novosibirsk
Krasnojarsk
Irkutsk
Ohotsk
Petropavlovsk-Kamčatski
Aleutian Is. (USA)
Sakhalin
Kuril Is.
Habarovsk
Harbin
RUSSIA
C. I. S.
Berlin
Warsaw
Kiev
UKRAINE
KAZAKHSTAN
Ulan-Bator
MONGOLIA
Shenyang
Sapporo
P'yongyang
KOREA
JAPAN
Seoul
Tōkyō
Ōsaka
Beijing
Tientsin
Nanjing
Xi'an
Shanghai
Wuhan
Alma Ata
Taškent
Ürümqi
Shache
Tbilisi
Yerevan
Baku
Istanbul
Ankara
Athens
TURKEY
Ašgabat
Tehrān
Kabul
AFGHANISTAN
Islāmābād
PAKISTAN
Baghdad
IRAQ
IRAN
Benghazi
Cairo
KUWAIT
EGYPT
SAUDI ARABIA
Riyadh
Mecca
Muscat
Delhi
Karachi
NEPAL
BHUTAN
Lhasa
CHINA
Kunming
Canton
Taipei
TAIWAN
Ryukyu Is.
Tropic of Cancer
Hanoi
Xianggang (Hong Kong)
Hainan
Luzon
INDIA
Calcutta
MYANMAR (BURMA)
Yangon
THAILAND
LAOS
VIETNAM
Mumbai
Quezon Cy.
Manila
PHILIPPINES
Northern Mariana Is. (USA)
MARSHALL IS.
Guam (USA)
Micronesia
FEDERATED STATES OF MICRONESIA
Caroline Is.
PALAU
Mindanao
Khartoum
SUDAN
YEMEN
Socotra (Yemen)
Chennai
Andaman Is. (India)
Bangkok
Ho Chi Minh
Adis Abeba
ETHIOPIA
SOMALIA
Lakshadweep (India)
Colombo
SRI LANKA
Nicobar Is. (India)
Kuala Lumpur
MALAYSIA
BRUNEI
SINGAPORE
Djamena
Bangui
Congo
DEM. REP. OF CONGO
Kinshasa
KENYA
Mogadishu
MALDIVES
Sumatra
Borneo
Celebes
Melanesia
Jayapura
NAURU
Nairobi
TANZANIA
Dar es Salaam
Dodoma
SEYCHELLES
INDIAN OCEAN
Chagos Archipelago
INDONESIA
PAPUA NEW GUINEA
Jakarta
Java
Dili
Pulau Timor
Pulau Sumbawa
Pulau Flores
SOLOMON IS.
ZAMBIA
MOZAMBIQUE
COMOROS
Harare
Cocos Is. (Austr.)
Darwin
VANUATU
MADAGASCAR
Antananarivo
MAURITIUS
Mascarene Is.
Tropic of Capricorn
Townsville
New Caledonia (Fr.)
BOTSWANA
Pretoria
Maputo
SWAZILAND
SOUTH AFRICA
LESOTHO
Cape Town
AUSTRALIA
Brisbane
Perth
Île Amsterdam (Fr.)
Île Saint Paul (Fr.)
Sydney
Adelaide
Canberra
Melbourne
Prince Edward Is. (South Africa)
Îles Crozet (Fr.)
Îles Kerguelen (Fr.)
Tasmania
Hobart
NEW ZEALAND
North Island
Wellington
South Island
Macquarie (Austr.)
Auckland Is. (N.Z.)
PACIFIC OCEAN
TURKEY
60 East
Nicosia
Aleppo
SYRIA
CYPRUS
Beirut
LEBANON
Damascus
IRAQ
ISRAEL
Amman
Jerusalem
JORDAN
EGYPT
SAUDI ARABIA
Scale 1 : 140 000 000
0 1000 2000 3000 4000 km

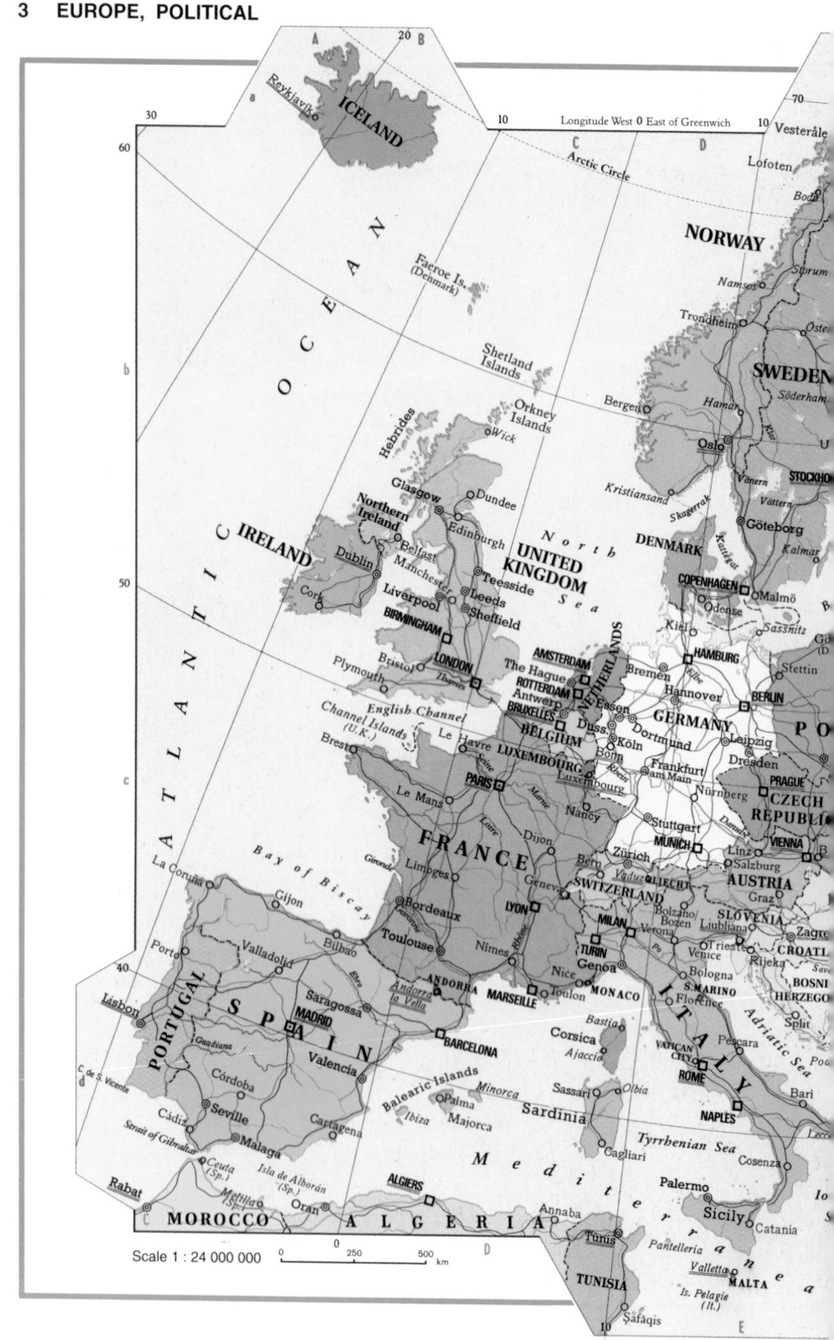
ICELAND
Reykjavík
Longitude West 0 East of Greenwich
Arctic Circle
ATLANTIC OCEAN
Faeroe Is. (Denmark)
Shetland Islands
Orkney Islands
Hebrides
NORWAY
SWEDEN
Lofoten
Vesterålen
Trondheim
Bergen
Oslo
Kristiansand
Skagerrak
Göteborg
STOCKHOLM
DENMARK
COPENHAGEN
Malmö
North Sea
UNITED KINGDOM
IRELAND
Northern Ireland
Dublin
Belfast
Glasgow
Dundee
Edinburgh
Manchester
Liverpool
Leeds
Sheffield
Teesside
BIRMINGHAM
LONDON
Bristol
Plymouth
Cork
English Channel
Channel Islands (U.K.)
NETHERLANDS
AMSTERDAM
ROTTERDAM
The Hague
Antwerp
BRUXELLES
BELGIUM
LUXEMBOURG
Luxembourg
GERMANY
HAMBURG
Bremen
Hannover
BERLIN
Essen
Düss
Dortmund
Köln
Bonn
Frankfurt am Main
Leipzig
Dresden
Nürnberg
Stuttgart
MUNICH
PRAGUE
CZECH REPUBLIC
VIENNA
AUSTRIA
Linz
Salzburg
Graz
FRANCE
PARIS
Le Havre
Brest
Le Mans
Nancy
Dijon
Limoges
Bordeaux
Toulouse
LYON
Nîmes
MARSEILLE
Toulon
Nice
MONACO
Bay of Biscay
SWITZERLAND
Bern
Zürich
Geneva
LIECHT.
Vaduz
SLOVENIA
Ljubljana
CROATIA
Zagreb
ITALY
MILAN
TURIN
Genoa
Verona
Venice
Trieste
Bologna
S.MARINO
Florence
VATICAN CITY
ROME
NAPLES
Pescara
Bari
Cosenza
Adriatic Sea
Tyrrhenian Sea
Corsica
Bastia
Ajaccio
Sardinia
Sassari
Olbia
Cagliari
Sicily
Palermo
Catania
Valletta
MALTA
SPAIN
MADRID
PORTUGAL
Lisbon
Porto
La Coruña
Gijon
Bilbao
Valladolid
Saragossa
ANDORRA
Andorra la Vella
BARCELONA
Valencia
Córdoba
Seville
Cádiz
Malaga
Cartagena
Strait of Gibraltar
Balearic Islands
Minorca
Majorca
Palma
Ibiza
Mediterranean
MOROCCO
Rabat
Ceuta (Sp.)
Melilla (Sp.)
ALGERIA
ALGIERS
Oran
Annaba
TUNISIA
Tunis
Şafāqis
Pantelleria
Is. Pelagie (It.)
Scale 1 : 24 000 000
0 250 500 km

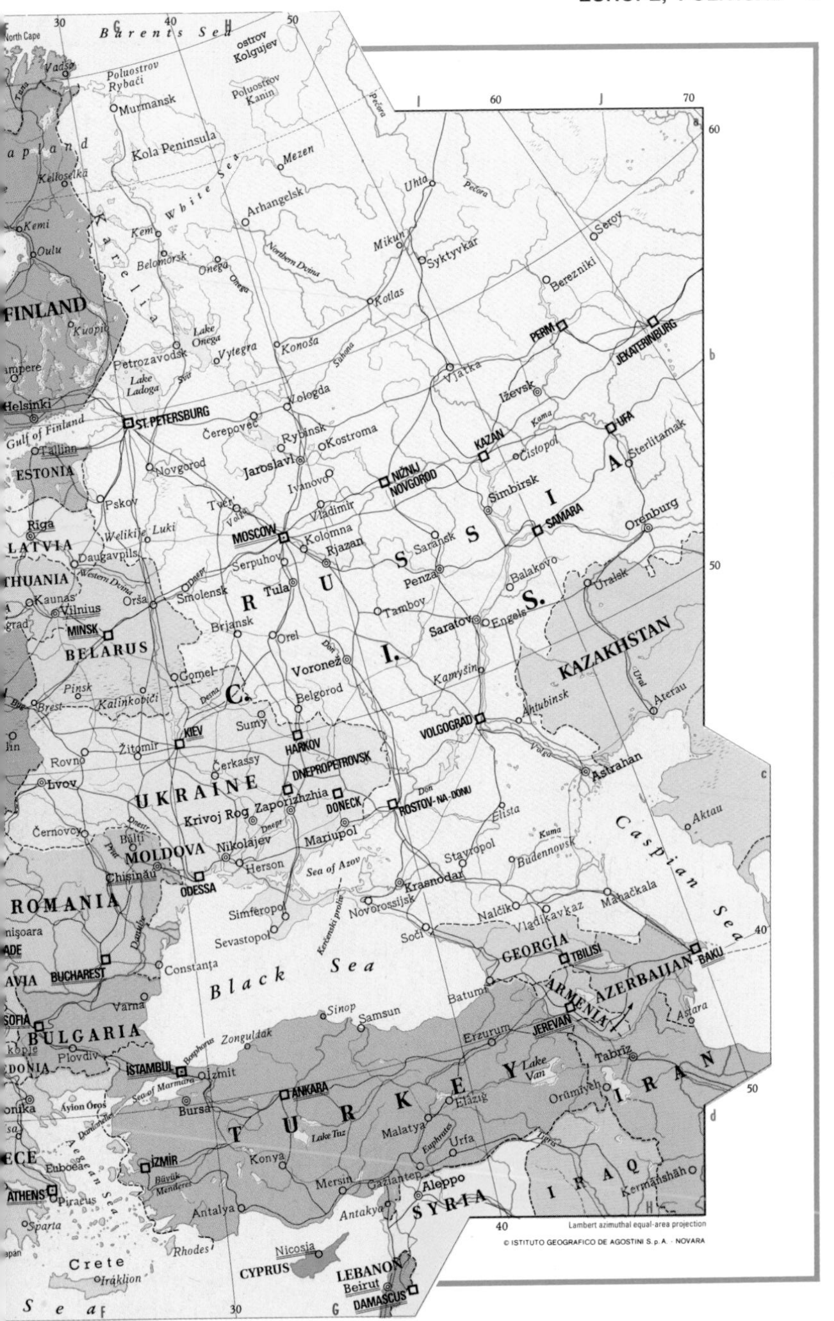
Barents Sea
White Sea
Black Sea
Caspian Sea
Sea of Azov
FINLAND
ESTONIA
LATVIA
BELARUS
UKRAINE
MOLDOVA
ROMANIA
BULGARIA
RUSSIA
KAZAKHSTAN
GEORGIA
ARMENIA
AZERBAIJAN
TURKEY
IRAN
IRAQ
SYRIA
LEBANON
CYPRUS
MOSCOW
ST. PETERSBURG
KIEV
MINSK
BUCHAREST
SOFIA
ATHENS
ANKARA
TBILISI
JEREVAN
BAKU
DAMASCUS
Lambert azimuthal equal-area projection
© ISTITUTO GEOGRAFICO DE AGOSTINI S.p.A. - NOVARA

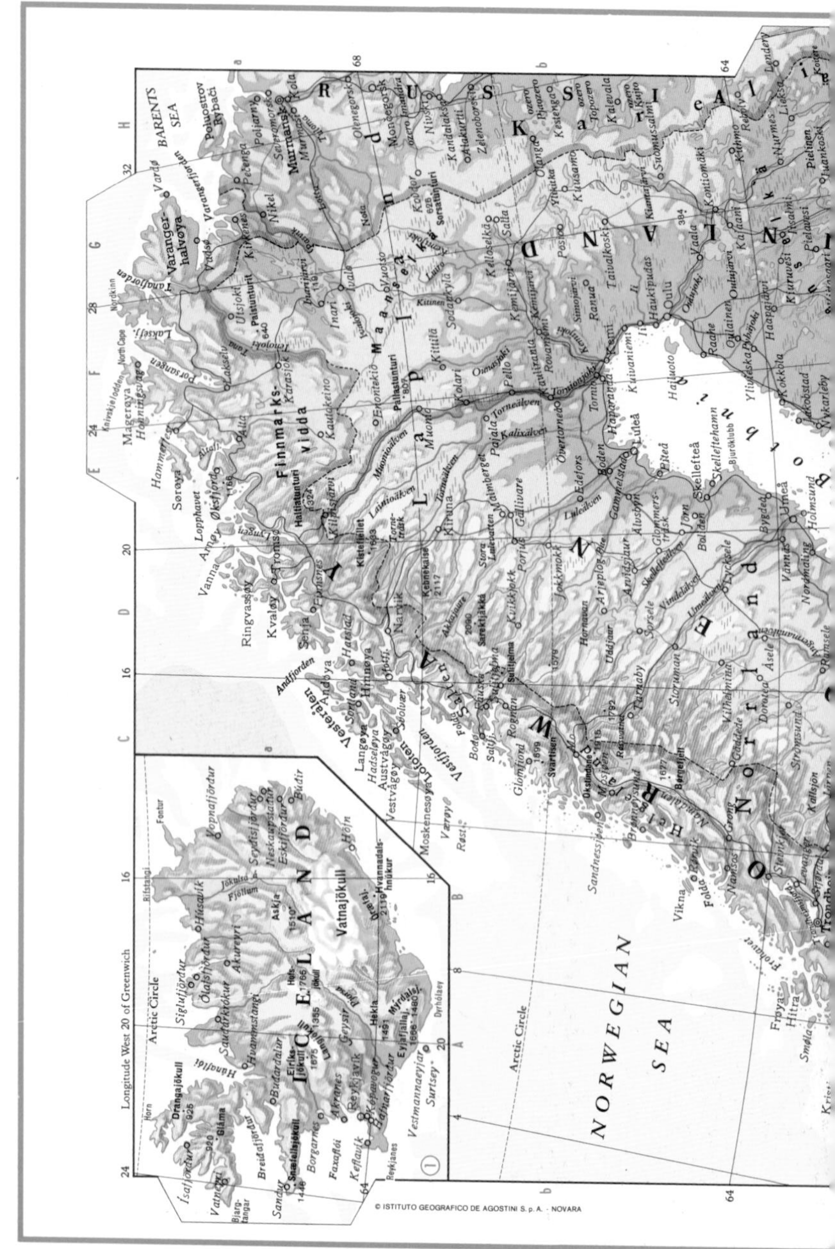
BARENTS SEA
NORWEGIAN SEA
ICELAND
Vatnajökull
Longitude West 20 of Greenwich
Arctic Circle
© ISTITUTO GEOGRAFICO DE AGOSTINI S.p.A. - NOVARA

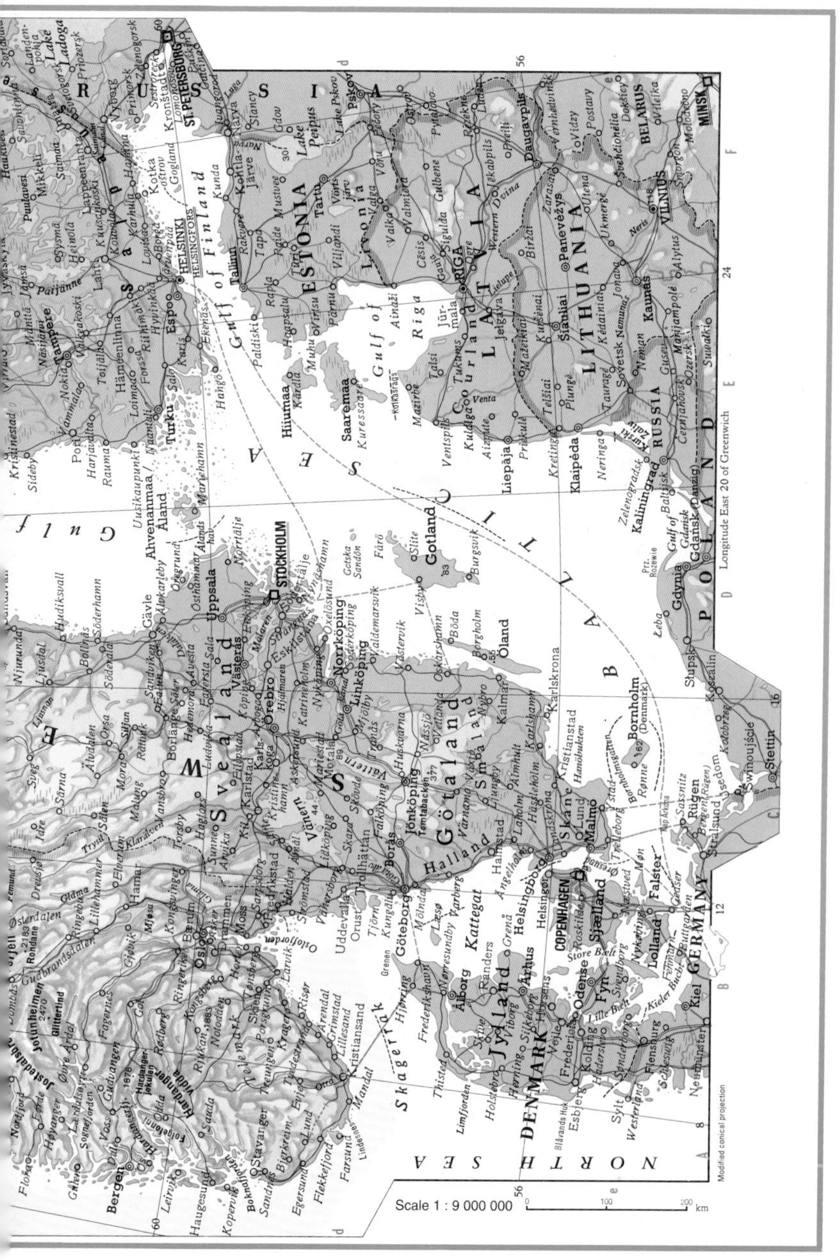
Scale 1 : 9 000 000
0
100
200
km
Modified conical projection
Longitude East 20 of Greenwich
NORTH SEA
BALTIC SEA
Gulf of Finland
Gulf of Riga
Skagerrak
Kattegat
Lake Ladoga
Lake Peipus
ESTONIA
LATVIA
LITHUANIA
BELARUS
RUSSIA
POLAND
GERMANY
DENMARK
Jylland
Svealand
Götaland
HELSINKI
HELSINGFORS
ST. PETERSBURG
STOCKHOLM
COPENHAGEN
RIGA
VILNIUS
MINSK
Tallinn
Tartu
Daugavpils
Kaunas
Klaipeda
Kaliningrad
Gdańsk (Danzig)
Gdynia
Stettin
Oslo
Bergen
Stavanger
Göteborg
Malmö
Uppsala
Västerås
Norrköping
Linköping
Jönköping
Örebro
Gotland
Öland
Saaremaa
Hiiumaa
Bornholm
(Denmark)
Åland
Turku
Tampere
Espoo
Ålborg
Århus
Odense
Fyn
Sjælland
Lolland
Falster
Rügen
Kiel
Flensburg
Helsingborg
Helsingør
Esbjerg
Kristiansand
Hardangervidda
Jotunheimen
Vänern
Vättern

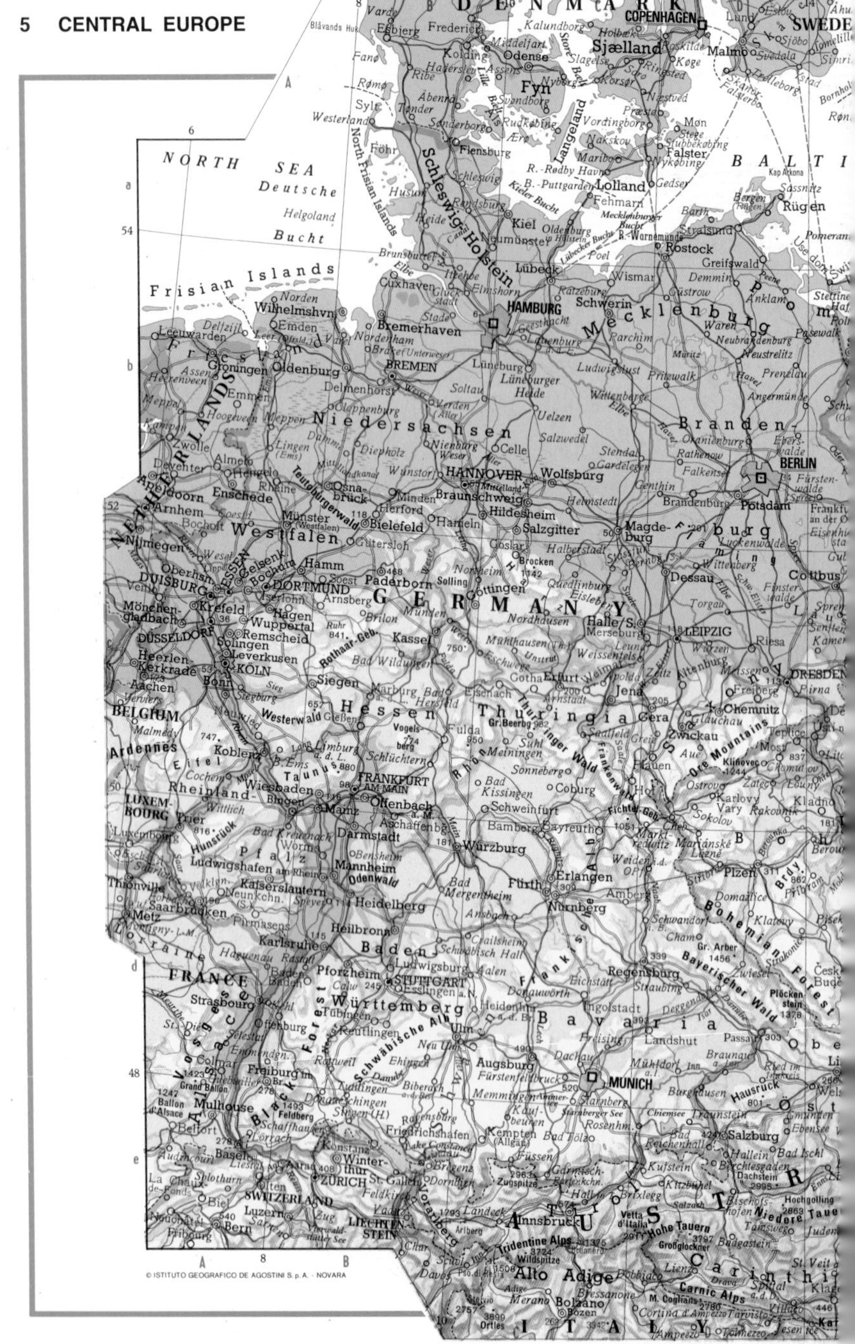
DENMARK
COPENHAGEN
Sjælland
Fyn
Odense
Esbjerg
Kolding
Langeland
Lolland
Falster
Malmö
SWEDEN
NORTH SEA
Deutsche Bucht
Helgoland
Frisian Islands
North Frisian Islands
Schleswig-Holstein
Flensburg
Kiel
Lübeck
Rostock
Rügen
Stralsund
Greifswald
Wismar
Schwerin
Mecklenburg
HAMBURG
Cuxhaven
Bremerhaven
Wilhelmshvn
Emden
BREMEN
Oldenburg
Groningen
Leeuwarden
Friesland
NETHERLANDS
Niedersachsen
Lüneburg
Lüneburger Heide
Uelzen
Celle
HANNOVER
Wolfsburg
Braunschweig
Hildesheim
Salzgitter
Magdeburg
BERLIN
Potsdam
Brandenburg
Osnabrück
Münster
Bielefeld
Teutoburgerwald
Westfalen
Hamm
DORTMUND
ESSEN
Bochum
Gelsenk.
DUISBURG
Krefeld
Mönchengladbach
DÜSSELDORF
Wuppertal
Remscheid
Solingen
Leverkusen
KÖLN
Bonn
Aachen
Hagen
Iserlohn
Paderborn
Kassel
Göttingen
Harz
Brocken
Dessau
Halle
LEIPZIG
Wittenberg
Cottbus
GERMANY
Rothaar-Geb.
Siegen
Westerwald
Hessen
Thuringia
Thüringer Wald
Erfurt
Jena
Gera
Gotha
Eisenach
Weimar
DRESDEN
Chemnitz
Zwickau
Ore Mountains
BELGIUM
Ardennes
Eifel
Koblenz
Taunus
Wiesbaden
FRANKFURT AM MAIN
Offenbach
Mainz
Darmstadt
Rheinland-Pfalz
Hunsrück
LUXEMBOURG
Trier
Saarbrücken
Metz
Lorraine
Ludwigshafen
Mannheim
Heidelberg
Kaiserslautern
Würzburg
Bamberg
Bayreuth
Erlangen
Fürth
Nürnberg
Plzeň
Bohemian Forest
Bayerischer Wald
Regensburg
Heilbronn
Karlsruhe
Pforzheim
STUTTGART
Baden-Württemberg
FRANCE
Strasbourg
Vosges
Alsace
Black Forest
Schwäbische Alb
Ulm
Augsburg
Ingolstadt
Bavaria
MUNICH
Landshut
Passau
Freiburg
Mulhouse
Colmar
Basel
Lake Constance
ZÜRICH
SWITZERLAND
Luzern
Bern
LIECHTENSTEIN
Innsbruck
Salzburg
AUSTRIA
Tridentine Alps
Alto Adige
Bolzano
Hohe Tauern
Carinthia
Carnic Alps
ITALY

© ISTITUTO GEOGRAFICO DE AGOSTINI S. p. A. - NOVARA

Long. East 20 of Greenwich

RUSSIA
Kaliningrad
Gulf of Gdańsk
Gdynia
Sopot
Gdańsk (Danzig)
Elbląg
Słupsk
Koszalin
Olsztyn
Eastern Prussia
Pojezierze Mazurskie
LITHUANIA
Grodno
Białystok
BELARUS
Bydgoszcz
Toruń
Włocławek
Płock
POZNAŃ
Great Poland
WARSAW
POLAND
Kalisz
ŁÓDŹ
Radom
Lublin
Brest
BRESLAU
Opole
Częstochowa
Kielce
Little Poland
Katowice
Gliwice
KRAKÓW
Tarnów
Rzeszów
Przemyśl
LVOV
UKRAINE
Ostrava
Olomouc
Brno
WESTERN CARPATHIANS
Beskidy Zachodnie
Vysoké Tatry
Nízke Tatry
SLOVAKIA
Košice
Užgorod
Bratislava
VIENNA
Miskolc
Nyíregyháza
Debrecen
Oradea
BUDAPEST
Győr
Székesfehérvár
Bakony Mountains
HUNGARY
ROMANIA

Modified conical projection
Scale 1 : 6 000 000
0 50 100 150 km

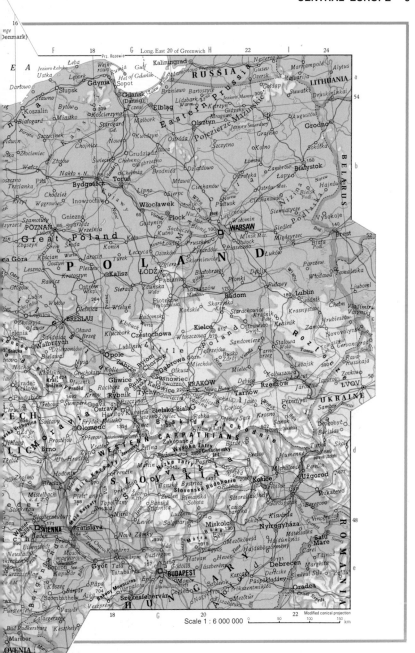

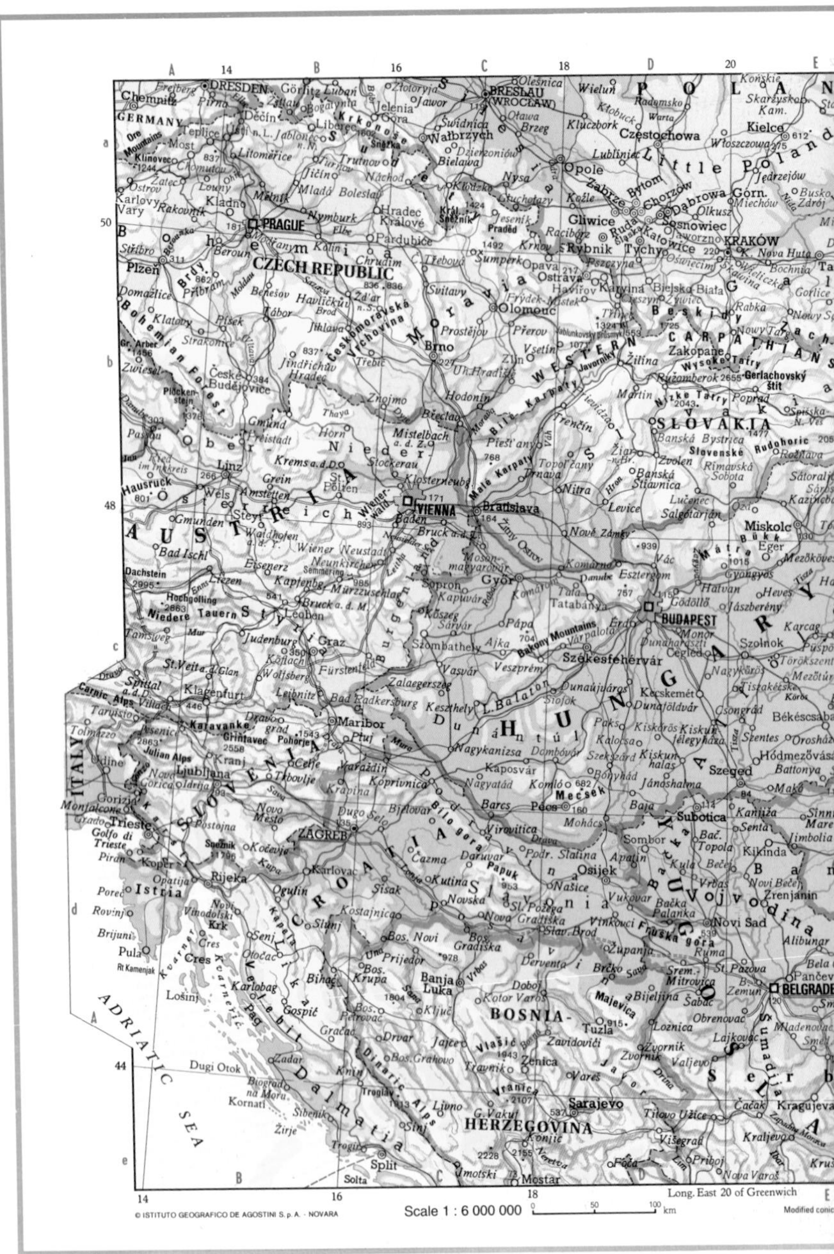

Scale 1 : 6 000 000

Long. East 20 of Greenwich

© ISTITUTO GEOGRAFICO DE AGOSTINI S.p.A. · NOVARA

Modified conic.

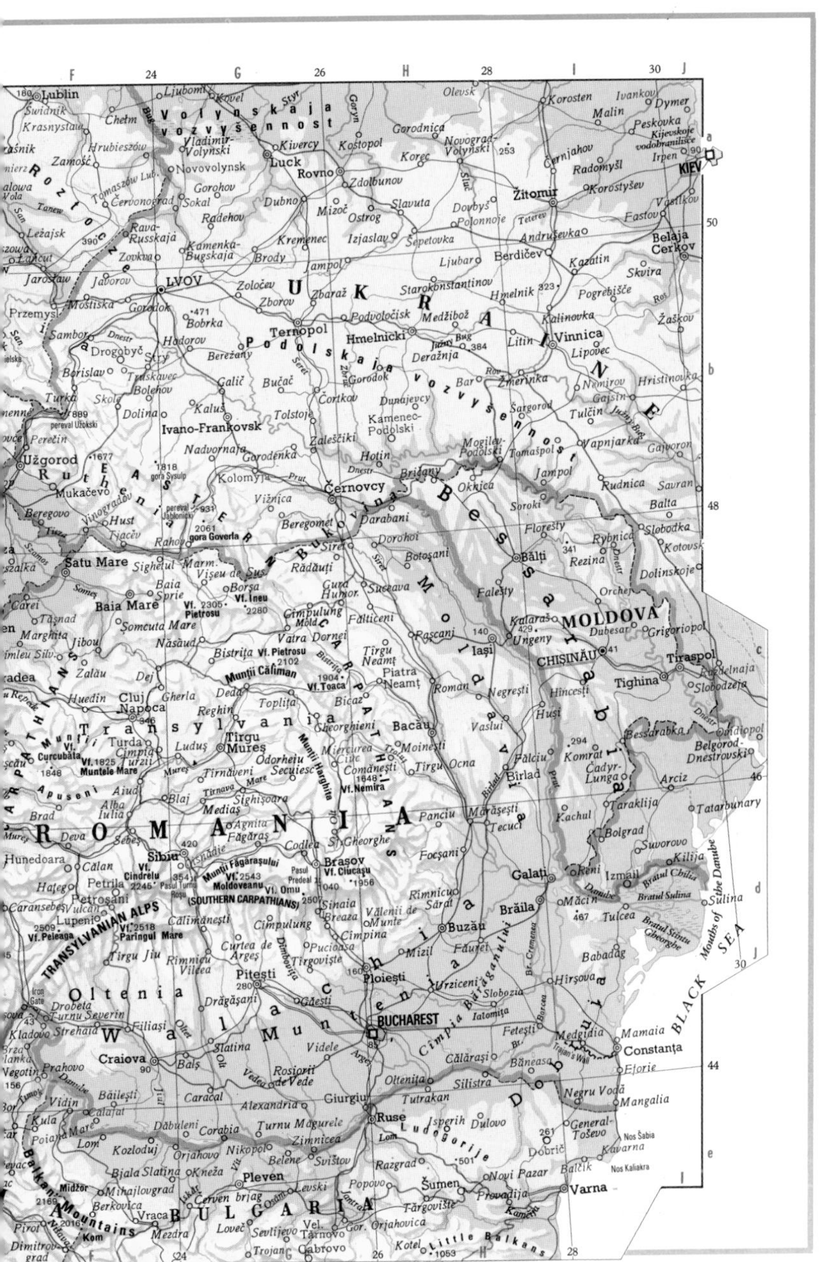

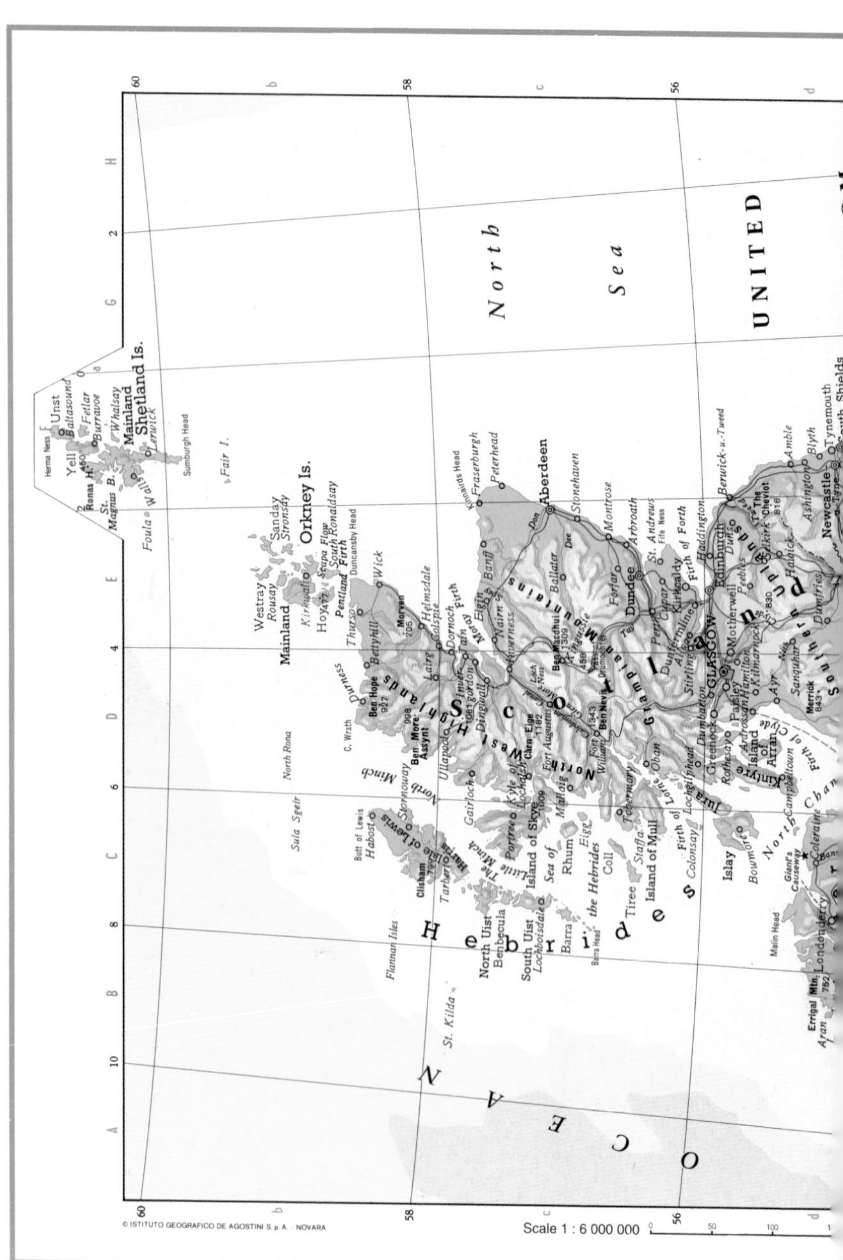
North Sea
UNITED
Shetland Is.
Orkney Is.
Mainland
Unst
Yell
Fetlar
Whalsay
Lerwick
Foula
Fair I.
Sumburgh Head
Westray
Rousay
Sanday
Stronsay
Kirkwall
Hoy
Scapa Flow
South Ronaldsay
Pentland Firth
Duncansby Head
Wick
Thurso
Helmsdale
Dornoch Firth
Moray Firth
Kinnairds Head
Fraserburgh
Peterhead
Aberdeen
Stonehaven
Montrose
Arbroath
Dundee
St. Andrews
Firth of Forth
Edinburgh
Berwick-u.-Tweed
Haddington
Perth
Kirkcaldy
Dunfermline
Stirling
GLASGOW
Motherwell
Hamilton
Paisley
Greenock
Dumbarton
Kilmarnock
Ayr
Dumfries
Hawick
Peebles
The Cheviot
Amble
Blyth
Ashington
Tynemouth
Newcastle
Inverness
Nairn
Elgin
Banff
Dingwall
Ullapool
Gairloch
Portree
Mallaig
Fort William
Fort Augustus
Ben Nevis
1343
Ben Macdhui
1309
Oban
Tobermory
Grampian Mountains
Scotland
North West Highlands
Ben Hope
927
Ben More Assynt
998
C. Wrath
Durness
North Rona
Sula Sgeir
Butt of Lewis
Stornoway
Isle of Lewis
Harris
North Minch
Little Minch
The Minch
Island of Skye
Sea of the Hebrides
Rhum
Eigg
Coll
Tiree
Staffa
Island of Mull
Jura
Islay
Colonsay
Kintyre
Island of Arran
Firth of Clyde
Campbeltown
North Channel
North Uist
Benbecula
South Uist
Barra
Flannan Isles
St. Kilda
Hebrides
Giant's Causeway
Coleraine
Londonderry
Malin Head
Errigal Mtn.
752
OCEAN
© ISTITUTO GEOGRAFICO DE AGOSTINI S. p. A. - NOVARA
Scale 1 : 6 000 000

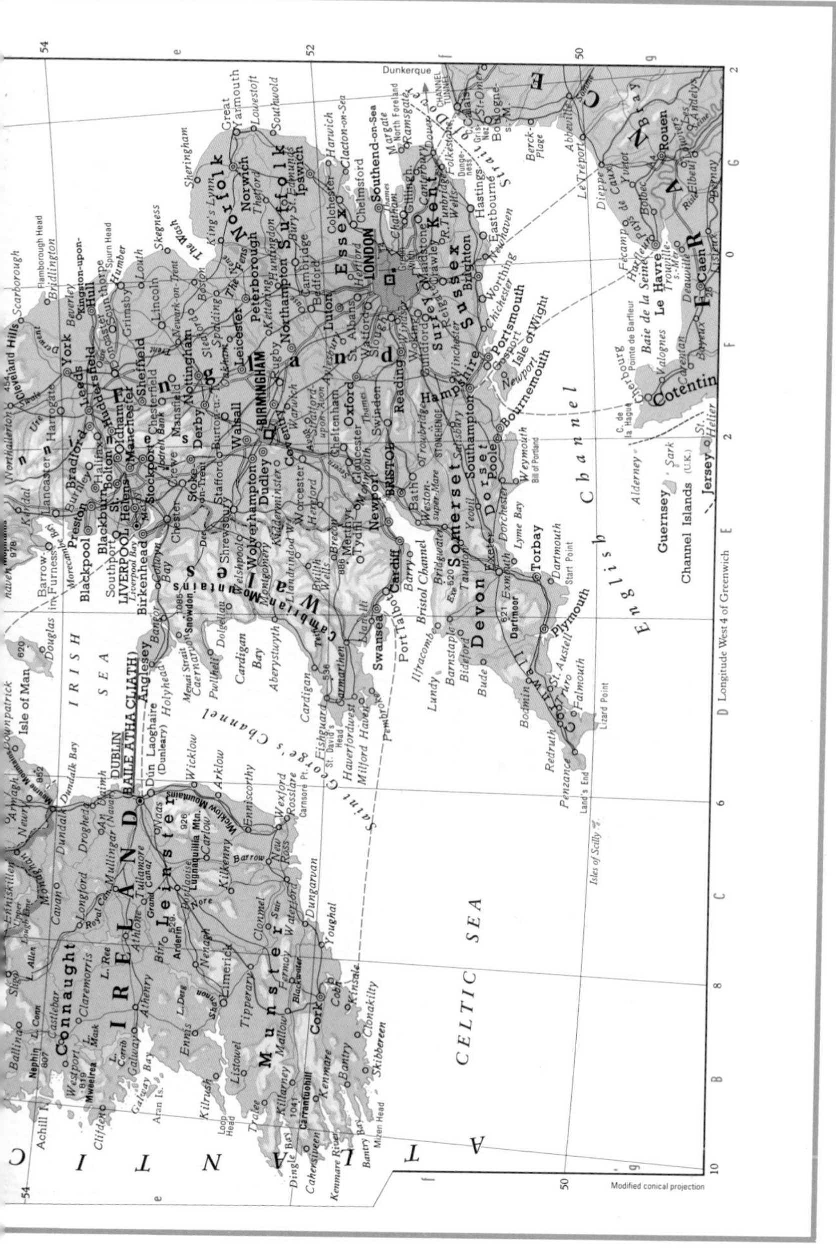
IRELAND
Connaught
Leinster
Munster
DUBLIN
BAILE ATHA CLIATH
Cork
Limerick
Galway
Waterford
Wexford
Kilkenny
Tipperary
Dundalk
Drogheda
Athlone
Isle of Man
Douglas
IRISH SEA
CELTIC SEA
St. George's Channel
Bristol Channel
English Channel
Wales
Cambrian Mountains
Snowdon
Anglesey
Cardigan Bay
Cardiff
Swansea
Newport
England
LONDON
BIRMINGHAM
BRISTOL
LIVERPOOL
Manchester
Leeds
Sheffield
York
Nottingham
Leicester
Coventry
Wolverhampton
Oxford
Reading
Southampton
Portsmouth
Brighton
Plymouth
Exeter
Bournemouth
Norwich
Ipswich
Peterborough
Northampton
Norfolk
Suffolk
Essex
Kent
Sussex
Surrey
Hampshire
Dorset
Somerset
Devon
Cornwall
Isle of Wight
The Wash
Channel Islands (U.K.)
Guernsey
Jersey
Alderney
Sark
Isles of Scilly
Land's End
Lizard Point
Cotentin
Cherbourg
Le Havre
Rouen
Caen
Dieppe
Calais
Boulogne
Dunkerque
FRANCE
CHANNEL TUNNEL
Strait of Dover
Longitude West 4 of Greenwich
Modified conical projection

NORTH SEA
ATLANTIC
English Channel
UNITED KINGDOM
NETHERLANDS
BELGIUM
GERMANY
LUXEMBOURG
FRANCE
Ardennes
Lorraine
Champagne
Picardy
Flanders
Normandie
Bretagne
Beauce
Orléanais
Maine
Cotentin
Île de France
Channel Islands (U.K.)
Guernsey
Jersey
Alderney
Sark
LONDON
PARIS
BRUXELLES/BRUSSEL
AMSTERDAM
THE HAGUE
ROTTERDAM
BIRMINGHAM
BRISTOL
Modified conical projection
Longitude East 2 of Greenwich

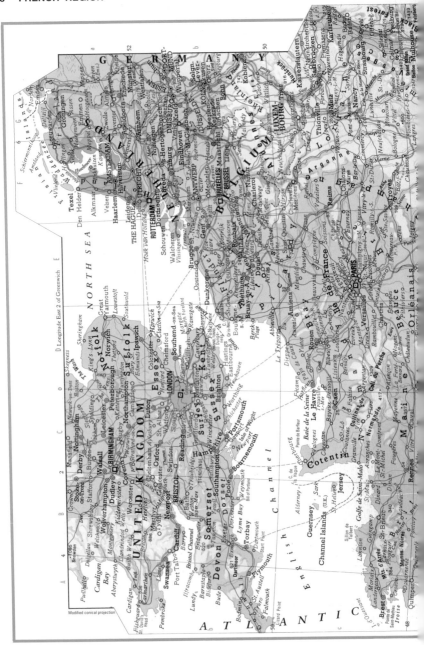

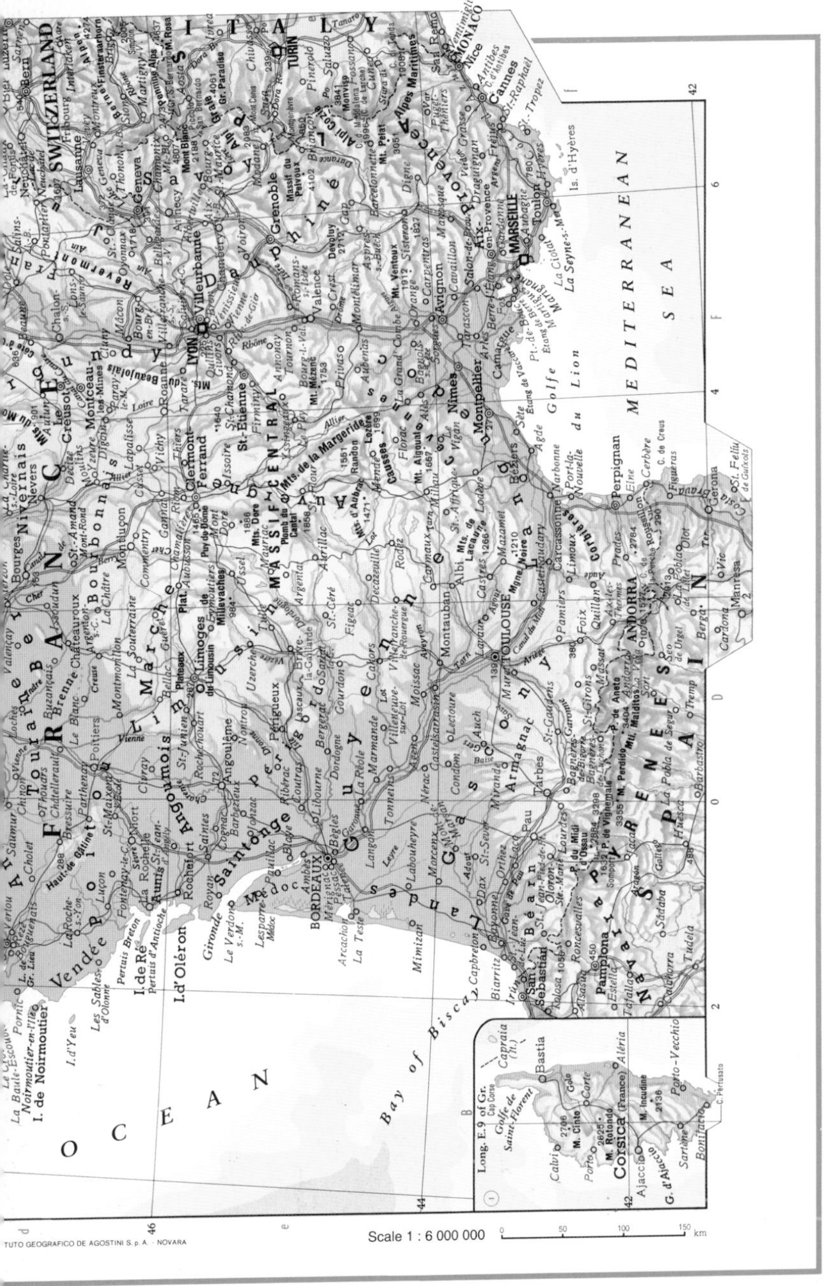
FRANCE
SWITZERLAND
ITALY
ANDORRA
Corsica (France)
MASSIF CENTRAL
OCEAN
Bay of Biscay
MEDITERRANEAN SEA
Golfe du Lion
PYRENEES
Alpes Maritimes
Provence
Dauphiné
Bordeaux
Toulouse
Lyon
Marseille
Grenoble
Limoges
Clermont-Ferrand
Montpellier
Nîmes
Avignon
Perpignan
Toulon
Nice
Cannes
Monaco
Turin
Geneva
Lausanne
Bern
Bastia
Ajaccio
Scale 1 : 6 000 000
TUTO GEOGRAFICO DE AGOSTINI S. p. A. - NOVARA

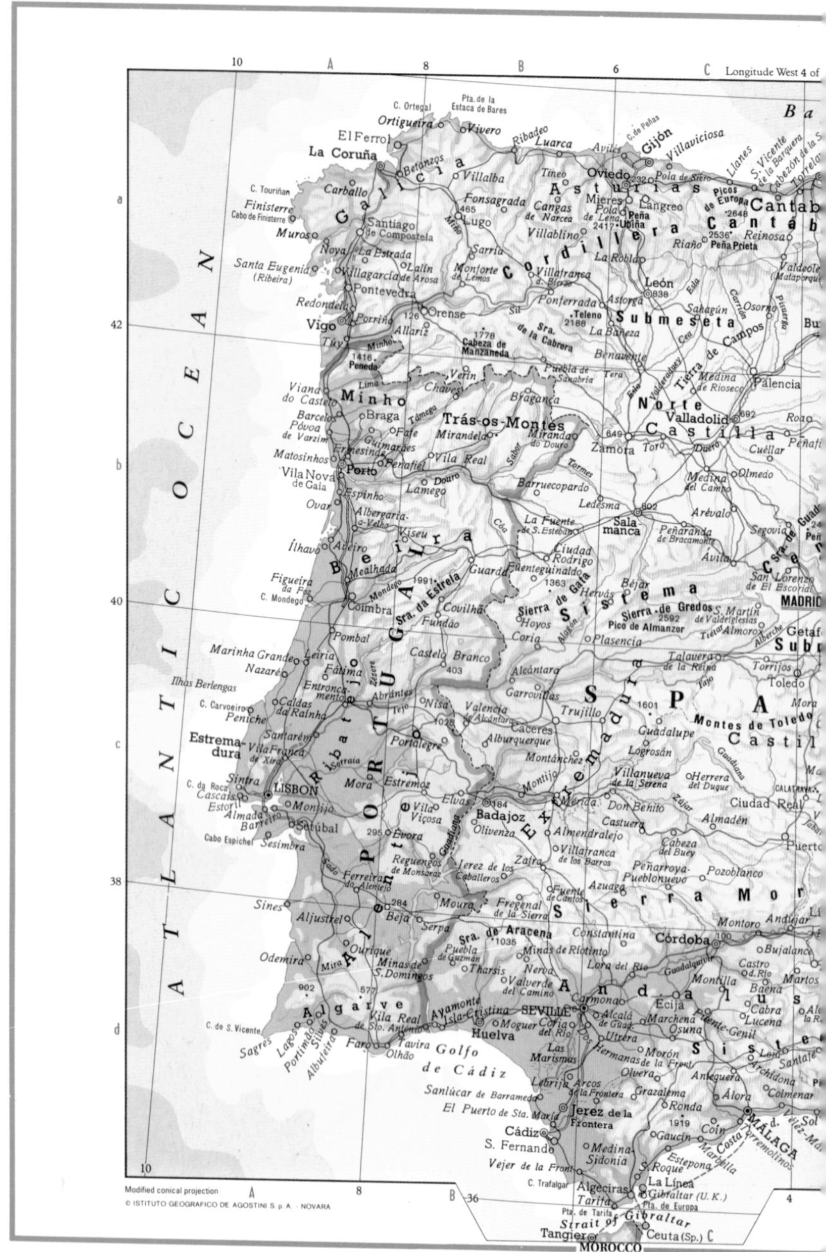
Longitude West 4 of
ATLANTIC OCEAN
PORTUGAL
SPAIN
Galicia
Asturias
Cordillera Cantábrica
Trás-os-Montes
Minho
Beira
Estremadura
Ribatejo
Alentejo
Algarve
Andalusia
Extremadura
Sistema Central
Sierra Morena
LISBON
Porto
MADRID
SEVILLE
Córdoba
MÁLAGA
Golfo de Cádiz
Strait of Gibraltar
MOROCCO
Modified conical projection
© ISTITUTO GEOGRAFICO DE AGOSTINI S. p. A. - NOVARA

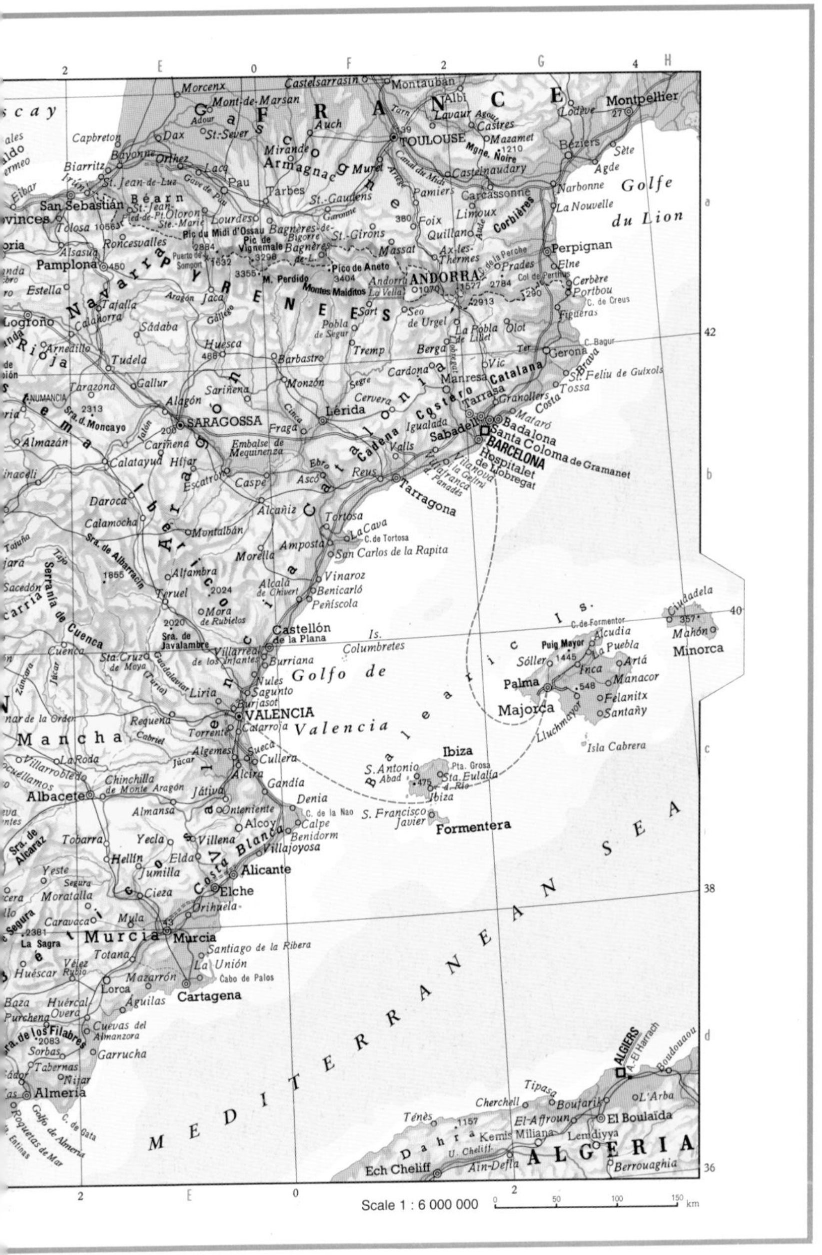
FRANCE
Morcenx
Castelsarrasin
Montauban
Mont-de-Marsan
Albi
Lavaur
Castres
Montpellier
Lodève
Auch
Dax
St.-Sever
Capbreton
Bayonne
Orthez
Mirande
TOULOUSE
Mazamet
Mgne. Noire
1210
Béziers
Sète
Agde
Biarritz
Lacq
Armagnac
Muret
Castelnaudary
Canal du Midi
St.-Jean-de-Luz
Pau
Tarbes
Narbonne
Golfe
du Lion
Irún
San Sebastián
Béarn
St.-Gaudens
Pamiers
Carcassonne
La Nouvelle
St.-Jean-Pied-de-Port
Oloron-Ste.-Marie
Lourdes
Foix
Limoux
Corbières
Tolosa
Pic du Midi d'Ossau
Bagnères-de-Bigorre
St.-Girons
Quillan
Roncesvalles
Pic de Vignemale
Bagnères-de-L.
Massat
Ax-les-Thermes
Perpignan
Alsasua
Pamplona
450
2884
3298
Pico de Aneto
Prades
Elne
Estella
3355
M. Perdido
3404
Montes Malditos
Andorra
La Vella
ANDORRA
2784
Col de Perthus
Cerbère
Portbou
C. de Creus
Navarra
PYRENEES
Aragón
Jaca
Sort
Seo de Urgel
2913
Figueras
Logroño
Tafalla
Calahorra
Sádaba
Pobla de Segur
La Pobla de Lillet
Olot
Rioja
Arnedillo
Huesca
Tremp
Berga
C. Bagur
Gerona
Costa Brava
Tudela
Barbastro
Vic
Ter
St. Feliu de Guixols
Tarazona
Gallur
Monzón
Segre
Cardona
Manresa
Catalana
Tossa
NUMANCIA
Alagón
Sariñena
Cervera
Tarrasa
Granollers
2313
Sra. d. Moncayo
SARAGOSSA
Lérida
Cordillera Costera
Igualada
Mataró
Fraga
Sabadell
Badalona
Almazán
Cariñena
Embalse de Mequinenza
Valls
Santa Coloma de Gramanet
BARCELONA
Hospitalet de Llobregat
Calatayud
Híjar
Ebro
Reus
Vilanova i la Geltrú
Vilafranca d. Panadés
Escatrón
Caspe
Ascó
Tarragona
Daroca
Alcañiz
Tortosa
Calamocha
Montalbán
La Cava
C. de Tortosa
Amposta
San Carlos de la Rapita
Sra. de Albarracín
Morella
Serranía de Cuenca
1855
Alfambra
Alcalá de Chivert
Vinaroz
Benicarló
Peñíscola
Teruel
2024
Mora de Rubielos
Ciudadela
Mahón
Minorca
357
2020
Sra. de Javalambre
Castellón de la Plana
Is. Columbretes
C. de Formentor
Alcudia
Puig Mayor
1445
La Puebla
Cuenca
Sta. Cruz de Moya
Villarreal de los Infantes
Burriana
Sóller
Artá
Inca
Manacor
Golfo de Valencia
Nules
Sagunto
Palma
548
Felanitx
Liria
Majorca
Santañy
Burjasot
VALENCIA
Requena
Catarroja
Torrente
Llucmayor
Mancha
Cabriel
Isla Cabrera
Algemesí
Sueca
Cullera
Júcar
La Roda
Villarrobledo
Ibiza
Pta. Grosa
S. Antonio Abad
475
Sta. Eulalia
Chinchilla de Monte Aragón
Alcira
Gandía
Albacete
Játiva
Denia
C. de la Nao
Almansa
Ontenient
S. Francisco Javier
Formentera
Alcoy
Calpe
Benidorm
Tobarra
Yecla
Villena
Villajoyosa
Hellín
Elda
Costa Blanca
Yeste
Jumilla
Alicante
Segura
Moratalla
Cieza
Elche
Orihuela
Caravaca
Mula
43
2381
La Sagra
Murcia
Santiago de la Ribera
Totana
La Unión
Vélez Rubio
Huéscar
Mazarrón
Cabo de Palos
Lorca
Cartagena
Águilas
Baza
Huércal-Overa
Purchena
Cuevas del Almanzora
Sra. de los Filabres
2083
Sorbas
Garrucha
Tabernas
Níjar
Almería
C. de Gata
Golfo de Almería
Roquetas de Mar
MEDITERRANEAN SEA
ALGIERS
El Harrach
Boudouaou
Tipasa
Cherchell
Boufarik
L'Arba
Ténès
1157
El-Affroun
El Boulaïda
Dahra
Kemis Miliana
Lemdiyya
U. Cheliff
Ech Cheliff
Aïn-Defla
ALGERIA
Berrouaghia
42
40
38
36
2
E
0
F
G
4
H
a
b
c
d
Scale 1 : 6 000 000
0
50
100
150
km

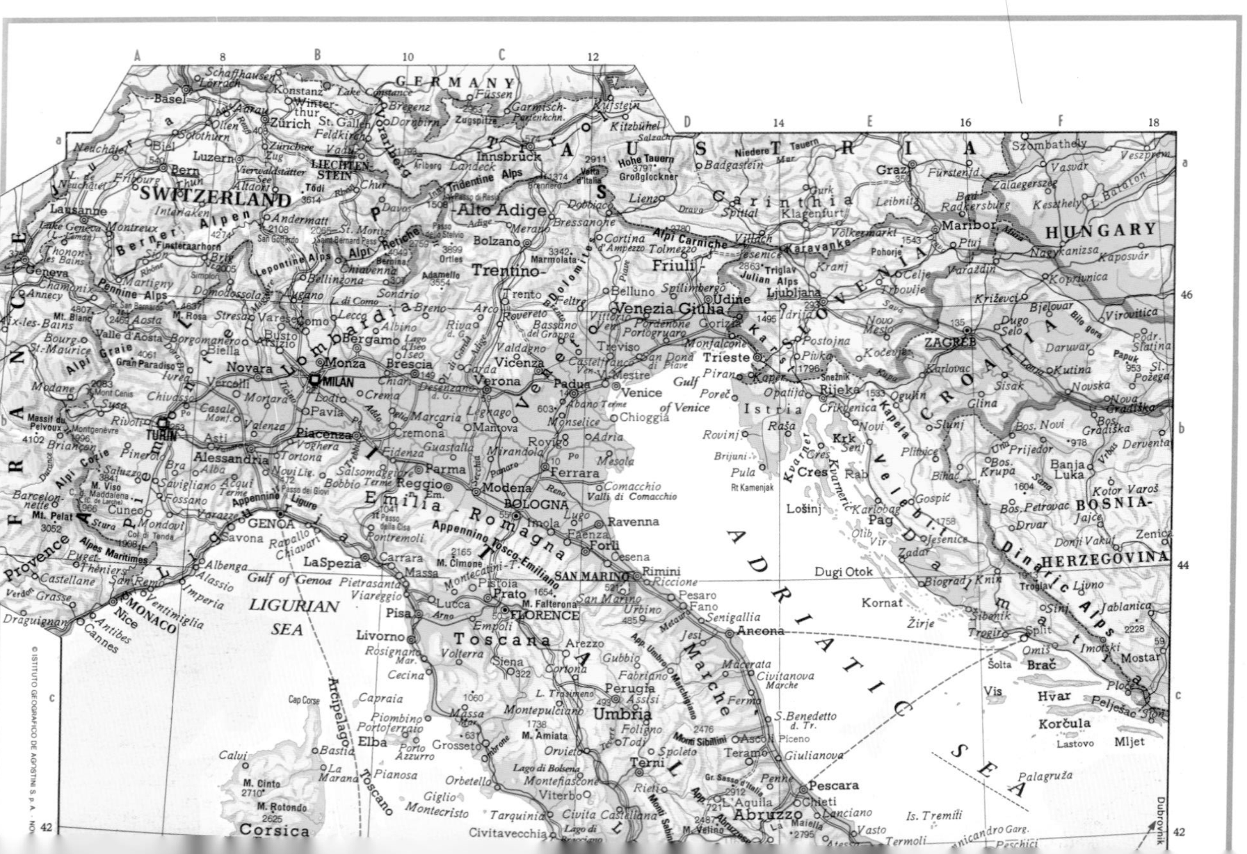
GERMANY
AUSTRIA
HUNGARY
SWITZERLAND
LIECHTENSTEIN
SLOVENIA
CROATIA
BOSNIA-
HERZEGOVINA
FRANCE
SAN MARINO
MONACO
ADRIATIC SEA
LIGURIAN SEA
Arcipelago Toscano
Gulf of Venice
Gulf of Genoa
Corsica
Dinaric Alps
Velebit
Dalmatia
Istria
Carinthia
Tirol
Alto Adige
Trentino-
Veneto
Lombardia
Piemonte
Liguria
Emilia-Romagna
Toscana
Umbria
Marche
Abruzzo
Lazio
Friuli-
Venezia Giulia
Provence
MILAN
TURIN
GENOA
Venice
BOLOGNA
FLORENCE
ZAGREB
Ljubljana
Trieste
Verona
Padua
Pisa
Livorno
Ancona
Pescara
Perugia
Nice
Cannes
Dubrovnik
© ISTITUTO GEOGRAFICO DE AGOSTINI S. p. A. - NOV

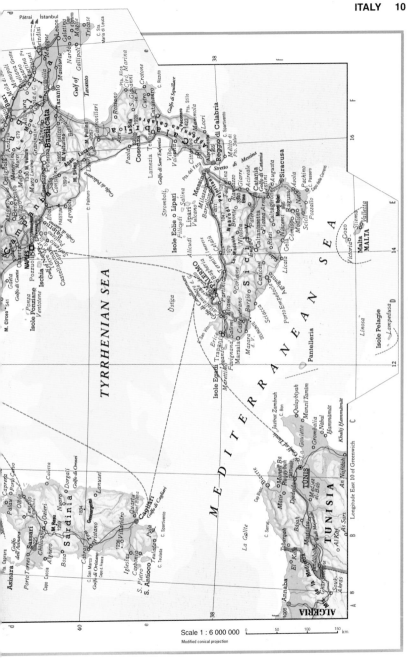

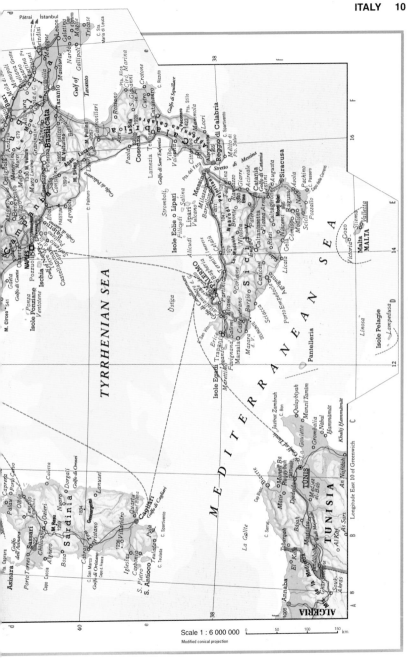

TYRRHENIAN SEA

MEDITERRANEAN SEA

Scale 1 : 6 000 000

Modified conical projection

0 50 100 150 km

Longitude East 10 of Greenwich

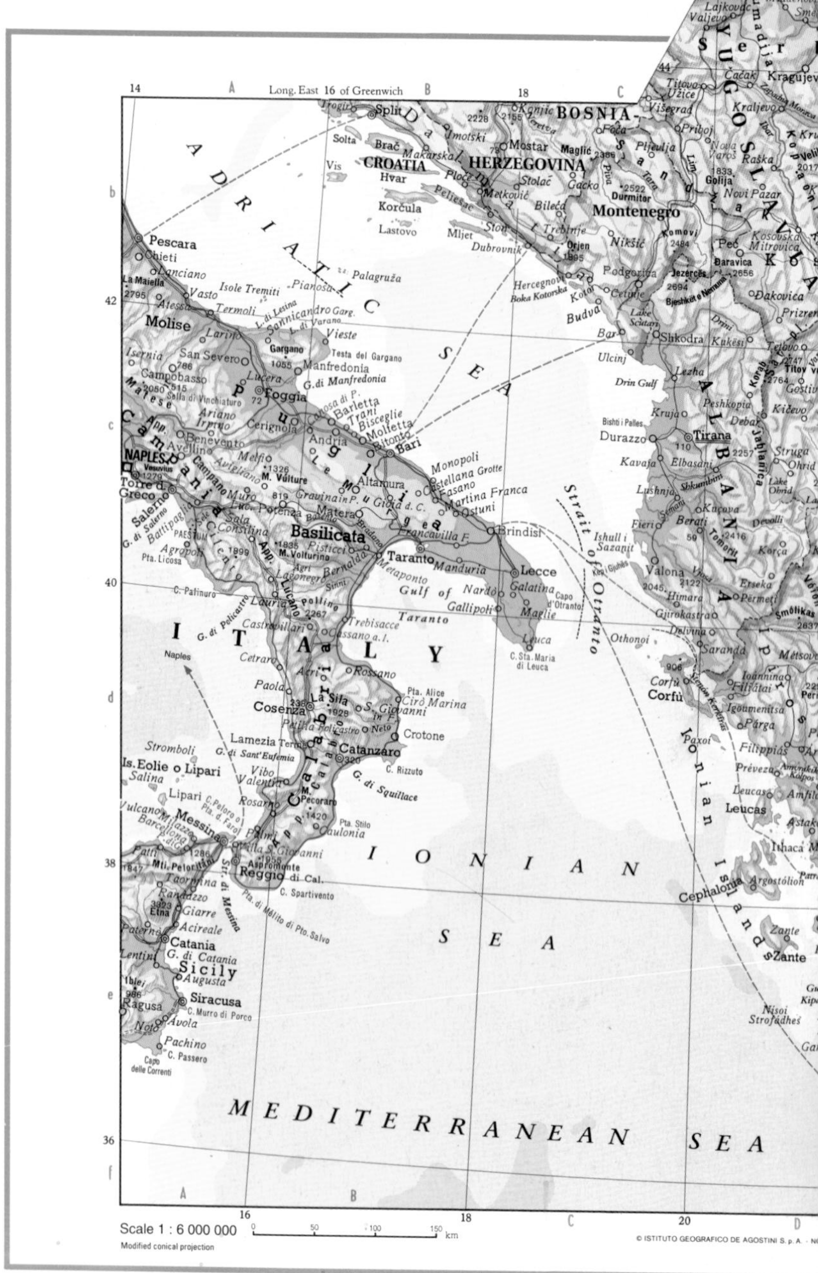

Scale 1 : 6 000 000

0   50   100   150 km

Modified conical projection

© ISTITUTO GEOGRAFICO DE AGOSTINI S.p.A. NE

ROMANIA
BUCHAREST
Muntenia
Oltenia
Craiova
Dobruja
Constanța
BULGARIA
SOFIA
Plovdiv
Varna
Burgas
Balkan Mountains
Central Balkans
Little Balkans
Rhodope Mountains
BLACK SEA
Thrace
Macedonia
SALONIKA
Chalcidice
Gulf of Salonika
İSTANBUL (CONSTANTINOPLE)
Sea of Marmara
BURSA
Dardanelles
TURKEY
İZMİR
AEGEAN SEA
Northern Sporades
Lesbos
Chios
Sámos
Límnos
Thásos
Euboea
Attica
ATHENS
Gulf of Corinth
Cyclades
Náxos
Páros
Dodecanese
Rhodes
Kárpathos
Kos
Cythera
Crete
Iráklion
Khaniá

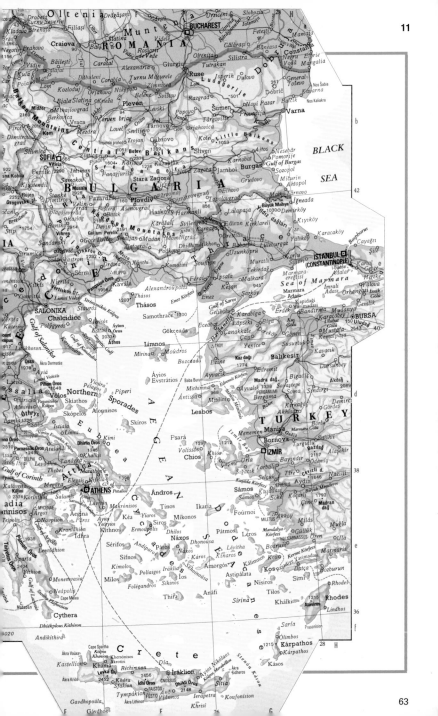

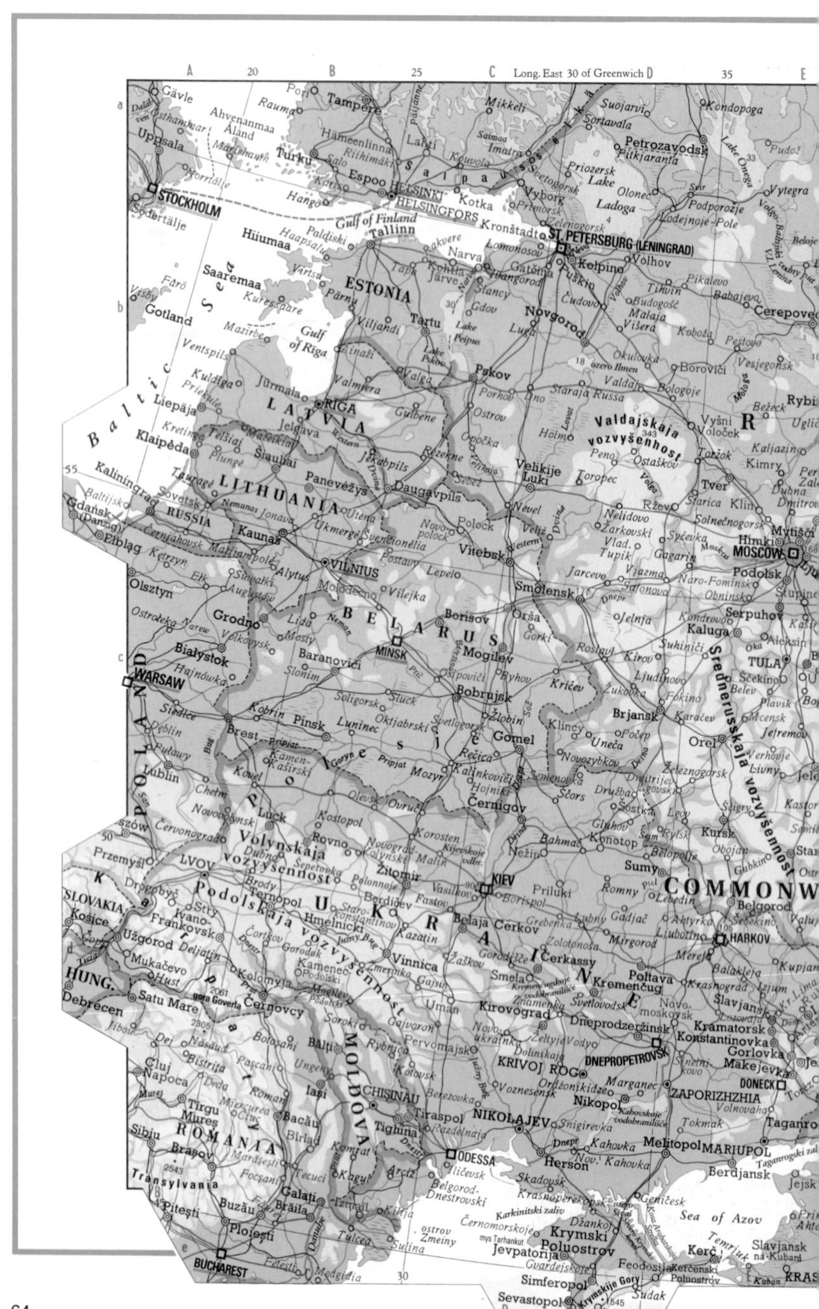
Long. East 30 of Greenwich
STOCKHOLM
HELSINKI
HELSINGFORS
Gulf of Finland
Tallinn
ST. PETERSBURG (LENINGRAD)
ESTONIA
Gulf of Riga
RIGA
LATVIA
LITHUANIA
RUSSIA
VILNIUS
BELARUS
MINSK
MOSCOW
WARSAW
POLAND
UKRAINE
KIEV
HARKOV
COMMONW
MOLDOVA
CHIŞINĂU
ODESSA
ROMANIA
BUCHAREST
SLOVAKIA
HUNG.
DNEPROPETROVSK
ZAPORIZHZHIA
DONECK
MARIUPOL
Sea of Azov
Baltic Sea
Gotland
Saaremaa
Hiiumaa
Lake Ladoga
Lake Peipus
Valdajskaja vozvyšennost
Srednerusskaja vozvyšennost
Volynskaja vozvyšennost
Podolskaja vozvyšennost
Krymski Poluostrov
Transylvania
Pskov
Novgorod
Smolensk
Vitebsk
Gomel
Mogilev
Brest
Grodno
Kaunas
Kaliningrad
Gdańsk (Danzig)
Klaipėda
Liepāja
Daugavpils
Tver
Tula
Kaluga
Orel
Kursk
Brjansk
Poltava
Vinnica
Žitomir
Rovno
Lvov
Ternopol
Černovcy
Nikolajev
Herson
Simferopol
Sevastopol
Jalta
Kerč
Melitopol
Kirovograd
Krivoj Rog
Čerkassy
Černigov
Tampere
Turku
Espoo
Petrozavodsk
Vyborg
Narva
Tartu
Pärnu
Šiauliai
Panevėžys
Białystok
Lublin
Iaşi
Galaţi
Brăila
Ploieşti

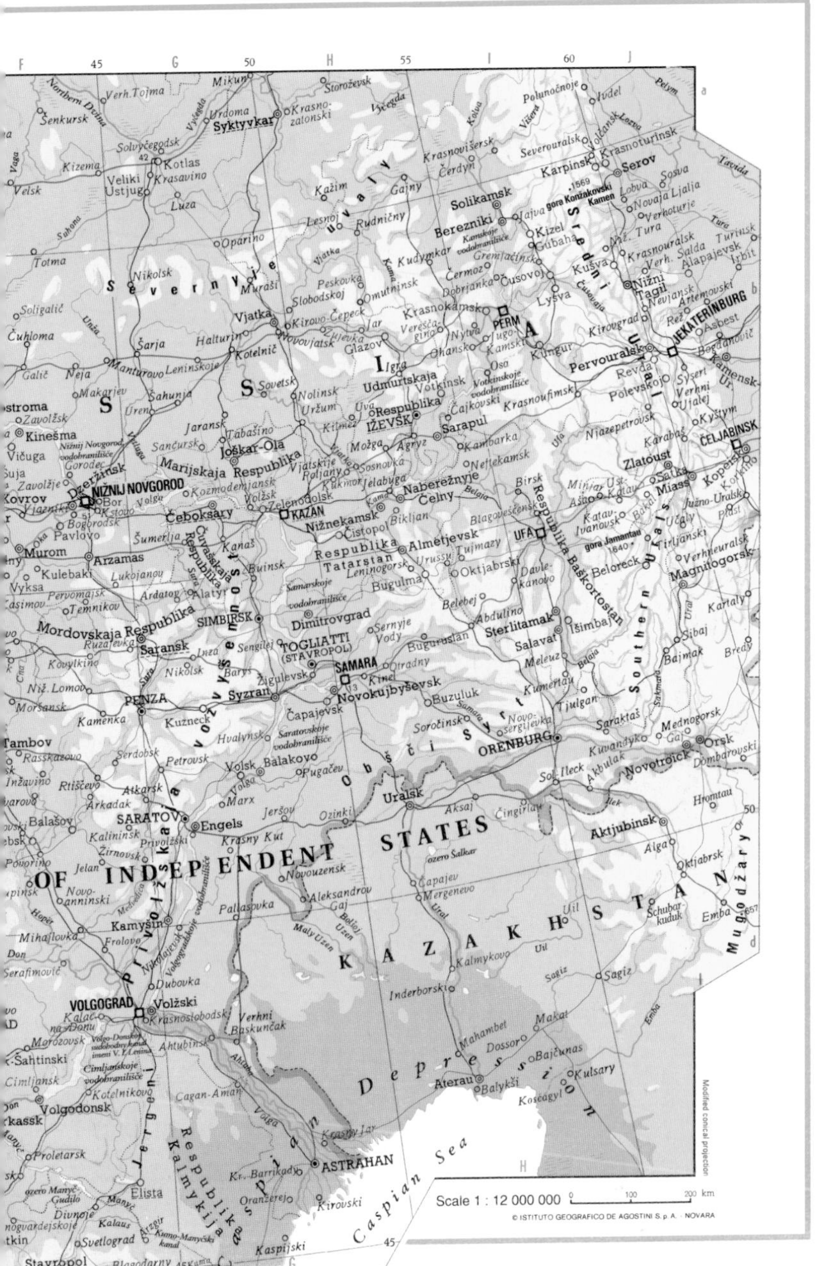

Scale 1 : 12 000 000

© ISTITUTO GEOGRAFICO DE AGOSTINI S.p.A. · NOVARA

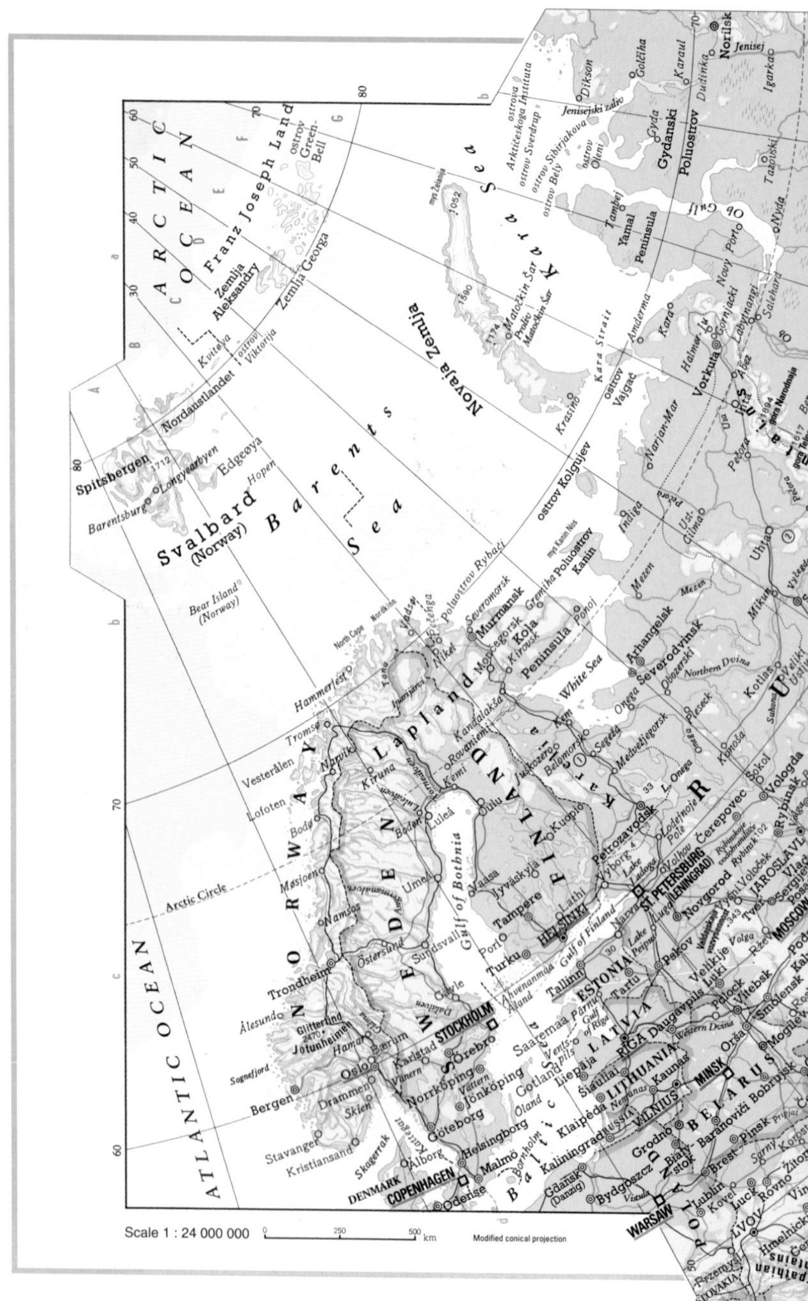
ARCTIC OCEAN
Franz Joseph Land
Barents Sea
Kara Sea
Novaja Zemlja
Svalbard (Norway)
Spitsbergen
Bear Island (Norway)
ATLANTIC OCEAN
NORWAY
SWEDEN
FINLAND
Lapland
White Sea
Kola Peninsula
Gulf of Bothnia
Gulf of Finland
Baltic Sea
ESTONIA
LATVIA
LITHUANIA
BELARUS
POLAND
DENMARK
COPENHAGEN
STOCKHOLM
HELSINKI
ST. PETERSBURG (LENINGRAD)
MOSCOW
RIGA
VILNIUS
MINSK
WARSAW
Tallinn
Oslo
Bergen
Trondheim
Murmansk
Arhangelsk
Vorkuta
Norilsk
Yamal Peninsula
Gydanski Poluostrov
Ob Gulf
Kara Strait
Arctic Circle
Scale 1 : 24 000 000
0 250 500 km
Modified conical projection

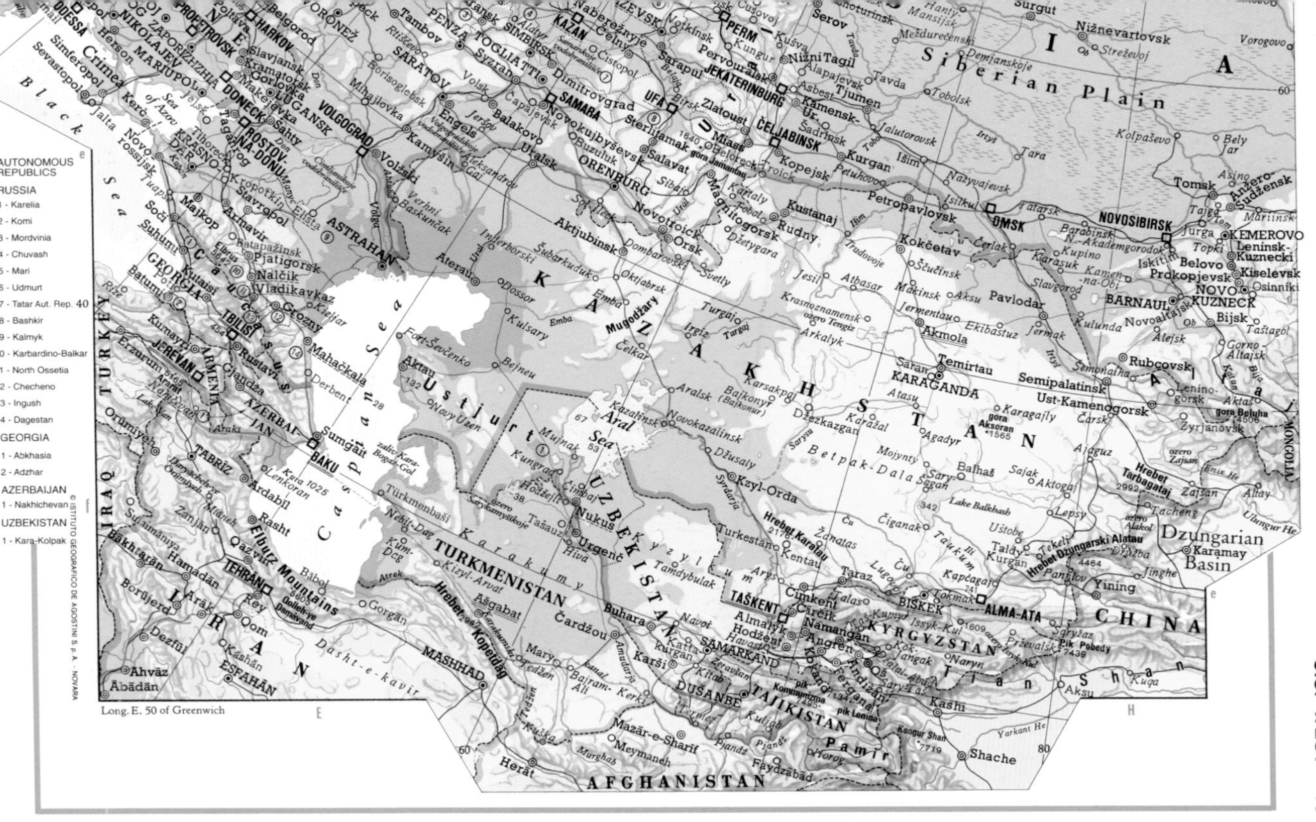
AUTONOMOUS REPUBLICS
RUSSIA
1 - Karelia
2 - Komi
3 - Mordvinia
4 - Chuvash
5 - Mari
6 - Udmurt
7 - Tatar Aut. Rep.
8 - Bashkir
9 - Kalmyk
10 - Karbardino-Balkar
11 - North Ossetia
12 - Checheno
13 - Ingush
14 - Dagestan
GEORGIA
1 - Abkhasia
2 - Adzhar
AZERBAIJAN
1 - Nakhichevan
UZBEKISTAN
1 - Kara-Kolpak
Siberian Plain
KAZAKHSTAN
UZBEKISTAN
TURKMENISTAN
KYRGYZSTAN
TAJIKISTAN
AFGHANISTAN
CHINA
MONGOLIA
IRAN
IRAQ
TURKEY
ARMENIA
GEORGIA
AZERBAIJAN
Black Sea
Sea of Azov
Caspian Sea
Aral Sea
Dzungarian Basin
Elburz Mountains
Betpak-Dala
Ustjurt
Karakumy
Kyzylkum
Pamir
Tien Shan
Long. E. 50 of Greenwich
© ISTITUTO GEOGRAFICO DE AGOSTINI S. p. A. - NOVARA

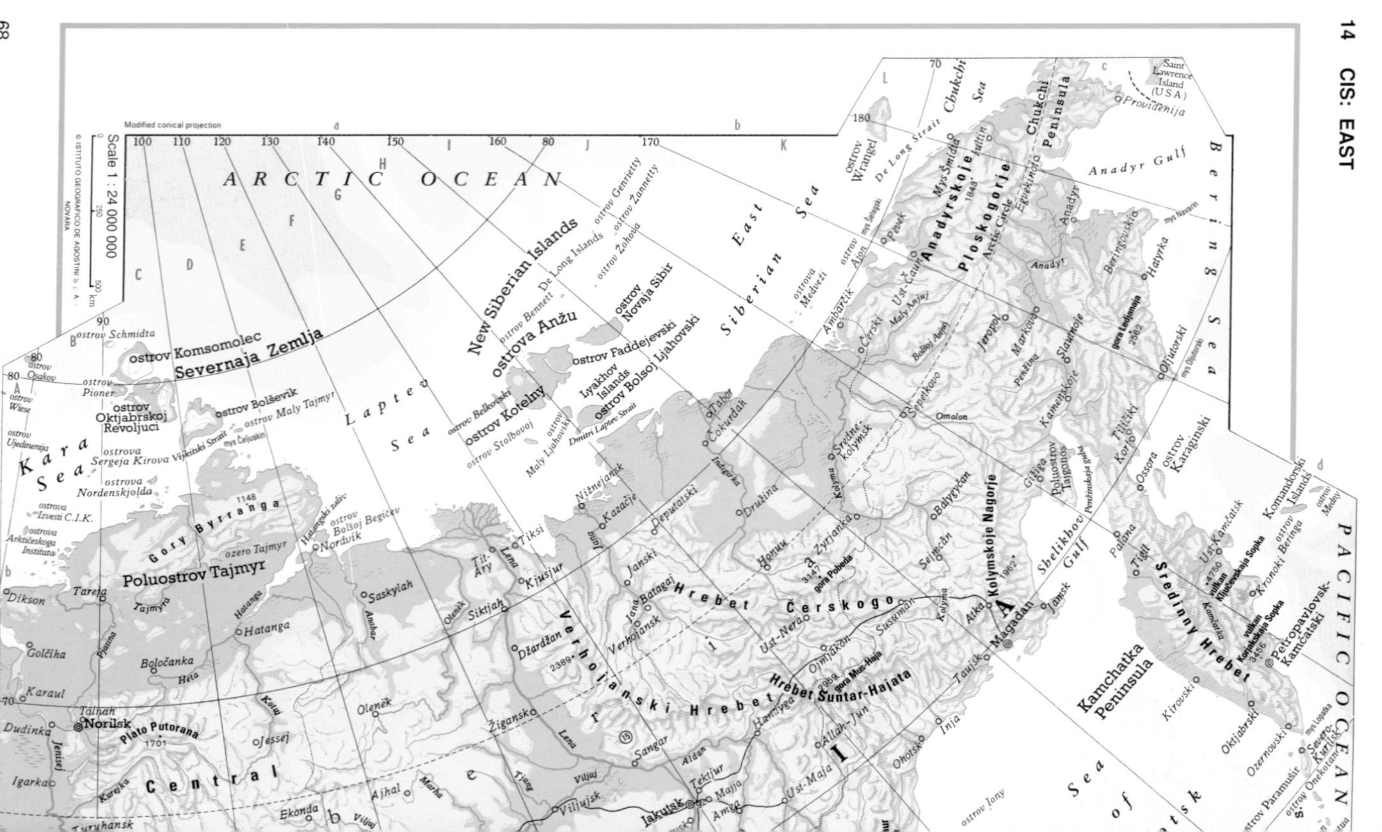
PACIFIC OCEAN
Bering Sea
Sea of Okhotsk
Kamchatka Peninsula
Sredinny Hrebet
Petropavlovsk-Kamčatski
Komandorski Islands
Anadyr Gulf
Chukchi Peninsula
Chukchi Sea
Anadyrskoje Ploskogorje
Kolymskoje Nagorje
Magadan
Shelikhov Gulf
Hrebet Čerskogo
Hrebet Suntar-Hajata
Verhojanski Hrebet
Jakutsk
East Siberian Sea
ostrov Wrangel
New Siberian Islands
Lyakhov Islands
Laptev Sea
ARCTIC OCEAN
Severnaja Zemlja
Poluostrov Tajmyr
Gory Byrranga
Kara Sea
Plato Putorana
Norilsk
Central
Scale 1 : 24 000 000
Modified conical projection
0 250 500 km

© ISTITUTO GEOGRAFICO DE AGOSTINI S.p.A. - NOVARA

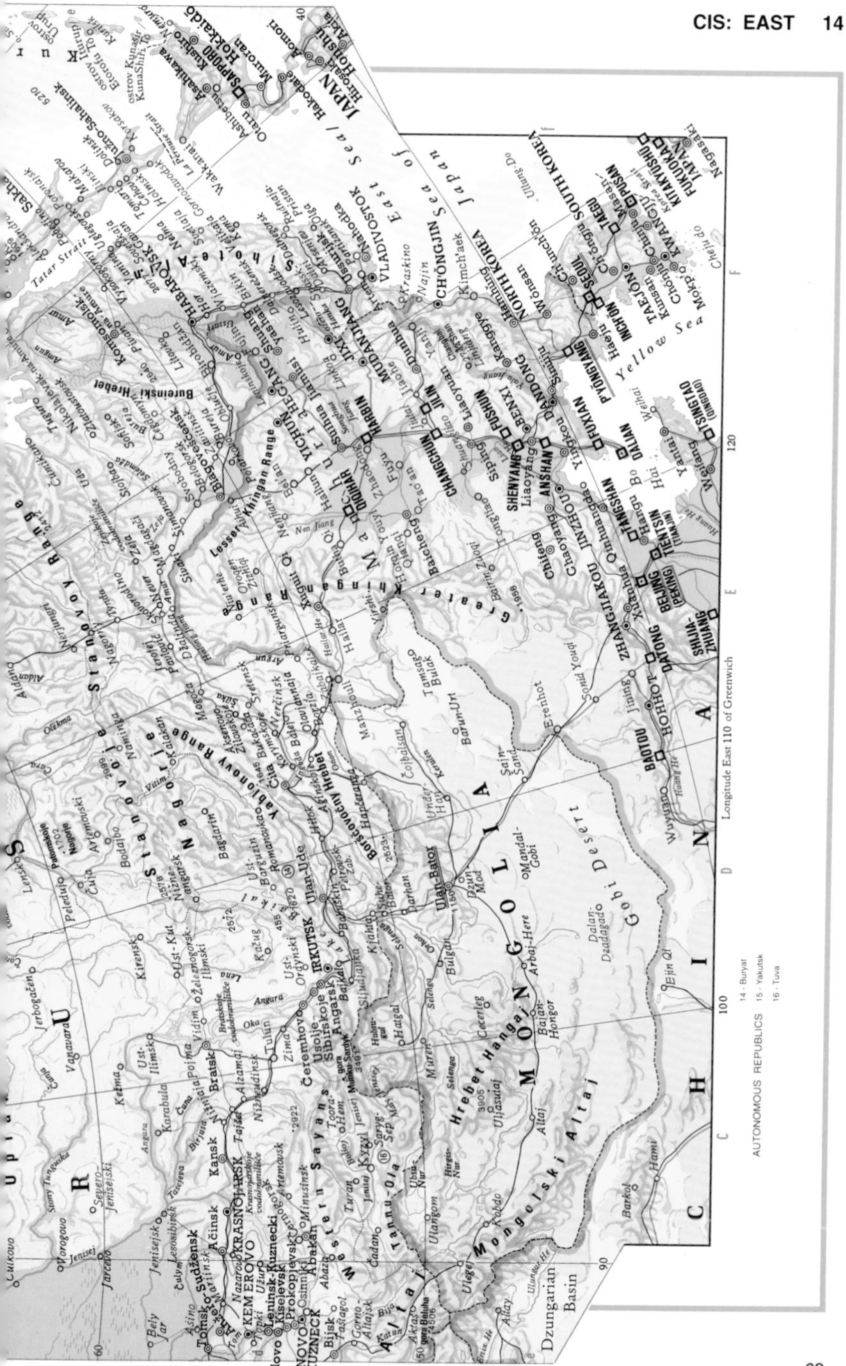

AUTONOMOUS REPUBLICS   14. Buryat   15. Yakutsk   16. Tuva

Longitude East 110 of Greenwich

JAPAN

Sea of Japan / East Sea

CHINA

MONGOLIA

Gobi Desert

Ulan-Bator

Mongolski Altaj

Dzungarian Basin

Tannu-Ola

Altai

Sayan

Stanovoy Range

Yablonovy Range

Greater Khingan Range

Lesser Khingan Range

Bureinski Hrebet

Tatar Strait

Sihote Alin

KHABAROVSK

VLADIVOSTOK

CHONGJIN

NORTH KOREA

SOUTH KOREA

PYONGYANG

SEOUL

INCHON

TAEJON

TAEGU

PUSAN

KWANGJU

Yellow Sea

BEIJING (PEKING)

TIENTSIN (TIANJIN)

SHIJIA-ZHUANG

DATONG

HOHHOT

BAOTOU

TANGSHAN

SHENYANG

ANSHAN

FUSHUN

CHANGCHUN

HARBIN

QIQIHAR

JILIN

DALIAN

QINGDAO

TAIYUAN

ZHANGJIAKOU

MUDANJIANG

JIXI

JIAMUSI

IRKUTSK

Ulan-Ude

Angarsk

Bratsk

Kansk

ACINSK

KRASNOYARSK

ABAKAN

NOVO-KUZNECK

KEMEROVO

Leninsk-Kuznecki

Belovo

Biisk

Tomsk

Tajget

KUZNECK

Yenisei

Lena

Angara

Amur

69

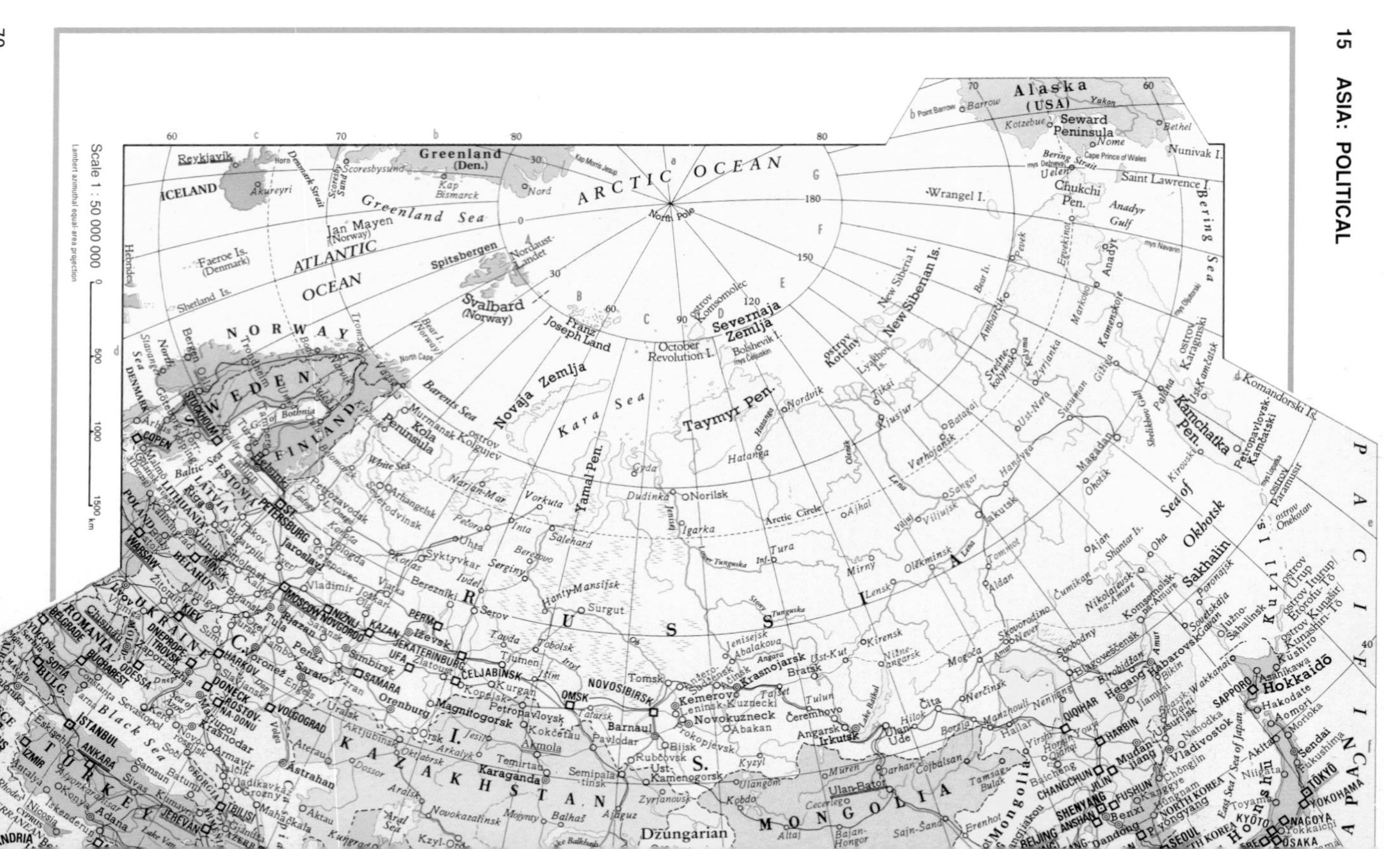

PACIFIC
ARCTIC OCEAN
North Pole
ATLANTIC OCEAN
Greenland Sea
Greenland (Den.)
Bering Sea
Sea of Okhotsk
Kara Sea
Barents Sea
Black Sea
Alaska (USA)
Seward Peninsula
Chukchi Pen.
Kamchatka Pen.
Wrangel I.
New Siberian Is.
Severnaja Zemlja
Taymyr Pen.
Franz Joseph Land
Novaja Zemlja
Svalbard (Norway)
Spitsbergen
Jan Mayen (Norway)
Kola Peninsula
Yamal Pen.
Sakhalin
Hokkaidō
Kuril Is.
ICELAND
NORWAY
SWEDEN
FINLAND
RUSSIA
KAZAKHSTAN
MONGOLIA
UKRAINE
TURKEY
ROMANIA
ESTONIA
LATVIA
LITHUANIA
BELARUS
POLAND
DENMARK
Reykjavik
STOCKHOLM
Helsinki
ST. PETERSBURG
MOSCOW
KIEV
WARSAW
MINSK
ISTANBUL
ANKARA
NOVOSIBIRSK
OMSK
Irkutsk
Ulan-Bator
Magadan
Vladivostok
Habarovsk
TOKYO
SAPPORO
Scale 1 : 50 000 000
0
500
1000
1500 km
Lambert azimuthal equal-area projection

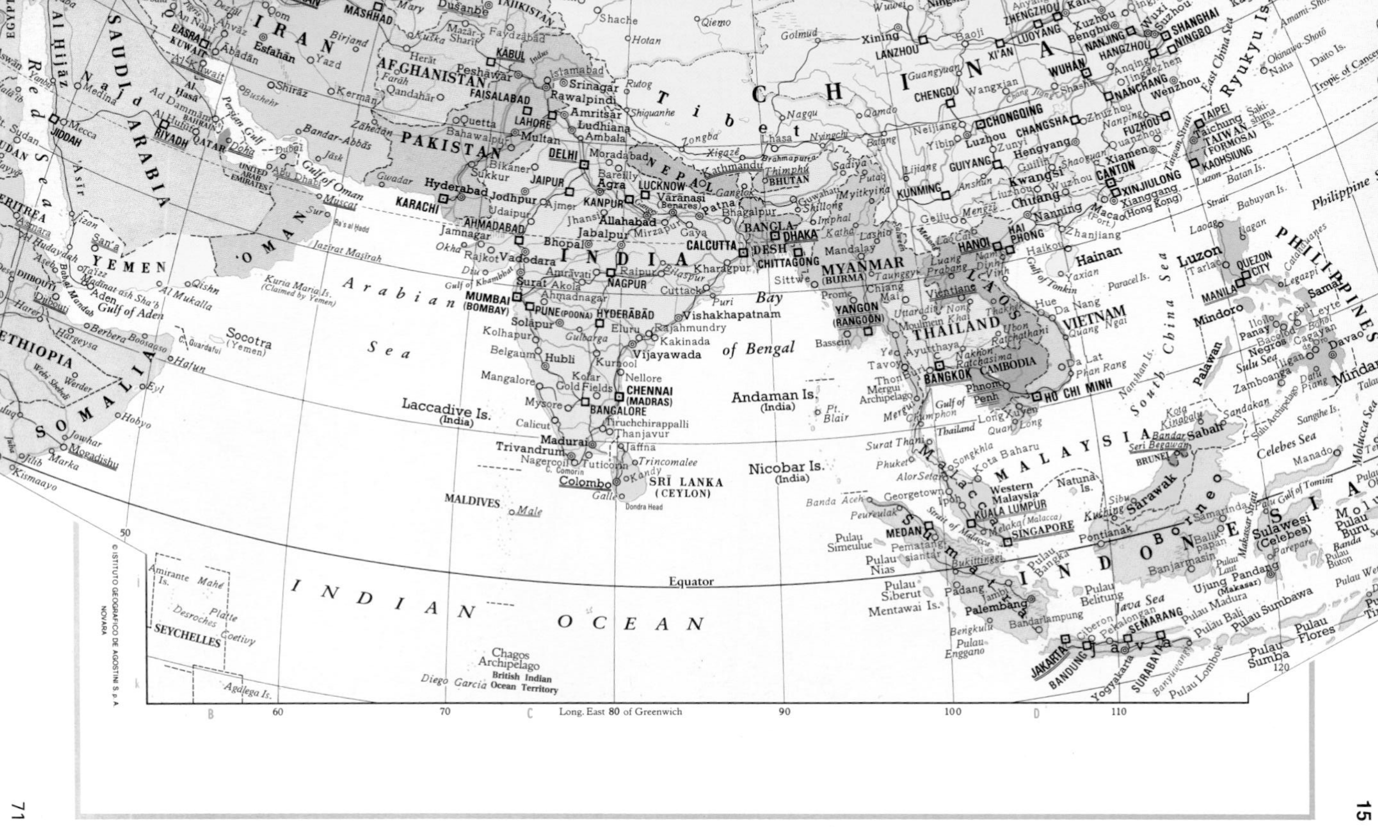
INDIAN OCEAN
Arabian Sea
Bay of Bengal
South China Sea
Philippine Sea
Red Sea
Gulf of Aden
Gulf of Oman
Persian Gulf
Java Sea
Celebes Sea
Equator
Tropic of Cancer
Long. East 80 of Greenwich
SAUDI ARABIA
YEMEN
OMAN
IRAN
AFGHANISTAN
PAKISTAN
INDIA
NEPAL
BHUTAN
BANGLADESH
MYANMAR (BURMA)
THAILAND
LAOS
VIETNAM
CAMBODIA
MALAYSIA
INDONESIA
PHILIPPINES
CHINA
Tibet
SRI LANKA (CEYLON)
MALDIVES
SOMALIA
ETHIOPIA
ERITREA
SEYCHELLES
Chagos Archipelago
British Indian Ocean Territory
Laccadive Is. (India)
Andaman Is. (India)
Nicobar Is. (India)
Socotra (Yemen)
KARACHI
DELHI
MUMBAI (BOMBAY)
CALCUTTA
CHENNAI (MADRAS)
BANGALORE
HYDERĀBĀD
DHAKA
YANGON (RANGOON)
BANGKOK
HANOI
HO CHI MINH
KUALA LUMPUR
SINGAPORE
JAKARTA
MANILA
CANTON
SHANGHAI
TAIPEI
KABUL
RIYADH
JIDDAH
Colombo
Male

© ISTITUTO GEOGRAFICO DE AGOSTINI S. p. A.
NOVARA

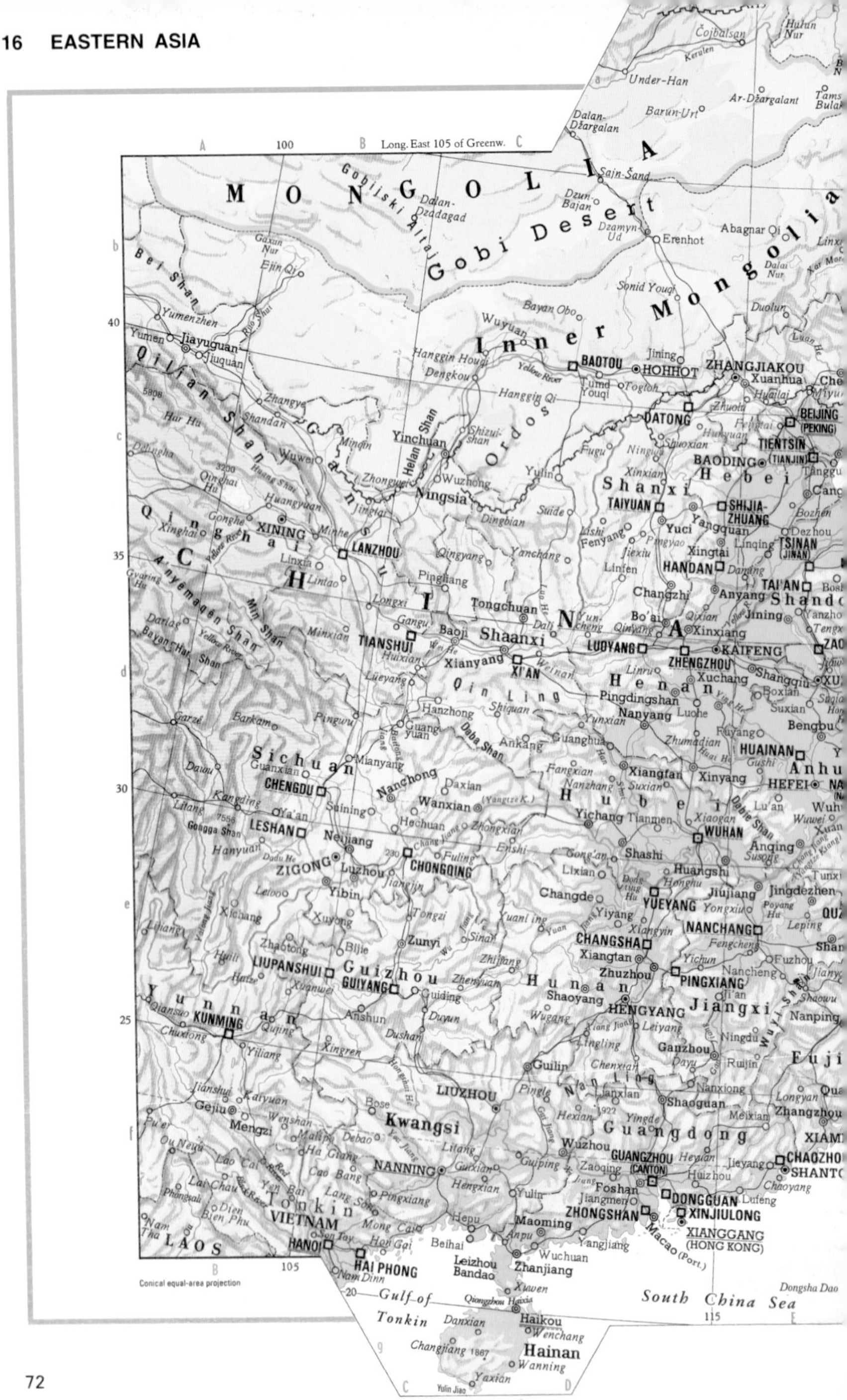

M O N G O L I A

Gobi Desert

Gobliski Altaj

Dalan-Daddagad

Dalan-Dzargalan

Barun-Urt

Under-Han

Ar-Dzargalant

Cojbalsan

Kerulen

Hubun Nur

Tams Bula

Dzun Bajan

Sain-Sand

Dzamyn Ud

Erenhot

Abagnar Qi

Linxi

Dalai Nur

Kar Mo

Sonid Youqi

Duolun

Luoto

I n n e r　M o n g o l i a

Bei Shan

Gaxun Nur

Ejin Qi

Yumenzhen

Yumen

Jiayuguan

Liuquan

Q i l i a n　S h a n

Subei

Dulan

Qaidam

Bayan Obo

Wuyuan

Hanggin Houqi

Dengkou

BAOTOU

HOHHOT

Jining

Tumd Youqi

Togtoh

Yellow River

ZHANGJIAKOU

Xuanhua

Huailai

Huailai

Che

DATONG

Shuoxian

Pingwang

Ningwu

Hunyuan

BEIJING (PEKING)

TIENTSIN (TIANJIN)

Tangu

G a n s u

Hur Ha

Sogo

Shandan

Zhangye

Linze

Hei Shui He

Minqin

Wuwei

Gulang

Yongdeng

Yinchuan

Helan Shan

Dingyuan

Shizui-shan

Wuzhong

Zhongwei

Ningsia

Yulin

Fugu

Xinxian

Ninpu

BAODING

Hebei

SHIJIA-ZHUANG

Dezhou

O R D O S

Qinghai Hu

Gonghe

Minhe

XINING

LANZHOU

Lintao

Linxia

Qingyang

Dingbian

Suide

Yanchang

Lishi

Fenyang

Fenyang

Jiexiu

TAIYUAN

Yuci

Yangquan

Pingyao

Linqing

JINAN

Qingyang

Pipglang

S h a n x i

Cang

JINAN

Gyaring Hu

Ayemaqen Shan

Bayan Har Shan

Yellow River

Min Shan

Maqu

Barkam

Longxi

Gangu

Minxian

TIANSHUI

Huixian

Lüeyang

Baoji

Dali

Longxian

Qian

Chengg

Qixan

Tongchuan

Shaanxi

Xianyang

XI'AN

Bo'ai

Qinshui

Xinxiang

KAIFENG

ZHENGZHOU

LUOYANG

Linru

Yun

Linfen

HANDAN

Anyang

Xingtai

TAI'AN

Shando

Jining

Tengxi

ZAO

XU

Changzhi

N A

H e n a n

Qin Ling

Hanzhong

Shiquan

Pingdingshan

Xuchang

Shangqiu

Boxian

Nanyang

Luohe

Suixian

S i c h u a n

Daba Shan

Ankang

Yunxian

Guanghua

Zhumadian

Bengbu

HUAINAN

Anhu

HEFEI

NA

Dingiu

Kangding

Gonga Shan

Hanyuan

Dadu He

LESHAN

Guanxian

CHENGDU

Mianyang

Nanchong

Daxian

Wanxian

Fangxian

Xiangfan

Xinyang

Gushi

Lu'an

Wuwei

Xuan

Ya'an

Neijiang

Hechuan

Zhongxian

Fengjie

Yichang

Tianmen

Xiaogan

WUHAN

Anqing

Tunxi

Q

Xichang

ZIGONG

Luzhou

Fuling

Enshi

H u b e i

Shashi

Huangshi

Susong

Yibin

CHONGQING

Gong'an

Lixian

Jiujiang

Jingdezhen

QU

Zhaotong

Leibo

Xuyong

Bijie

Zunyi

Sinan

Yuanling

Changde

Yiyang

Henghu

Honghu

YUEYANG

Yongxiu

Poyang Hu

Leping

Shan

Luoxi

Zhijiang

Xiangyin

NANCHANG

Fuzhou

Jiangy

Huili

Weining

Zhenyuan

CHANGSHA

Yichun

Fengcheng

Liuanshui

GUIYANG

G u i z h o u

Kaili

Guiding

Xiangtan

Zhuzhou

Nancheng

Jiangx

Shaowu

Nanping

Yunnan

KUNMING

Anshun

Dushan

Duyun

Shaoyang

H u n a n

PINGXIANG

Ji'an

Euji

Qujing

Yiliang

Luxi

Xingren

Wucang

HENGYANG

Leiyang

J i a n g x i

Chuxiong

Xingyi

Jingling

Ganzhou

Ruijin

Tianshui

Taiyuan

Weishan

Guilin

N a n n i n g

Chenxian

Nanxiong

Longyan

Zhangzhou

Gejiu

Mengzi

Malin

Debao

Litang

Hexian

Yineda

Shaoguan

Meixian

CHAOZHOU

SHANTO

Lao Cai

Ha Giang

Wuzhou

GUANGZHOU (CANTON)

Heyuan

Jieyang

Bai

Cao Bang

Lang Son

Hengxian

Yulin

Zaoqing

Foshan

Huizhou

Chaoyang

Lufeng

K w a n g s i

NANNING

Guiping

Pingxiang

G u a n g d o n g

XIAM

Dien Bien Phu

VIETNAM

LAOS

HANOI

HAI PHONG

Hepu

Beihai

Leizhou Bandao

Maoming

ZHONGSHAN

DONGGUAN

XINJIULONG

XIANGGANG (HONG KONG)

Macao (Port.)

Wuchuan

Yangjiang

Zhanjiang

Anpu

Haikou

Wenchang

Danxian

Changjiang

Hainan

Yaxian

Wanning

Dongsha Dao

South China Sea

Gulf of Tonkin

Conical equal-area projection

Long. East 105 of Greenw.

Scale 1 : 18 000 000

© ISTITUTO GEOGRAFICO DE AGOSTINI S.p.A. - NOVARA

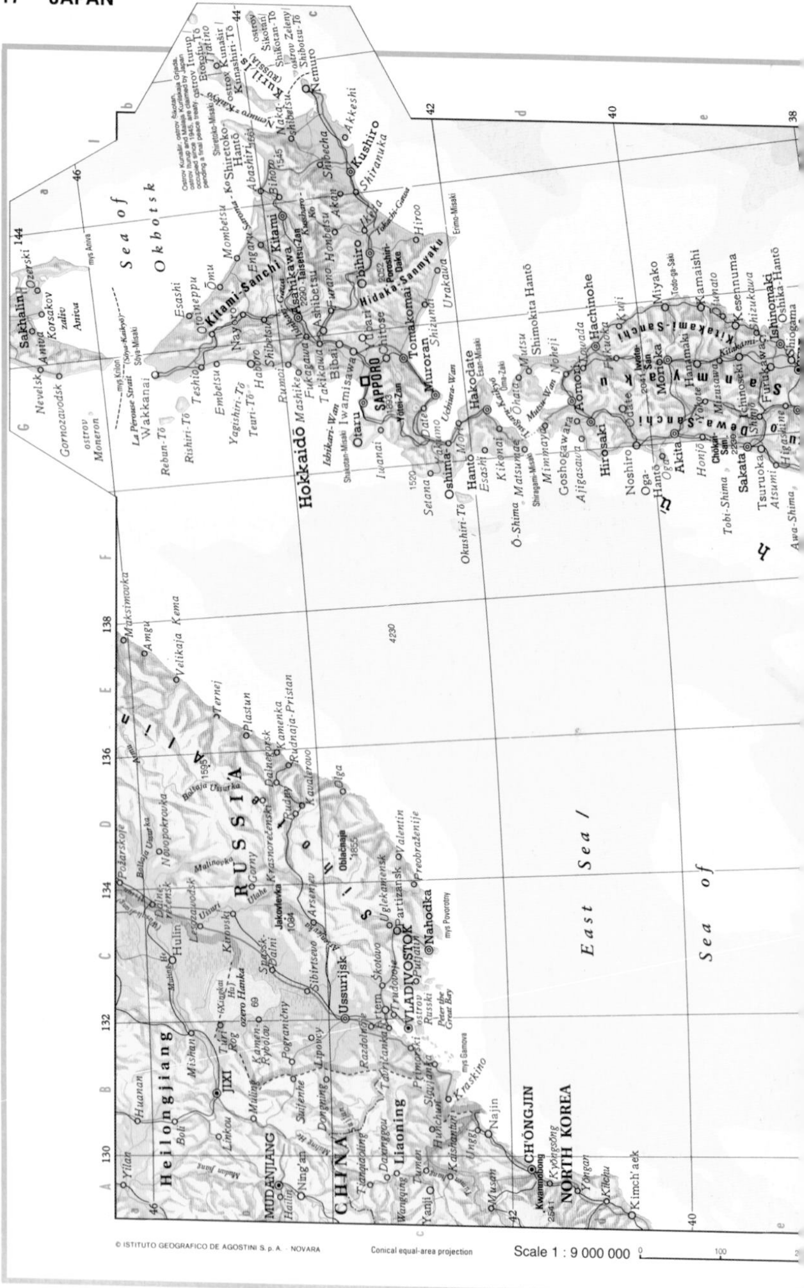

Sea of Okhotsk

Sahalin

Sea of Japan / East Sea

HOKKAIDŌ

SAPPORO

Kitami-Sanchi

Hidaka-Sammyaku

Muroran
Hakodate

RUSSIA

CHINA

Heilongjiang

MUDANJIANG

Jilin

Liaoning

NORTH KOREA

CH'ŌNGJIN

Ussurijsk

VLADIVOSTOK

Najin

Kimch'aek

Hachinohe

Morioka

Kitakami-Sanchi

Akita

Sakata

© ISTITUTO GEOGRAFICO DE AGOSTINI S.p.A. - NOVARA   Conical equal-area projection   Scale 1 : 9 000 000

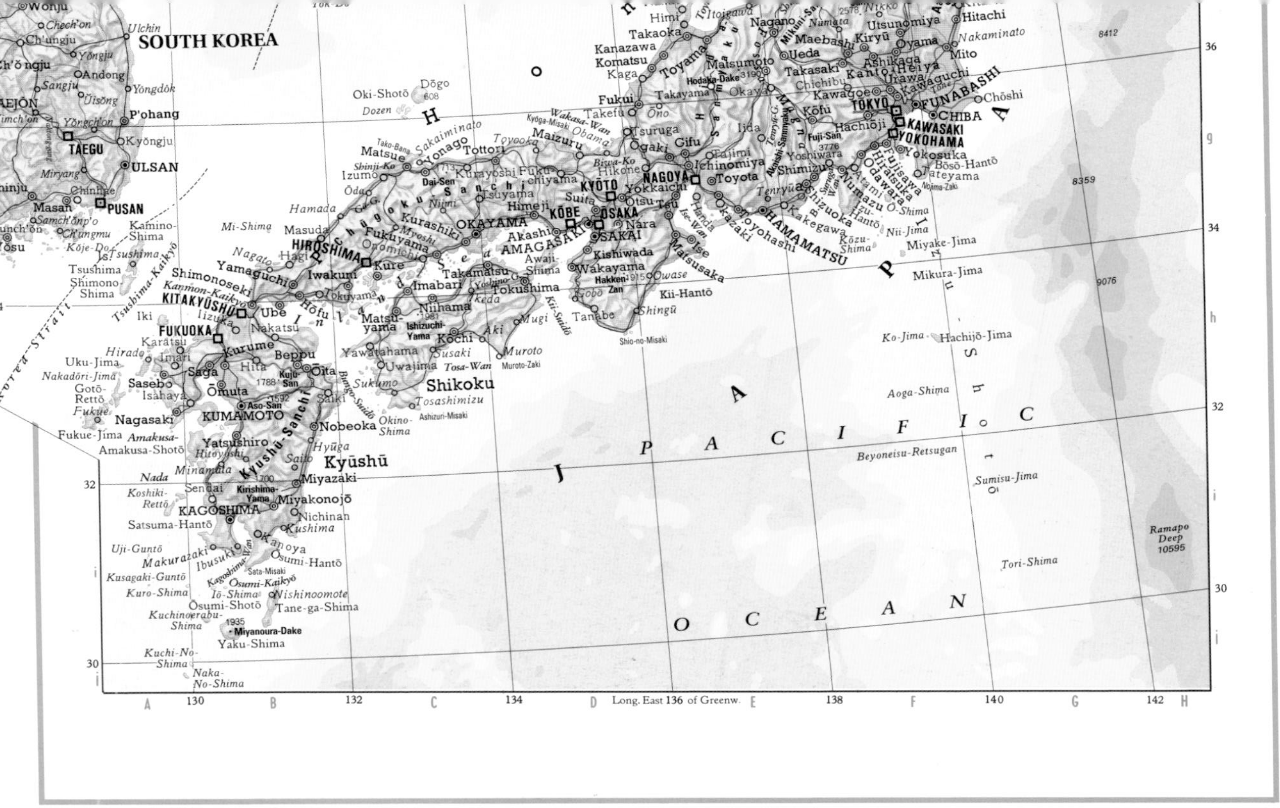
SOUTH KOREA
PUSAN
TAEGU
ULSAN
P'ohang
Kyŏngju
Andong
Ch'ŏngju
TAEJŎN
Chinju
Masan
Yŏsu
Korea Strait
Tsushima-Kaikyō
Tsushima
Iki
FUKUOKA
KITAKYŪSHŪ
Shimonoseki
Yamaguchi
Nagasaki
Sasebo
Saga
Kurume
Ōmuta
KUMAMOTO
Beppu
Ōita
Kyūshū
Miyazaki
Miyakonojō
KAGOSHIMA
Nobeoka
Yaku-Shima
Tane-ga-Shima
Shikoku
Matsuyama
Kōchi
Takamatsu
Tokushima
HIROSHIMA
Kure
Fukuyama
OKAYAMA
Kurashiki
Matsue
Izumo
Tottori
Oki-Shotō
KŌBE
ŌSAKA
SAKAI
KYŌTO
Nara
Wakayama
Kii-Hantō
NAGOYA
Gifu
Toyota
Toyohashi
HAMAMATSU
Shizuoka
Fukui
Kanazawa
Toyama
Nagano
Matsumoto
Kōfu
Fuji-San
TŌKYŌ
YOKOHAMA
KAWASAKI
CHIBA
FUNABASHI
Mito
Hitachi
Chōshi
Hachijō-Jima
Miyake-Jima
Tori-Shima
Ramapo Deep 10595
PACIFIC OCEAN
Long. East 136 of Greenw.

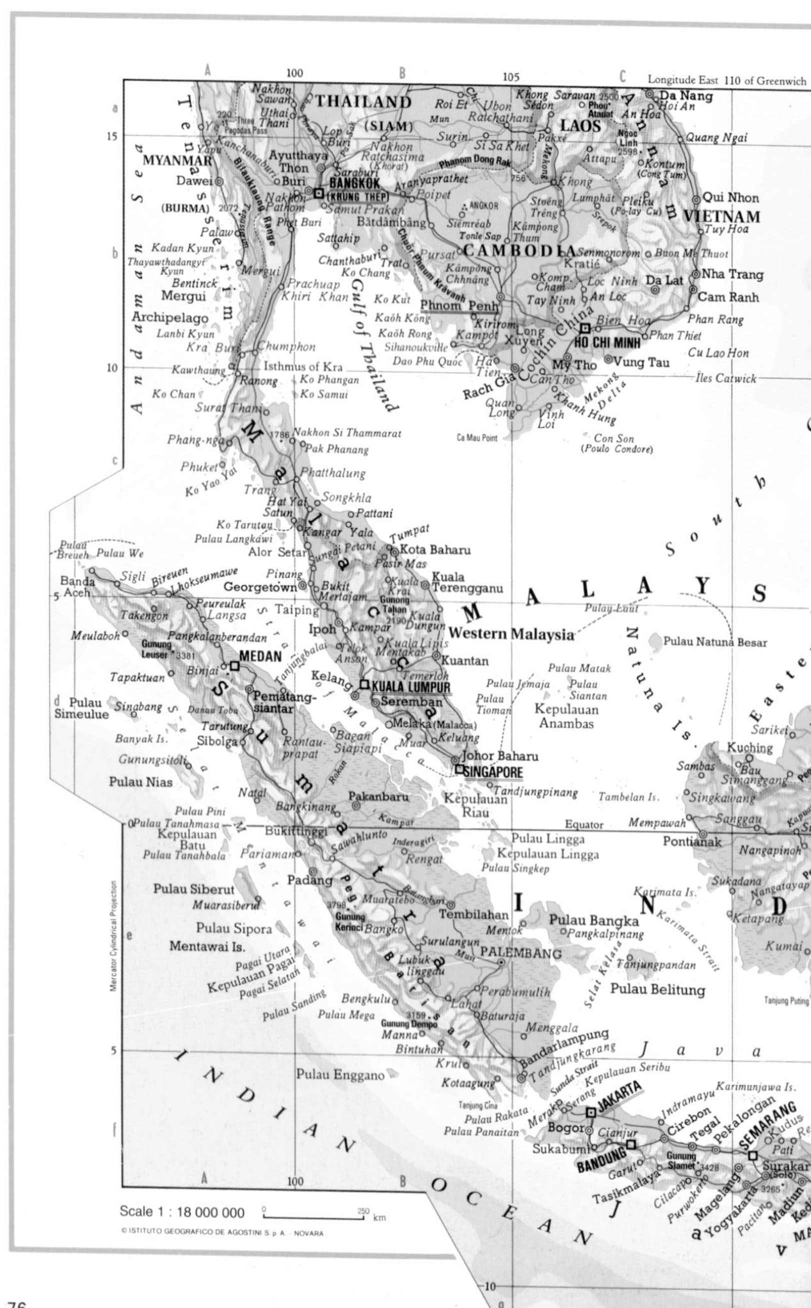
THAILAND
(SIAM)
BANGKOK
(KRUNG THEP)
MYANMAR
(BURMA)
LAOS
CAMBODIA
VIETNAM
Phnom Penh
HO CHI MINH
Gulf of Thailand
Andaman Sea
Western Malaysia
KUALA LUMPUR
SINGAPORE
MEDAN
Sumatra
PALEMBANG
JAKARTA
BANDUNG
SEMARANG
INDIAN OCEAN
Java
Christmas Island
Equator
Longitude East 110 of Greenwich
Mercator Cylindrical Projection
Scale 1 : 18 000 000
© ISTITUTO GEOGRAFICO DE AGOSTINI S.p.A. - NOVARA

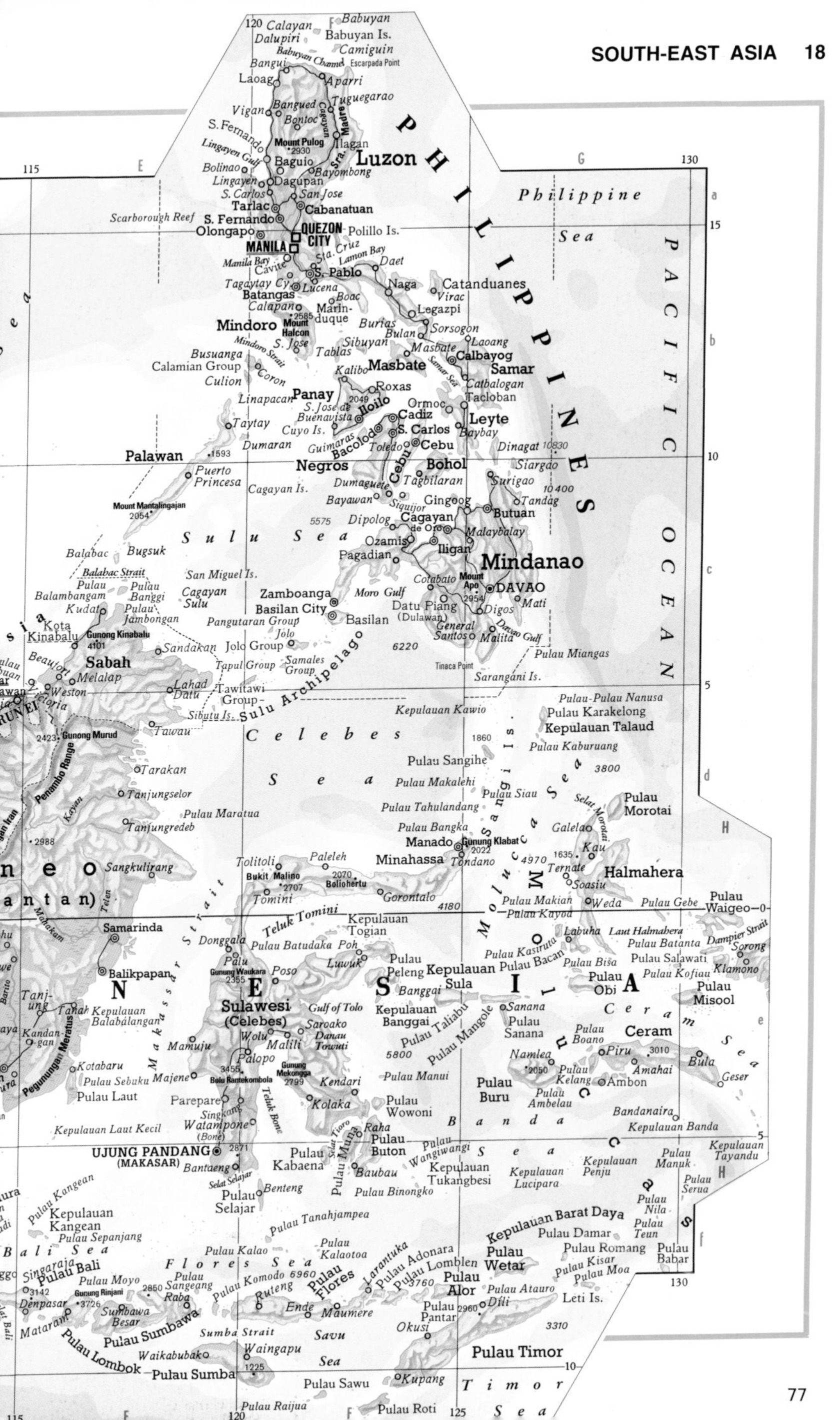

120 *Calayan* — *Babuyan*
Dalupiri — Babuyan Is.
Babuyan Chann. — *Camiguin*
Bangui — *Escarpada Point*
Laoag○ — ○Aparri
Vigan○ — ○Tuguegarao
S. Fernando○ — *Bangued*○ ○*Bontoc*
Lingayen Gulf — Mount Pulog○ — ○Ilagan
Bolinao○ — ∆2930 — Baguio○ — Luzon
Lingayen○ — ○Dagupan — ○Bayombong
S. Carlos○ — ○San Jose — *S. Carlos*
Scarborough Reef⁺ — Tarlac○ — ○Cabanatuan — *Philippine*
S. Fernando○ — Polillo Is. — *Sea*
Olongapo○ — QUEZON — G — 130
Manila Bay — MANILA■CITY — 15 — a
Calvite○ — *Sta. Cruz* — *Lamon Bay*
Tagaytay Cy○ — ○S. Pablo — ○*Daet*
Batangas○ — ○Lucena — Naga○ — ○Catanduanes
Calapan○ — *Boac* — ○*Virac*
Mindoro — Marin- — *Burias* — ○Legazpi
Mount — duque — *Bulan*○ — ○Laoang
Halcon — *Sibuyan* — ○Sorsogon
∆2586 — Tablas — *Masbate* — ○Calbayog
Busuanga○ — S. Jose○ — ○*Kalibo* — *Masbate*○ — Samar
Calamian Group — ○Roxas — ○Catbalogan
Culion — Panay — ○*Catbalogan*
○Coron — ○*S. Jose* — Iloilo○ — Ormoc○ — Tacloban
Linapacan — ○*Buenavista* — Cadiz○ — S. Carlos○ — Leyte
Taytay○ — Cuyo Is. — Toledo○ — Baybay○
○Dumaran — *Guimaras* — ○Cebu — Dinagat 10830
Palawan — ∆1593 — Negros — Bohol — ○Siargao
○*Puerto* — *Dumaguete*○ — Tagbilaran○ — Surigao○ — ○*Tandag*
Princesa — Cagayan Is. — Bayawan○ — ○Gingoog — 10400
∆5575 — *Siquijor* — ○Butuan
Mount Mantalingajan — Dipolog○ — Cagayan — ○Malaybalay
∆2054 — Ozamis○ — de Oro○ — ○Iligan
Sulu Sea — ○Pagadian — Mindanao
Balabac — Bugsuk — San Miguel Is. — Cotabato○ — Mount
Balabac Strait — *Pulau* — Zamboanga○ — Apo
Balambangan — *Pulau* — Cagayan — ○Digos
Kudato — *Banggi* — Sulu — Basilan City○ — *Datu Piang*○ — ∆2954 — ●DAVAO
Pulau — *Pangutaran* — ○Basilan — (*Dulawan*) — ○Mati
Jambongan — *Sulu* — Moro Gulf — General — *Davao Gulf*
Kota — Sandakan○ — Jolo Group — Jolo — Santos○ — ○*Matila*
Kinabalu — ○*Tapul Group* — *Samales* — ○Sarangani Is.
Gunong Kinabalu — *Group* — 6220 — *Tinaca Point*
∆4101 — Sabah — ○Lahad — *Tawitawi* — *Sarangani Is.*
Beaufort○ — *Datu* — *Group* — Pulau-Pulau Nanusa
○Melalap — *Sibutu Is.* — Sulu Archipelago — Pulau Karakelong
BRUNEI — ○Weston — *Tawau* — Kepulauan Talaud
○*Keria* — ○Tawau — Kepulauan Kawio — Pulau Kaburuang
∆2423 — Gunong Murud — *Celebes* — 1860
Penubuhan Range — ○*Tarakan* — *Sea* — Pulau Sangihe — Pulau Siau — 3800
Tanjungselor○ — Pulau Makalehi — Selat Siau — Pulau
neo — *Tanjungredeb*○ — Pulau Tahulandang — Morotai
(antan) — *Sangkulirang*○ — Pulau Bangka — Galelao
∆2988 — Manado○ — Gunung Klabat — *Kau*
N — Toliltoli○ — *Paleleh* — Minahassa — ∆2022 — 1635 — Halmahera
Samarinda● — Bukit Malino — Tendano — 4970 — Ternate○ — ○Soasiu
○*Donggala* — ∆2707 — Gorontalo○ — M — Pulau
Pulau Batudaka — Ballohertu — 4180 — Pulau Makian○ — Gebe — Waigeo○
Balikpapan● — Teluk Tomini — Pulau Kayoa○ — ○Weda — Pulau Gebe — Dampier Strait
Tanj- — *Poso*○ — Kepulauan — Pulau Kasiruta○ — Pulau Batanta — Sorong○
ung — *Palu*○ — Togian — Peleng — Kepulauan — Pulau Bacan○ — Pulau Salawati — Klamono○
Gunung Wankara — *Luwuk* — Sula — Pulau Bisa○ — Pulau Kofiau — Pulau
∆2351 — Kepulauan — Obi — A — Misool
Tanah Grogot○ — I — Banggai — Sanana○ — N — Ceram — Pulau
N — Kendari — E — Pulau — Pulau Obi — e — Misool
Kepulauan — Sulawesi — S — *Banggai* — *Talabu* — *Sanana* — *Ceram Sea*
Balabalangan — (Celebes) — Gulf of Tolo — Pulau Talabu — Namlea○ — Piru○ — 3010
○*Kotabaru* — Saroako○ — Pulau Mangole — ∆2090 — Amahai○ — *Bula*○
Mamuju○ — *Danau* — Pulau — Namlea — Ambon● — ○Geser
Pulau Sebuku○ — Majene○ — Gunung — *Towuti* — Sanana — Pulau
Pulau Laut — ∆3455 — *Mekongga* — Kelang
Kepulauan Laut Kecil — Parepare○ — ∆2799 — Pulau — Pulau — Bandanaira○
Singkang — Kolaka○ — Wowoni — Ambelau — ○Kepulauan Banda
○*Watampone* — Pulau — Banda — Sea — Kepulauan
UJUNG PANDANG● — (Bone) — Raha○ — *Pulau* — ○*Wangiwangi* — *Tayandu*
(MAKASAR) — ∆2871 — Pulau — Kepulauan — Kepulauan — Kepulauan — Pulau
Bantaeng○ — Buton — *Wangiwangi* — Tukangbesi — Lucipara — Penju — Manuk○
Selat Selajar — Baubau○ — Pulau — Kepulauan — Kepulauan — Pulau
Benteng○ — Pulau Binongko — Tukangbesi — Lucipara — Penju — *Serua*
Pulau — Pulau — Kepulauan — Pulau
Selajar — Pulau Tanahjampea — Barat Daya — *Nila*
○*Teun*
Kepulauan — Pulau Kalao — Pulau Damar — Pulau
Kangean — Kalaotoa — *Teun*
Pulau — *Pulau* — Kepulauan Barat Daya — Pulau
Kepulauan — *Kalao* — Pulau — Pulau — *Babar*
Sepanjang — 6960 — *Adonara* — Pulau Romang — Pulau
Bali Sea — Pulau Komodo — *Larantuka*○ — *Kisar* — Moa — *Bahar*
Singaraja○ — *Flores Sea* — Pulau — Pulau Lomblen — Pulau
∆3142 — Pulau Moyo — *Sangeang* — Flores — 3760 — Pulau Atauro○ — Leti Is.
Denpasar○ — ∆2850 — ○*Ruteng* — Pulau Alor — Dili○
∆3726 — Gunung Rinjani — *Raba*○ — Ende○ — 960
Pulau — Sumbawa — ○*Maumere* — *Pantar*
Lombok — *Besar* — *Okusi*○ — 3310
Pulau Sumbawa — Sumba Strait — *Savu* — Pulau Timor
○*Waikabubak* — *Waingapu*○ — *Sea*
1225 — ○*Kupang* — Timor
Pulau Sumba — Pulau Sawu○ — ○*Pulau Roti* — *Sea*
Pulau Raijua○ — 125

115 — E — 120 — F — 125

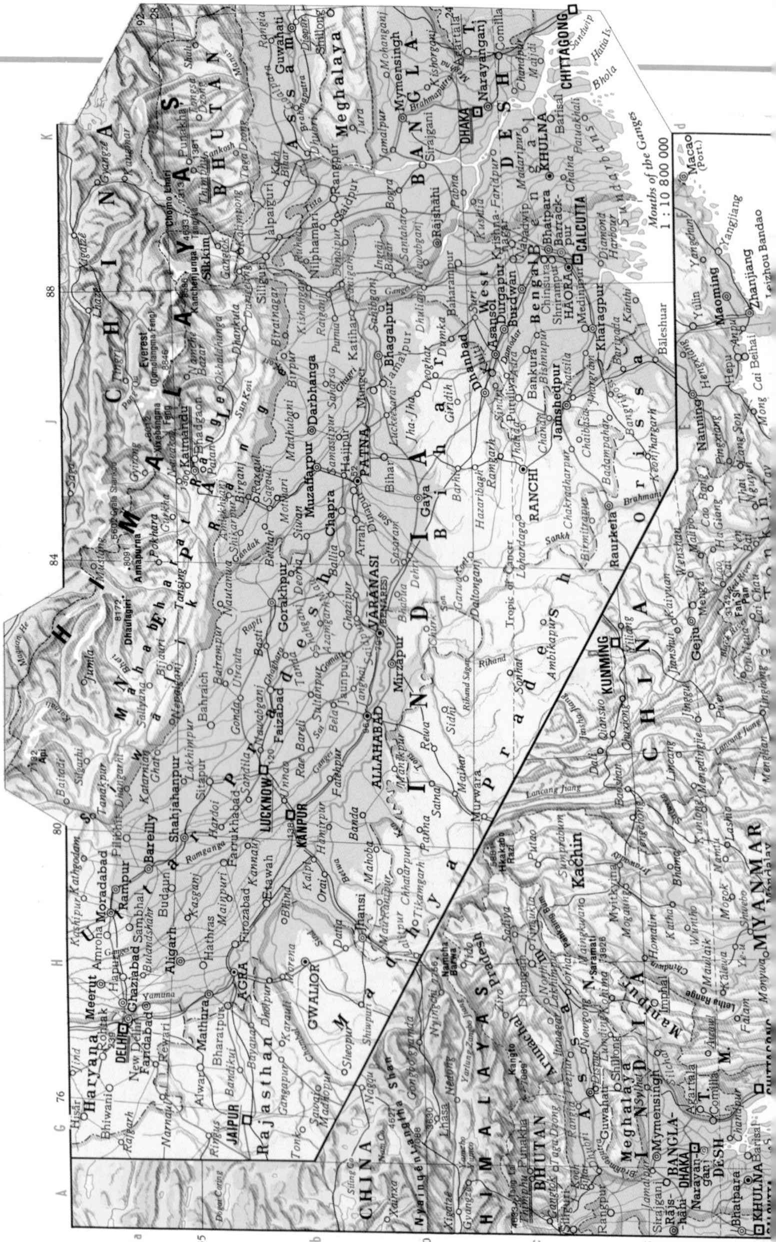

CHINA

HIMALAYA

BHUTAN

Meghalaya

ASSAM

BANGLADESH

DHAKA

CHITTAGONG

Macao (Port.)

Sikkim

Everest

Kathmandu

NEPAL

West Bengal

KHULNA

CALCUTTA

HAORA

Orissa

KUNMING

CHINA

MYANMAR

Kachin

MANIPUR

NAGALAND

PATNA

Bihar

RANCHI

Jamshedpur

Gaya

VARANASI

ALLAHABAD

LUCKNOW

KANPUR

Uttar Pradesh

AGRA

GWALIOR

DELHI

New Delhi

Haryana

Rajasthan

JAIPUR

Madhya Pradesh

Mouths of the Ganges

1 : 10 800 000

Tropic of Cancer

Meghalaya

BHUTAN

DHAKA

KHULNA

BANGLADESH

CHINA

HIMALAYA

Mymensingh

© ISTITUTO GEOGRAFICO DE AGOSTINI S.p.A. NOVARA

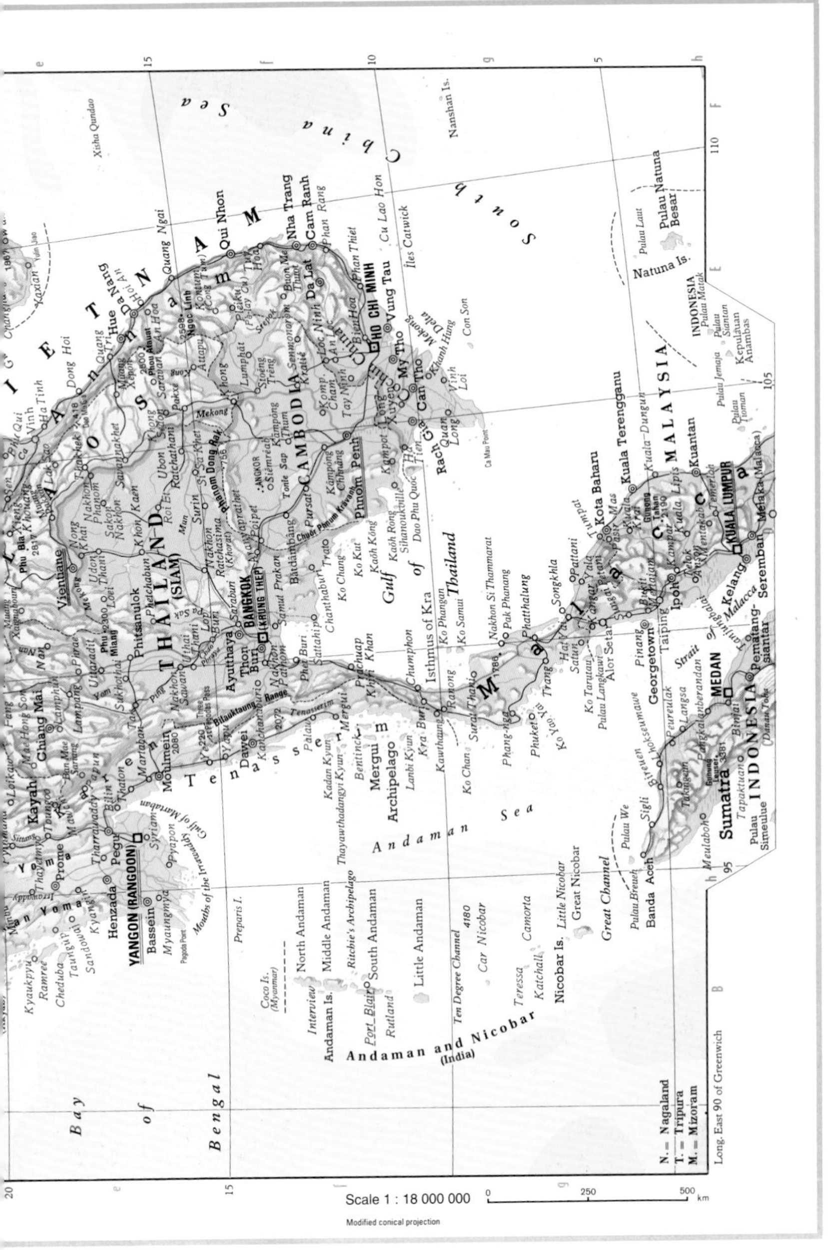
THAILAND
(SIAM)
CAMBODIA
MALAYSIA
INDONESIA
Andaman and Nicobar
(India)
South China Sea
Gulf of Thailand
Andaman Sea
Bay of Bengal
Gulf of Martaban
Strait of Malacca
Isthmus of Kra
Mergui Archipelago
Mouths of the Irrawaddy
Great Channel
Ten Degree Channel
Natuna Is.
Nanshan Is.
Nicobar Is.
Andaman Is.
Coco Is.
(Myanmar)
BANGKOK
(KRUNG THEP)
HO CHI MINH
Phnom Penh
Vientiane
YANGON (RANGOON)
KUALA LUMPUR
MEDAN
Sumatra
Kota Baharu
Kuala Terengganu
Kuantan
Ipoh
Georgetown
Taiping
Seremban
Melaka (Malacca)
Kelang
Alor Setar
Songkhla
Phuket
Chiang Mai
Lampang
Phitsanulok
Ayutthaya
Moulmein
Bassein
Henzada
Pegu
Prome
Mergui
Dawei
Qui Nhon
Nha Trang
Cam Ranh
Da Lat
Vung Tau
My Tho
Can Tho
Hue
Da Nang
Banda Aceh
Port Blair
N. = Nagaland
T. = Tripura
M. = Mizoram
Long. East 90 of Greenwich
Scale 1 : 18 000 000
0
250
500
km
Modified conical projection

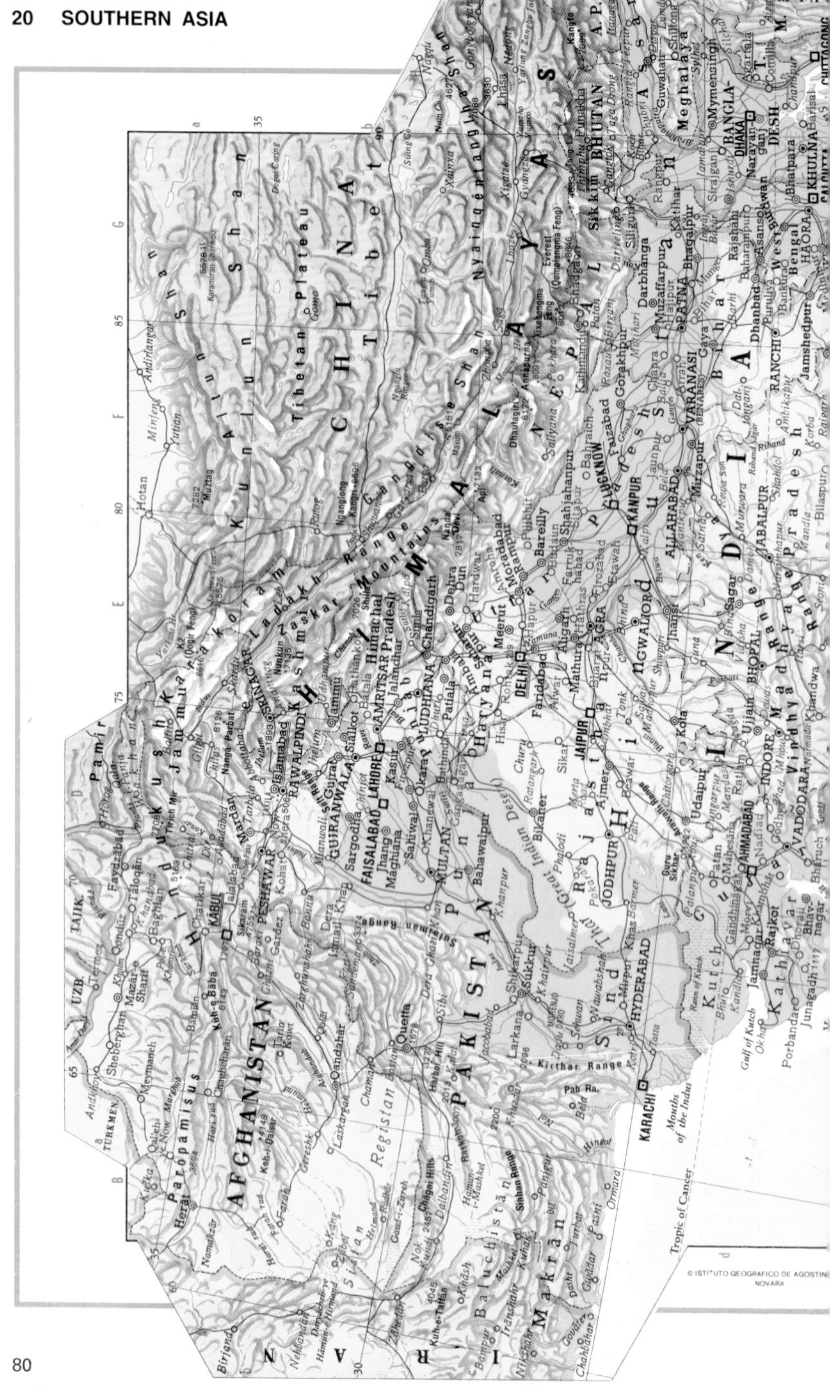
AFGHANISTAN
PAKISTAN
CHINA
INDIA
NEPAL
BHUTAN
BANGLA-DESH
Tibetan Plateau
H I M A L A Y A
Karakoram
Hindu Kush
Kunlun Shan
Altun Shan
Nyainqêntanglha Shan
Ladakh Range
Zaskar Mountains
Kirthar Range
Sulaiman Range
Vindhya Range
Aravalli Range
Great Indian Desert
Thar Desert
Registan
Paropamisus
Baluchistan
Makran
Punjab
Sind
Rajasthan
Uttar Pradesh
Madhya Pradesh
Bihar
West Bengal
Himachal Pradesh
Haryana
Jammu and Kashmir
Sikkim
Meghalaya
Assam
Kathiawar
Kutch
Gulf of Kutch
Mouths of the Indus
Tropic of Cancer
KABUL
ISLAMABAD
DELHI
KATHMANDU
THIMPHU
DHAKA
Lhasa
KARACHI
LAHORE
PESHAWAR
RAWALPINDI
SRINAGAR
AMRITSAR
LUDHIANA
FAISALABAD
GUJRANWALA
MULTAN
HYDERABAD
JODHPUR
JAIPUR
AGRA
KANPUR
LUCKNOW
ALLAHABAD
VARANASI
PATNA
AHMADABAD
VADODARA
INDORE
BHOPAL
JABALPUR
GWALIOR
RANCHI
KHULNA
Quetta
Herat
Kandahar
Mazar-e Sharif
Everest
K2
Nanga Parbat
Annapurna
Dhaulagiri
© ISTITUTO GEOGRAFICO DE AGOSTINI NOVARA

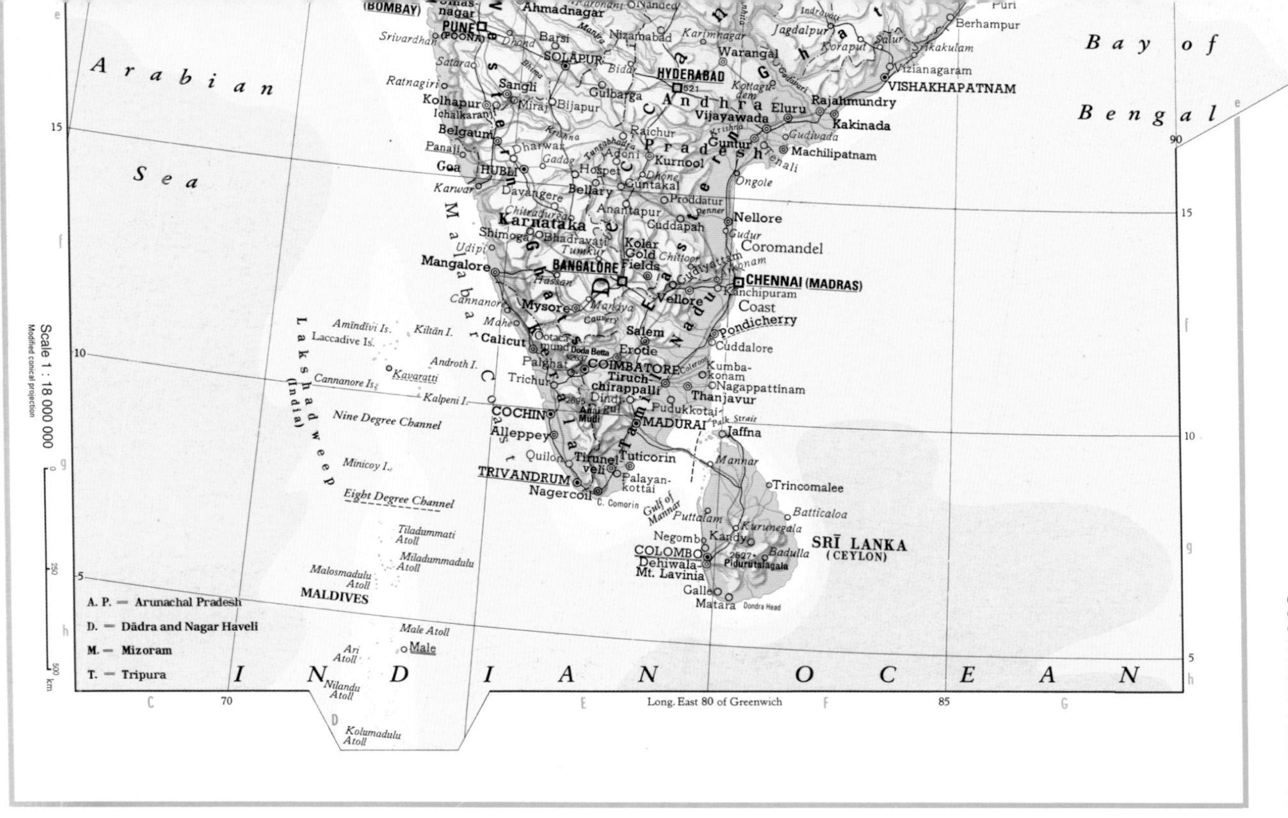

(BURMA)

Bay of Bengal

Arabian Sea

INDIAN OCEAN

Long. East 80 of Greenwich

Puri
Berhampur
VISHAKHAPATNAM
Vizianagaram
Kakinada
Rajahmundry
Eluru
Machilipatnam
Vijayawada
Warangal
HYDERABAD
Ongole
Nellore
Coromandel
CHENNAI (MADRAS)
Pondicherry
Coast
Cuddalore
Nagappattinam
Thanjavur
Tiruchchirappalli
MADURAI
Tuticorin
C. Comorin
Trincomalee
Batticaloa

SRĪ LANKA
(CEYLON)

Negombo
Kandy
COLOMBO
Dehiwala
Mt. Lavinia
Galle
Matara

Jaffna
Mannar

Puttalam

HUBLI
Goa
Panaji
PUNE
(BOMBAY)
Ahmadnagar
SOLAPUR
Kolhapur
Belgaum
Sangli
Ratnagiri
Mangalore
Karwar

Karnataka
BANGALORE
Mysore
Salem
COIMBATORE
Erode
COCHIN
Alleppey
Quilon
TRIVANDRUM
Nagercoil

Maldives

Laccadive Is.
Amindivi Is.
Minicoy I.
Nine Degree Channel
Eight Degree Channel
Laksh adweep
(India)

MALDIVES
Male
Arī Atoll
Male Atoll
Tiladummati Atoll
Miladummadula Atoll
Maalhosmadula Atoll
Nilandu Atoll
Kolamadulu Atoll

A. P. — Arunachal Pradesh
D. — Dādra and Nagar Haveli
M. — Mizoram
T. — Tripura

Scale 1 : 18 000 000
Modified conical projection
0   250   500 km

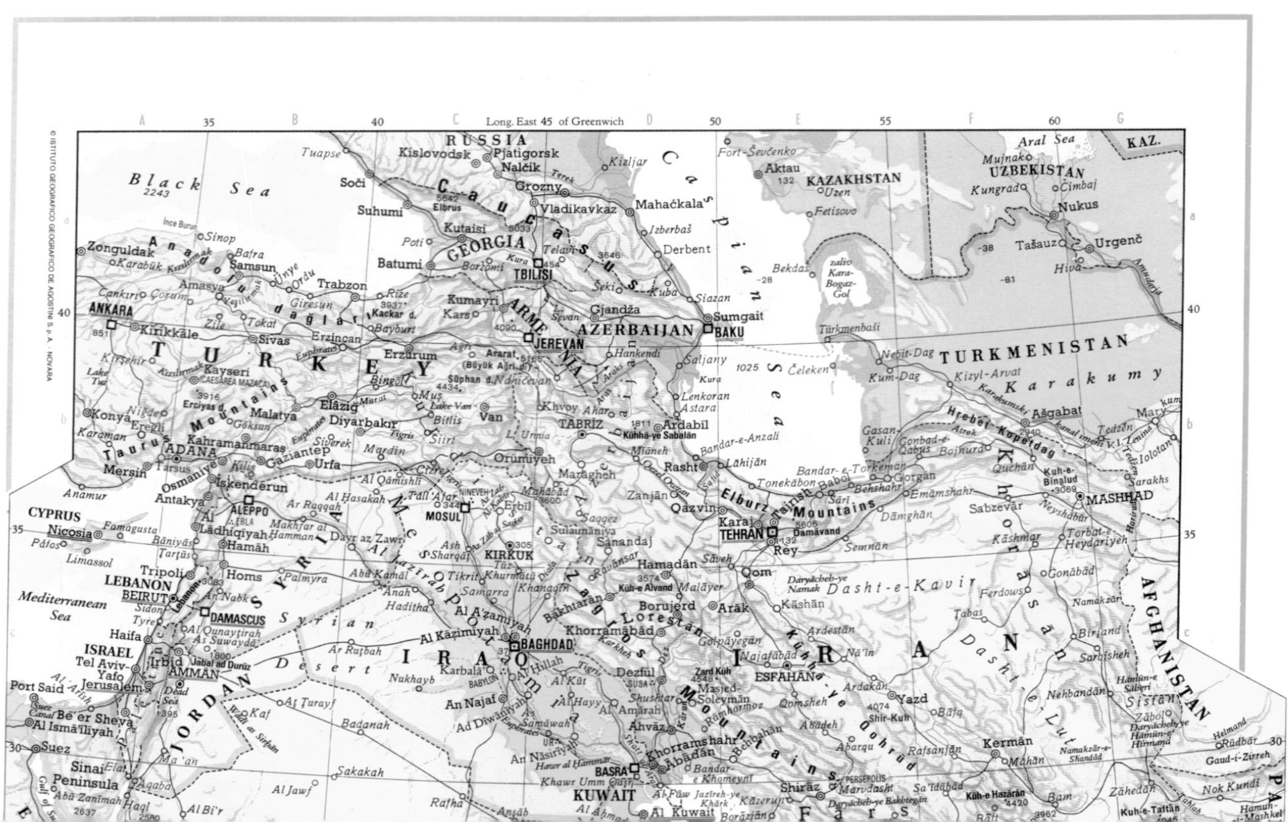

PA

KAZ.

Aral Sea

UZBEKISTAN

Mujnako
Kungrad
Nukus
Urgenç
Hiva
Çimbaj

AFGHANISTAN

Amudarja

TURKMENISTAN
K a r a k u m y

Taşauz

MASHHAD

Qum-Dag
Vsegli-Dag
Heyat
Aşgabat
K h o r a s a n

Dasht-e Lut

KAZAKHSTAN

Fort-Ševčenko
Aktau

Caspian Sea

Kara-
Bogaz-
Gol

Krasnovodsk

Gasan-Kuli

Elburz Mountains
TEHRAN
Karaj
Rey

Kerman

Qom

I R A N

ESFAHAN

Zagros Mountains

Mahačkala
Derbent
Sumgait
BAKU

RUSSIA

Kislovodsk
Pjatigorsk
Nalčik
Groznyj
Vladikavkaz

Elbrus

C a u c a s u s

GEORGIA
Kutaisi
Batumi
TBILISI

Kumajri
Kars

ARMENIA
YEREVAN

AZERBAIJAN
Gandža
Stepanakert

Ardabil
Rasht

Zanjan
Qazvin
Hamadan

Ahvaz
Abadan

Suhumi
Soči

Trabzon
Erzurum

TURKEY

Lenkoran
Astara

Tabriz
Urümiye

Orumiyeh

KUWAIT

BASRA

Tuapse

Black Sea

Sinop
Samsun
Ordu
Giresun

Sivas

ANKARA
Kayseri

Malatya
Kahramanmaraş

ADANA

Diyarbakir
Elazig

Urfa
Gaziantep

Siirt
Bitlis
Van

MOSUL
KIRKUK

I R A Q
BAGHDAD
Karbala
An Najaf

Ar Rutbah

Syrian Desert

Zonguldak
Iskenderun
Anakya
ALEPPO
LADHIQIYAH
Homs
HAMAH

Mersin

Konya

Tarsus

Antakya

Tripoli
BEIRUT

LEBANON
DAMASCUS

Palmyra

JORDAN
AMMAN

CYPRUS
Nicosia
Limassol

ISRAEL
Tel Aviv
Haifa
Jerusalem

Mediterranean Sea

Port Said
Suez

Gulf of

Sinai

Long East 45 of Greenwich

© ISTITUTO GEOGRAFICO GEOGRAFICO DE AGOSTINI S.p.A. · NOVARA

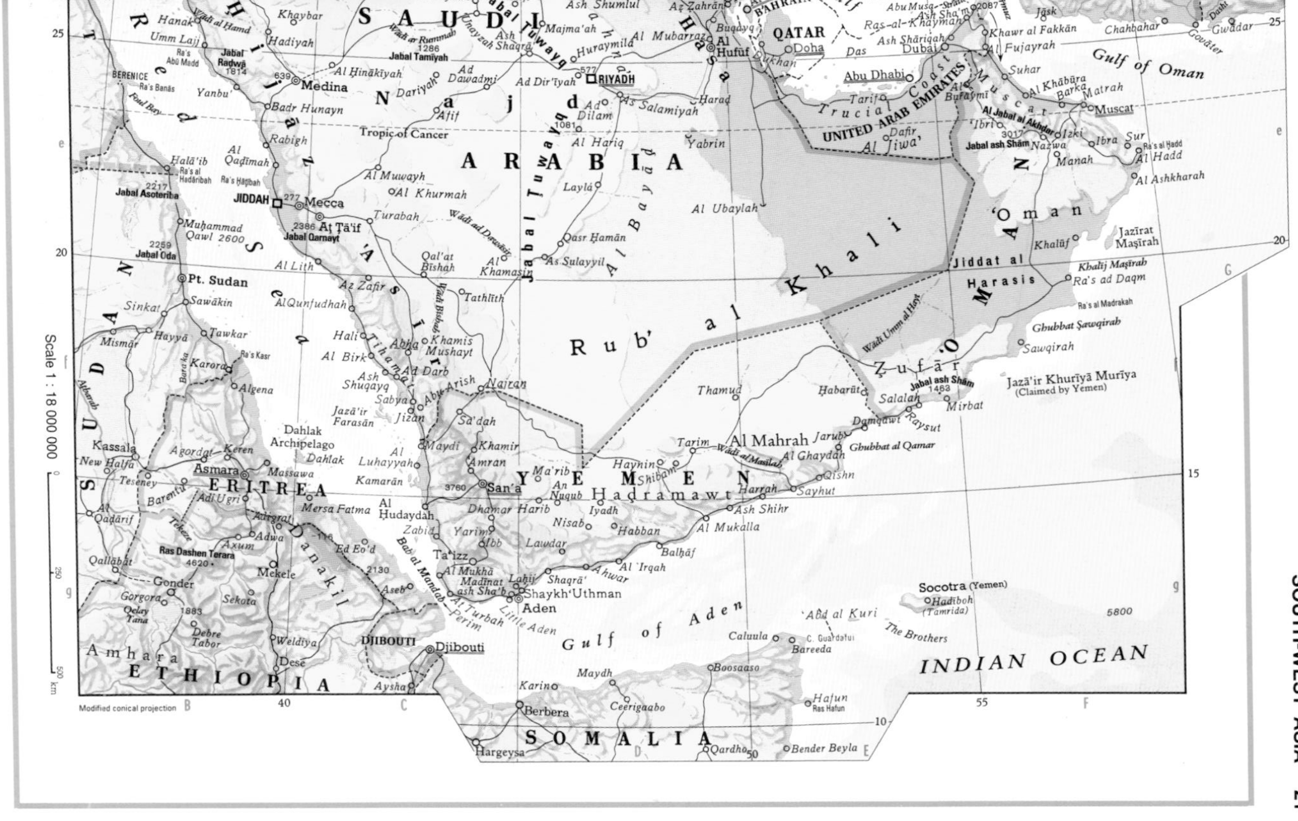
SAUDI ARABIA
YEMEN
'Oman
OMAN
UNITED ARAB EMIRATES
QATAR
BAHRAIN
ERITREA
ETHIOPIA
SOMALIA
DJIBOUTI
SUDAN
INDIAN OCEAN
Gulf of Aden
Gulf of Oman
Red Sea
Rub' al Khali
Hadramawt
Najd
Hijaz
'Asir
Tihamah
Zufar
Danakil
Amhara
Jiddat al Harasis
Trucial Coast
Jabal Tuwayq
Al Bayad
RIYADH
Mecca
Medina
JIDDAH
At Ta'if
San'a
Aden
Muscat
Abu Dhabi
Dubai
Doha
Al Hufuf
Djibouti
Asmara
Pt. Sudan
Massawa
Kassala
Gonder
Berbera
Hargeysa
Socotra (Yemen)
Jazā'ir Khurīyā Murīya
(Claimed by Yemen)
Tropic of Cancer
Bab al Mandab
Perim
Little Aden
Al Mukalla
Salalah
Jazīrat Maşīrah
Ras Dashen Terara 4620
The Brothers
Dahlak Archipelago
Modified conical projection
Scale 1 : 18 000 000
0
250
500
km

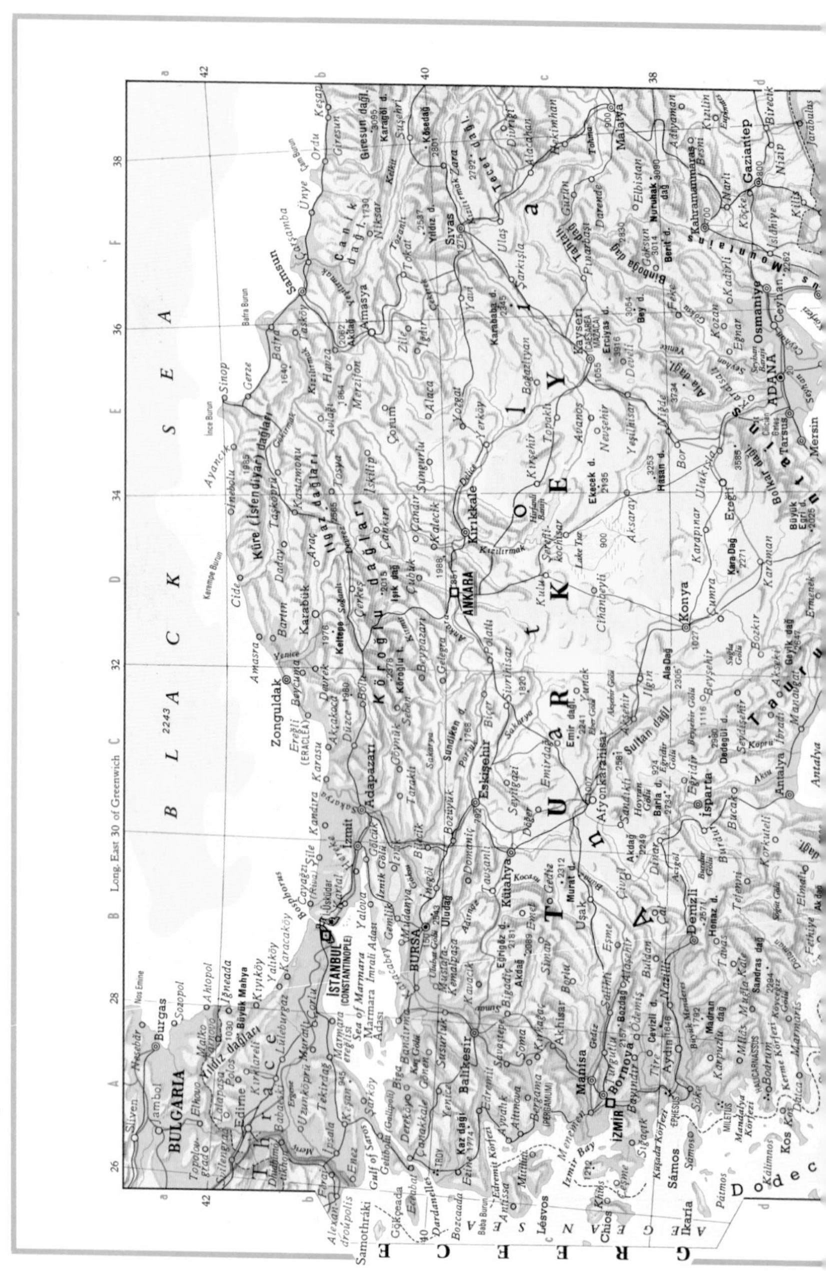
BLACK SEA
TURKEY
GREECE
BULGARIA
Thrace
Long. East 30 of Greenwich
ISTANBUL (CONSTANTINOPLE)
ANKARA
İZMIR
BURSA
ADANA
Konya
Kayseri
Sivas
Samsun
Eskişehir
Zonguldak
Malatya
Gaziantep
Mersin
Antalya
Sea of Marmara
Gulf of Saros
Dardanelles
Bosporus
İzmir Bay
Sinop
Kırıkkale
Kütahya
Afyonkarahisar
Isparta
Denizli
Aydın
Manisa
Balıkesir
Edirne
Tekirdağ
Adapazarı
İzmit
Lésvos
Chios
Sámos
Ikaria
Kos
Samothráki
Gökçeada
Bozcaada
Taurus Mountains
Köroğlu dağları
Küre (İsfendiyar) dağları
Tecer dağl.
Dodec

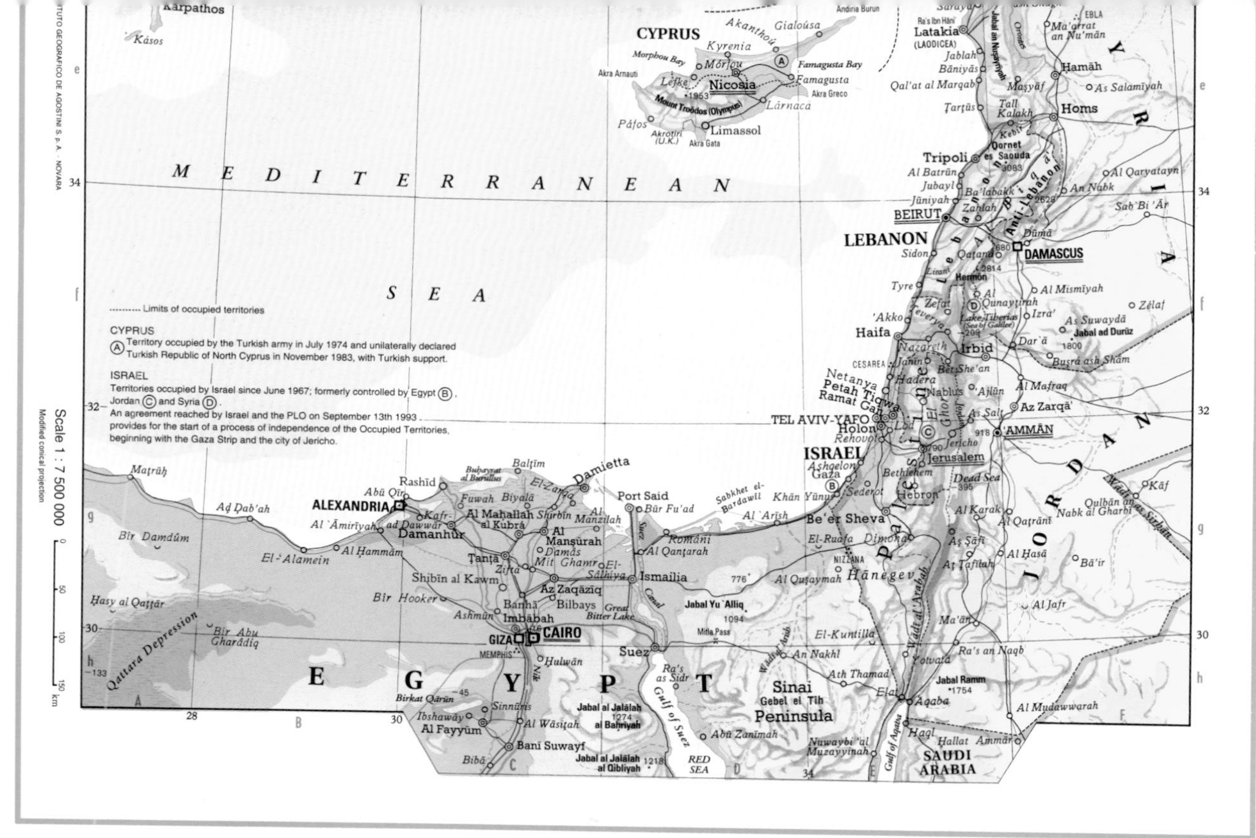

ISTITUTO GEOGRAFICO DE AGOSTINI S.p.A. · NOVARA

Scale 1 : 7 500 000   0   50   100   150 km
Modified conical projection

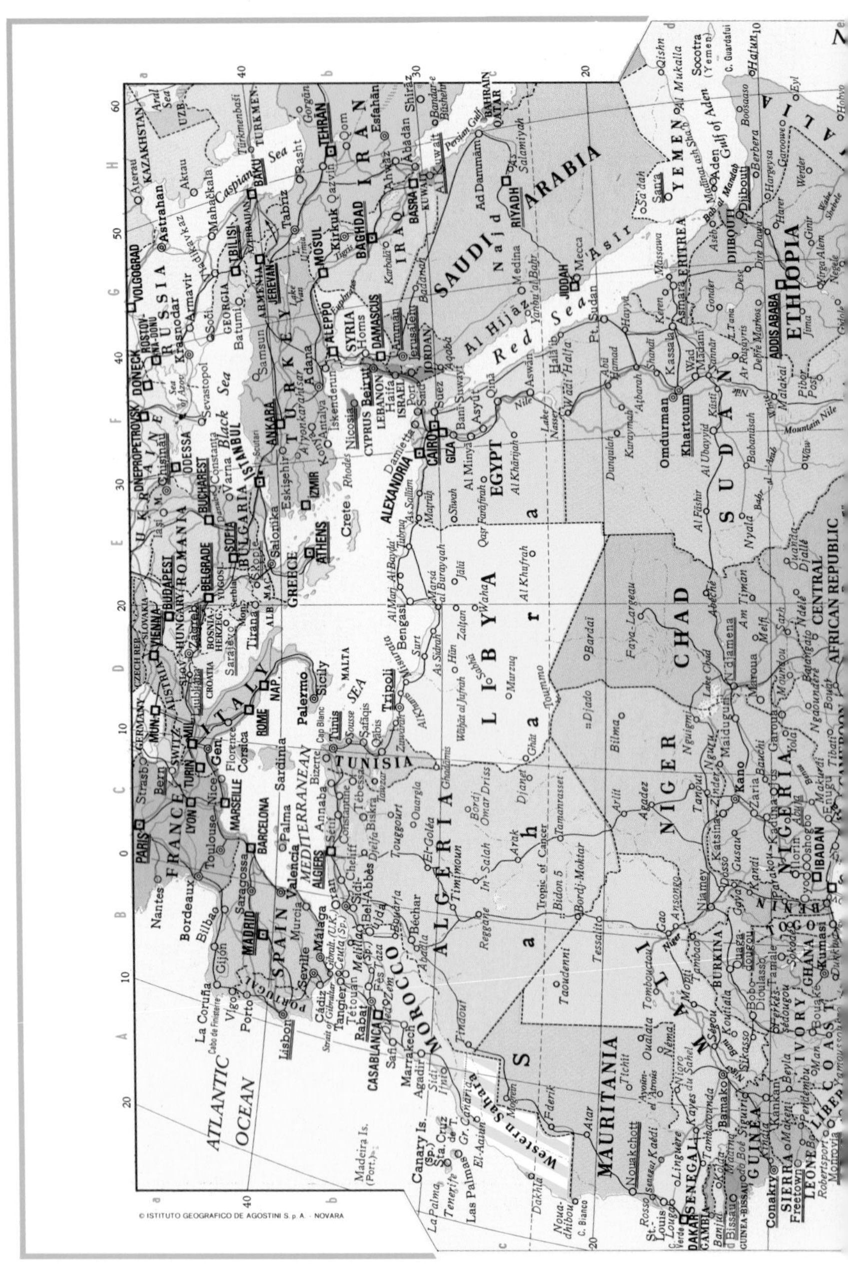
ATLANTIC OCEAN
MEDITERRANEAN SEA
Black Sea
Caspian Sea
Red Sea
Persian Gulf
Gulf of Aden
Madeira Is. (Port.)
Canary Is. (Sp.)
Western Sahara
MOROCCO
ALGERIA
TUNISIA
LIBYA
EGYPT
SUDAN
CHAD
NIGER
MALI
MAURITANIA
SENEGAL
GAMBIA
GUINEA-BISSAU
GUINEA
SIERRA LEONE
LIBERIA
IVORY COAST
GHANA
BURKINA
NIGERIA
CENTRAL AFRICAN REPUBLIC
ETHIOPIA
ERITREA
DJIBOUTI
SAUDI ARABIA
YEMEN
IRAN
IRAQ
SYRIA
JORDAN
ISRAEL
LEBANON
CYPRUS
TURKEY
GREECE
ITALY
SPAIN
PORTUGAL
FRANCE
ROMANIA
BULGARIA
UKRAINE
RUSSIA
GEORGIA
KAZAKHSTAN
Sahara
Tropic of Cancer
CAIRO
ALEXANDRIA
KHARTOUM
Omdurman
ADDIS ABABA
RIYADH
JIDDAH
Mecca
BAGHDAD
TEHRAN
DAMASCUS
ANKARA
ISTANBUL
ATHENS
ROME
MADRID
ALGIERS
Tripoli
Tunis
CASABLANCA
Rabat
DAKAR
Bamako
Niamey
N'djamena
Kano
IBADAN
Nouakchott
Freetown
Conakry
© ISTITUTO GEOGRAFICO DE AGOSTINI S. p. A. - NOVARA

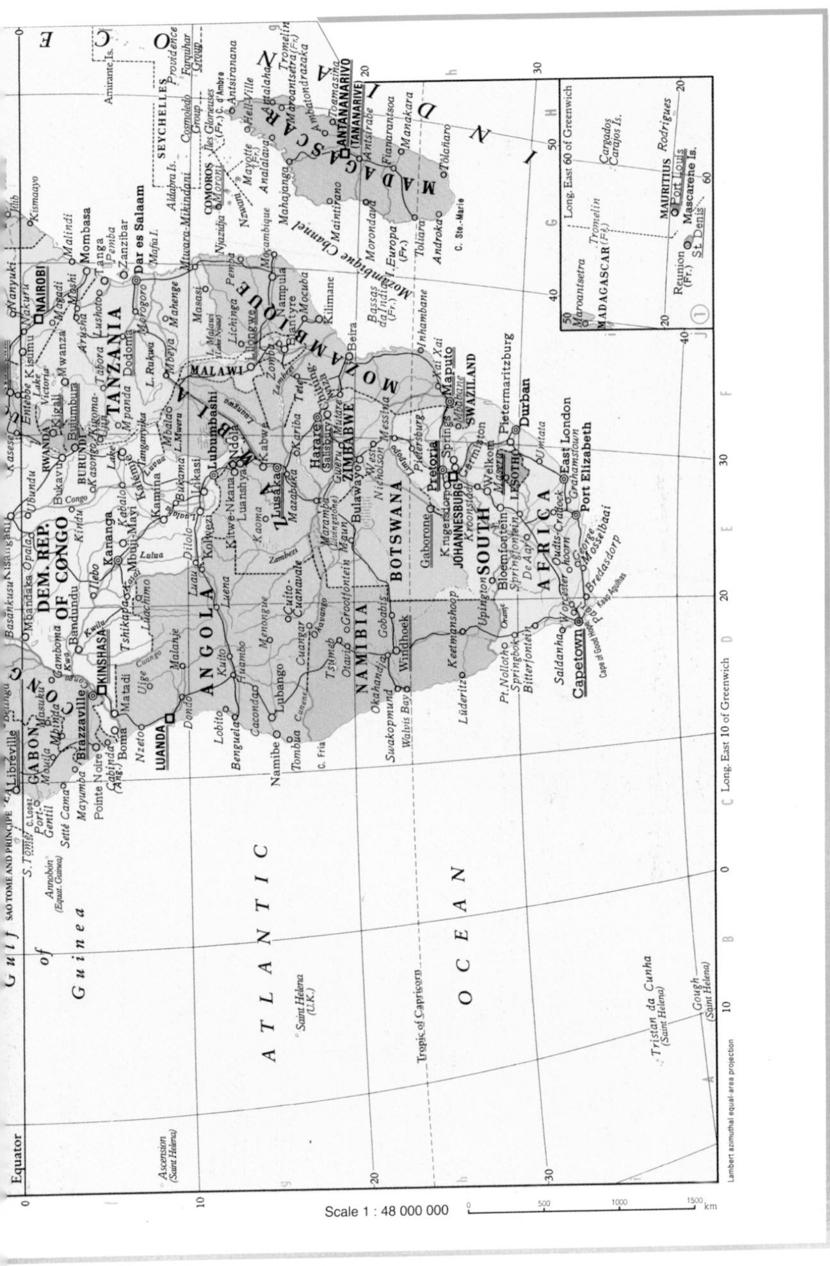
ATLANTIC
OCEAN
Gulf of Guinea
Equator
Tropic of Capricorn
Mozambique Channel
GABON
DEM. REP. OF CONGO
CONGO
ANGOLA
NAMIBIA
BOTSWANA
ZAMBIA
ZIMBABWE
MOZAMBIQUE
MALAWI
TANZANIA
RWANDA
BURUNDI
SOUTH AFRICA
LESOTHO
SWAZILAND
MADAGASCAR
SEYCHELLES
COMOROS
MAURITIUS
SAO TOME AND PRINCIPE
LUANDA
KINSHASA
Brazzaville
Libreville
NAIROBI
Dar es Salaam
Dodoma
Lusaka
Harare
Windhoek
Gaborone
Pretoria
JOHANNESBURG
Maputo
Mbabane
Maseru
ANTANANARIVO
Moroni
Port Louis
St Denis
Capetown
Port Elizabeth
East London
Durban
Pietermaritzburg
Bloemfontein
Lubumbashi
Kananga
Kisangani
Mombasa
Zanzibar
Beira
Bulawayo
Ndola
Kitwe-Nkana
Walvis Bay
Lüderitz
Saint Helena (U.K.)
Ascension (Saint Helena)
Tristan da Cunha (Saint Helena)
Gough (Saint Helena)
Annobon (Equat. Guinea)
Réunion (Fr.)
Rodrigues
Mascarene Is.
Long. East 10 of Greenwich
Long. East 60 of Greenwich
Lambert azimuthal equal-area projection
Scale 1 : 48 000 000
0 500 1000 1500 km

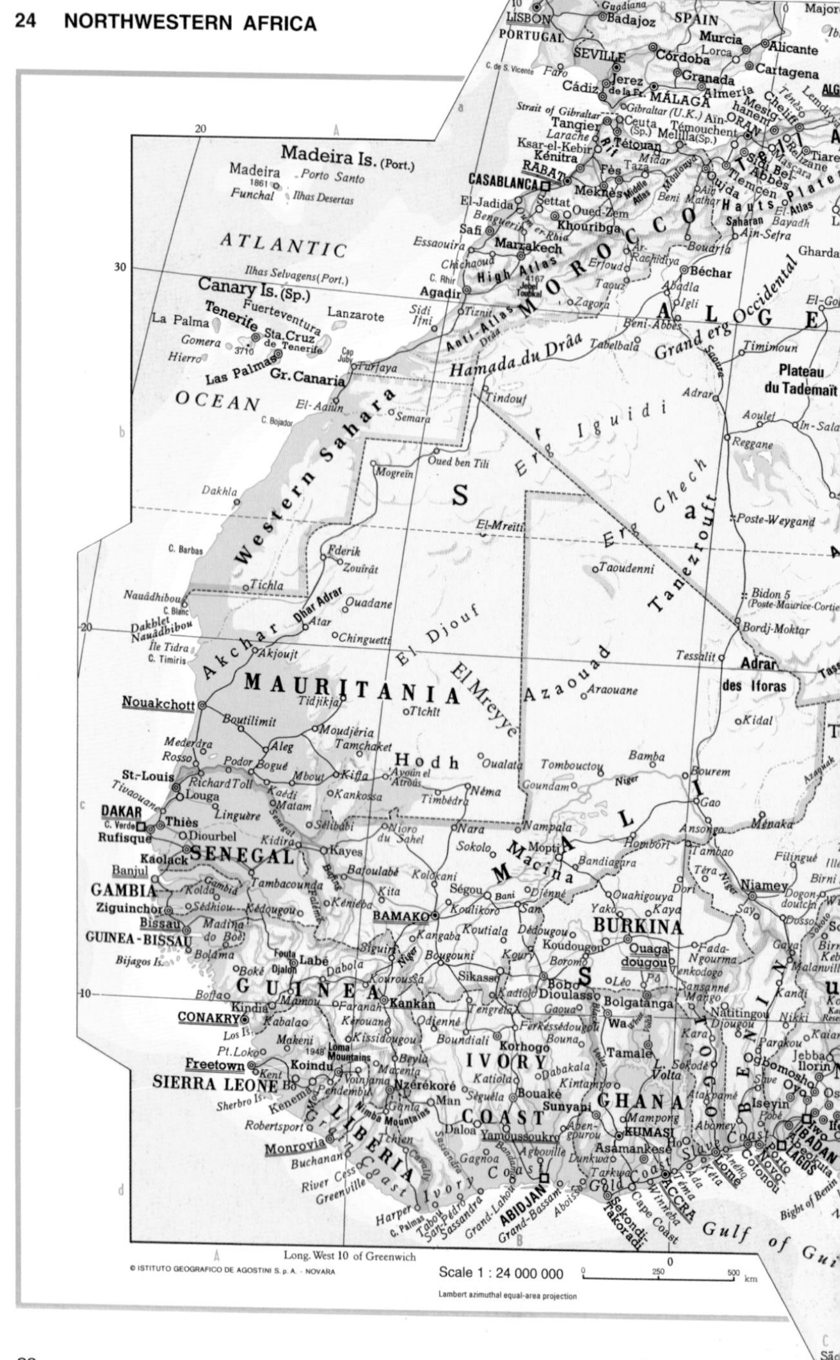

Scale 1 : 24 000 000

Lambert azimuthal equal-area projection

© ISTITUTO GEOGRAFICO DE AGOSTINI S. p. A. - NOVARA

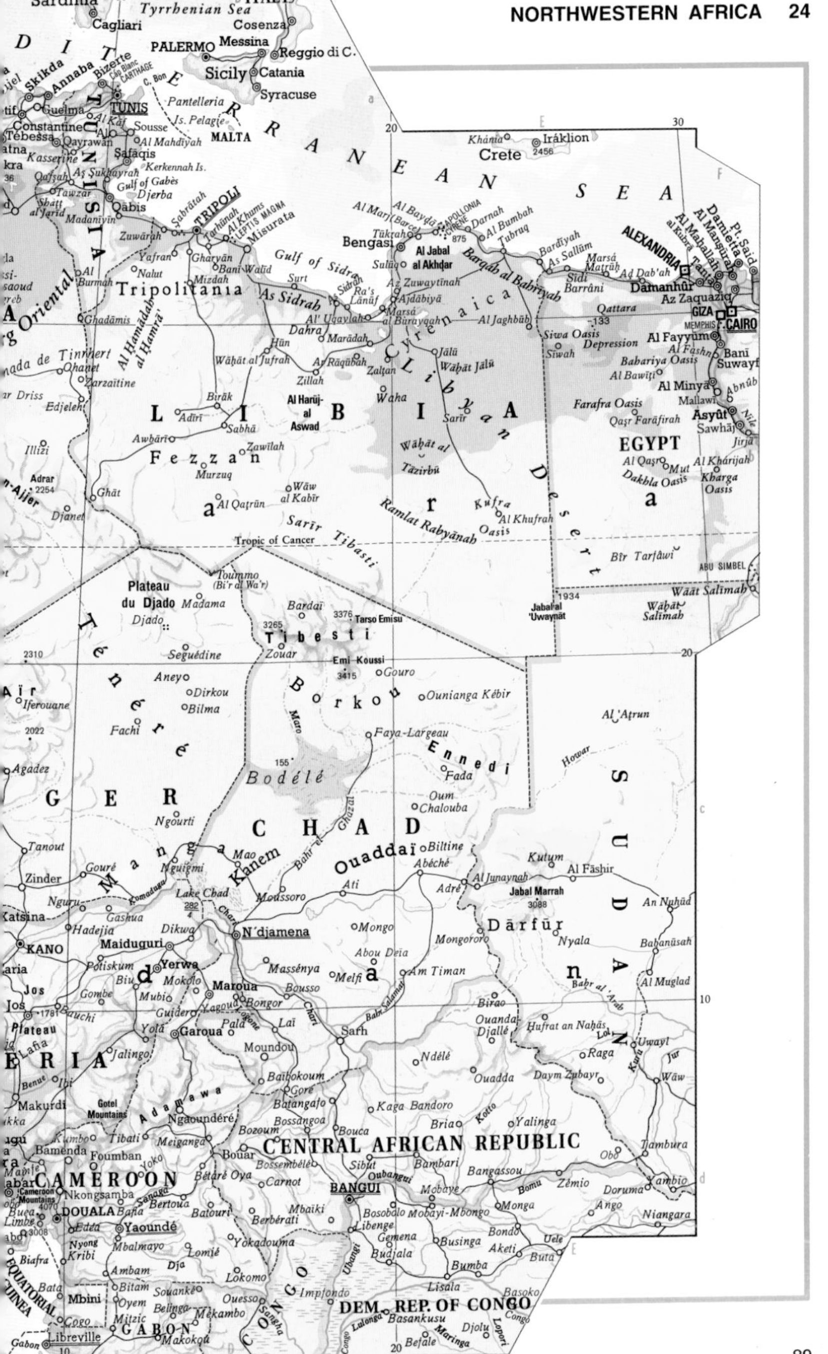
Sardinia
Cagliari
Tyrrhenian Sea
ITALY
Cosenza
PALERMO
Messina
Reggio di C.
Sicily
Catania
Syracuse
Skikda
Annaba
Bizerte
TUNIS
Guelma
Constantine
Tébessa
Qayrawān
Sousse
Al Mahdīyah
Pantelleria
Is. Pelagie
MALTA
Ṣafāqis
Kasserine
Kerkennah Is.
Qafṣah
Aṣ Ṣukhayrah
Gulf of Gabès
Tawzar
Djerba
Qābis
Madanīyīn
Zuwārah
Ṣabrātah
TRIPOLI
Al Khums
LEPTIS MAGNA
Misurata
Tarhūnah
Yafran
Gharyān
Nalut
Mizdah
Banī Walīd
Tripolitania
Gulf of Sidra
Surt
As Sidrah
Ra's Lānūf
Ghadāmis
Al Ḥamādah al Ḥamrā'
Wāḥāt al Jufrah
Hūn
Dahra
Marādah
Ar Rāqūbah
Zaltan
Zillah
Ohanet
Zarzaïtine
Edjeleh
Birāk
Adīrī
Sabhā
Awbārī
Fezzan
Zawīlah
Murzuq
Illizi
Adrar
2254
Ghāt
Djanet
Al Qaṭrūn
Wāw al Kabīr
MEDITERRANEAN SEA
Khánia
Iráklion
Crete
2456
Al Marj (Barce)
Al Bayḍā'
APOLLONIA
CYRENE
Darnah
Al Bumbah
Tubruq
Bengasi
Tūkrah
875
Al Jabal al Akhḍar
Sulūq
Az Zuwaytīnah
Ajdābiyā
Marsá al Burayqah
Al' Uqaylah
Cyrenaica
Al Jaghbūb
Barqah al Baḥrīyah
Bardīyah
As Sallūm
Marsá Maṭrūḥ
Sīdī Barrānī
Ad Dab'ah
ALEXANDRIA
Damanhûr
Az Zaqaziq
Damietta
Pt. Said
Al Manṣūrah
Al Maḥallah al Kubrá
Ṭanṭā
Qattara Depression
-133
GIZA
MEMPHIS
CAIRO
Siwa Oasis
Sīwah
Al Fayyūm
Al Fashn
Banī Suwayf
Babariya Oasis
Al Bawīṭī
Al Minyā
Abnūb
Mallawī
Asyūt
Sawhāj
Nile
Jirjā
Farafra Oasis
Qaṣr Farāfirah
EGYPT
Al Qaṣr
Mut
Dakhla Oasis
Al Khārijah
Kharga Oasis
Jālū
Wāḥāt Jālū
Waha
Al Harūj al Aswad
LIBYA
Libyan Desert
Sarīr
Wāḥāt al Tāzirbū
Kufra
Al Khufrah Oasis
Ramlat Rabyānah
Sarīr Tibasti
Tropic of Cancer
Bīr Tarfāwī
ABU SIMBEL
Wāat Salīmah
Wāḥāt Salīmah
Jabal al 'Uwaynāt
1934
Toummo (Bi'r al Wa'r)
Plateau du Djado
Madama
Djado
Bardaï
3376
Tarso Emisu
3265
Tibesti
Zouar
Emi Koussi
3415
Gouro
Seguédine
2310
Ténéré
Aney
Dirkou
Bilma
Aïr
Iferouane
2022
Fachi
Borkou
Ounianga Kébir
Al 'Aṭrun
Faya-Largeau
Maro
Ennedi
Howar
155
Bodélé
Fada
Agadez
NIGER
Ngourti
Oum Chalouba
SUDAN
CHAD
Tanout
Manga
Mao
Kanem
Bahr el Ghazal
Ouaddaï
Biltine
Abéché
Kutum
Al Fāshir
Gouré
Nguigmi
Zinder
Lake Chad
282
Moussoro
Ati
Al Junaynah
Adré
Jabal Marrah
3088
An Nahūd
Nguru
Komadugu
Katsina
Gashua
Hadejia
Dikwa
Chari
N'djamena
Mongo
Mongororo
Dārfūr
Nyala
Babanūsah
KANO
Maiduguri
Yerwa
Potiskum
Massénya
Abou Deïa
Melfi
Am Timan
Al Muglad
Jos
Biu
Mokolo
Maroua
Bousso
Gombe
Mubi
Bahr al 'Arab
Bauchi
1781
Plateau
Guider
Yagoua
Bongor
Birao
Lafia
Yola
Garoua
Pala
Laï
Bahr Salamat
Ouanda Djallé
Hufrat an Naḥās
Lol
Uwayl
NIGERIA
Jalingo
Moundou
Sarh
Ndélé
Raga
Jur
Benue
Ibi
Baïbokoum
Goré
Ouadda
Daym Zubayr
Wāw
Makurdi
Gotel Mountains
Adamawa
Batangafo
Kaga Bandoro
Kotto
Ngaoundéré
Bossangoa
Bozoum
Bouca
Bria
Yalinga
Kumbo
Tibati
Meiganga
CENTRAL AFRICAN REPUBLIC
Tambura
Bamenda
Foumban
Bouar
Yoko
Bossembélé
Sibut
Bambari
Obo
Bétaré Oya
Bangassou
Bomu
Zémio
Yambio
Doruma
CAMEROON
Cameroon Mountains
4070
Nkongsamba
Carnot
BANGUI
Oubangui
Mobaye
DOUALA
Sanaga
Bertoua
Bafia
Mbaïki
Bosobolo
Mobayi-Mbongo
Monga
Ango
Niangara
Buea
Limbe
Edéa
Yaoundé
Batouri
Berbérati
Libenge
Bondo
3008
Uele
Nyong
Kribi
Mbalmayo
Yokadouma
Gemena
Businga
Aketi
Buta
Biafra
Lomié
Ubangi
Budjala
Ambam
Dja
Bumba
EQUATORIAL GUINEA
Bata
Lokomo
Bitam
Souanké
Mbini
Oyem
Belinga
Ouesso
Impfondo
Lisala
Basoko
CONGO
Mékambo
Sangha
DEM. REP. OF CONGO
Cogo
Mitzic
Lulonga
Basankusu
Congo
Libreville
GABON
Makokou
Djolu
Lopori
Gabon
Maringa
Befale
10
20
30

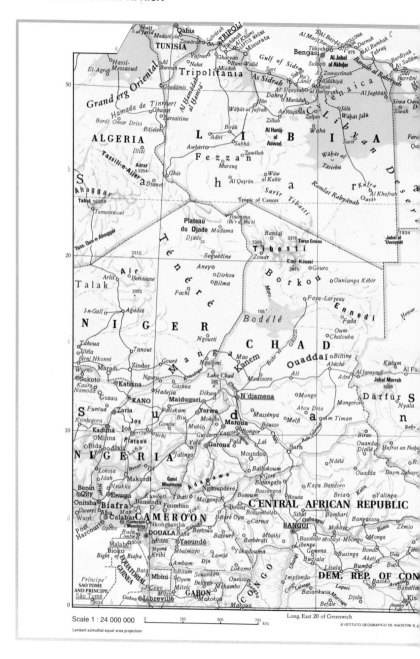

Scale 1 : 24 000 000

Lambert azimuthal equal-area projection

0   250   500   750 km

Long. East 20 of Greenwich

© ISTITUTO GEOGRAFICO DE AGOSTINI S.p.

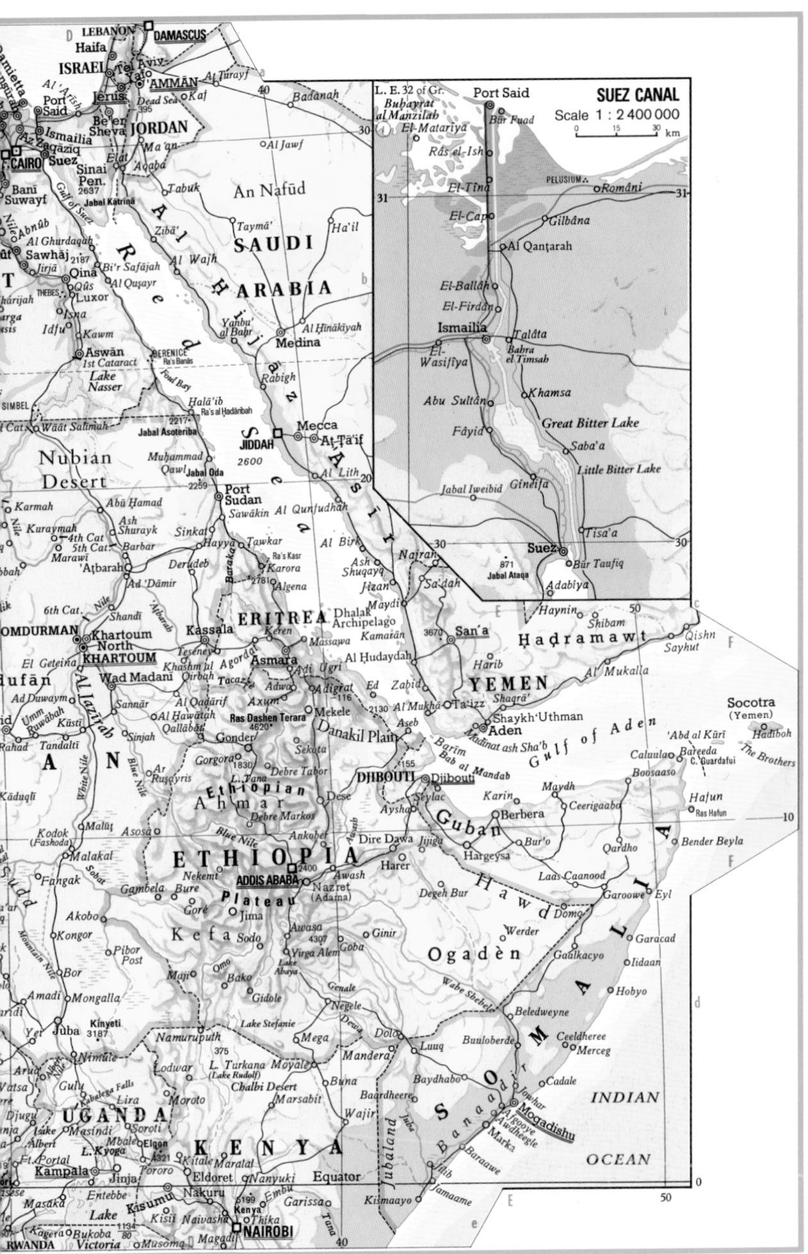

SUEZ CANAL

Scale 1 : 2 400 000

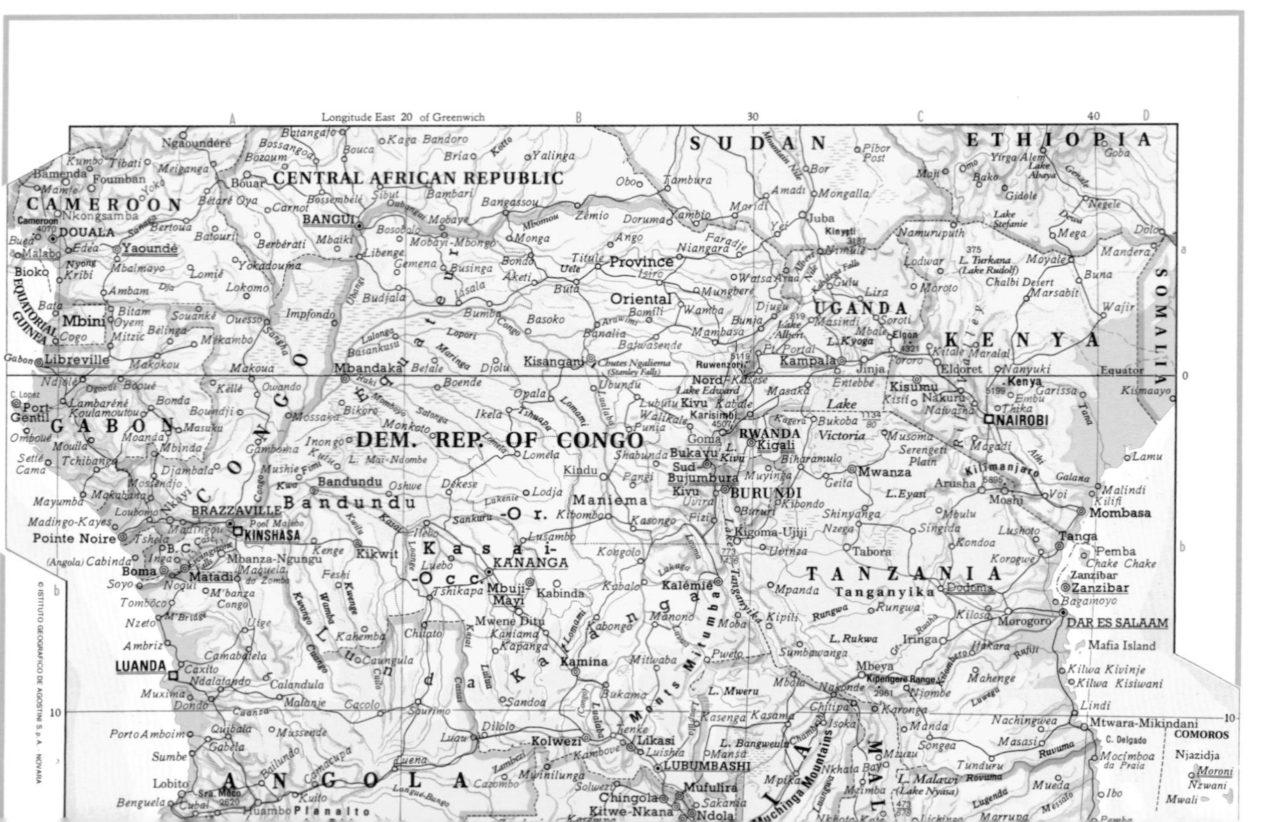

Longitude East 20 of Greenwich
SUDAN
ETHIOPIA
SOMALIA
CENTRAL AFRICAN REPUBLIC
CAMEROON
EQUATORIAL GUINEA
GABON
CONGO
DEM. REP. OF CONGO
UGANDA
KENYA
RWANDA
BURUNDI
TANZANIA
ANGOLA
COMOROS
NAIROBI
Kampala
Kigali
BURUNDI
DAR ES SALAAM
Dodoma
BANGUI
KINSHASA
BRAZZAVILLE
LUANDA
Yaoundé
Libreville
DOUALA
Mombasa
Zanzibar
Lake Victoria
Tanganyika
KANANGA
LUBUMBASHI
Kisangani
Mbandaka
Equator
© ISTITUTO GEOGRAFICO DE AGOSTINI S. p. A. - NOVARA

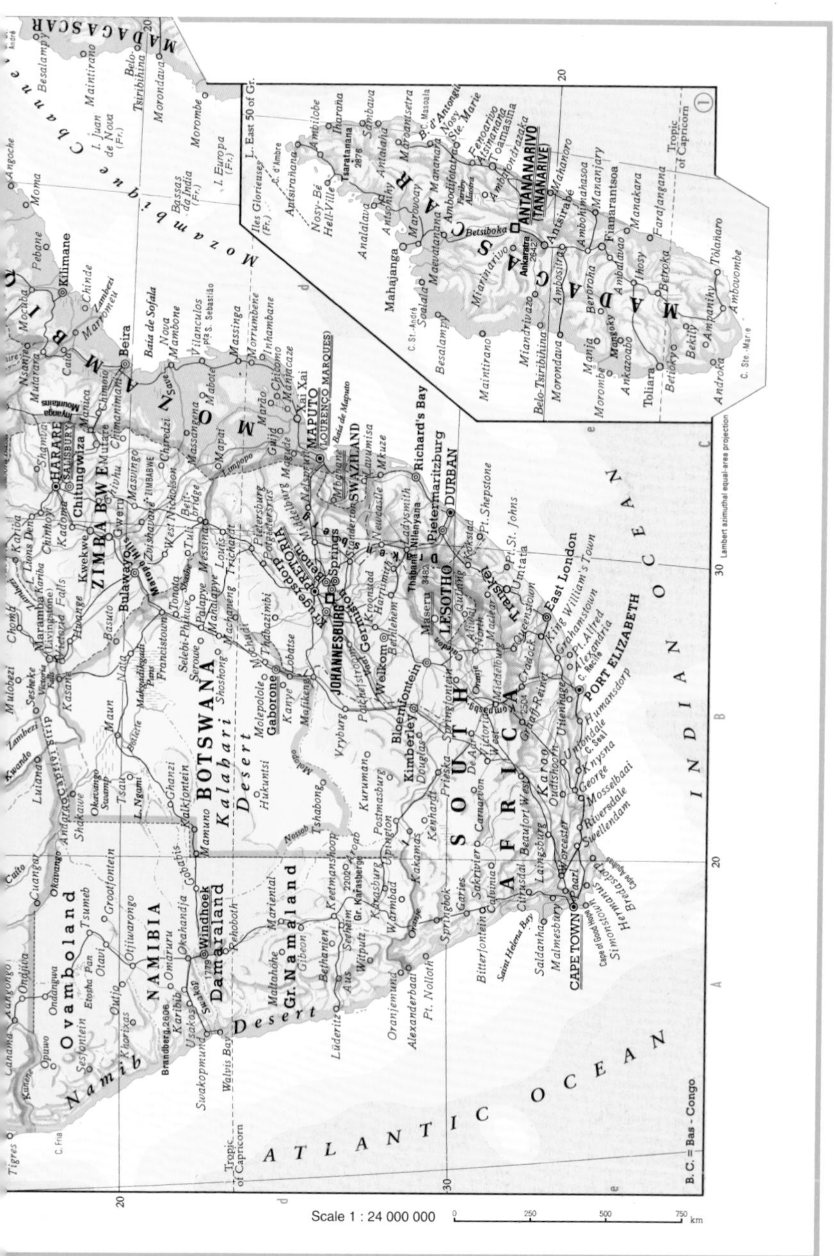
ATLANTIC OCEAN
INDIAN OCEAN
SOUTH AFRICA
BOTSWANA
NAMIBIA
ZIMBABWE
MOZAMBIQUE
MADAGASCAR
LESOTHO
SWAZILAND
Mozambique Channel
Kalahari Desert
Namib Desert
Ovamboland
Damaraland
Gr. Namaland
Transkei
Karoo
CAPE TOWN
PORT ELIZABETH
DURBAN
JOHANNESBURG
PRETORIA
MAPUTO (LOURENÇO MARQUES)
HARARE (SALISBURY)
ANTANANARIVO (TANANARIVE)
Windhoek
Gaborone
Bloemfontein
Kimberley
East London
Pietermaritzburg
Richard's Bay
Bulawayo
Beira
Kilimane
Maseru
Walvis Bay
Lüderitz
Swakopmund
Mahajanga
Toliara
Fianarantsoa
Tropic of Capricorn
Scale 1 : 24 000 000
0 250 500 750 km
B. C. = Bas - Congo
Lambert azimuthal equal-area projection

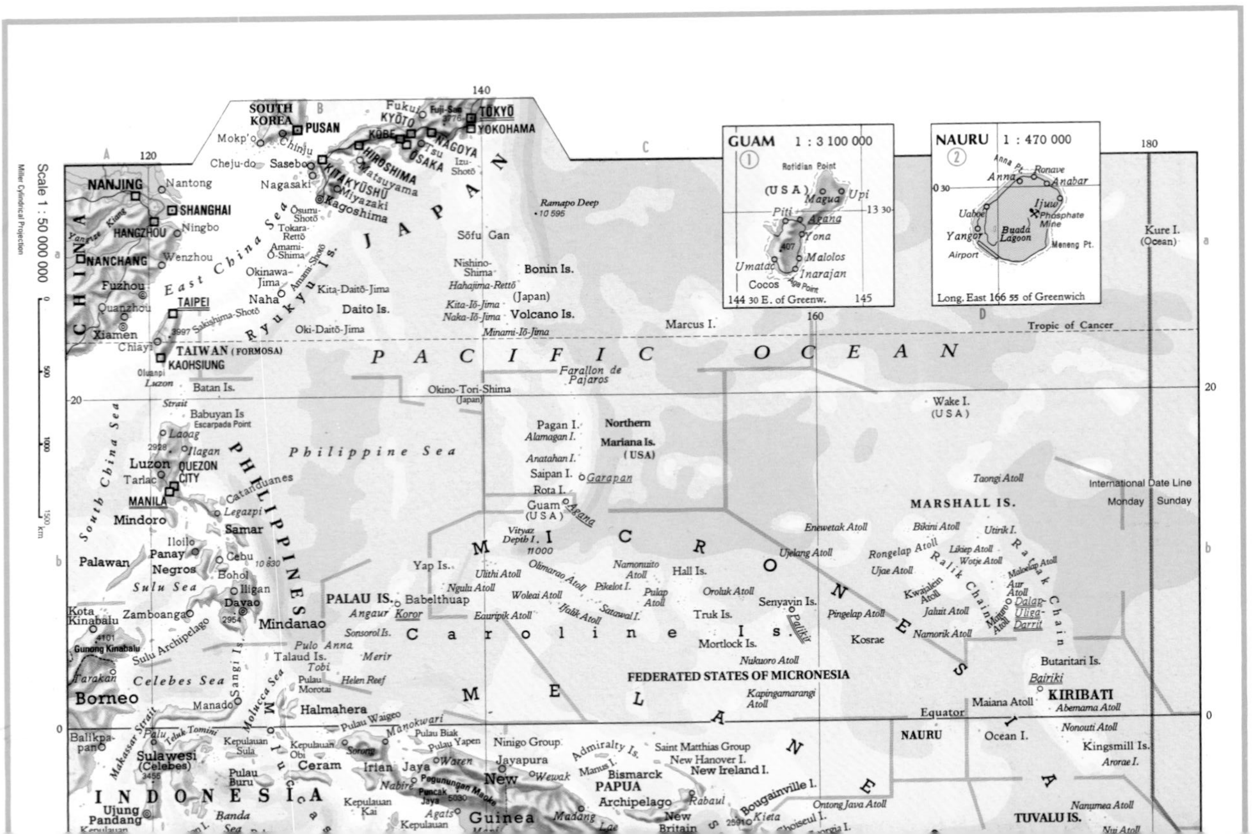

NAURU 1 : 470 000

GUAM 1 : 3 100 000

Scale 1 : 50 000 000

Miller Cylindrical Projection

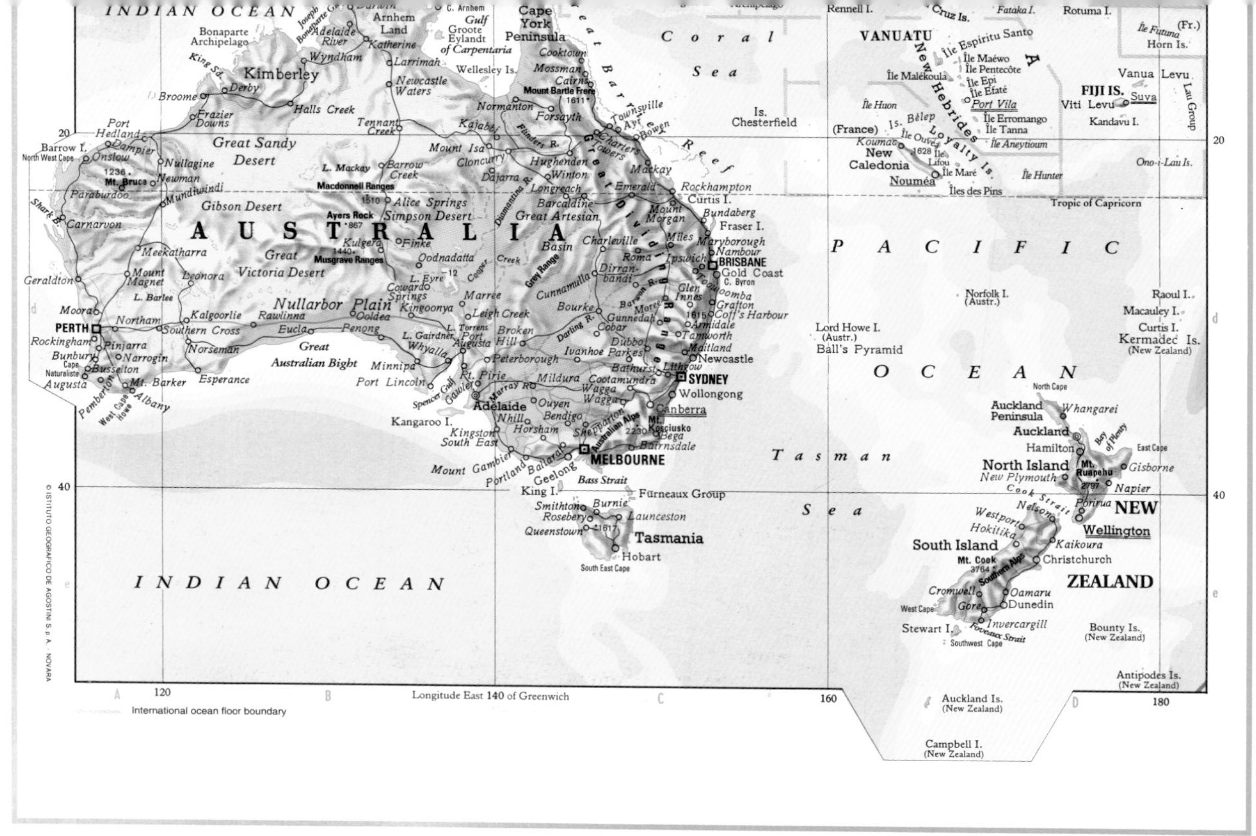

INDIAN OCEAN
Coral Sea
PACIFIC OCEAN
Tasman Sea
AUSTRALIA
NEW ZEALAND
North Island
South Island
Tasmania
New Caledonia
VANUATU
New Hebrides
Loyalty Is.
FIJI IS.
Great Barrier Reef
Great Dividing Range
Great Artesian Basin
Great Sandy Desert
Gibson Desert
Great Victoria Desert
Simpson Desert
Nullarbor Plain
Great Australian Bight
Kimberley
Arnhem Land
Cape York Peninsula
Gulf of Carpentaria
Bass Strait
Cook Strait
Tropic of Capricorn
PERTH
BRISBANE
SYDNEY
MELBOURNE
Canberra
Adelaide
Hobart
Auckland
Wellington
Christchurch
Dunedin
Nouméa
Suva
Port Vila
Longitude East 140 of Greenwich
International ocean floor boundary
© ISTITUTO GEOGRAFICO DE AGOSTINI S. p. A. · NOVARA

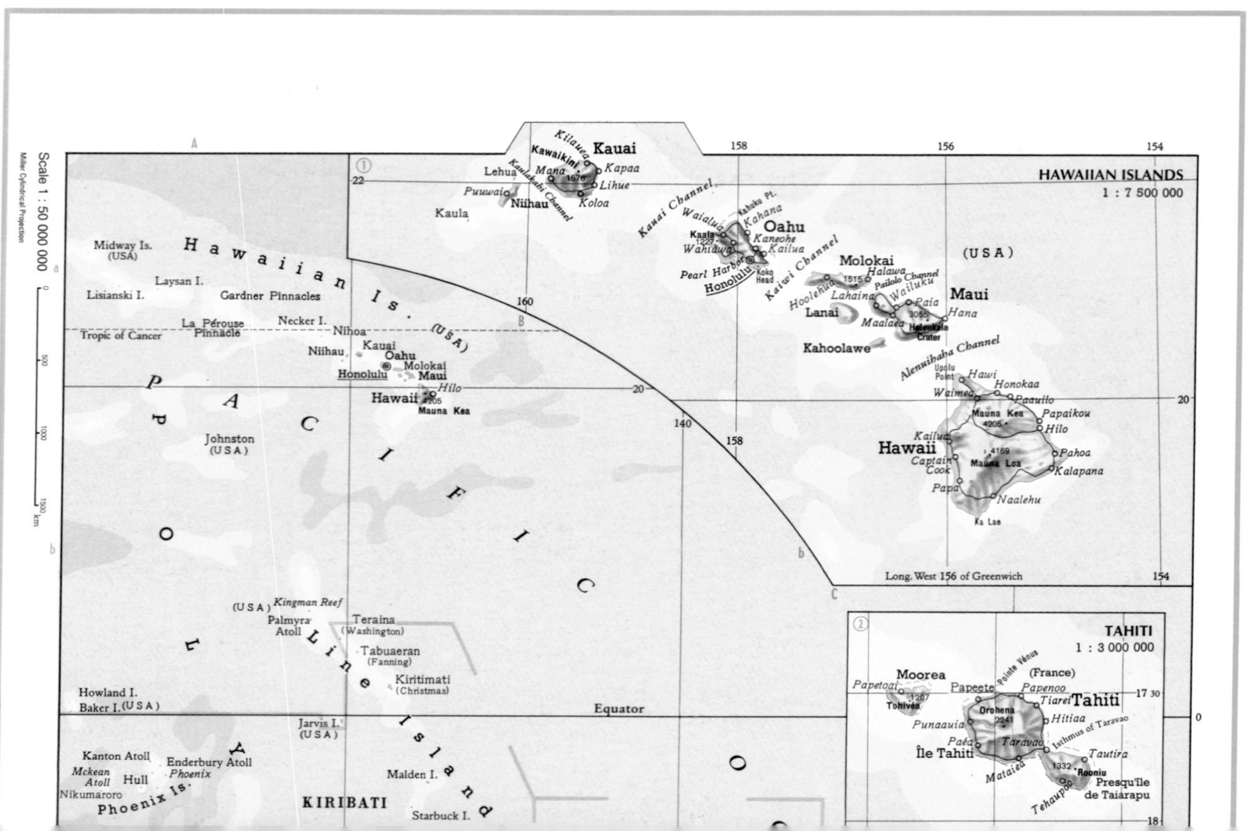

HAWAIIAN ISLANDS
1 : 7 500 000

Long. West 156 of Greenwich

Kauai
Kilauea · Kawaihau · Kapaa · Anahola
Waimea · Makaweli · Lihue
Koloa
Niihau
Lehua · Kaulakahi Channel · Puuwai
Kaula

Oahu (U S A)
Kaena Pt. · Waialua · Kahana Pt.
Wahiawa · Kaneohe · Kailua
Honolulu · Waipahu
Kaimuki · Pearl Harbor
Kaena · Kaiwi Channel
Kauai Channel

Molokai
Pailolo Channel · Kalaupapa
Hoolehua · Lahaina · Wailuku
Lanai · Maunalei
Kahoolawe

Maui (U S A)
Halawa · Honokohau
Waihee · Wailuku · Paia · Hana
Kahului · Puunene
Lanai · Maalaea

Hawaii
Hawi · Honokaa
Waimea · Ookala · Papaikou
Mauna Kea · Hilo
4206 · Kilauea · Pahoa
Mauna Loa · Kalapana
4169 · Keauhou
Captain Cook · Pahala
Papa · Naalehu
Ka Lae

Kaiwi Channel
Nihoa

H a w a i i a n   I s.   (U S A)
Midway Is. (USA)
Lisianski I.
Laysan I.
Gardner Pinnacles
Tropic of Cancer
La Pérouse Pinnacle
Necker I.
Nihoa
Kauai · Oahu · Molokai · Maui · Mauna Kea
Honolulu · Hilo
Hawaii (U S A)

Johnston I. (USA)

Kingman Reef (U S A)
Palmyra Atoll (USA)

Teraina (Washington)
Tabuaeran (Fanning)
Kiritimati (Christmas)

Jarvis I. (USA)

Malden I.
Starbuck I.
L i n e   I s l a n d s

KIRIBATI

Howland I.
Baker I. (USA)

Kanton Atoll · Enderbury Atoll
Mckean · Hull · Phoenix
Nikumaroro · **Phoenix Is.**

P A C I F I C   O C E A N

Equator

TAHITI
1 : 3 000 000
(France)

Moorea
Papetoai · Teavaro
Tohivea · 1207

Papeete
Faaa · Paea · Pirae · Arue
Punaauia · Papara
Mataiea · Orohena · 2241 · Papenoo
Tiarei · Hitiaa
Tautira
Tahiti
Mahina · Taravao
Ile Tahiti
Presqu'île de Taiarapu

Scale 1 : 50 000 000
0 · 500 · 1000 · 1500 km
Miller Cylindrical Projection

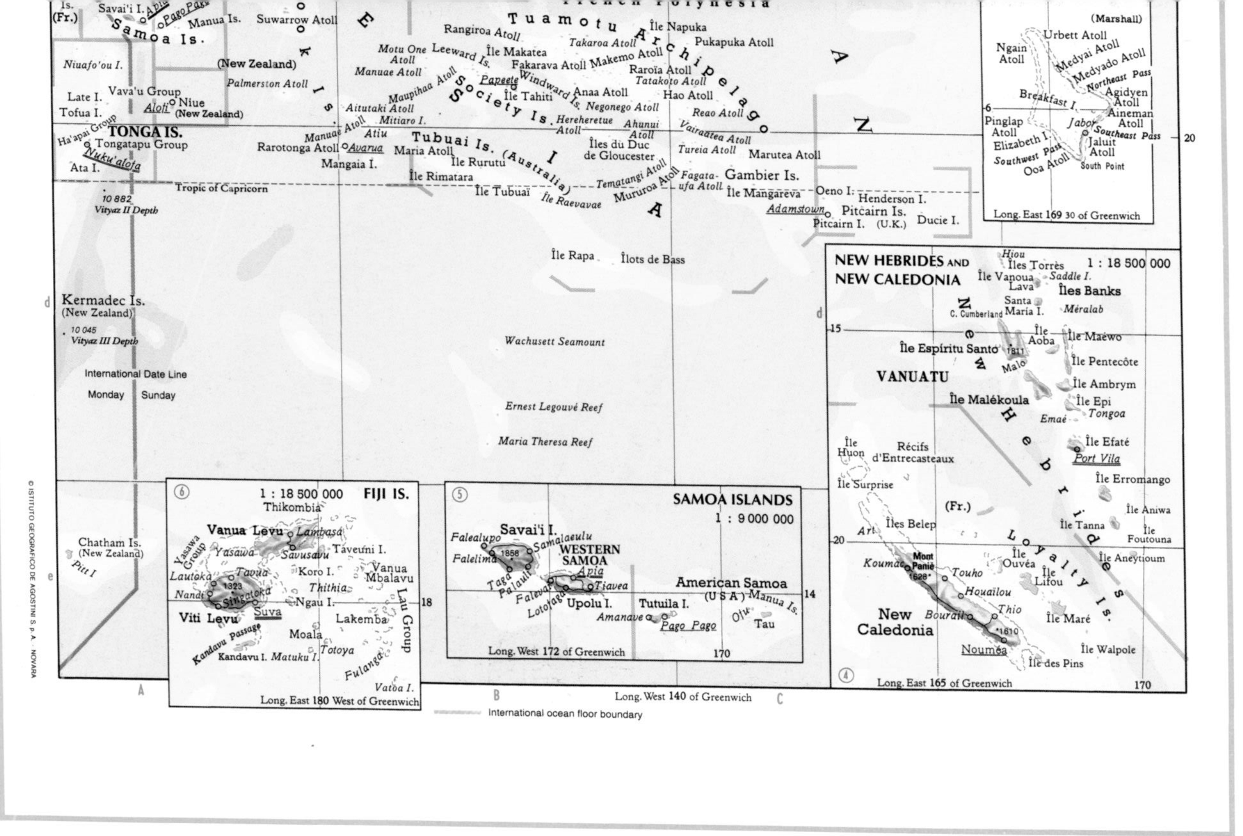
Tuamotu Archipelago
Rangiroa Atoll
Île Napuka
Takaroa Atoll
Pukapuka Atoll
Île Makatea
Fakarava Atoll
Makemo Atoll
Raroïa Atoll
Tatakoto Atoll
Anaa Atoll
Hao Atoll
Negonego Atoll
Reao Atoll
Society Is.
Leeward Is.
Windward Is.
Papeete
Île Tahiti
Motu One Atoll
Manuae Atoll
Maupihaa Atoll
Aitutaki Atoll
Mitiaro I.
Manuae Atoll
Atiu
Rarotonga Atoll
Avarua
Mangaia I.
Cook Is.
Suwarrow Atoll
Palmerston Atoll
(New Zealand)
Samoa Is.
Savai'i I.
Apia
Pago Pago
Manua Is.
(Fr.)
Niuafo'ou I.
Late I.
Tofua I.
Vava'u Group
Alofi
Niue
(New Zealand)
TONGA IS.
Ha'apai Group
Tongatapu Group
Nuku'alofa
Ata I.
Tropic of Capricorn
10 882
Vityaz II Depth
Tubuai Is. (Australia)
Maria Atoll
Île Rurutu
Île Rimatara
Île Tubuaï
Île Raevavae
Hereheretue Atoll
Ahunui Atoll
Îles du Duc de Gloucester
Vairaatea Atoll
Tureia Atoll
Marutea Atoll
Tematangi Atoll
Mururoa Atoll
Fagataufa Atoll
Gambier Is.
Île Mangareva
Oeno I.
Henderson I.
Adamstown
Pitcairn Is.
Pitcairn I.
(U.K.)
Ducie I.
Île Rapa
Îlots de Bass
Kermadec Is.
(New Zealand)
10 045
Vityaz III Depth
International Date Line
Monday
Sunday
Wachusett Seamount
Ernest Legouvé Reef
Maria Theresa Reef
Chatham Is.
(New Zealand)
Pitt I.
(Marshall)
Ngain Atoll
Urbett Atoll
Medyai Atoll
Medyado Atoll
Northeast Pass
Agidyen Atoll
Breakfast I.
Pinglap Atoll
Elizabeth I.
Jabor
Aineman Atoll
Southeast Pass
Jaluit Atoll
Southwest Pass
Ooa Atoll
South Point
Long. East 169 30 of Greenwich
NEW HEBRIDES AND NEW CALEDONIA
1 : 18 500 000
Hiou
Îles Torrès
Saddle I.
Île Vanoua Lava
Îles Banks
Santa Maria I.
Méralab
C. Cumberland
Île Aoba
Île Maéwo
Île Espíritu Santo
1811
Malo
Île Pentecôte
VANUATU
Île Ambrym
Île Malékoula
Île Epi
Emaé
Tongoa
New Hebrides
Île Huon
Récifs d'Entrecasteaux
Île Efaté
Port Vila
Île Surprise
Île Erromango
(Fr.)
Île Aniwa
Art
Îles Belep
Île Tanna
Île Foutouna
Koumac
Mont Panié
1628
Touho
Île Ouvéa
Île Lifou
Île Aneytioum
Houaïlou
Loyalty Is.
Thio
New Caledonia
Bourail
Île Maré
1610
Nouméa
Île des Pins
Île Walpole
Long. East 165 of Greenwich
1 : 18 500 000
FIJI IS.
Thikombia
Vanua Levu
Lambasa
Savusavu
Taveuni I.
Yasawa Group
Yasawa
Vanua Mbalavu
Lautoka
Tavua
Koro I.
1323
Thithia
Nandi
Singatoka
Ngau I.
Suva
Viti Levu
Lakemba
Lau Group
Kandavu Passage
Moala
Totoya
Kandavu I.
Matuku I.
Fulanga
Vatoa I.
Long. East 180 West of Greenwich
SAMOA ISLANDS
1 : 9 000 000
Falealupo
Savai'i I.
Samalaeulu
Falelima
1858
WESTERN SAMOA
Apia
Taga
Palauli
Tiavea
Falealili
Lotofaga
Upolu I.
Tutuila I.
American Samoa
(U S A)
Manua Is.
Amanave
Pago Pago
Olu
Tau
Long. West 172 of Greenwich
Long. West 140 of Greenwich
International ocean floor boundary
© ISTITUTO GEOGRAFICO DE AGOSTINI S. p. A. - NOVARA

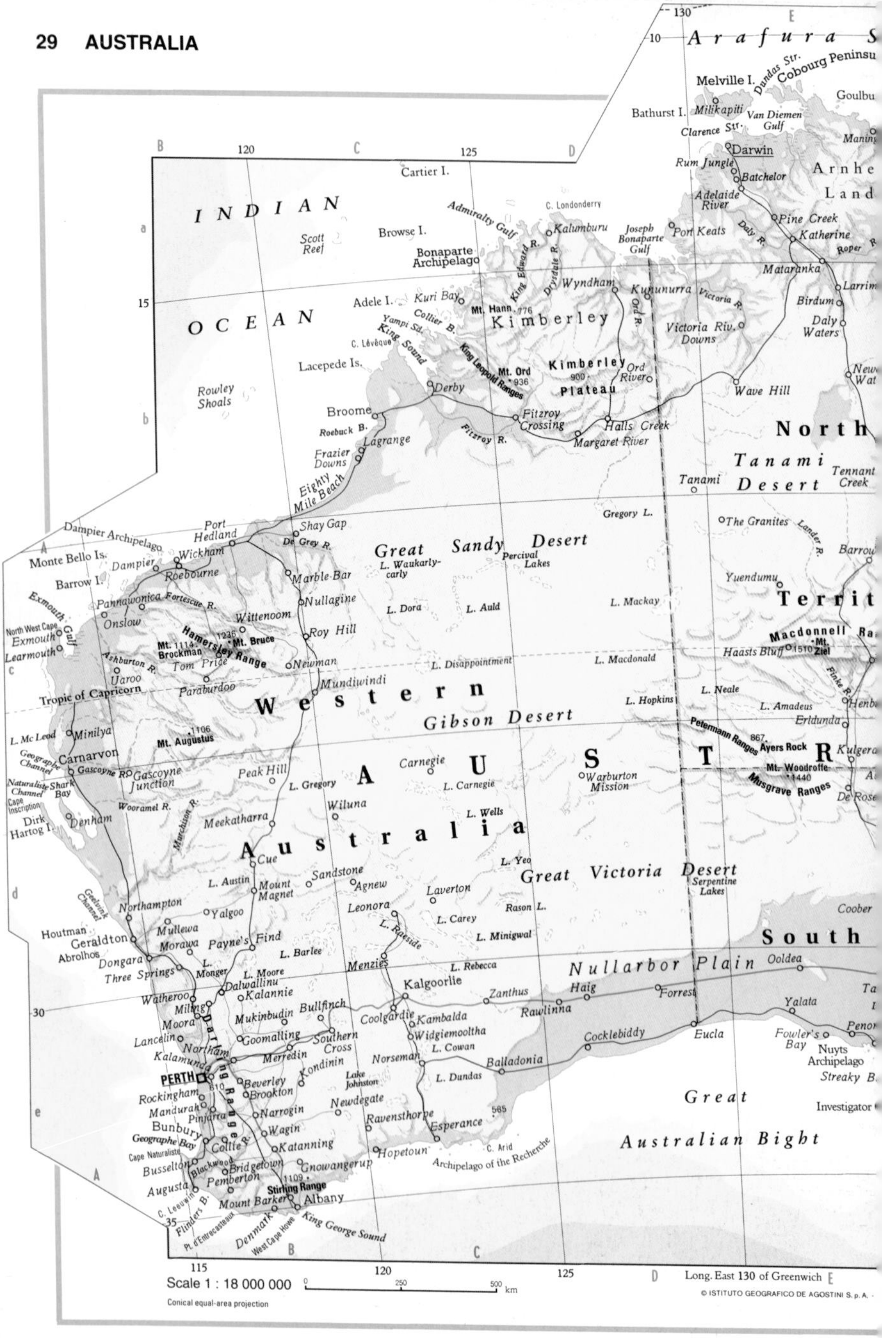

A r a f u r a S

130 E
10

Melville I. Dundas Str. Cobourg Peninsu
Bathurst I. *Milikapiti* Van Diemen Goulbu
Clarence Str. Gulf *Manin*
Rum Jungle o**Darwin**
Adelaide o*Batchelor* *Arnhe*
River o*Pine Creek* Land
Joseph o Port Keats *Katherine*
C. Londonderry Bonaparte *Deb R.* *Roper R.*
Admiralty Gulf oKalumburu Gulf o*Mataranka* *Larrim*
Browse I. *King Edward R.* oWyndham o*Birdum*
Adele I. Kuri Bay o**Mt. Hann.** 976 *Victoria R.* *Daly*
Collier B. **K I M B E R L E Y** *Kununurra* *Waters*
Yampi Sd. **Mt. Ord** *Ord R.* o*New*
C. Lévêque o King Leopold Ranges 936 **Kimberley** oWave Hill *Wat*
Lacepede Is. 900 **Plateau**
oDerby Fitzroy *Ord River*
Broome Crossing Halls Creek **North**
Roebuck B. o oLagrange Fitzroy R. Margaret River *T a n a m i*
Frazier *D e s e r t* Tennant
Downs *Tanami* Creek
Eighty oThe Granites *Landor*
Mile Beach Gregory L. *Barrou*

I N D I A N

O C E A N

Scott
Reef

Rowley
Shoals

Cartier I.

120 C 125 D

a

15

b

Dampier Archipelago, Port oShay Gap *Yuendumu*
Monte Bello Is. Hedland De Grey R. **Great Sandy Desert** *Territ*
Dampier o oWickham *L. Waukarly-* Percival
Barrow I. oRoebourne Marble Bar carly Lakes
North West Cape o Pannawonica oFortescue R. Nullagine L. Dora L. Auld L. Mackay **Macdonnell Ra**
Exmouth oOnslow oWittenoom oRoy Hill Haasts Bluff *Mt.*
Learmonth **Mt. 1113** 1236 **Mt. Bruce** *Zeil* 1510
Brockman oNewman L. Disappointment L. Macdonald oHenb
o Uaroo Tom Price Mundiwindi L. Amadeus Erldunda
Tropic of Capricorn oParaburdoo **Gibson Desert** L. Hopkins L. Neale *Kulgera*
L. Mc Leod oMinilya **Mt. Augustus** 1106 *Petermann Ranges* 867 Ayers Rock *A*
George R. oCarnarvon Carnegie **Mt. Woodroffe** 1440 *De Rose*
Naturaliste oShark Gascoyne R. **A U S T R A L I A** Warburton *Musgrave Ranges*
Channel RP Gascoyne Peak Hill L. Gregory Mission
Cape o Bay Junction oWiluna L. Carnegie
Inscription oDenham Wooramel R. oMeekatharra L. Wells
Dirk Murchison R. oCue L. Yeo **Great Victoria Desert**
Hartog I. Serpentine
L. Austin oSandstone Lakes *Cooper*
oYalgoo Mount oAgnew
Houtman Northampton Magnet Leonora L. Carey **South**
Abrolhos oGeraldton oMullewa Payne's Find L. Raeside L. Minigwal
oMorawa oLaverton *Ta*
Three Springs L. Barlee Rason L. Yalata *l*
Dongara o L. Moore oMenzies L. Rebecca *Fowler's* Penor
Walkaway o oMingenew Kalgoorlie **Nullarbor Plain** Ooldea *Bay*
Milin oMoora Dalwallinu Zanthus Haig Forrest Nuyts
Lancelin oKalannie Coolgardie Rawlinna *Archipelago*
Kalamunda Mukinbudin Bulfinch Kambalda Cocklebiddy oEucla *Streaky B.*
PERTHo Goomalling Widgiemooltha *Investigator I*
Rockingham Merredin Southern L. Cowan
Mandurah Northam Cross oNorseman **Great**
Pinjarra Beverley Kondinin L. Johnston
Bunbury Brookton Balladonia **Australian Bight**
oNarrogin Newdegate L. Dundas
oWagin Ravensthorpe 565
Busselton oKatanning oEsperance C. Arid
Augusta Bridgetown oHopetoun Archipelago of the Recherche
C. Leeuw Pemberton 1109
Stirling Range
Mount Barker o oAlbany
Denmark King George Sound
West Cape Howe

c

Tropic of Capricorn

d

30

e

35

A

B

Western

115 120 125 D
Scale 1 : 18 000 000 0 250 500 km
Conical equal-area projection Long. East 130 of Greenwich E
© ISTITUTO GEOGRAFICO DE AGOSTINI S.p.A.

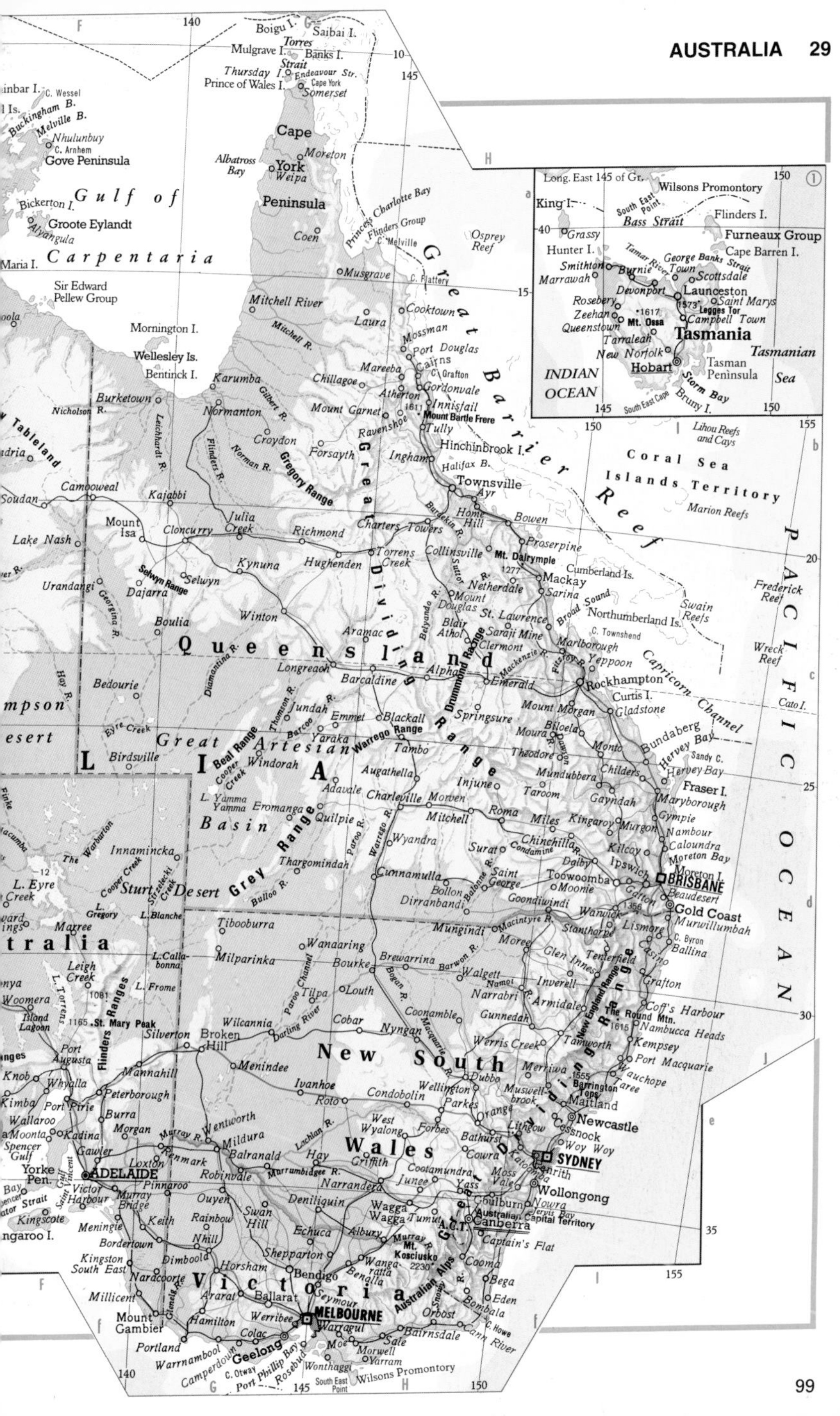

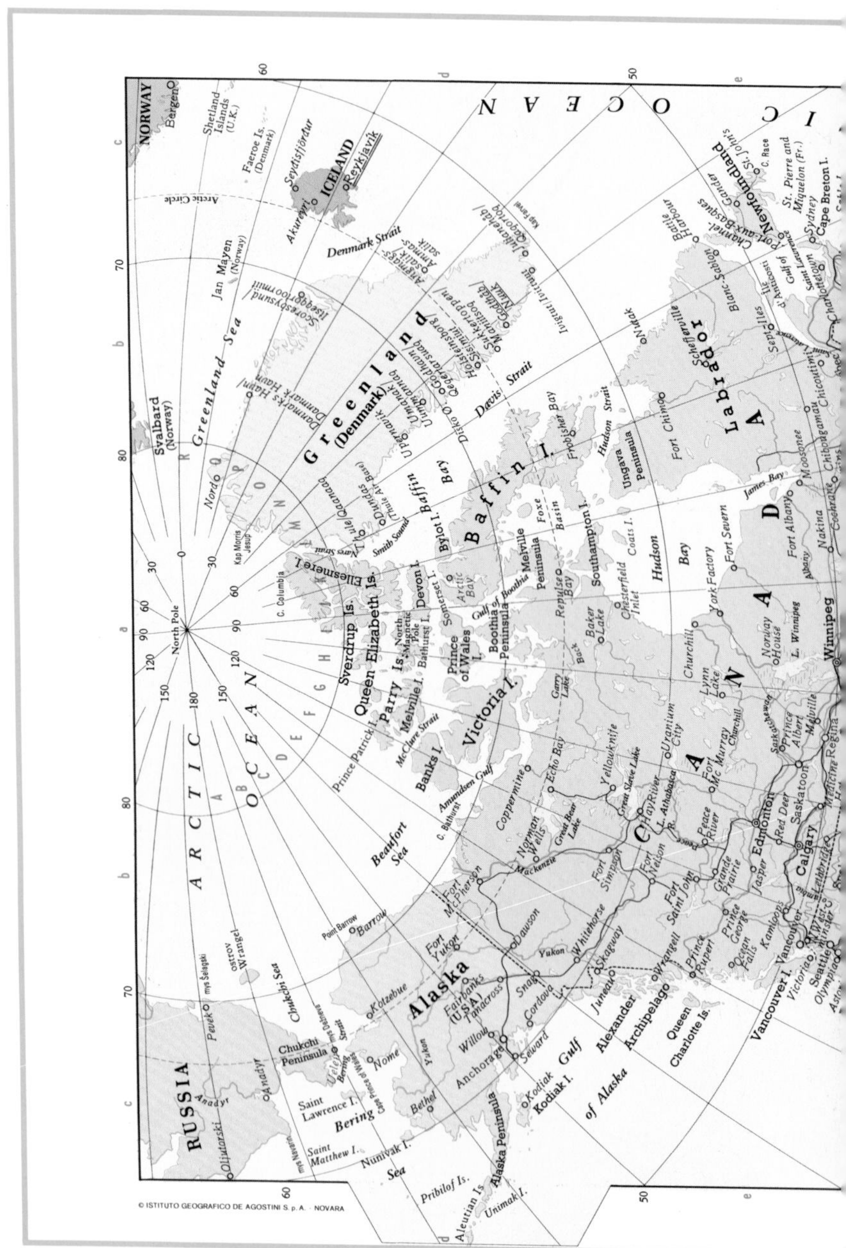
ARCTIC OCEAN
North Pole
NORWAY
Bergen
Shetland Islands (U.K.)
Faeroe Is. (Denmark)
ICELAND
Reykjavík
Akureyri
Seydisfjördur
Arctic Circle
Jan Mayen (Norway)
Denmark Strait
Greenland Sea
Svalbard (Norway)
Greenland (Denmark)
Scoresbysund
Angmagssalik
Danmarks Havn
Nord
Thule
Qaanaaq
Upernavik
Umanak
Godhavn
Disko
Holsteinsborg
Godthåb
Nuuk
Julianehåb
Kap Farvel
Davis Strait
Baffin Bay
Baffin I.
Bylot I.
Smith Sound
Nares Strait
Ellesmere I.
C. Columbia
Kap Morris Jesup
Queen Elizabeth Is.
Sverdrup Is.
Parry Is.
Devon I.
North Magnetic Pole
Bathurst I.
Melville I.
Prince Patrick I.
McClure Strait
Banks I.
Victoria I.
Prince of Wales I.
Somerset I.
Arctic Bay
Gulf of Boothia
Boothia Peninsula
Melville Peninsula
Foxe Basin
Repulse Bay
Southampton I.
Frobisher Bay
Hudson Strait
Ungava Peninsula
Fort Chimo
Labrador
Nain
Schefferville
Hudson Bay
James Bay
Coats I.
Chesterfield Inlet
Baker Lake
Churchill
York Factory
Fort Severn
Moosonee
Fort Albany
Nakina
Chibougamau
Chicoutimi
Sept-Îles
Île d'Anticosti
Gulf of Saint Lawrence
Blanc-Sablon
Battle Harbour
Newfoundland
St. John's
C. Race
Gander
Port-aux-Basques
St. Pierre and Miquelon (Fr.)
Cape Breton I.
Sydney
Charlottetown
CANADA
Winnipeg
L. Winnipeg
Norway House
Lynn Lake
Prince Albert
Saskatoon
Regina
Medicine Hat
Edmonton
Red Deer
Calgary
Lethbridge
Jasper
Grande Prairie
Peace River
Fort McMurray
Uranium City
L. Athabasca
Great Slave Lake
Yellowknife
Hay River
Great Bear Lake
Norman Wells
Coppermine
Echo Bay
Amundsen Gulf
C. Bathurst
Beaufort Sea
Fort Simpson
Fort Nelson
Fort Saint John
Prince George
Kamloops
Vancouver
Vancouver I.
Victoria
Seattle
Olympia
Prince Rupert
Ocean Falls
Queen Charlotte Is.
Wrangell
Juneau
Skagway
Whitehorse
Dawson
Fort McPherson
Mackenzie
Yukon
Alaska (USA)
Fort Yukon
Fairbanks
Tanacross
Cordova
Anchorage
Seward
Willow
Kodiak
Kodiak I.
Gulf of Alaska
Alexander Archipelago
Barrow
Point Barrow
Kotzebue
Nome
Bering Strait
Bering Sea
Bethel
Saint Lawrence I.
Saint Matthew I.
Nunivak I.
Pribilof Is.
Alaska Peninsula
Aleutian Is.
Unimak I.
Chukchi Sea
Chukchi Peninsula
ostrov Wrangel
mys Šelagski
Pevek
Anadyr
RUSSIA
Oljutorski

© ISTITUTO GEOGRAFICO DE AGOSTINI S. p. A. · NOVARA

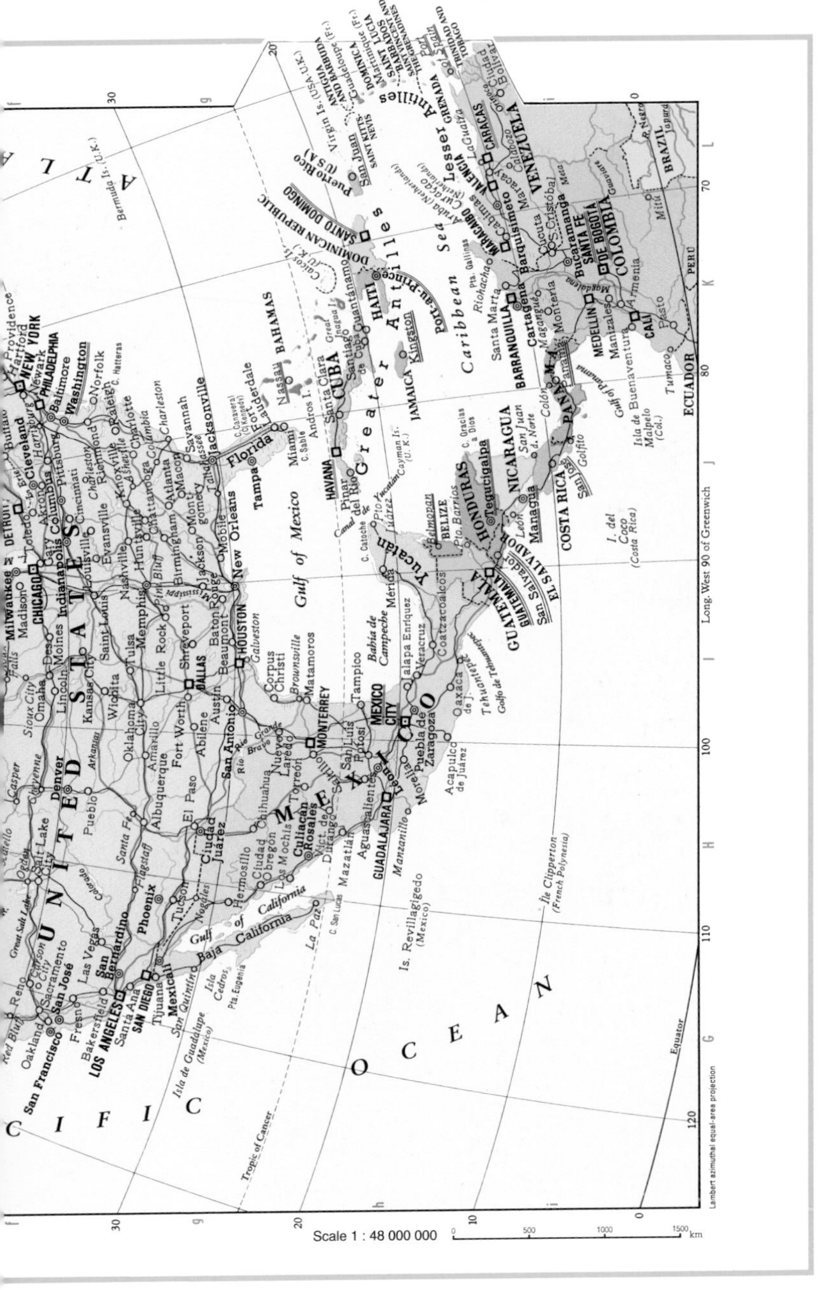

Scale 1 : 48 000 000

Lambert azimuthal equal-area projection

Long. West of 90 of Greenwich

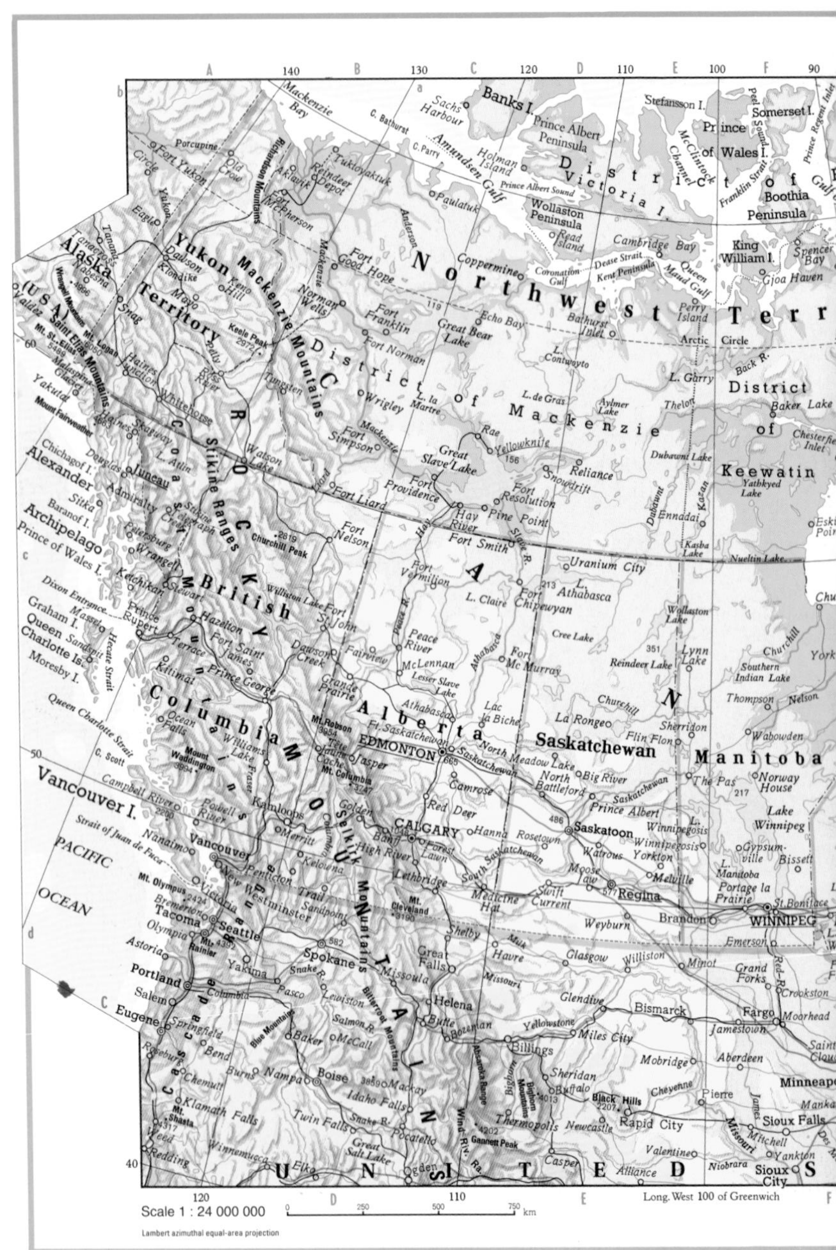

Scale 1 : 24 000 000

0   250   500   750 km

Lambert azimuthal equal-area projection

Long. West 100 of Greenwich

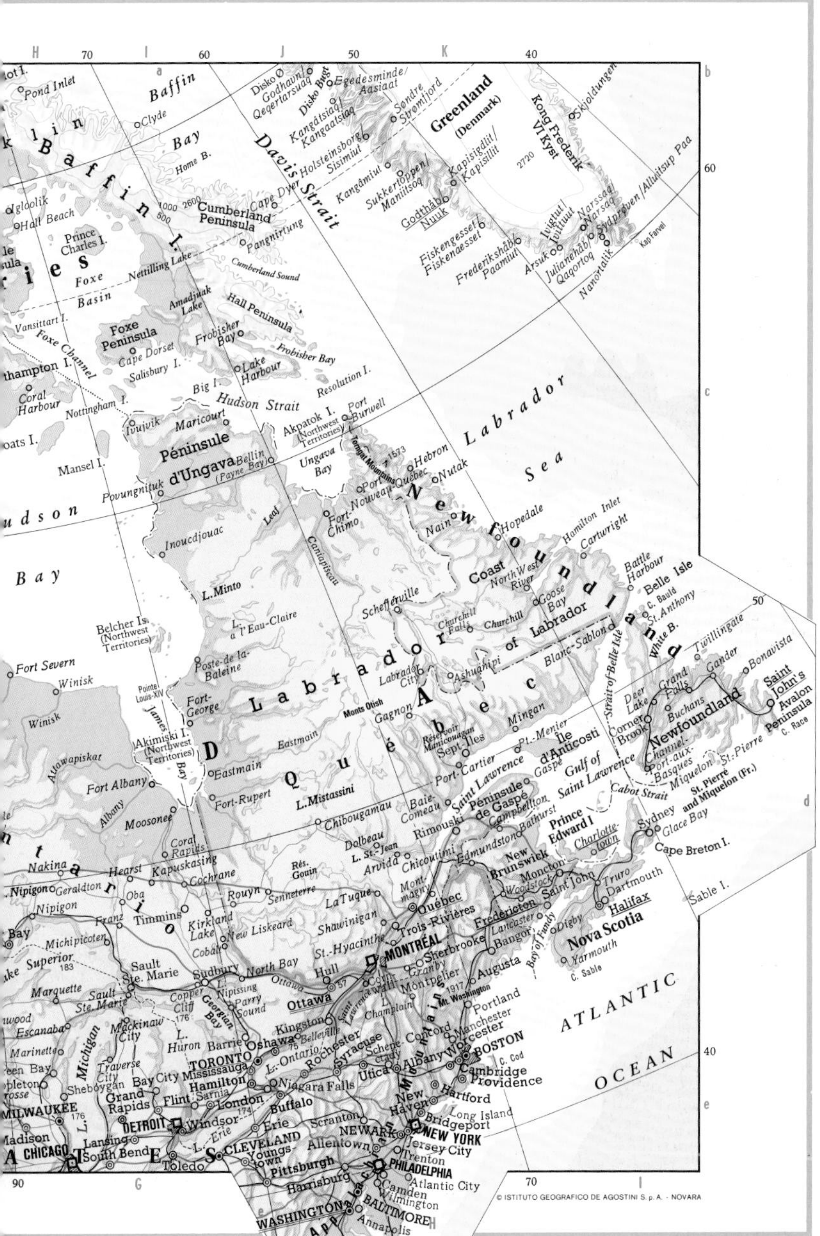
Baffin Bay
Davis Strait
Greenland (Denmark)
Cumberland Peninsula
Foxe Basin
Foxe Peninsula
Hudson Strait
Péninsule d'Ungava
Ungava Bay
Labrador Sea
Newfoundland
Labrador
Québec
Hudson Bay
Gulf of Saint Lawrence
Nova Scotia
New Brunswick
Prince Edward I.
ATLANTIC OCEAN
MONTRÉAL
Ottawa
TORONTO
BOSTON
NEW YORK
PHILADELPHIA
WASHINGTON
BALTIMORE
CHICAGO
DETROIT
CLEVELAND
MILWAUKEE
Québec
Halifax
Saint John's

© ISTITUTO GEOGRAFICO DE AGOSTINI S. p. A. - NOVARA

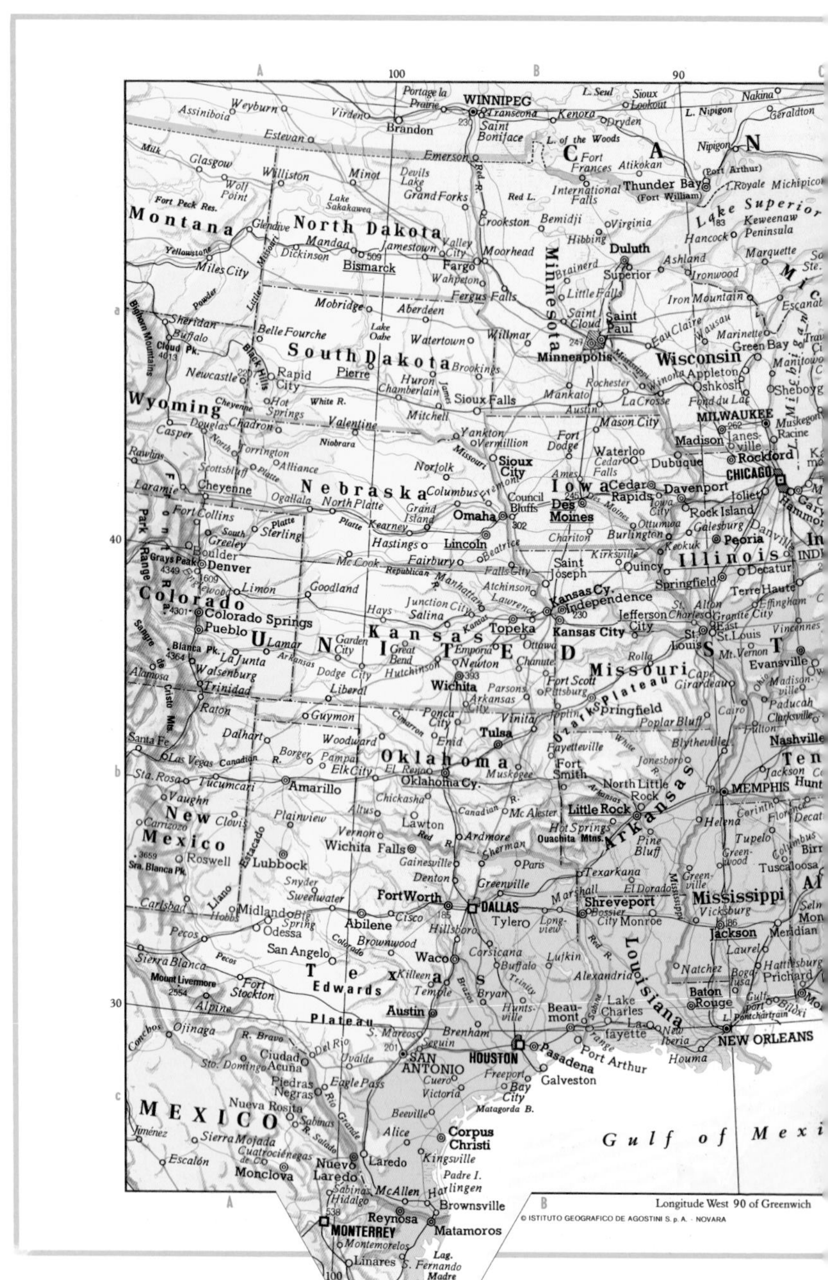

A
100
B
90
C
Portage la Prairie
WINNIPEG
Transcona
Saint Boniface
L. Seul
Sioux Lookout
Kenora
Dryden
Nakina
Geraldton
L. Nipigon
Nipigon
Assiniboia
Weyburn
Virden
Brandon
Estevan
Emerson
L. of the Woods
Fort Frances
Atikokan
Thunder Bay
(Fort William)
(Port Arthur)
I. Royale
Michipicoten
Milk
Glasgow
Wolf Point
Williston
Minot
Devils Lake
Grand Forks
Red R.
Red L.
International Falls
Fort Peck Res.
Lake Sakakawea
Montana
Glendive
North Dakota
Mandan
Dickinson
Bismarck
509
Jamestown
Valley City
Fargo
Moorhead
Wahpeton
Fergus Falls
Crookston
Bemidji
Virginia
Hibbing
Duluth
Superior
Brainerd
Little Falls
Minnesota
Lake Superior
83
Keweenaw Peninsula
Hancock
Marquette
Ashland
Ironwood
Iron Mountain
Escanaba
Yellowstone
Miles City
Powder
Little Missouri
Missouri
Mobridge
Aberdeen
Lake Oahe
Bighorn Mountains
Sheridan
Buffalo
Cloud Pk.
4013
Belle Fourche
Black Hills
South Dakota
Watertown
Willmar
Saint Cloud
Saint Paul
247
Minneapolis
Eau Claire
Wausau
Marinette
Green Bay
Wisconsin
Manitowoc
Newcastle
2207
Rapid City
Pierre
Huron
Chamberlain
James
Brookings
Sioux Falls
Rochester
Mankato
Winona
La Crosse
Appleton
Oshkosh
Fond du Lac
Sheboygan
Wyoming
Cheyenne
Hot Springs
White R.
Mitchell
Austin
Mississippi
MILWAUKEE
262
Muskegon
Casper
Douglas
Chadron
Valentine
Niobrara
Yankton
Vermillion
Mason City
Madison
Janesville
Racine
North Platte
Torrington
Alliance
Fort Dodge
Waterloo
Cedar Falls
Dubuque
Rockford
Rawlins
Scottsbluff
Norfolk
Sioux City
Ames
CHICAGO
Laramie
Cheyenne
Nebraska
Columbus
Fremont
Iowa
Cedar Rapids
Davenport
Joliet
Gary
Hammond
Ogallala
North Platte
Grand Island
Council Bluffs
Des Moines
245
Iowa City
Rock Island
Galesburg
Front Range
Fort Collins
South Platte
Sterling
Platte
Kearney
Omaha
302
Ottumwa
Burlington
Park Range
Greeley
Boulder
Hastings
Lincoln
Chariton
Keokuk
Peoria
Danville
Grays Peak
4349
Denver
1609
Englewood
McCook
Fairbury
Beatrice
Republican
Kirksville
Saint Joseph
Quincy
Illinois
Decatur
IND
Colorado
Limon
Goodland
Manhattan
Falls City
Atchison
Springfield
Terre Haute
4301
Colorado Springs
Pueblo
Hays
Junction City
Salina
Lawrence
Kansas Cy.
Independence
230
Jefferson City
St. Charles
Alton
Effingham
Granite City
Sangre de Cristo Mts.
Blanca Pk.
4364
La Junta
Lamar
United States
Garden City
Kansas
Topeka
Kansas City
East St. Louis
St. Louis
Vincennes
Alamosa
Walsenburg
Arkansas
Dodge City
Great Bend
Hutchinson
Emporia
Newton
Ottawa
Chanute
Rolla
Missouri
Mt. Vernon
Evansville
Trinidad
Liberal
393
Wichita
Parsons
Fort Scott
Pittsburg
Ozark Plateau
Cape Girardeau
Ohio
Madisonville
Paducah
Raton
Guymon
Cimarron
Ponca City
Arkansas City
Joplin
Springfield
Poplar Bluff
Cairo
Clarksville
Fulton
Santa Fe
Dalhart
Woodward
Enid
Tulsa
Vinita
Blytheville
Nashville
Las Vegas
Canadian R.
Borger
Pampa
Elk City
Oklahoma
El Reno
Oklahoma Cy.
Muskogee
Fayetteville
Fort Smith
Jonesboro
White R.
Tennessee
Jackson
Sta. Rosa
Tucumcari
Amarillo
Chickasha
North Little Rock
Little Rock
Arkansas
79
MEMPHIS
Huntsville
Vaughn
New Mexico
Clovis
Plainview
Altus
Lawton
Canadian R.
Mc Alester
Hot Springs
Ouachita Mtns.
Helena
Corinth
Florence
Decatur
Carrizozo
Estacado
Vernon
Red R.
Ardmore
Pine Bluff
Tupelo
Columbus
Birmingham
3659
Sra. Blanca Pk.
Roswell
Lubbock
Wichita Falls
Gainesville
Sherman
Paris
Texarkana
Greenwood
Tuscaloosa
Snyder
Sweetwater
Denton
Greenville
El Dorado
Greenville
Carlsbad
Llano
Hobbs
Midland
Big Spring
Odessa
Abilene
Cisco
Fort Worth
185
DALLAS
Marshall
Shreveport
Bossier City
Monroe
Mississippi
Vicksburg
186
Jackson
Meridian
Selma
Montgomery
Pecos
Tyler
Longview
Hillsboro
Colorado
Brownwood
San Angelo
Waco
Corsicana
Lufkin
Louisiana
Laurel
Sierra Blanca
Pecos
Buffalo
Red R.
Alexandria
Natchez
Bogalusa
Hattiesburg
Prichard
Mount Livermore
2554
Fort Stockton
Texas
Edwards Plateau
Killeen
Temple
Brazos
Bryan
Trinity
Baton Rouge
Gulfport
Biloxi
Alpine
Austin
Huntsville
Beaumont
Sabine
Lake Charles
Lafayette
New Iberia
L. Pontchartrain
Mobile
Conchos
Ojinaga
R. Bravo
Del Rio
S. Marcos
Brenham
Seguin
201
SAN ANTONIO
HOUSTON
Pasadena
Orange
Port Arthur
NEW ORLEANS
Houma
Ciudad Acuña
Sto. Domingo
Uvalde
Freeport
Galveston
Piedras Negras
Eagle Pass
Rio Grande
Cuero
Victoria
Bay City
Matagorda B.
MEXICO
Nueva Rosita
Sabinas
Beeville
Jiménez
Sierra Mojada
R. Salado
Alice
Corpus Christi
Gulf of Mexico
Cuatrociénegas de C.
Escalón
Monclova
Nuevo Laredo
Laredo
Kingsville
Padre I.
Sabinas Hidalgo
McAllen
Harlingen
Brownsville
538
Reynosa
Matamoros
MONTERREY
Montemorelos
Linares
Lag. S. Fernando Madre
100
40
30
a
b
c
Longitude West 90 of Greenwich
© ISTITUTO GEOGRAFICO DE AGOSTINI S. p. A. - NOVARA

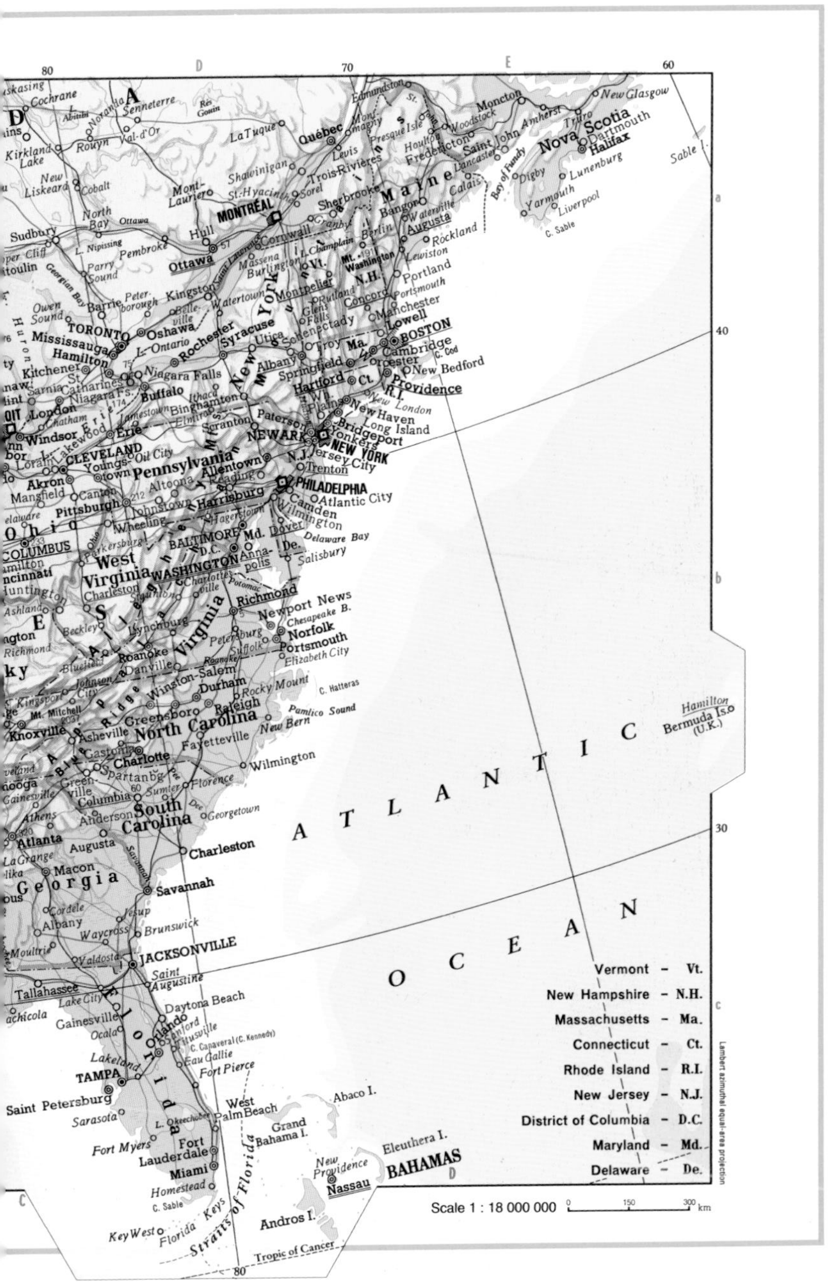

Vermont — Vt.
New Hampshire — N.H.
Massachusetts — Ma.
Connecticut — Ct.
Rhode Island — R.I.
New Jersey — N.J.
District of Columbia — D.C.
Maryland — Md.
Delaware — De.

Scale 1 : 18 000 000   0   150   300 km

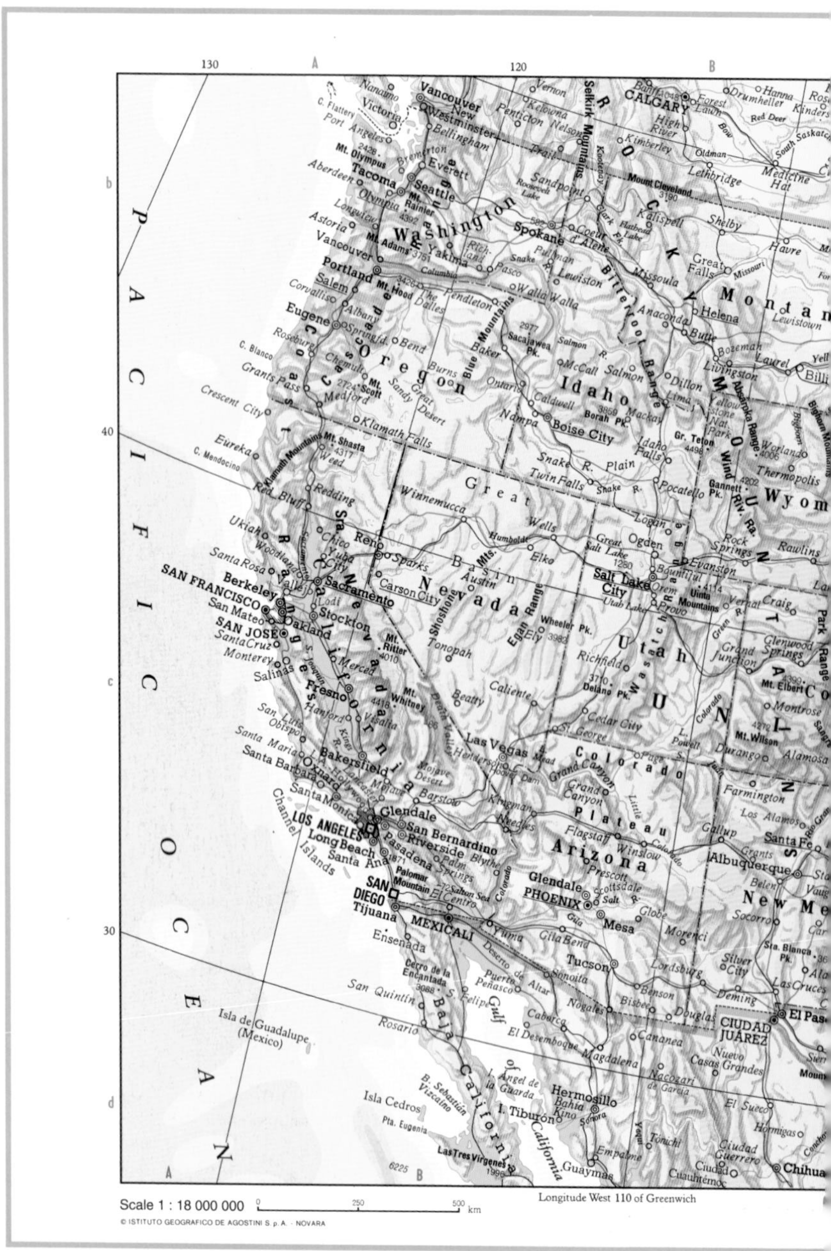

Scale 1 : 18 000 000

Longitude West 110 of Greenwich

© ISTITUTO GEOGRAFICO DE AGOSTINI S.p.A. · NOVARA

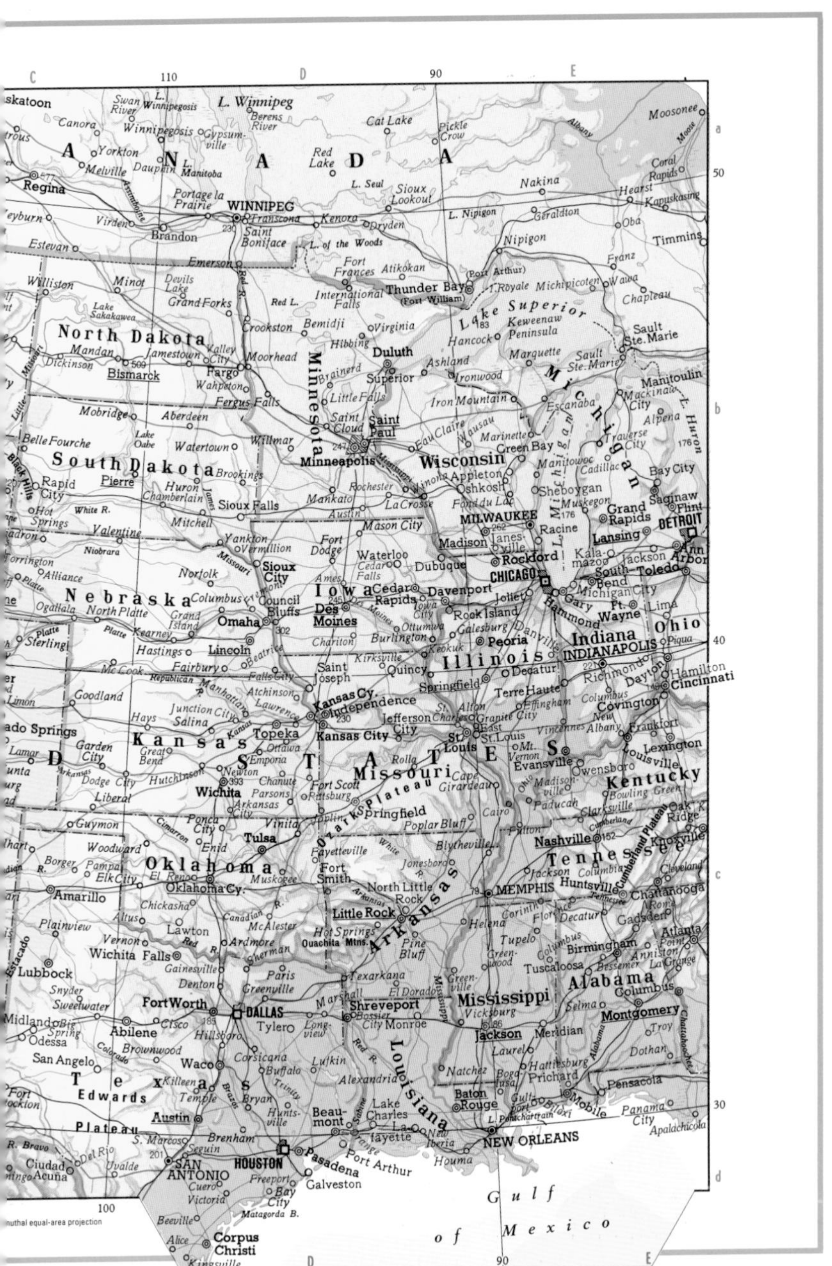
C
110
D
90
E
L. Winnipeg
L. Winnipegosis
Cat Lake
Pickle Crow
Moosonee
Canora
Winnipegosis
Yorkton
Melville
Dauphin
L. Manitoba
Red Lake
Regina
Portage la Prairie
WINNIPEG
Transcona
Saint Boniface
Brandon
Virden
Estevan
Kenora
Dryden
L. Seul
Sioux Lookout
L. of the Woods
Nakina
Hearst
Kapuskasing
Geraldton
L. Nipigon
Nipigon
Oba
Timmins
Coral Rapids
Emerson
Fort Frances
Atikokan
International Falls
Thunder Bay
(Port Arthur)
(Fort William)
I. Royale
Michipicoten
Wawa
Chapleau
Franz
Williston
Minot
Devils Lake
Grand Forks
Lake Sakakawea
Red L.
Crookston
Bemidji
Virginia
Lake Superior
Keweenaw Peninsula
Hancock
Sault Ste. Marie
North Dakota
Mandan
Dickinson
Bismarck
Jamestown
Valley City
Fargo
Moorhead
Wahpeton
Fergus Falls
Hibbing
Duluth
Superior
Ashland
Ironwood
Marquette
Manitoulin
Mackinac City
Minnesota
Brainerd
Little Falls
Iron Mountain
Escanaba
Michigan
Mobridge
Aberdeen
Lake Oahe
Saint Cloud
Saint Paul
Alpena
L. Huron
Belle Fourche
Watertown
Willmar
Minneapolis
Eau Claire
Wausau
Marinette
Green Bay
Traverse City
South Dakota
Black Hills
Rapid City
Pierre
Huron
Chamberlain
Brookings
Sioux Falls
Wisconsin
Appleton
Oshkosh
Manitowoc
Cadillac
Bay City
Saginaw
Flint
Rochester
Winona
Mankato
La Crosse
Fond du Lac
Sheboygan
Muskegon
Grand Rapids
DETROIT
Hot Springs
White R.
Mitchell
Austin
Mason City
MILWAUKEE
Racine
Lansing
Valentine
Yankton
Vermillion
Madison
Janesville
Niobrara
Fort Dodge
Waterloo
Cedar Falls
Dubuque
Rockford
Kalamazoo
Jackson
Ann Arbor
Torrington
Alliance
Norfolk
Sioux City
Ames
CHICAGO
South Bend
Toledo
Nebraska
Columbus
Council Bluffs
Iowa
Cedar Rapids
Davenport
Joliet
Michigan City
Gary
Hammond
Lima
Ogallala
North Platte
Grand Island
Omaha
Des Moines
Iowa City
Rock Island
Ft. Wayne
Ohio
Sterling
Kearney
Ottumwa
Galesburg
Peoria
Indiana
Piqua
Chariton
Burlington
Keokuk
Hastings
Lincoln
Beatrice
Kirksville
Illinois
INDIANAPOLIS
McCook
Fairbury
Falls City
Saint Joseph
Quincy
Decatur
Richmond
Dayton
Hamilton
Cincinnati
Limon
Goodland
Atchinson
Lawrence
Kansas Cy.
Independence
Springfield
Terre Haute
Effingham
Columbus
Covington
Junction City
Manhattan
Salina
Hays
Jefferson City
St. Charles
Alton
Granite City
New Albany
Frankfort
Colorado Springs
Garden City
Kansas
Topeka
Kansas City
St. Louis
East St. Louis
Vincennes
Lexington
Great Bend
Ottawa
Emporia
Rolla
Mt. Vernon
Evansville
Louisville
Dodge City
Hutchinson
Newton
Wichita
Chanute
Fort Scott
Missouri
Cape Girardeau
Madisonville
Owensboro
Kentucky
Liberal
Parsons
Pittsburg
Arkansas City
Ozark Plateau
Paducah
Bowling Green
Oak Ridge
Guymon
Ponca City
Vinita
Joplin
Springfield
Poplar Bluff
Cairo
Clarksville
Knoxville
Cimarron
Woodward
Enid
Tulsa
Fulton
Nashville
Cumberland Plateau
Blytheville
Fayetteville
Borger
Pampa
Elk City
Oklahoma
Muskogee
Fort Smith
Jonesboro
Tennessee
Jackson
Columbia
Cleveland
Amarillo
Oklahoma Cy.
North Little Rock
MEMPHIS
Huntsville
Chattanooga
Chickasha
Little Rock
Arkansas
Corinth
Florence
Decatur
Rome
Gadsden
Plainview
Altus
Lawton
McAlester
Hot Springs
Ouachita Mtns.
Pine Bluff
Helena
Tupelo
Atlanta
Vernon
Wichita Falls
Ardmore
Sherman
Greenwood
Columbus
Birmingham
Anniston
La Grange
Lubbock
Gainesville
Paris
Tuscaloosa
Bessemer
Snyder
Denton
Greenville
Texarkana
El Dorado
Greenville
Alabama
Sweetwater
Fort Worth
DALLAS
Marshall
Shreveport
Bossier City
Monroe
Mississippi
Selma
Columbus
Montgomery
Midland
Big Spring
Odessa
Abilene
Cisco
Hillsboro
Tyler
Longview
Vicksburg
Jackson
Meridian
Troy
Brownwood
Corsicana
Louisiana
Laurel
Dothan
San Angelo
Waco
Buffalo
Lufkin
Natchez
Hattiesburg
Bogalusa
Prichard
Texas
Killeen
Temple
Bryan
Alexandria
Edwards Plateau
Fort Stockton
Pensacola
Baton Rouge
Gulfport
Biloxi
Mobile
Panama City
Apalachicola
Austin
Huntsville
Beaumont
Lake Charles
L. Pontchartrain
Brenham
Lafayette
New Iberia
NEW ORLEANS
R. Bravo
Del Rio
S. Marcos
Seguin
HOUSTON
Pasadena
Port Arthur
Houma
Ciudad Acuña
Uvalde
SAN ANTONIO
Freeport
Galveston
Cuero
Victoria
Bay City
Matagorda B.
Gulf of Mexico
100
Beeville
Corpus Christi
Alice
Kingsville
a
b
c
d
50
40
30

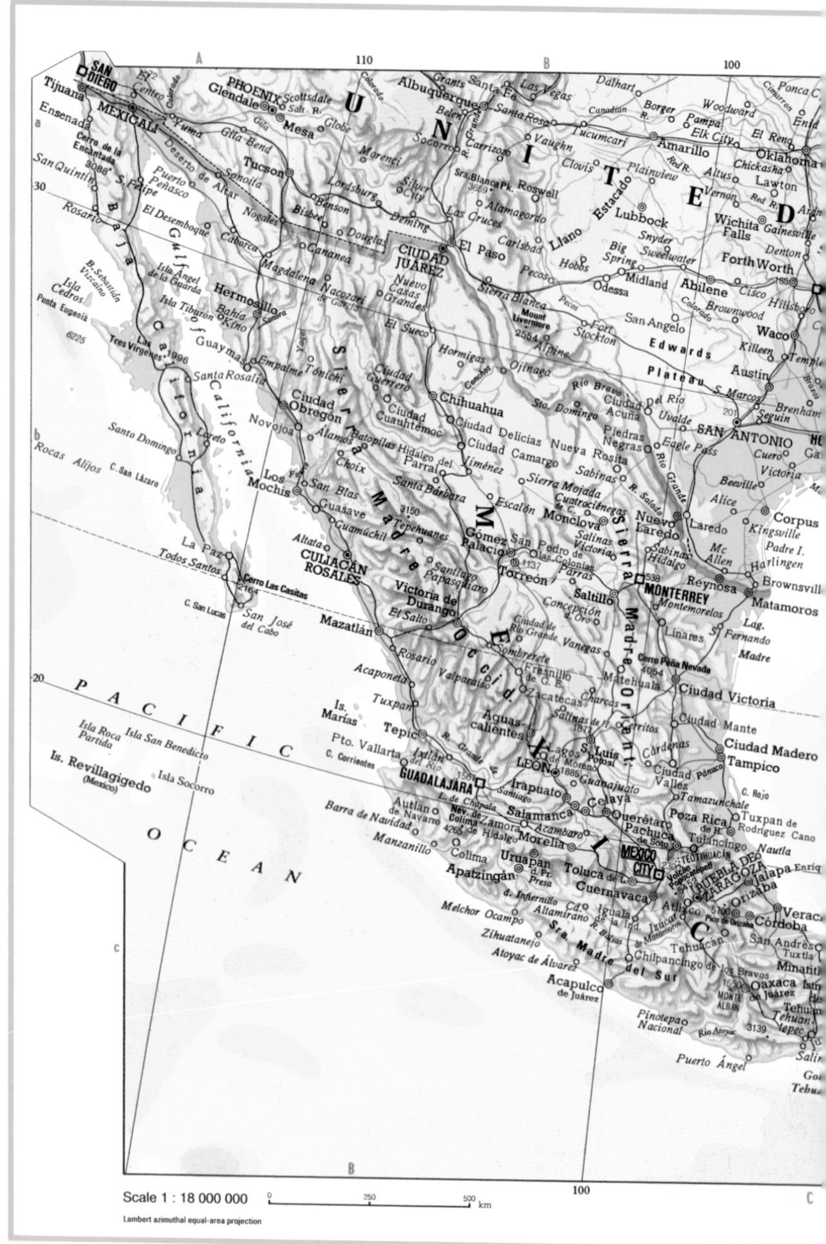

A
110
B
100
SAN DIEGO
Tijuana
MEXICALI
Ensenada
Cerro de la Encantada 3088
San Quintín
S. Felipe
Rosario
Baja
California
Yuma
Gila
Gila Bend
PHOENIX
Glendale
Scottsdale
Salt R.
Mesa
Globe
Tucson
Sonoita
Puerto Peñasco
Deserto de Altar
Nogales
Bisbee
Benson
Lordsburg
Douglas
Cananea
Caborca
El Desemboque
Magdalena
Nacozari de García
Gulf of California
Isla Ángel de la Guarda
Isla Tiburón
Hermosillo
Bahía Kino
B. Sebastián Vizcaíno
Isla Cedros
Punta Eugenia
Tres Vírgenes 1996
Guaymas
Empalme
Santa Rosalía
Tónichi
Ciudad Obregón
Novojoa
Álamos
Loreto
Santo Domingo
Rocas Alijos
C. San Lázaro
Los Mochis
San Blas
Guasave
Guamúchil
Altata
CULIACÁN ROSALES
La Paz
Todos Santos
Cerro Las Casitas 2164
C. San Lucas
San José del Cabo
Mazatlán
Albuquerque
Santa Fe
Las Vegas
Grants
Belen
Santa Rosa
Socorro
Carrizozo
Vaughn
Morenci
Silver City
Deming
Las Cruces
Sra. Blanca Pk. 3659
Roswell
Alamogordo
El Paso
CIUDAD JUÁREZ
Nuevo Casas Grandes
Carlsbad
Hobbs
Pecos
Sierra Blanca
Mount Livermore 2554
Alpine
El Sueco
Hormigas
Ojinaga
Sierra Madre Occidental
Ciudad Guerrero
Chihuahua
Ciudad Cuauhtémoc
Ciudad Delicias
Ciudad Camargo
Batopilas
Hidalgo del Parral
Jiménez
Choix
Santa Bárbara
Sierra Mojada
Escalón
Tepehuanes
3150
Gómez Palacio
Torreón
San Pedro de las Colonias
Santiago Papasquiaro
Victoria de Durango
El Salto
Rosario
Acaponeta
Tuxpan
Is. Marías
Tepic
Pto. Vallarta
C. Corrientes
Ixtlán del Río
GUADALAJARA
L. de Chapala
Autlán de Navarro
Barra de Navidad
Manzanillo
Colima
Nev. de Colima 4265
Zamora de Hidalgo
Uruapan
Apatzingán
Melchor Ocampo
Zihuatanejo
Atoyac de Álvarez
Acapulco de Juárez
Fresnillo de G. E.
Zacatecas
Sombrerete
Aguascalientes
Lagos de Moreno
LEÓN
Irapuato
Salamanca
Guanajuato
Celaya
Querétaro
Acámbaro
Morelia
Toluca de L.
MEXICO CITY
TEOTIHUACÁN
Pachuca de Soto
Volcán Popocatépetl 5452
PUEBLA DE ZARAGOZA
Cuernavaca
Iguala de la Ind.
Chilpancingo de los Bravos
Sra. Madre del Sur
Altamirano
Izúcar de Matamoros
Tehuacán
Orizaba
Pico de Orizaba 5700
Córdoba
Jalapa Enríquez
Veracruz
San Andrés Tuxtla
Minatitlán
Oaxaca de Juárez
MONTE ALBÁN
Pinotepa Nacional
Puerto Ángel
Salina Cruz
Tehuantepec
3139
Poza Rica
Tuxpan de Rodríguez Cano
Tulancingo
Nautla
Ciudad Valles
Tamazunchale
Ciudad Madero
Tampico
C. Rojo
Ciudad Mante
Ciudad Victoria
Cerro Peña Nevada 4054
Matehuala
Charcas
Salinas de H.
San Luis Potosí
Cárdenas
Linares
Montemorelos
MONTERREY
Saltillo
Concepción del Oro
Vanegas
Sierra Madre Oriental
Monclova
Cuatrociénegas
Sabinas
Nueva Rosita
Piedras Negras
Ciudad Acuña
Nuevo Laredo
Laredo
Sabinas Hidalgo
Reynosa
Matamoros
Brownsville
Lag. Madre
San Fernando
Corpus Christi
Kingsville
Padre I.
Harlingen
Mc Allen
Alice
Beeville
Victoria
Cuero
SAN ANTONIO
Seguin
Brenham
Austin
Temple
Killeen
Waco
Edwards Plateau
San Angelo
Fort Stockton
Odessa
Midland
Big Spring
Abilene
Brownwood
Fort Worth
Denton
Wichita Falls
Lubbock
Llano Estacado
Snyder
Sweetwater
Amarillo
Dalhart
Borger
Pampa
Tucumcari
Clovis
Plainview
Canadian R.
Woodward
Elk City
El Reno
Oklahoma City
Chickasha
Lawton
Altus
Vernon
Red R.
Gainesville
Río Bravo del Norte
Río Grande
Eagle Pass
Uvalde
Del Río
UNITED
MEXICO
PACIFIC OCEAN
Is. Revillagigedo (Mexico)
Isla Socorro
Isla San Benedicto
Isla Roca Partida
20
30
a
b
c
Scale 1 : 18 000 000
0
250
500
km
Lambert azimuthal equal-area projection

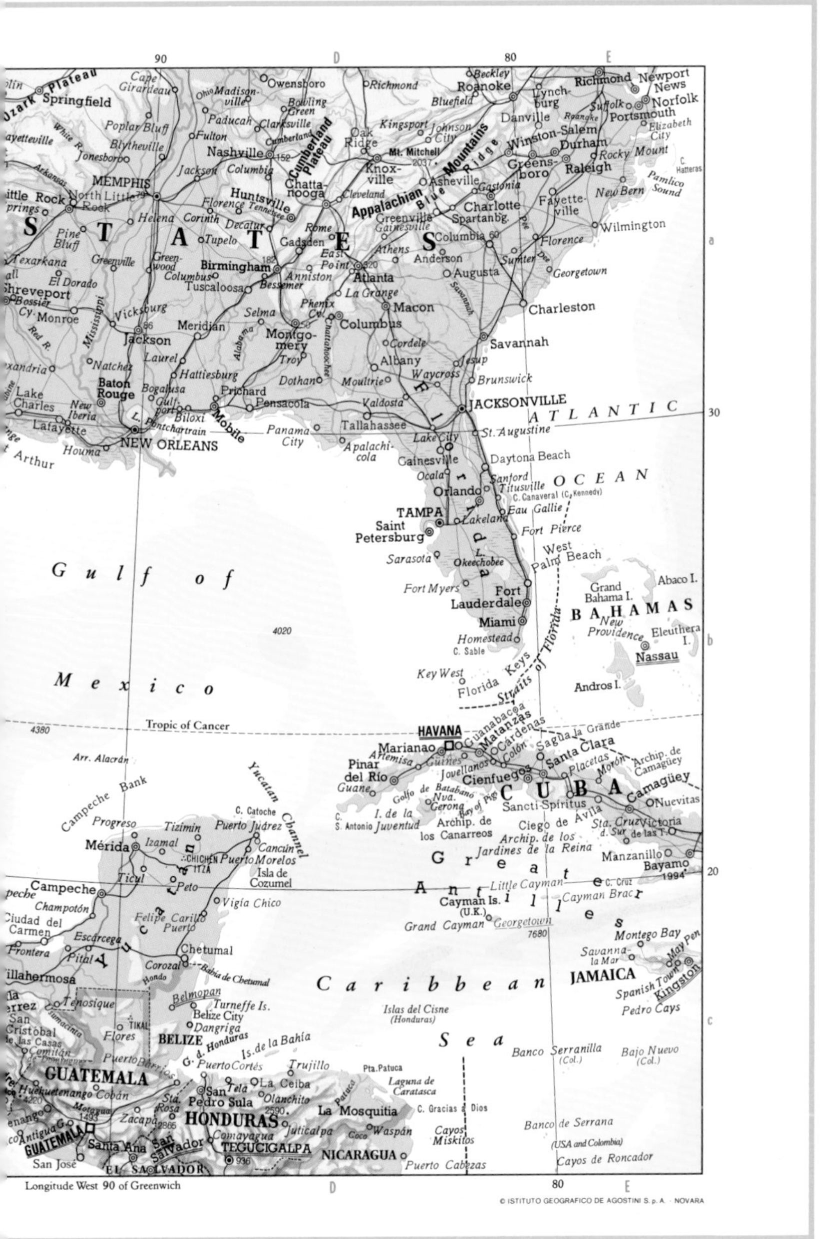

Ozark Plateau Cape Girardeau Ohio Madison-ville Owensboro Richmond Beckley Roanoke Richmond Newport News
Springfield Poplar Bluff Bowling Green Paducah Clarksville Bluefield Lynch-burg Suffolk Portsmouth
ayetteville Fulton Kingsport Johnson Danville Roanoke Elizabeth City
Jonesboro Nashville Oak Ridge Mt. Mitchell Winston-Salem Durham Norfolk
MEMPHIS Jackson Columbia Knox-ville Cumberland Plateau Greens-boro Raleigh Rocky Mount
little Rock North Little Huntsville Chatta-nooga Cleveland Asheville Gastonia Fayette-ville New Bern Pamlico Sound
springs Helena Corinth Florence Tennessee Appalachian Charlotte Spartanbg. Hatteras
S T A T E S Decatur Rome Gadsden Athens Columbia Wilmington
exarkana Pine Bluff Greenville Green-wood Birmingham East Point Anderson Sumter Georgetown
all El Dorado Columbus Anniston Atlanta Augusta a
hreveport Bossier Tuscaloosa Bessemer La Grange Florence Charleston
CY Monroe Vicksburg Meridian Selma Phenix Macon Savannah
xandria Natchez Jackson Montgo-mery Troy Columbus Cordele
Lake Laurel Hattiesburg Albany Waycross Brunswick
Charles New Iberia Baton Rouge Bogalusa Dothan Moultrie Valdosta
Lafayette Gulf-port Prichard Pensacola Tallahassee JACKSONVILLE ATLANTIC 30
Arthur Houma NEW ORLEANS Pontchartrain Panama City Apalachi-cola Lake City St. Augustine
Gulf of Daytona Beach OCEAN
Ocala Sanford Titusville (C. Kennedy)
Orlando C. Canaveral (C. Kennedy)
TAMPA Lakeland Eau Gallie
Saint Petersburg Fort Pierce
M e x i c o Sarasota Okeechobee West Palm Beach
4020 Fort Myers Fort Lauderdale Grand Bahama I. Abaco I.
Miami B A H A M A S
Homestead New Providence Eleuthera I.
C. Sable Nassau
4380 Tropic of Cancer Key West Florida Keys Andros I.
Arr. Alacrán Straits of Florida
Campeche Bank Yucatan Channel HAVANA Matanzas
Progreso Tizimín C. Catoche Marianao Sagua la Grande Archip. de
Mérida Izamal Puerto Juárez Pinar del Río Jovellanos Cárdenas Santa Clara Placetas Morón Camagüey
Ticul Peto CHICHEN ITZA Puerto Morelos Cancún Guane Golfo de Batabanó Gerona Nva. C U B A Nuevitas
Campeche Vigía Chico Isla de Cozumel I. de la S. Antonio Juventud los Canarreos Ciego de Ávila Sta. Cruz Victoria 20
peche Champotón Felipe Carillo Archip. de G r e a t d. Sur de las Manzanillo Bayamo
Ciudad del Carmen Escárcega Puerto Jardines de la Reina A n t i l l e s 1994
Frontera Pital Chetumal C. Cruz
illahermosa Coroal Little Cayman C. Cruz
Honda Bahía de Chetumal C a r i b b e a n Cayman Is. Cayman Brac
rrez Tenosique Belmopan Turneffe Is. (U.K.) Georgetown JAMAICA Montego Bay
la Belize City Grand Cayman 7680 Savanna Hoy Pen
San TIKAL Islas del Cisne la Mar Kingston
Cristobal Flores BELIZE Dangriga Isla de Bahía (Honduras) S e a Spanish Town
las Casas Comitán G. Honduras Banco Serranilla Bajo Nuevo Pedro Cays
GUATEMALA Puerto Barrios Puerto Cortés Trujillo (Col.) (Col.)
Huehuetenango Cobán San Pedro Sula La Ceiba Pta. Patuca
Zacapa Olanchito Banco de Serrana
GUATEMALA Santa Ana San HONDURAS Juticalpa La Mosquitia C. Gracias a Dios (USA and Colombia)
San José EL SALVADOR Comayagua Coco Waspán Cayos Miskitos Cayos de Roncador
TEGUCIGALPA NICARAGUA Puerto Cabezas

Longitude West 90 of Greenwich

© ISTITUTO GEOGRAFICO DE AGOSTINI S.p.A. - NOVARA

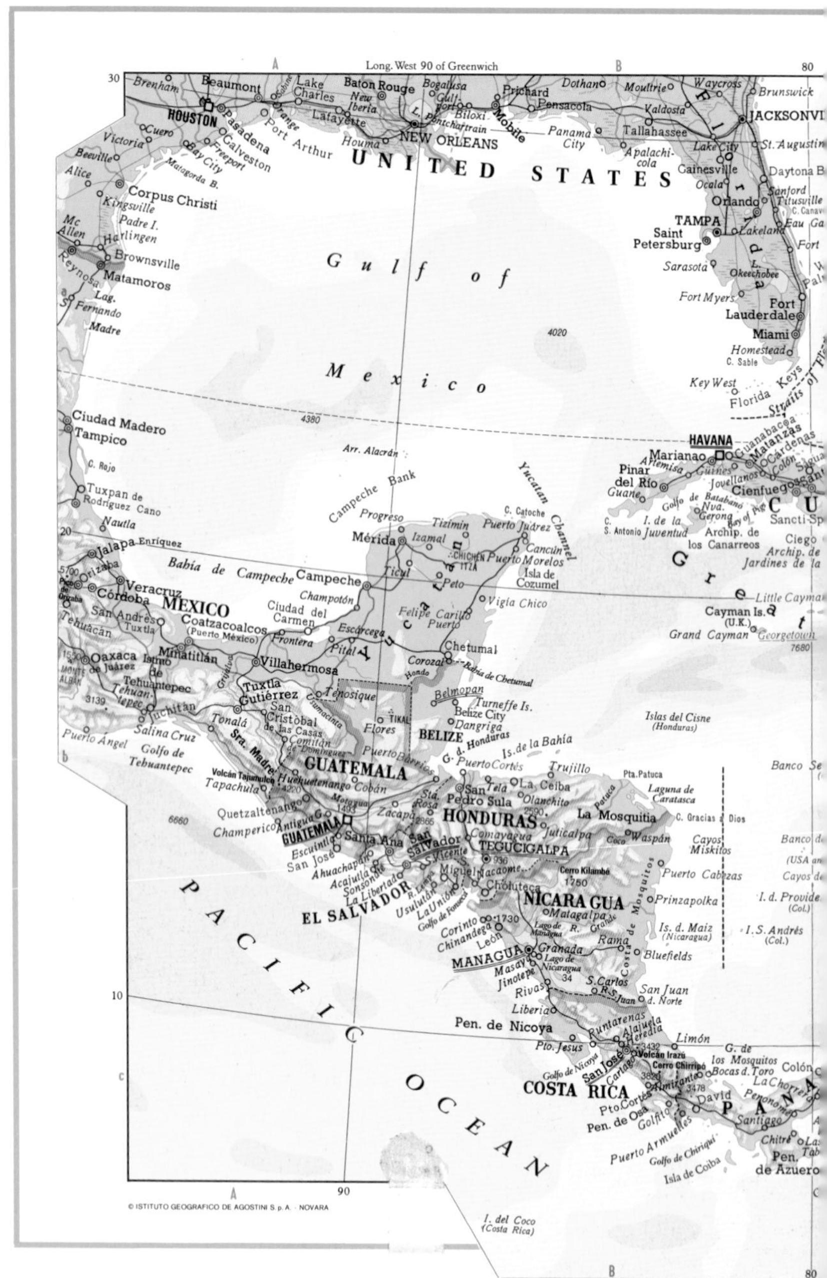
Long. West 90 of Greenwich
U N I T E D S T A T E S
Gulf of Mexico
HOUSTON
Beaumont
Baton Rouge
NEW ORLEANS
Mobile
Pensacola
Tallahassee
JACKSONVILLE
TAMPA
Saint Petersburg
Orlando
Fort Lauderdale
Miami
Key West
Florida Keys
Corpus Christi
Brownsville
Matamoros
Ciudad Madero
Tampico
HAVANA
Pinar del Río
Cienfuegos
Yucatan Channel
Campeche Bank
Mérida
Campeche
Bahía de Campeche
Veracruz
MEXICO
Coatzacoalcos
Villahermosa
Chetumal
Cayman Is. (U.K.)
Belmopan
Belize City
BELIZE
GUATEMALA
Islas del Cisne (Honduras)
San Pedro Sula
HONDURAS
TEGUCIGALPA
SAN SALVADOR
EL SALVADOR
NICARAGUA
MANAGUA
COSTA RICA
San José
PANAMA
PACIFIC OCEAN
I. del Coco (Costa Rica)

© ISTITUTO GEOGRAFICO DE AGOSTINI S. p. A. - NOVARA

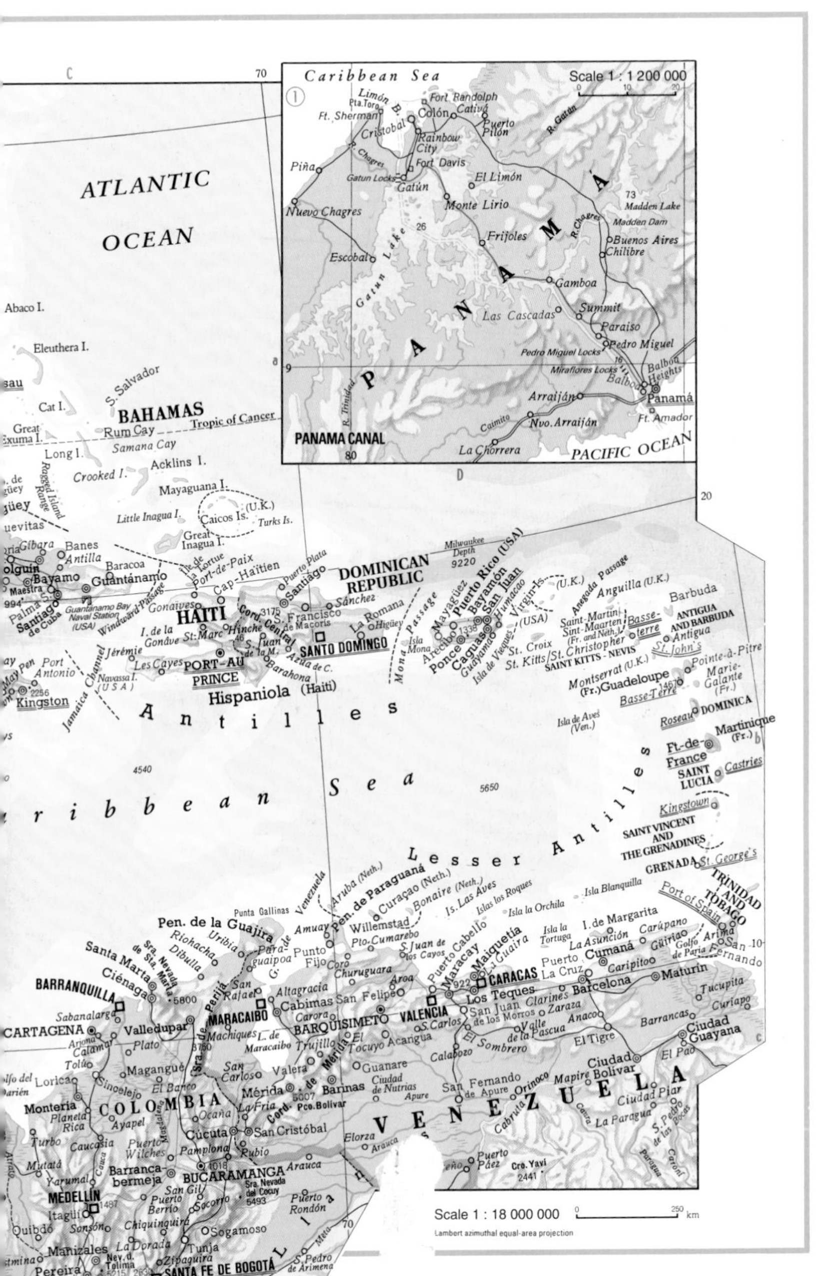

ATLANTIC

OCEAN

Abaco I.

Eleuthera I.

Cat I.

BAHAMAS
Great
Exuma I. Rum Cay — *Tropic of Cancer*
Long I. Samana Cay
Crooked I. Acklins I.
Mayaguana I.
(U.K.)
Little Inagua I. Caicos Is. · Turks Is.
Great
Inagua I.

Caribbean Sea   Scale 1 : 1 200 000

Limón
Pta.Toro   Ft. Randolph
Ft. Sherman   Colón Cativá
Cristóbal   Puerto Pilón   R.Gatún
Rainbow
Piña   City   R.Chagres
Fort Davis
El Limón
Gatún Locks
Nuevo Chagres   Gatún   Monte Lirio   73
Madden Lake
26   Madden Dam
Escobal   Frijoles   Buenos Aires
Chilibre
Gamboa
Las Cascadas
Summit
Paraíso
Pedro Miguel Locks   Pedro Miguel
Miraflores Locks   76
Arraiján   Balboa
Nvo. Arraiján   Panamá
PANAMA CANAL   La Chorrera   Ft. Amador
80   PACIFIC OCEAN

DOMINICAN
REPUBLIC
HAITI
Santiago
Francisco
Sánchez
Romana
SANTO DOMINGO
Hispaniola (Haiti)

Puerto Rico (USA)
San Juan
Ponce
Mona Passage
(U.K.)
St. Croix
SAINT KITTS - NEVIS
Montserrat
(Fr.)Guadeloupe
Basse-Terre
(Fr.)

Anguilla (U.K.)
Barbuda
ANTIGUA
AND BARBUDA
Antigua
St. John's
Pointe-à-Pitre
Marie-
Galante
(Fr.)

Roseau DOMINICA
Ft.-de Martinique
France (Fr.)
SAINT Castries
LUCIA

Kingstown
SAINT VINCENT
AND
THE GRENADINES
GRENADA St. George's
TRINIDAD
AND
TOBAGO
Port of Spain

Antilles

Caribbean Sea

Lesser Antilles

Isla de Aves
(Ven.)

Aruba (Neth.)   Curaçao (Neth.)
Bonaire (Neth.)
Willemstad
Pto.Cumarebo
Punta Gallinas
Pen. de la Guajira   Amuay Pen. de Paraguaná
Las Aves
Islas los Roques
Isla Orchila   Isla Blanquilla
I. de Margarita
La Asunción   Carúpano
Isla la   San
Tortuga   Porlamar   Fernando
VENEZUELA
CARACAS
Los Teques
Barcelona   Maturín
Puerto Cumaná   Güiria
Cabello
Valencia
MARACAIBO
VALENCIA
BARRANQUILLA
CARTAGENA   Valledupar
Maracaibo
BARQUISIMETO   San Carlos
COLOMBIA   Mérida   Barinas
Ciudad Bolívar
Ciudad
Guayana
El Pao
Ciudad Piar
VENEZUELA
BUCARAMANGA
MEDELLÍN
SANTA FE DE BOGOTÁ

Scale 1 : 18 000 000   0   250
km
Lambert azimuthal equal-area projection

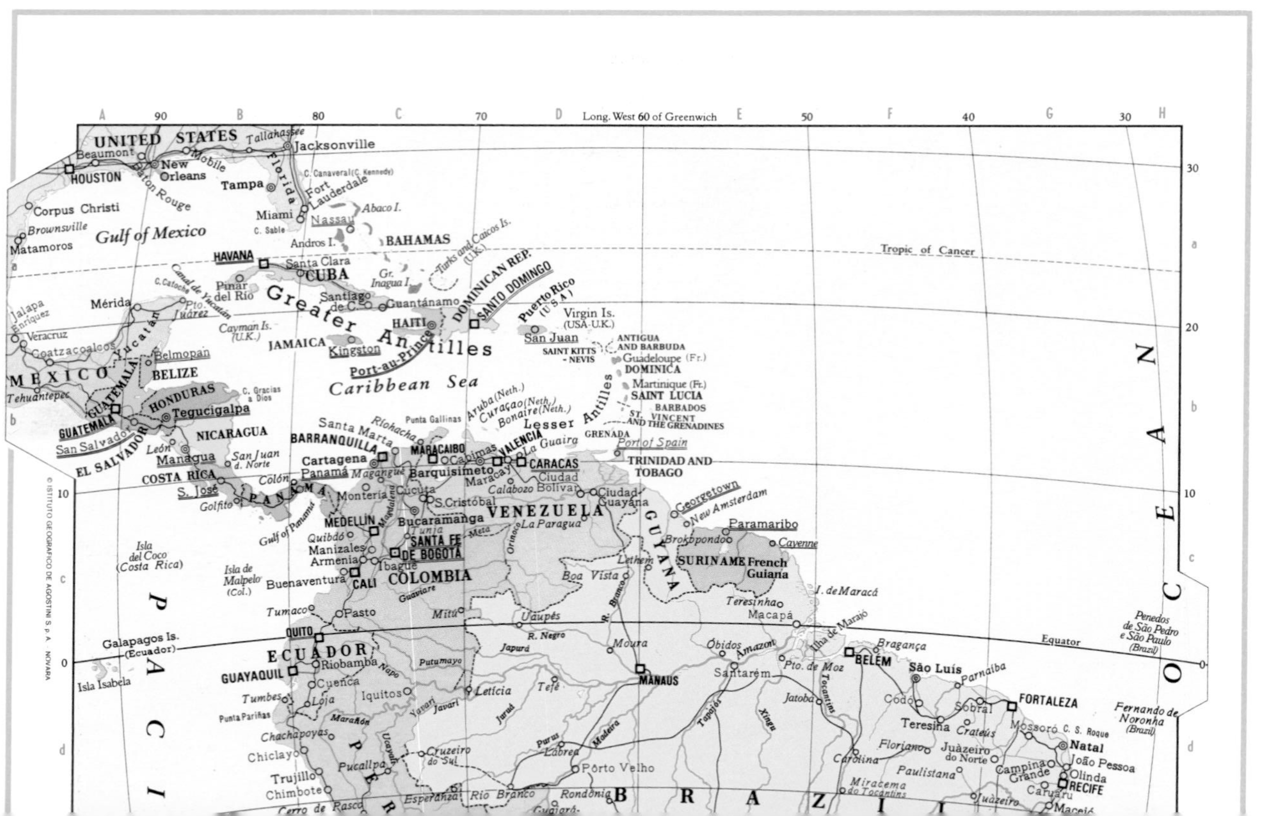

Long. West 60 of Greenwich
Tropic of Cancer
Equator
UNITED STATES
Gulf of Mexico
MEXICO
BAHAMAS
CUBA
JAMAICA
HAITI
DOMINICAN REP.
Greater Antilles
Lesser Antilles
Caribbean Sea
BELIZE
GUATEMALA
HONDURAS
EL SALVADOR
NICARAGUA
COSTA RICA
PANAMA
TRINIDAD AND TOBAGO
VENEZUELA
COLOMBIA
GUYANA
SURINAME
French Guiana
ECUADOR
Galapagos Is. (Ecuador)
CARACAS
SANTA FE DE BOGOTÁ
QUITO
MANAUS
BELÉM
FORTALEZA
RECIFE
© ISTITUTO GEOGRAFICO DE AGOSTINI S.p.A. - NOVARA

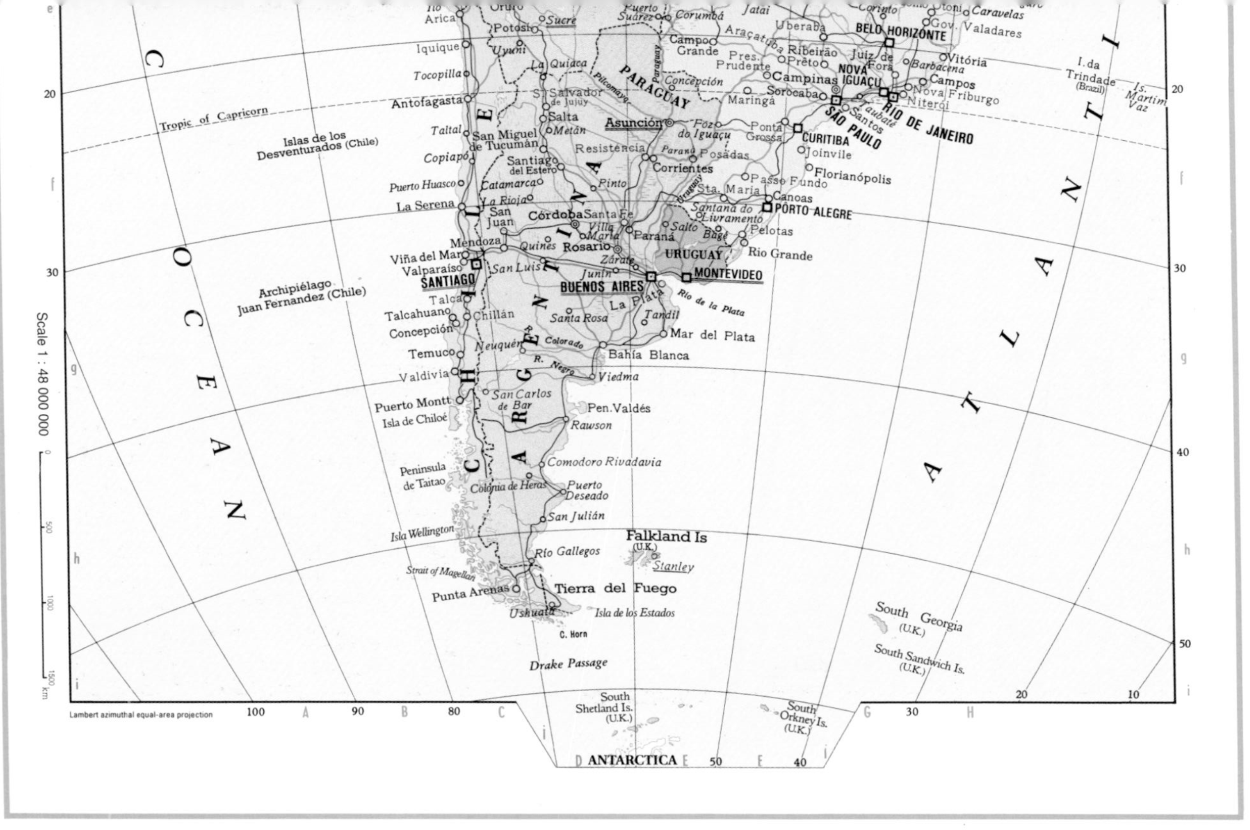

Scale 1 : 48 000 000   0   500   1000   1500 km

Lambert azimuthal equal-area projection

Caribbean

Pen. de la Guajira
Punta Gallinas
Aruba (Neth.)
Pen. de Parag
Willemstad
Cura

Santa Marta
Ciénaga
Riohacha
Uribia
Paraguaipoa
Punta
Pto. Cumarebo
Churuguara
BARRANQUILLA
Sabanalarga
Dibulla
5800
Srá. Nevada
de Sta. Marta
San Rafael
Fijo Coro
Altagracia
VAL
CARTAGENA
Calam
Valledupar
Machiques
Coro
El Tocuyo
BARQUISIMETO
Arjona
3750
Lago de
Maracaibo
Cabimas
San Felipe
MARACAIBO
Tolú
San Carlos
del Zulia
Trujillo
Golfo del
Magangué
Plato
Darién
Lorica
El Banco
Valera
MÉRIDA
Guanare
Montería
Sincelejo
Ocaña
Mérida
5007
Pen. Bolívar
Barinas
Planeta
Rica
Ayapel
La Fría
Ciudad de Nutri
Apure
Arch. del
las Perlas
La Palma
Tibú
Puerto
Wilches
Cúcuta
Pamplona
San Cristóbal
Elora
Arauca
Arauca
V
Yarumal
Barranca-
bermeja
San Gil
BUCARAMANGA
Rubio
Puerto C
MEDELLÍN
Puerto
Berrío
Socorro
Sierra Nevada
del Cocuy
5493
Puerto
Rondón
Itaguí
Chiquinquirá
Sonsón
La Dorada
Zipaquirá
Tunja
Sogamoso
Quibdó
Manizales
Nev.
Tolima
5215
S. Pedro
de Arimena
C. Corrientes
Pereira
SANTA FE DE BOGOTÁ
Armenia
Girardot
Villavicencio
S. José
de Ocune
Vichada
Istmina
Tuluá
Ibagué
Río Guaviare
Palmira
COLOMBIA
Buenaventura
CALI
S. Martín
Isla Gorgona
Nev. del Huila
5750
Neiva
San José
del Guaviare
Inírida
Guapi
Popayán
Garzón
Mesa de
Yambí
Tumaco
Patía
S. Agustín
Florencia
Miraflores
Vaupés
Mitú
Barbacoas
2594
Mocoa
Caquetá
Tres Esquinas
Iauareté
San Lorenzo
Ipiales
Pasto
Puerto Huitoto
Vaupés
Esmeraldas
Ibarra
Tulcán
Puerto
Asís
Punta Galera
Muisne
Otavalo
QUITO
Volcán Cayambe
5790
Puerto
Leguízamo
Bahía de Caráquez
Volcán
Cotopaxi
5897
Napo
Portoviejo
Manta
Latacunga
ECUADOR
Nuevo
Rocafuerte
La Pedrera
Japurá
Jipijapa
Volcán Chimborazo
6310
Ambato
Puyo
Arica
Babahoyo
Riobamba
Macas
Puca Urco
Pebas
Tarapacá
Içá
Santo
do
GUAYAQUIL
Salinas
Cuenca
Azogues
Iquitos
106
Leticia
São Pau
de Oliven
I. Puná
Golfo de Guayaquil
Machala
Amazon
Zorritos
Tumbes
Loja
Borja
Benjamín
Constant
Talara
Zumba
Marañón
Requena
S
Punta Pariñas
Sullana
Paita
Chulucanas
Bellavista
Yurimaguas
Ipixuna
Eirunepe
Soled
Piura
Jaén
Moyobamba
Bahía de Sechura
Chachapoyas
Punta Aguja
Des. de
Sechura
Chiclayo
Bambamarca
Tarapoto
Contamana
Cruzeiro
do Sul
Envira
Is. Lobos
de Afuera
PERÚ
Chachapoyas
Ojuanjui
ACRE
Pacasmayo
Cajamarca
Pucallpa
Pôrto
Valter
Tarauacá
Feijó
Puerto Chicama
CHAN CHAN
Trujillo
Tingo
María
Esperanza
6220
Nevado Huascarán
6768
Aguaytía
Ihapari
Chimbote
Huaraz
Huánuco
Ambo
Oxapampa
Atalaya
Alto Purús
Xapur
Brasiléia
Nevado Yerupajá
6632
Cerro
de Pasco
Iberia
Paramonga
Canta
Tarma
R. de los Piedras
Huacho
La Oroya
Jauja
Guillabamba
Manu
CALLAO
Huancayo
3271
Miguel
Salcantay
6271
MACHUPICCHU
Urubamba
Cusco
LIMA
Huancavelica
Ayacucho
Abancay
5384
Nudo Ausangate
Ayaviri
S. Vicente
de Cañete
Chincha Alta
Is. de Chincha
Pisco
Afiplano
del Perú
Chalhuanca
Sicuani
Nevado
Pahinan
5993
Ica

PACIFIC OCEAN

NICARAGUA
San Juan
d. Norte
Bluefields
COSTA RICA
Limón
Cerro
Chirripó
3820
G. de
los Mosquitos
Colón
R. Toro
Bocas d. Toro
La Chorrera
Almirante
5478
PANAMA
David
Santiago
Chitré
Pen. Las Tablas
de Azuero
Golfo de Chiriquí
Isla de Coiba
Puerto
Armuelles
Puerto
Cortés
Gulf of Panama
Cupica
Isla de
Malpelo
(Col.)

© ISTITUTO GEOGRAFICO DE AGOSTINI S. p. A. - NOVARA

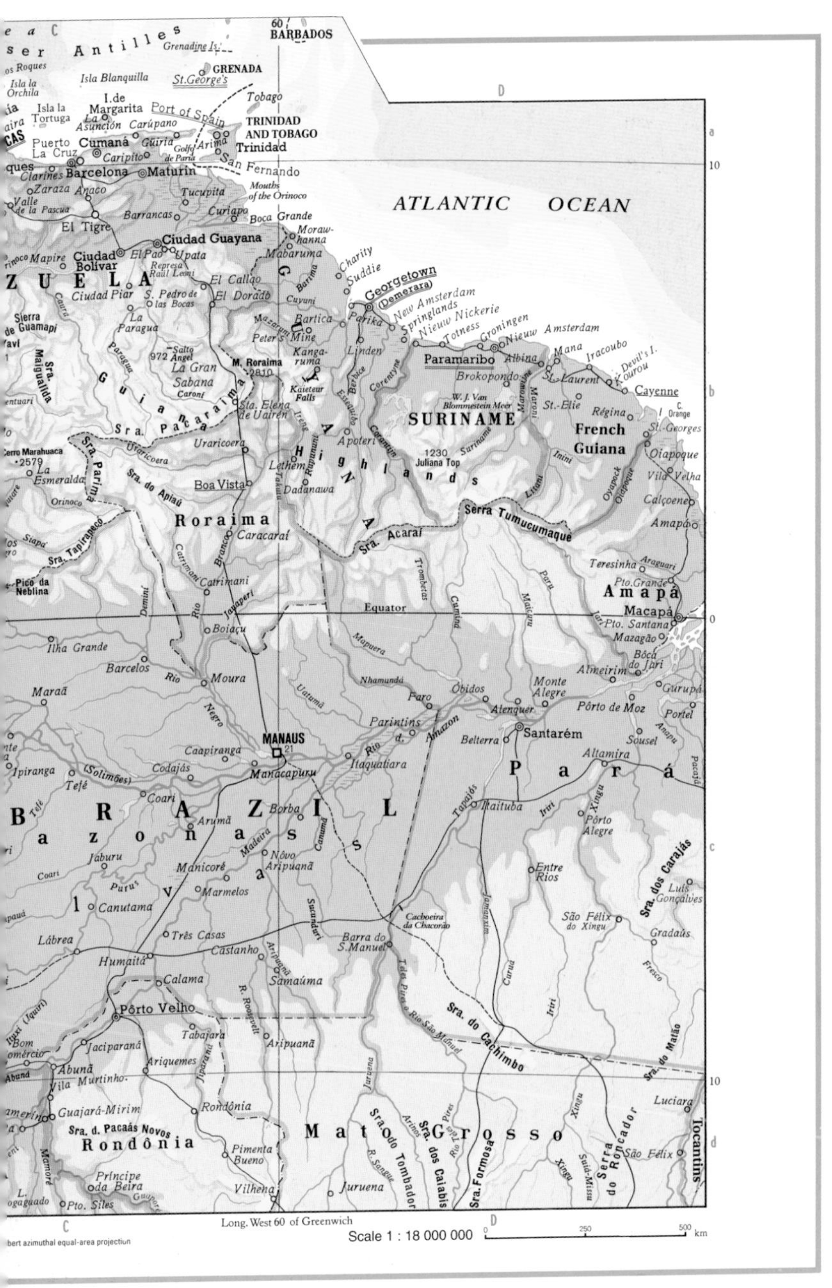

ATLANTIC   OCEAN

Scale 1 : 18 000 000

Long. West 60 of Greenwich

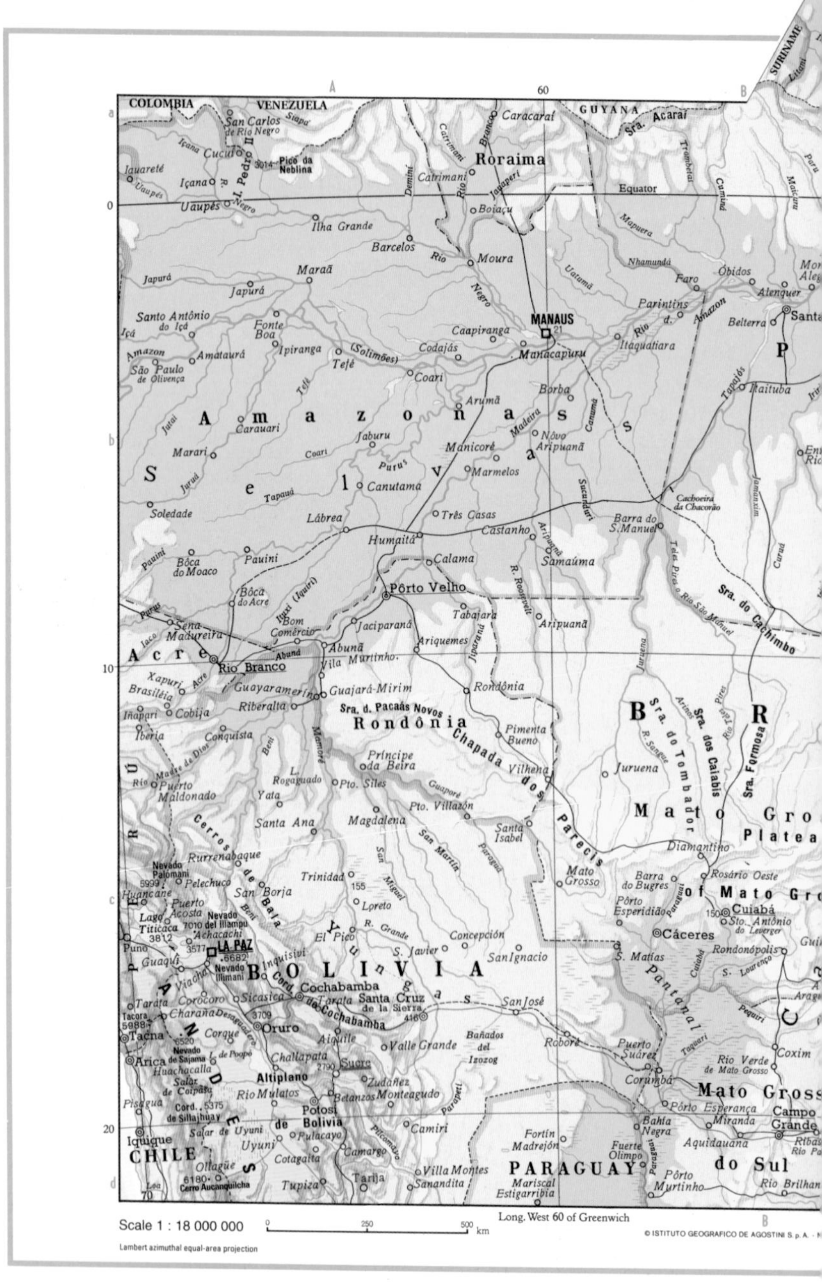

COLOMBIA   VENEZUELA   60   GUYANA   SURINAME

San Carlos de Rio Negro Siapa Caracaraí Sra. Acaraí

Iauareté Cucuí Pico da Neblina 3014 Catrimani Roraima

Içana Uaupés Uaupés Boiaçu Equator

Ilha Grande Maquera

Japurá Barcelos Rio Moura Nhamundá Óbidos Alenquer

Maraã Negro Faro Parintins Belterra Santa

Santo Antônio do Içá Fonte Boa Ipiranga (Solimões) Caapiranga MANAUS Itaquatiara

Içá São Paulo de Olivença Amaturá Tefé Codajás Manacapuru P

Amazon Coari Arumã Borba

A m a z o ñ a s

Marari Carauari Jaburu Manicoré Nôvo Aripuanã

S e l v Coari Purus Marmelos

Soledade Tapauá Canutama Três Casas Cachoeira da Chacorão

Lábrea Humaitá Castanho Barra do S. Manuel

Pauini Bôca do Moaco Pauini Calama Samaúma Sra. do Cachimbo

Bôca do Acre Bom Comércio Pôrto Velho Tabajara Aripuanã

A c r e Rio Branco Abunã Jaciparaná Ariquemes

Xapuri Vila Murtinho Rondônia

Brasiléia Guayaramerin Guajará-Mirim Sra. d. Pacaás Novos B R

Iñapari Cobija Riberalta R o n d ô n i a Pimenta Bueno

Iberia Chapada Vilhena Juruena Sra. do Tombador

Puerto Maldonado Príncipe da Beira Pto. Siles dos Sra. Farmosa

Rogaguado Pto. Villazón Santa Isabel M a t o G r o

Yata Magdalena Parecis Platea

Cerros Santa Ana San Martín Diamantino

Rurrenabaque Trinidad 155 Mato Grosso Barra do Bugres Rosário Oeste

Nevado Palomani 5974 Pelechuco San Borja Loreto Pôrto Esperidião Cuiabá of Mato Gro

Huaicane Puerto Acosta Nevado Achacachi R. Grande Concepción Sto. Antônio de Leverger

Lago Titicaca 7010 del Illampú 3812 El Pico S. Javier Cáceres Rondonópolis

Puno Achacachi Nevado Illimani 3577 San Ignacio S. Matías S. Lourenço Gui

LA PAZ 6882 Inquisivi B O L I V I A

P. Guaqui Corocoro Cochabamba Santa Cruz de la Sierra San José

Tarata Sicasica 3709 Cochabamba 416

Tacora 5989 Charaña Caracollo Oruro Aiquile Valle Grande Bañados del Izozog Rabori Puerto Suárez Rio Verde de Mato Grosso Coxim

Nevado de Sajama 6520 Corque Mato Grosso Corumbá Mato Gross

Arica Huachacalla A. de Pagog Challapata Sucre Zudáñez Pôrto Esperança Miranda Campo

Salar de Coipasa 5375 Altiplano 2790 Monteagudo Bahía Negra Aquidauana Grande

Pisigua Cord. 5375 de Sillahuay Rio Mulatos Betanzos Potosí Camiri

Iquique Salar de Uyuni de Bolivia O'Pulacayo Fortín Madrejón Fuerte Olimpo Mato Gross do Sul

CHILE Ollagüe Uyuni Cotagaita Camargo Villa Montes Bahía Negra Pôrto Murtinho Rio Brilhan

6180 Cerro Aucanquicha Tupiza Tarija Sanandita PARAGUAY do Sul

70 Mariscal Estigarribia

Scale 1 : 18 000 000 0 250 500 km Long. West 60 of Greenwich

Lambert azimuthal equal-area projection © ISTITUTO GEOGRAFICO DE AGOSTINI S.p.A. - M

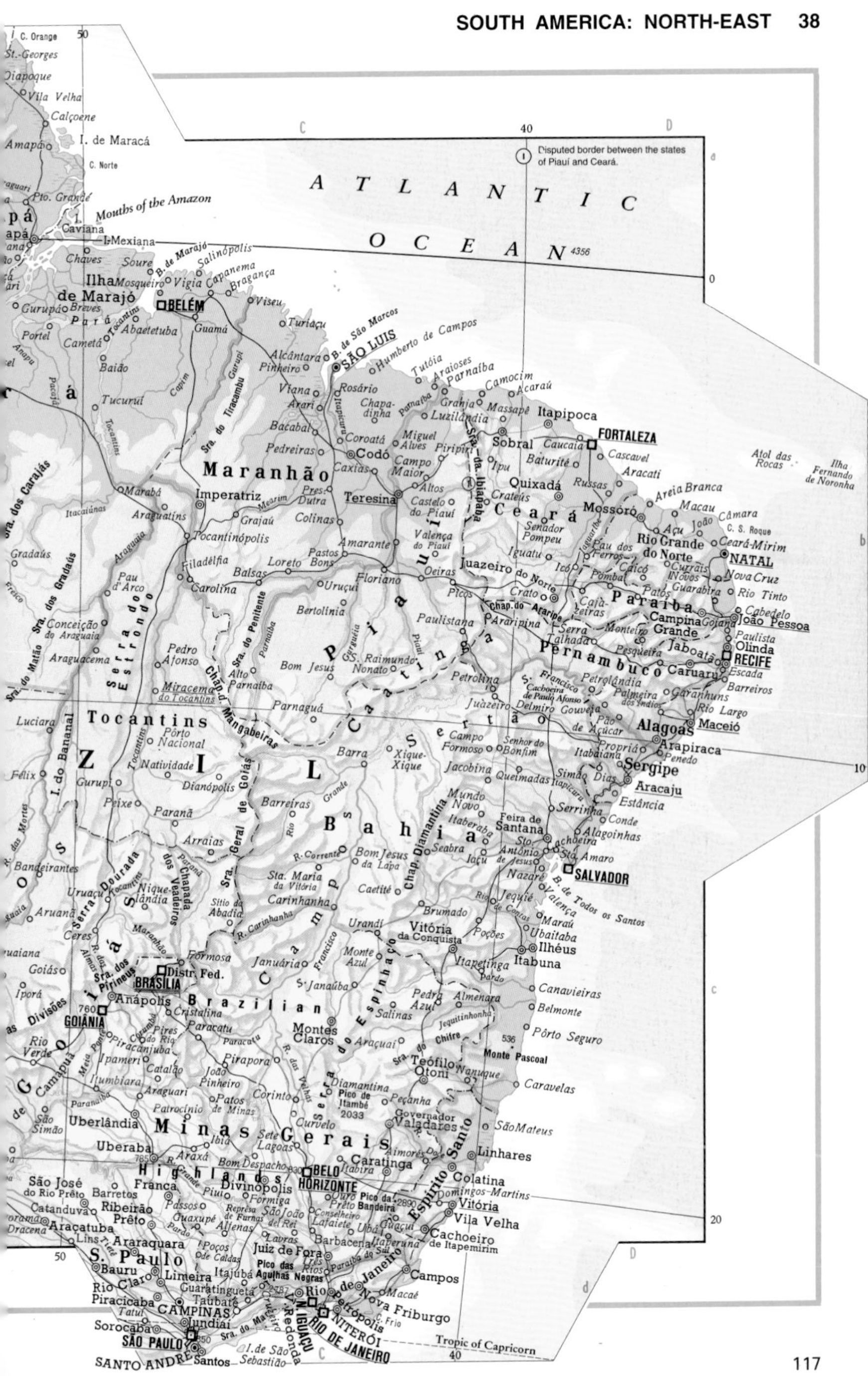
Disputed border between the states of Piauí and Ceará.
ATLANTIC OCEAN
Mouths of the Amazon
I. de Maracá
C. Orange
C. Norte
Ilha de Marajó
BELÉM
SÃO LUIS
FORTALEZA
NATAL
João Pessoa
RECIFE
Maceió
Aracaju
SALVADOR
Maranhão
Ceará
Piauí
Paraíba
Pernambuco
Alagoas
Sergipe
Bahia
Tocantins
Goiás
Minas Gerais
Espírito Santo
S. Paulo
Teresina
Imperatriz
Brazilian Highlands
Campos
Sertão
Chapada Diamantina
Serra do Espinhaço
BRASÍLIA
Distr. Fed.
GOIÂNIA
BELO HORIZONTE
RIO DE JANEIRO
SÃO PAULO
NITERÓI
CAMPINAS
SANTO ANDRÉ
Santos
Vitória
Tropic of Capricorn
Atol das Rocas
Ilha Fernando de Noronha
B. de Todos os Santos
Monte Pascoal
Pico da Bandeira
Campina Grande
Feira de Santana
Juazeiro do Norte
Montes Claros
Uberlândia
Uberaba
Juiz de Fora
Ilhéus
Vitória da Conquista
Governador Valadares
Teófilo Otoni
Anápolis
Petrolina
Juazeiro
Mossoró
Caruaru
Sobral
Caxias
Codó
Marabá
Carolina
Floriano
Barreiras
Jequié
Itabuna
Ribeirão Prêto
Bauru
Limeira
Piracicaba
Sorocaba
Jundiaí
Taubaté
Petrópolis
Nova Friburgo
Cachoeiro de Itapemirim
Colatina
Linhares
Caravelas
Pôrto Seguro
Parnaíba
Tutóia
Camocim
Arapiraca
Olinda
Cabedelo
Caicó
Areia Branca
Rio Grande do Norte
Ceará-Mirim
Macau
C. S. Roque
Crato
Iguatu
Quixadá
Crateús
Oeiras
Picos
Bom Jesus
Parnaguá
Barra
Xique-Xique
Jacobina
Senhor do Bonfim
Paulo Afonso
Alagoinhas
Estância
Penedo
Santo Amaro
Nazaré
Valença
Canavieiras
Belmonte
Diamantina
Curvelo
Pirapora
Paracatu
Patos de Minas
Araxá
Divinópolis
Barbacena
Lavras
Franca
Araraquara
Araçatuba
Catanduva
Barretos
São José do Rio Prêto
Rio Claro
Guaratinguetá
Itajubá
Volta Redonda
Nova Iguaçu
Macaé
C. Frio
I. de São Sebastião
Caratinga
Ipatinga
Conselheiro Lafaiete
Ubá
Muriaé
Cristalina
Formosa
Catalão
Itumbiara
Rio Verde
São Simão
Ceres
Uruaçu
Porangatu
Niquelândia
Gurupi
Natividade
Porto Nacional
Miracema do Tocantins
Araguaína
Tocantinópolis
Araguatins
Conceição do Araguaia
Santa Maria da Vitória
Bom Jesus da Lapa
Guanambi
Caetité
Brumado
Januária
Janaúba
Salinas
Araçuaí
Almenara
Pedra Azul
Chapada dos Veadeiros
Serra Geral de Goiás
Chap. das Mangabeiras
Serra do Estrondo
Sra. dos Carajás
Sra. dos Gradaús
Sra. do Penitente
Serra Dourada
Sra. dos Pirineus
Sra. da Ibiapaba
Chap. do Araripe
Caatinga
Tocantins
Araguaia
Xingu
Parnaíba
Rio Grande
R. Corrente
R. Carinhanha
São Francisco
R. das Velhas
Paranaíba
R. Grande
Tietê
Paraíba do Sul
Jequitinhonha
Pardo
Mearim
Gurupi
Capim
Guamá
Pacajá
Anapu
Itacaiúnas
Gradaús
Tucuruí
Bacabal
Pedreiras
Coroatá
Chapadinha
Piripiri
Campo Maior
Altos
Viana
Arari
Pinheiro
Alcântara
Turiaçu
Viseu
Bragança
Capanema
Salinópolis
Vigia
Mosqueiro
Abaetetuba
Cametá
Baião
Portel
Breves
Gurupá
Chaves
Soure
Caviana
I. Mexiana
Macapá
Amapá
Calçoene
Vila Velha
Oiapoque
St.-Georges
Humberto de Campos
Araioses
Granja
Luzilândia
Massapê
Acaraú
Itapipoca
Caucaia
Cascavel
Aracati
Baturité
Russas
Senador Pompeu
Açu
João Câmara
Currais Novos
Nova Cruz
Guarabira
Rio Tinto
Patos
Pombal
Cajàzeiras
Sousa
Monteiro
Serra Talhada
Pesqueira
Garanhuns
Palmeira dos Índios
Pão de Açúcar
Propriá
Itabaiana
Simão Dias
Serrinha
Conde
Cachoeira
Sto. Antônio de Jesus
Maraú
Ubaitaba
Itapetinga
Poções
Jaboatão
Paulista
Escada
Barreiros
Rio Largo
Salgueiro
Araripina
Paulistana
São Raimundo Nonato
Uruçuí
Bertolínia
Amarante
Valença do Piauí
Castelo do Piauí
Pastos Bons
Loreto
Balsas
Colinas
Pres. Dutra
Grajaú
Filadélfia
Pau d'Arco
Pedro Afonso
Alto Parnaíba
Dianópolis
Arraias
Paranã
Peixe
Bandeirantes
Aruanã
Goiás
Iporá
Jataí
Caçu
Luciara
Félix
I. do Bananal
Ipameri
Pires do Rio
Piracanjuba
Araguari
Patrocínio
Ibiá
Bom Despacho
Pitangui
Sete Lagoas
Corinto
Itabira
Ouro Prêto
São João del Rei
Piuí
Formiga
Passos
Guaxupé
Alfenas
Poços de Caldas
Represa de Furnas
Três Rios
Pico das Agulhas Negras
Pico de Itambé
Chifre
Nanuque
Aimorés
Domingos Martins
Vila Velha
São Mateus
Lins
Tatuí
Tupã
Dracena
Moji Mirim
Resende
Barra Mansa
Mundo Novo
Itaberaba
Iaçu
Seabra
Irecê
Queimadas
Campo Formoso
Delmiro Gouveia
Cachoeira de Paulo Afonso
Santana
Monte Azul
Urandi
Carinhanha
Sítio da Abadia
Itapicuru
Penedo

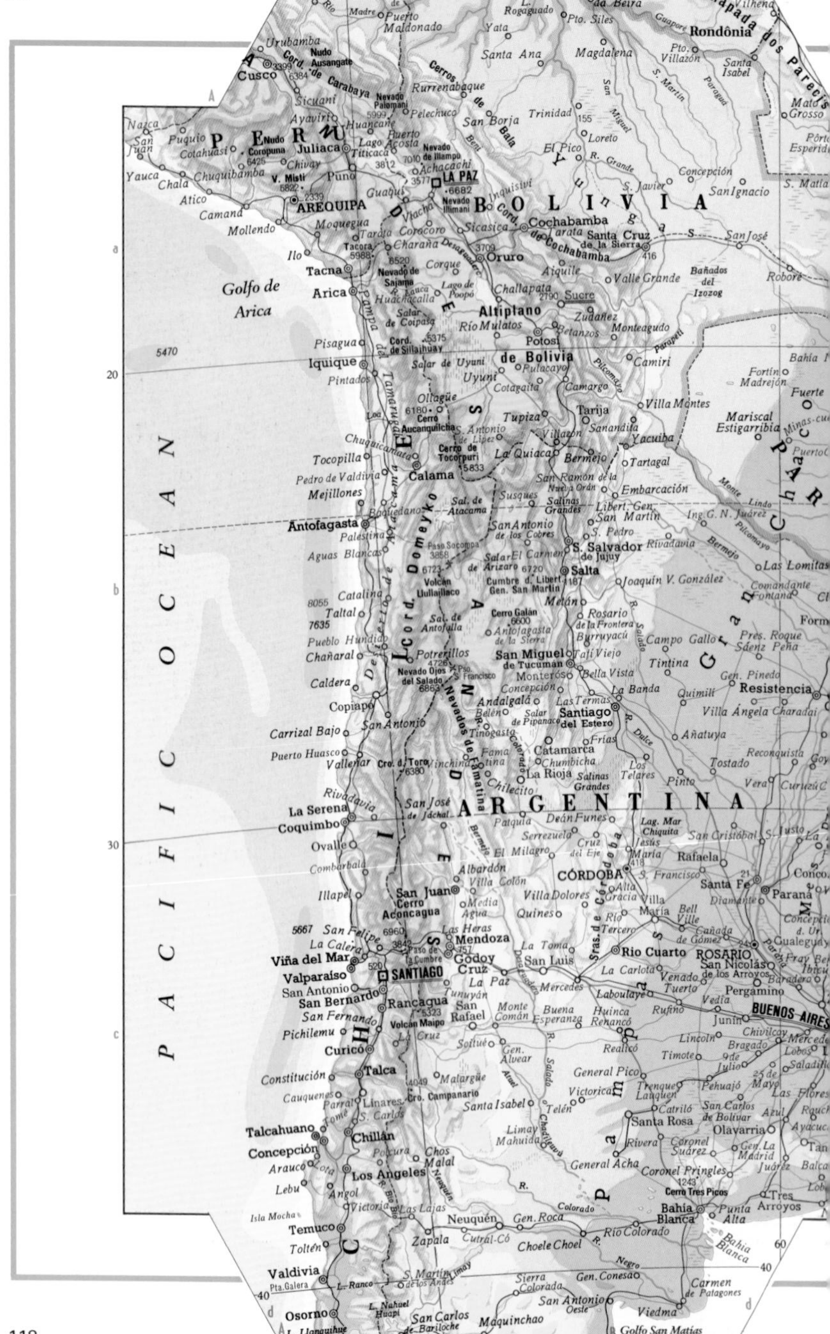
PERU
BOLIVIA
ARGENTINA
CHILE
PACIFIC OCEAN
Gran Chaco
Pampas
Golfo de Arica
Cusco
Arequipa
Juliaca
Puno
Lago Titicaca
LA PAZ
Nevado Illimani
Cochabamba
Oruro
Sucre
Potosí
Santa Cruz de la Sierra
Altiplano
Salar de Uyuni
Tacna
Arica
Iquique
Tocopilla
Calama
Antofagasta
Taltal
Chañaral
Copiapó
La Serena
Coquimbo
Viña del Mar
Valparaíso
SANTIAGO
Rancagua
Curicó
Talca
Chillán
Concepción
Talcahuano
Los Angeles
Temuco
Valdivia
Osorno
Salta
S. Salvador de Jujuy
San Miguel de Tucumán
Santiago del Estero
Catamarca
La Rioja
San Juan
Cerro Aconcagua
Mendoza
San Luis
CÓRDOBA
Rio Cuarto
ROSARIO
Santa Fe
Paraná
Resistencia
BUENOS AIRES
Santa Rosa
Bahía Blanca
Neuquén
Viedma
Golfo San Matías
Rondônia
Chapada dos Parecis
Trinidad
Cord. Domeyko
Nevados de Famatina
Desierto de Atacama
Lag. Mar Chiquita
Cerro Tres Picos
Nevado Ojos del Salado
6863
Volcán Llullaillaco
6723
Cerro Galán
6600
6960
20
30
40
60
70

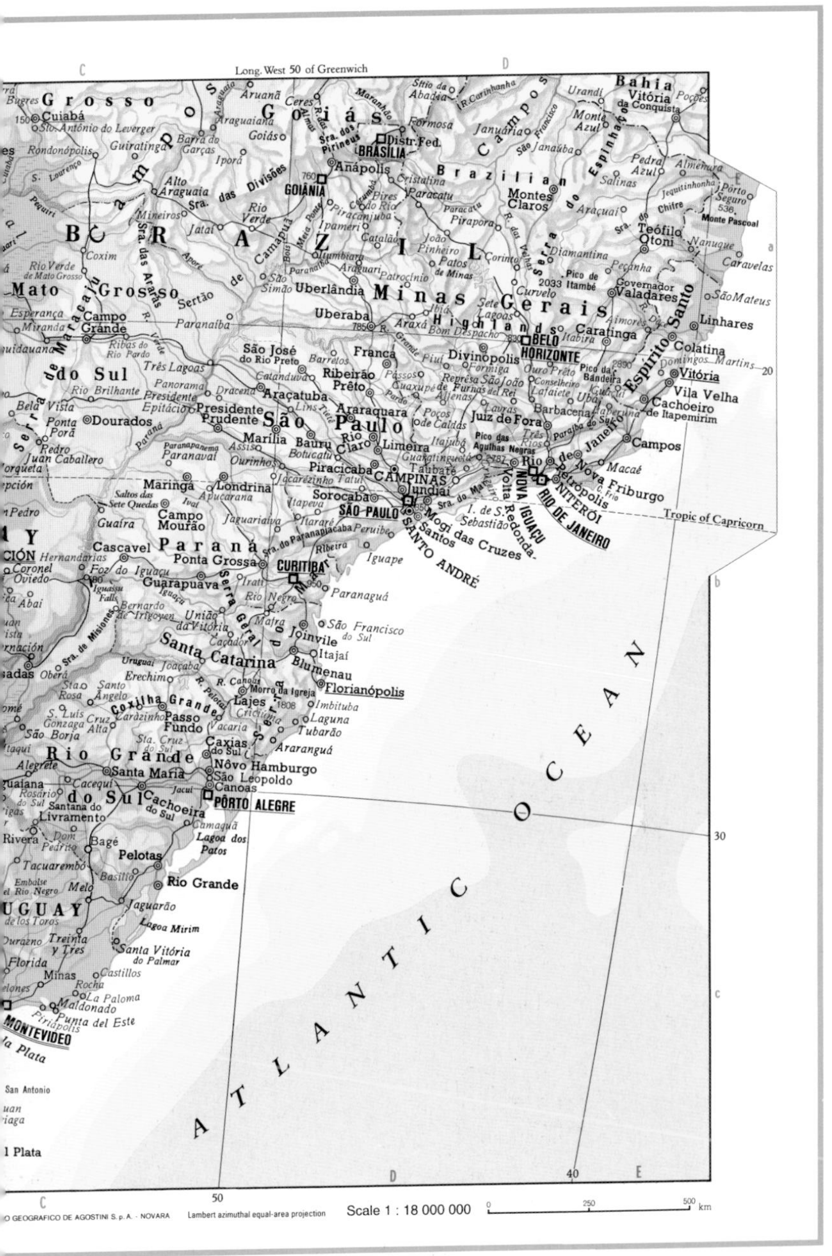
Long. West 50 of Greenwich
C
D
E
Bahia
Vitória da Conquista
Goiás
Grosso
Cuiabá
Sto. Antônio do Leverger
Rondonópolis
Guiratinga
Barra do Garças
Goiás
Iporá
Aruanã
Ceres
Araguaiana
Formosa
Distr. Fed.
BRASÍLIA
Anápolis
GOIÂNIA
Sra. dos Pirineus
Januária
São Francisco
Janaúba
Monte Azul
Urandi
Pedra Azul
Almenara
Salinas
Pôrto Seguro
536
Monte Pascoal
Chifre
Teófilo Otoni
Nanuque
Caravelas
Brazilian
Montes Claros
Araçuaí
Paracatu
Pirapora
Cristalina
Pires do Rio
Piracanjuba
Ipameri
Catalão
João Pinheiro
Alto Araguaia
Sra. das Divisões
Rio Verde
Jataí
Mineiros
Campos
BRAZIL
Coxim
Rio Verde de Mato Grosso
Mato Grosso
Sra. das Araras
Sertão
Campo Grande
Miranda
Esperança
Paranaíba
Itumbiara
Araguari
Patrocínio
Patos de Minas
Diamantina
Pico de Itambé
2033
Curvelo
Corinto
Governador Valadares
Peçanha
São Mateus
Minas Gerais
Uberlândia
São Simão
Uberaba
Araxá
Bom Despacho
Ibiá
Sete Lagoas
Highlands
BELO HORIZONTE
Itabira
Caratinga
Linhares
Espírito Santo
Colatina
Domingos Martins
Vitória
Vila Velha
Cachoeiro de Itapemirim
do Sul
Três Lagoas
Ribas do Rio Pardo
Rio Brilhante
Bela Vista
Ponta Porã
Dourados
Pedro Juan Caballero
Panorama
Presidente Epitácio
Presidente Prudente
Dracena
Araçatuba
São José do Rio Preto
Barretos
Franca
Ribeirão Prêto
Catanduva
Divinópolis
Formiga
Ouro Prêto
Pico da Bandeira
2890
Conselheiro Lafaiete
Ubá
Barbacena
Juiz de Fora
Represa de Furnas
São João del Rei
Alfenas
Lavras
Poços de Caldas
São Paulo
Araraquara
Rio Claro
Limeira
Marília
Bauru
Botucatu
Piracicaba
CAMPINAS
Jundiaí
Taubaté
Guaratinguetá
Pico das Agulhas Negras
2787
Campos
Macaé
Nova Friburgo
Petrópolis
C. Frio
NITERÓI
RIO DE JANEIRO
NOVA IGUAÇU
Volta Redonda
Paranavaí
Assis
Ourinhos
Maringá
Londrina
Apucarana
Jacarèzinho
Saltos das Sete Quedas
Campo Mourão
Sorocaba
Itapeva
Itararé
SÃO PAULO
Mogi das Cruzes
Santos
SANTO ANDRÉ
I. de S. Sebastião
Tropic of Capricorn
Jaguariaíva
Peruíbe
Iguape
Ribeira
Sra. do Paranapiacaba
Guaíra
Cascavel
Paraná
Ponta Grossa
CURITIBA
Foz do Iguaçu
Iguassu Falls
Guarapuava
Irati
Paranaguá
Rio Negro
Bernardo de Irigoyen
União da Vitória
Serra Geral
Mafra
Joinvile
São Francisco do Sul
Caçador
Santa Catarina
Itajaí
Blumenau
Joaçaba
Erechim
Sra. de Misiones
Oberá
Florianópolis
Lajes
Morro da Igreja
1808
Imbituba
Laguna
Tubarão
Criciúma
Araranguá
Coxilha Grande
Santo Ângelo
S. Luís Gonzaga
São Borja
Cruz Alta
Carazinho
Passo Fundo
Vacaria
Caxias do Sul
Rio Grande do Sul
Alegrete
Santa Maria
Nôvo Hamburgo
São Leopoldo
Canoas
PÔRTO ALEGRE
Cacequi
Jacuí
Rosário do Sul
Santana do Livramento
Cachoeira do Sul
Camaquã
Lagoa dos Patos
Rivera
Dom Pedrito
Bagé
Pelotas
Tacuarembó
Basilio
Rio Grande
Embalse del Rio Negro
Melo
Jaguarão
URUGUAY
Lagoa Mirim
Durazno
Treinta y Tres
Santa Vitória do Palmar
Florida
Minas
Castillos
Rocha
La Paloma
Maldonado
Punta del Este
Piriápolis
MONTEVIDEO
la Plata
San Antonio
1 Plata
ATLANTIC OCEAN
30
40
20
50
a
b
c
Lambert azimuthal equal-area projection
Scale 1 : 18 000 000
0
250
500 km

© GEOGRAFICO DE AGOSTINI S. p. A. - NOVARA

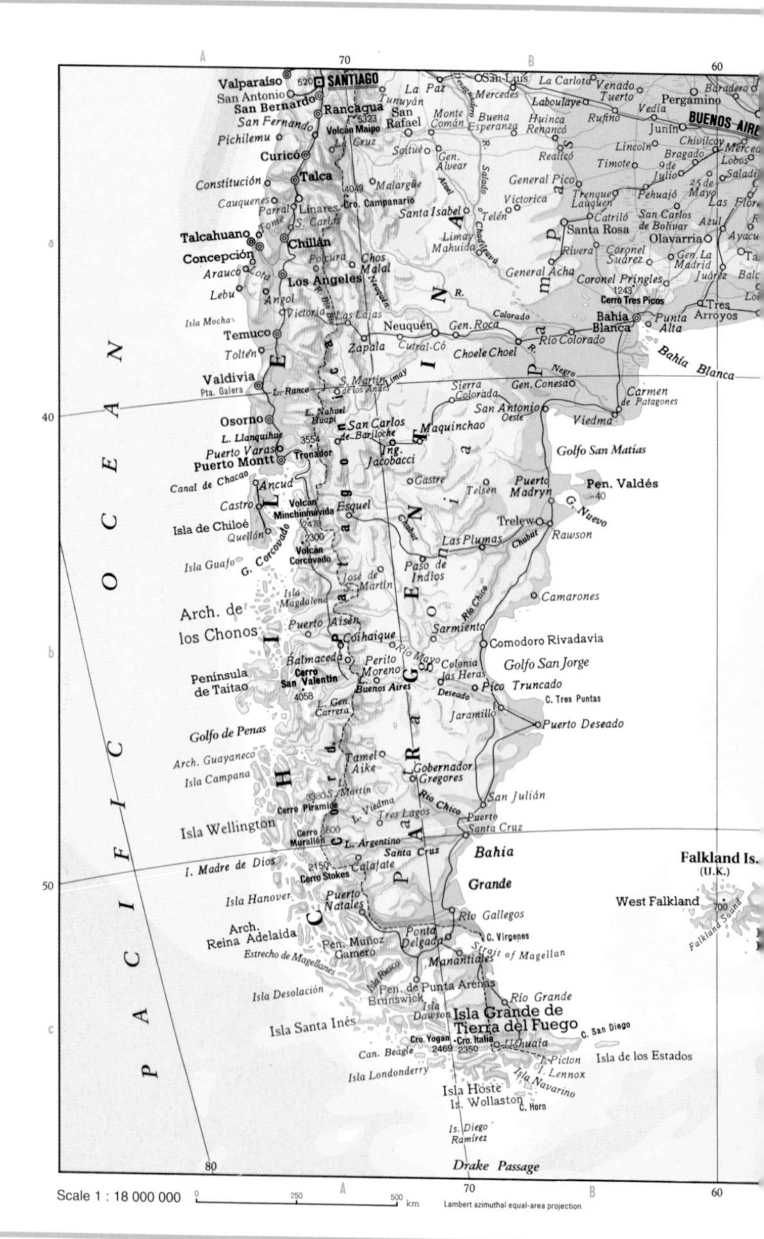

Valparaíso 520 · SANTIAGO · La Carlota · Venado · Baradero
San Antonio · San Luis · Mercedes · Laboulaye · Tuerto · Pergamino
San Bernardo · Rancagua · Tunuyán · Vedia · **BUENOS AIRES**
San · Monte · Rufino · Junín
San Fernando · Rafael · Comán · Buena Esperanza · Huinca Renancó · Lincoln · Chivilcoy
Pichilemu · Volcán Maipo · Realicó · Timote · Bragado · Lobos · Mercedes
Curicó · 9 de Julio · 25 de Mayo · Saladillo
Constitución · Malargüe · General Pico · Pehuajó · Las Flores
Talca · Cauquenes · Trenque Lauquen · San Carlos de Bolívar · Azul · Ayacucho
Parral · Linares · Cro. Campanario · Victorica · Catriló · Santa Rosa · Olavarría
Talcahuano · S. Carlos · Santa Isabel · Telén · Rivera · Coronel Suárez · Gen. La Madrid · Tandil · Balcarce
Concepción · Chillán · Limay Mahuida · General Acha · Coronel Pringles · Tres Arroyos
Arauco · Los Ángeles · 1243 · Cerro Tres Picos
Lebu · Angol · Bahía Blanca · Punta Alta
Isla Mocha · Victoria · Las Lajas · Colorado
Temuco · Neuquén · Gen. Roca · Río Colorado · Bahía Blanca
Toltén · Zapala · Cutral-Có · Choele Choel · Negro
Valdivia · L. Ranco · S. Martín · Sierra Colorada · Gen. Conesa · Carmen de Patagones
Pta. Galera · de los Andes · San Antonio Oeste · Viedma
Osorno · San Carlos de Bariloche · Maquinchao
L. Llanquihue · Vng. Tronador · Golfo San Matías
Puerto Varas · Jacobacci
Puerto Montt · Esquel · Puerto Madryn · Pen. Valdés
Canal de Chacao · Ancud · Gastre · Telsen · G. Nuevo
Castro · Volcán Minchinmávida · Trelew · Rawson
Isla de Chiloé · Quellón · Las Plumas · Chubut
Isla Guafo · Volcán Corcovado · Paso de Indios
G. Corcovado · José de San Martín · Camarones
Arch. de los Chonos · Puerto Aisén · Sarmiento
Coihaique · Comodoro Rivadavia
Balmaceda · Perito Moreno · Colonia las Heras · Golfo San Jorge
Península de Taitao · Cerro San Valentín · Buenos Aires · Pico Truncado · C. Tres Puntas
L. Gen. Carrera · Deseado · Jaramillo
Golfo de Penas · Puerto Deseado
Arch. Guayaneco · Tamel Aike · Gobernador Gregores
Isla Campana · Cerro Piramide · S. Martín · Viedma · San Julián
Tres Lagos · Río Chico · Santa Cruz
Isla Wellington · Cerro Murallón · L. Argentino · Santa Cruz · Bahía Grande
I. Madre de Dios · Cerro Stokes · Calafate · Río Gallegos
Isla Hanover · Puerto Natales · Punta Delgada · C. Vírgenes
Arch. Reina Adelaida · Pen. Muñoz Gamero · Manantiales · Strait of Magellan
Estrecho de Magallanes · Pen. de Brunswick · Punta Arenas · Río Grande
Isla Desolación · Isla Dawson · Isla Grande de Tierra del Fuego
Isla Santa Inés · Cro. Yogan · Cro. Italia · Ushuaia · C. San Diego
Can. Beagle · I. Picton · Isla de los Estados
Isla Londonderry · I. Lennox
Isla Hoste · Isla Navarino
Is. Wollaston · C. Horn
Is. Diego Ramírez

Falkland Is. (U.K.) · West Falkland · Falkland Sound

P A C I F I C   O C E A N

P A M P A

C O R D I L L E R A   P A T A G Ó N I C A

Drake Passage

Scale 1 : 18 000 000   0   250   500   km   Lambert azimuthal equal-area projection

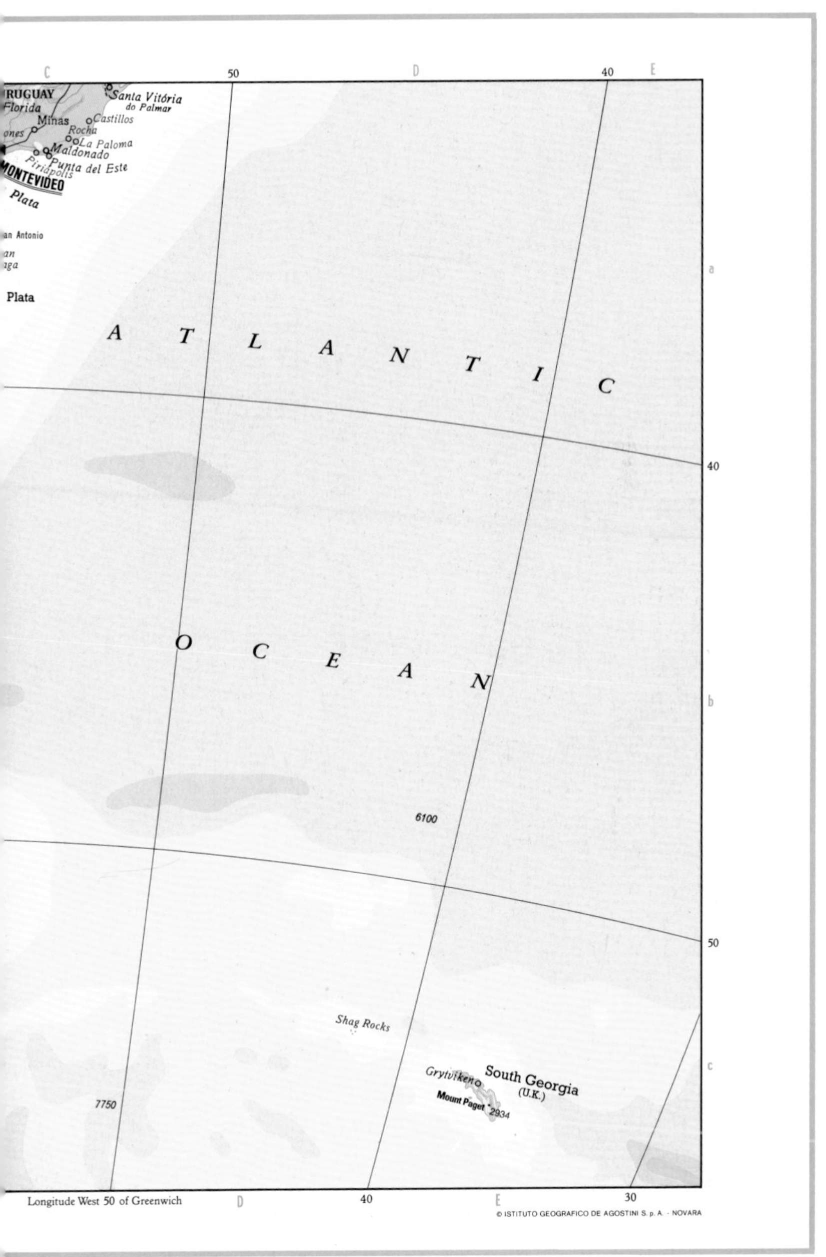

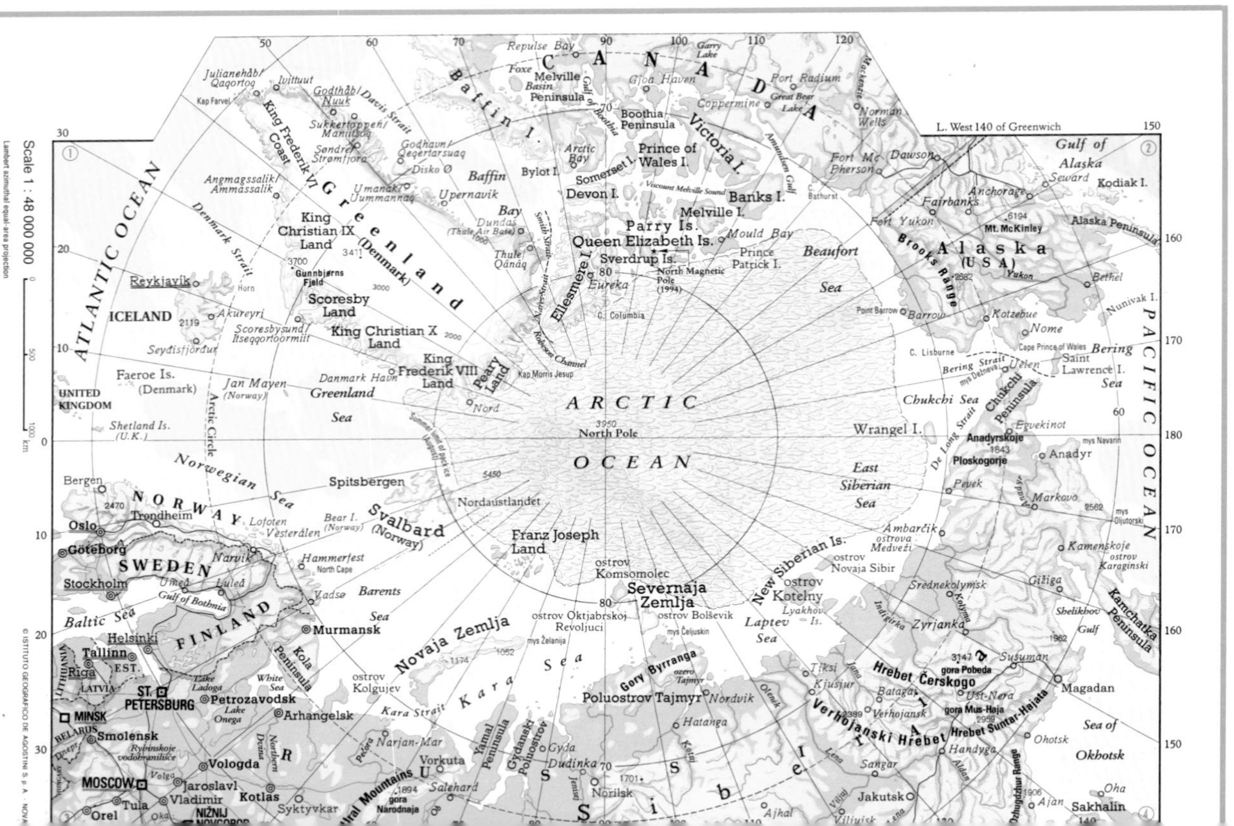

Scale 1 : 48 000 000

Lambert azimuthal equal-area projection

© ISTITUTO GEOGRAFICO DE AGOSTINI S.p.A. – NOVA

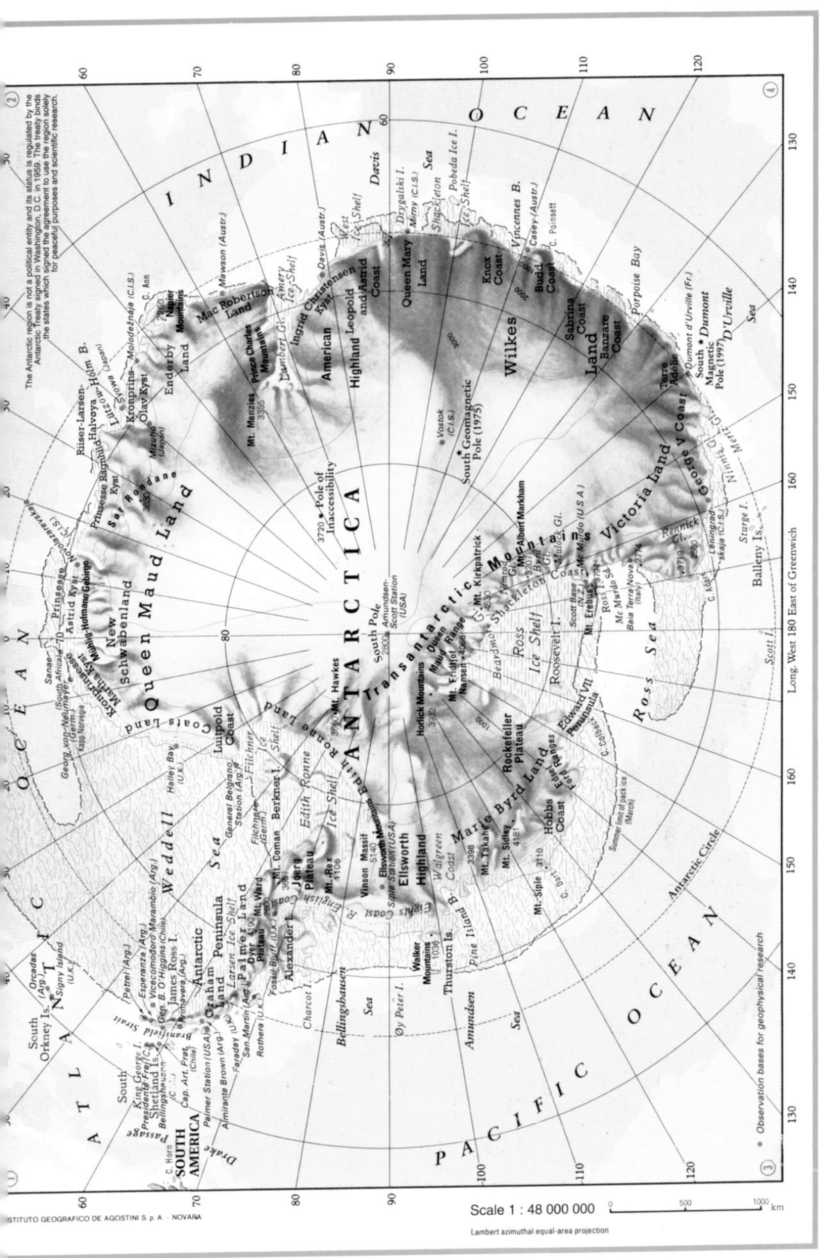

ISTITUTO GEOGRAFICO DE AGOSTINI S.p.A. - NOVARA

Scale 1 : 48 000 000

Lambert azimuthal equal-area projection

* Observation bases for geophysical research

INDEX

All the names shown on the maps are only listed once in the index and normally, the reference given is to the principle map on which they appear.

The individual maps in numerical order are divided by the lines of the meridian and the parallels into grid squares marked from left to right with upper case letters and from top to bottom with lower case letters.

The names which refer to the map inserts are followed by the words "map no."; those refering to the maps of the polar region are followed by the words "grid square no.".

The names referred to on The World Political map are followed only by the number of the map.

In general, names are listed in the index in full even if they are abbreviated on the maps.

All the names are listed in alphabetical order according to their international form, not taking into account any diacritic letter forms (e.g. ā, æ, ö, œ, ū, etc.).

Physical features composed of a proper name and a description are listed alphabetically by the proper name, followed by the description.

To ease understanding for physical features and administrative divisions, an abbreviation of the type of feature is shown in brackets in the index after its name.

In the case of two places with the same name, the political identity is shown in square brackets.

Abbreviations used in the index

at.	atoll
Aut. Reg.	Autonomous Region
Aut. Rep.	Autonomous Republic
b.	bay
c.	cave
can.	canal
cap.	cape
co.	County
Dep.	Dependency, Colony
des.	desert
g.	gulf
gl.	glacier
hist. reg.	historical region
i.	island
Ind. St.	Independent State
is.	islands
l.	lake
lag.	lagoon
mt.	mountain
mts.	mountains
p.	pass
pen.	peninsula
phys. reg.	physical region
plat.	plateau, upland
prov.	Province
r.	ruins
reg.	Region
res.	reservoir
rf.	reef
riv.	river
riv. m.	river mouth
sal. l.	salt lake
sc. stat.	scientific station
s. m.	salt marsh
str.	strait
sw.	swamp, marsh
v.	valley
volc.	volcano
w.	wadi
wf.	waterfall

© ISTITUTO GEOGRAFICO DE AGOSTINI S.p.A. - Novara

Abbr.	Full name	Abbr.	Full name	Abbr.	Full name
Ak.-U.S.	Alaska, U.S.	Id.-U.S.	Idaho, U.S.	Nor.	Norway
Al.-U.S.	Alabama, U.S.	Il.-U.S.	Illinois, U.S.	Nv.-U.S.	Nevada, U.S.
Alta.-Can.	Alberta, Canada	In.-U.S.	Indiana, U.S.	N.Y.-U.S.	New York, U.S.
Ant.	Antarctica	Indon.	Indonesia	N.Z.	New Zealand
Ar.-U.S.	Arkansas, U.S.	Ire.	Ireland	Oh.-U.S.	Ohio, U.S.
Arg.	Argentina	It.	Italy	Ont.-Can.	Ontario, Canada
Atg.	Antigua and	Jam.	Jamaica	Or.-U.S.	Oregon, U.S.
	Barbuda	Jap.	Japan	Pa.-U.S.	Pennsylvania, U.S.
Aus.	Austria	Jor.	Jordan	Pak.	Pakistan
Austl.	Australia	Kaz.	Kazakhstan	Pan.	Panama
Az.-U.S.	Arizona, U.S.	Ky.-U.S.	Kentucky, U.S.	Par.	Paraguay
Bah.	Bahamas	Kyrg.	Kyrgyzstan	Phil.	Philippines
Bel.	Belgium	La.-U.S.	Louisiana, U.S.	Pol.	Poland
Bela.	Belarus	Lbr.	Liberia	Port.	Portugal
Bngl.	Bangladesh	Leb.	Lebanon	Reu.	Reunion
Bol.	Bolivia	Lib.	Libya	Rom.	Romania
Braz.	Brazil	Ma.-U.S.	Massachusetts,	S. Afr.	South Africa
Bul.	Bulgaria		U.S.	S. Amer.	South America
Ca.-U.S.	California, U.S.	Mala.	Malaysia	S.C.-U.S.	South Carolina,
Can.	Canada	Me.-U.S.	Maine, U.S.		U.S.
C.A.R.	Central African	Mex.	Mexico	Scot.-U.K.	Scotland, U.K.
	Republic	Mi.-U.S.	Michigan, U.S.	S.D.-U.S.	South Dakota,
Cay. Is.	Cayman Islands	Mn.-U.S.	Minnesota, U.S.		U.S.
Co.-U.S.	Colorado, U.S.	Mo.-U.S.	Missouri, U.S.	Sp.	Spain
Col.	Colombia	Mold.	Moldova	Sud.	Sudan
C.R.	Costa Rica	Moz.	Mozambique	Sur.	Suriname
Cyp.	Cyprus	Ms.-U.S.	Mississippi, U.S.	Swe.	Sweden
Czech Rep.	Czech Republic	Mt.-U.S.	Montana, U.S.	Tn.-U.S.	Tennessee, U.S.
De.-U.S.	Delaware, U.S.	Mtna.	Mauritania	Trin.	Trinidad and
Dom. Rep.	Dominican	Mya.	Myanmar (Burma)		Tobago
	Republic	N. Amer.	North America	Tun.	Tunisia
Ec.	Ecuador	Nb.-U.S.	Nebraska, U.S.	Tur.	Turkey
Eg.	Egypt	N.B.-Can.	New Brunswick,	Tx.-U.S.	Texas, U.S.
El Sal.	El Salvador		Canada	U.K.	United Kingdom
Eng.-U.K.	England, U.K.	N.C.-U.S.	North Carolina,	Ukr.	Ukraine
Eth.	Ethiopia		U.S.	Ur.	Uruguay
Fl.-U.S.	Florida, U.S.	N.D.-U.S.	North Dakota, U.S.	U.S.	United States
Fr.	France	Nep.	Nepal	Va.-U.S.	Virginia, U.S.
Fr. Gui.	French Guiana	Neth.	Netherlands	Ven.	Venezuela
Fr. Poly.	French Polynesia	Newf.-Can.	Newfoundland,	Vt.-U.S.	Vermont, U.S.
Ga.-U.S.	Georgia, U.S.		Canada	Wa.-U.S.	Washington,
Ger.	Germany	N.H.-U.S.	New Hampshire,		U.S.
Grc.	Greece		U.S.	Wi.-U.S.	Wisconsin, U.S.
Guat.	Guatemala	Nic.	Nicaragua	W.V.-U.S.	West Virginia,
Hi.-U.S.	Hawaii, U.S.	Nig.	Nigeria		U.S.
Hond.	Honduras	N.Ire.-U.K.	Northern Ireland,	Wy.-U.S.	Wyoming, U.S.
Ia.-U.S.	Iowa, U.S.		U.K.	Yugo.	Yugoslavia
I.C.	Ivory Coast	N.M.-U.S.	New Mexico, U.S.	Zimb.	Zimbabwe

© ISTITUTO GEOGRAFICO DE AGOSTINI S p.A. - Novara

A

Aachen 5 Ac
Aaiún, El– 24 Ab
Aalen 5 Cd
Aalst 8 EFb
Äänekoski 4 Fc
Aansarîyé, Gebel– (mt.) 22 Fe
Aarau 5 Be
Aasiaat / Egedesminde 31 JKb
Aba 24 Cd
Abaco Island 32 Dc
Ābādān 21 Dc
Abādeh 21 Ec
Abaetetuba 38 Cb
Abagnar Qi 16 DEb
Abai 39 Cb
Abakan 14 BCd
Abalakova 14 Cd
Abancay 37 Bd
Abano Terme 10 Cb
Abarqu 21 Ec
Abashiri 16 Jb
Abaya, Lake– 25 Dd
Abaza 14 BCd
Abbeville 8 Db
Abbottabad 20 Db
Abd al Kuri (i.) 21 Eg
Abdulino 12 Hc
Abéché 25 Cc
Abemama Atoll 27 Db
Abengourou 24 Bd
Àbenrå 5 Ba
Abeokuta 24 Cd
Abercorn → Mbala 26 Cb
Aberdeen [S.D.–U.S.] 32 Ba
Aberdeen [U.K.] 7 EFc
Aberdeen [Wa.–U.S.] 33 Ab
Aberystwyth 7 De
Abez 13 Fc
Abha 21 Cf
Abidjan 24 Bd
Abilene 33 CDc
Abitibi Lake 32 Da
Abkhasia (Aut. Rep.) 13 De
Abminga 29 EFd
Abnûb 25 Db
Aboisso 24 Bd
Abomey 24 Cd
Abou Deïa 25 BCc
Abrántes 9 ABc
Abruzzo (reg.) 10 DEcd
Absaroka Range 33 BCb
Abu 20 Dd
Abū 'Alî 21 DEd
Abu Arish 21 Cf
Abu Dhabi 21 Ee
Abu Gharâdiq, Bîr– 22 Bgh
Abū Hamad 25 Dc
Abuja 24 Cd
Abū Kamâl 21 Cc
Abū Madd, Ra's– 21 Be
Abu Musa (i.) 21 EFd
Abunã (riv.) 37 Ccd
Abunã 37 Cc
Abū Qîr 22 BCg
Abu Simbel (r.) 25 CDb
Abu Sultân 25 map no.1
Abū Zanimah 21 Ad
Acajutla 35 ABb

Acámbaro 34 Bbc
Acaponeta 34 Bb
Acapulco de Juárez 34 Blh
Acaraí, Serra– (mts.) 38 Ba
Acaraú 38 CDb
Acarigua 37 Cb
Accra 24 BCd
Achacachi 39 Ba
Achill Island 7 ABe
Acıgöl 22 BCd
Ačinsk 14 Cd
Acireale 10 Ef
Acklins Island 35 Ca
Aconcagua, Cerro– (mt.) 39 ABc
Acqui Terme 10 Bb
Acre 39 Ba
Acre (State) 37 BCc
Acri 10 Fe
Acsu (riv.) 22 Cd
Açu 38 Db
Ada 24 Cd
Adabîya 25 map no.1
Adalar (is.) 11 Hc
Adama 25 DEd
Adamawa 24 Dd
Adamello (mt.) 10 Ca
Adams, Mount– 33 Ab
Adamstown 28 Cd
Adana 22 Ed
Adapazarı 22 Cb
Adare, Cape– 42 grid square no.4
Adavale 29 GHd
Adda (riv.) 10 Bb
Ad Dir'îyah 21 De
Addis Ababa 25 Dd
Adelaide 29 FGef
Adelaide River 29 Ea
Adele Island 29 Cb
Adélie, Terre– 42 grid square no.4
Aden 21 Dg
Aden, Gulf of– 25 EFc
Adige (riv.) 10 Ca
Adigrat 25 DEc
Adîrî 24 Db
Adırnaz (riv.) 22 Bc
Adi Ugri 21 Bg
Adıyaman 22 FGd
Admiralty (i.) 31 Bc
Admiralty Gulf 29 CDa
Admiralty Islands 27 Cc
Adonara, Pulau– (i.) 18 Ff
Adoni 20 Ee
Adour (riv.) 8 Cf
Adra [India] 19 Ik
Adra [Sp.] 9 Dd
Adrar 24 Bb
Adrar (mt.) 24 Cb
Adrar, Dhar– (mts.) 24 Ab
Adré 25 Cc
Adria 10 Db
Adriatic Sea 10 Ec
Adwa 25 Dc
Adzhar (Aut. Rep.) 13 De
Aegean Sea 11 FGde
Aegina (i.) 11 Ee
Ærø 5 Ca
Afghanistan (Ind. St.) 15 Cf
Afgooye 25 Ed
'Afîf 21 Ce
Afyonkarahisar 22 Cc

Agadez 24 Cc
Agadir 24 ABab
Agadyr 13 Ge
Agalega Islands 15 BCk
Agaña 27 map no.1
Aga Point (cap.) 27 map no.1
Agartala 19 Bd
Agats 27 Bc
Agboville 24 Bd
Agde 8 Ef
Agen 8 De
Agidyen Atoll 28 map no.3
Aginskoje 14 Ed
Agnew 29 Cc
Agnita 6 Gcd
Agordat 25 Dc
Agout (riv.) 8 DEf
Agra 15 Cg
Agreb, El– 24 Ca
Agrigento 10 Df
Agrinion 11 Dd
Agropoli 10 Ed
Agryz 12 Hb
Aguas Blancas 39 ABb
Aguascalientes 34 Bb
Águilas 9 Ed
Aguja, Punta– (cap.) 37 Ac
Agulhas, Cape– 26 ABe
Agulhas Negras, Pico das– (mt.) 39 Db
Ahaggar (mts.) 24 Cb
Ahar 21 Db
Ahmadabad 15 Cg
Ahmadî, Al– 21 Dd
Ahmadnagar 20 DEe
Ahmar (hist. reg.) 25 Dc
Ahtopol 11 GHb
Ahtuba (riv.) 13 De
Ahtubinsk 3 Hc
Ahtyrka 12 Ec
Ahuachapán 35 ABb
Ahunui Atoll 28 Bc
Åhus 5 Ea
Ahvāz 21 Dc
Ahvenanmaa / Åland (is.) 4 DEc
Ahwar 21 Dg
Aigoual, Mont– (mt.) 8 Ee
Aigues (riv.) 8 Fe
Aihui 16 Ga
Aim 14 Gd
Aimorés 39 Da
Ain (riv.) 8 Fd
Ainaži 4 EFd
Aïn–Beni Mathar 24 Ba
Aïn–Defla 9 FGd
Aineman Atoll 28 map no.3
Aïn–Sefra 24 BCa
Aïn–Témouchent 24 Ba
Aiquile 39 Ba
Aïr (mt.) 24 Cc
Aitutaki Atoll 28 ABc
Aiud 6 Fc
Aix–en–Provence 8 FGf
Aix–les–Bains 8 FGe
Aiyion 11 Ed
Aizawl 19 Bd
Aizpute 4 Ed
Aizuwakamatsu 16 IJc
Ajaccio 8 map no.1
Ajaccio, Golfe d'– 8 map no.1
Ajaguz 13 GHe
Ajan 14 Gd

Ajanta (r.) 20 Ed
Ajdābiyā 24 DEa
Ajhal 14 Ec
Ajigasawa 17 FGd
Ajka 6 Cc
'Ajlūn 22 EFf
Ajmer 20 Dc
Ajon, ostrov– (i.) 14 Jbc
Ajtos 11 Gb
Akademgorodok, Novosibirsk– 13 GHd
Akan 17 Hlc
Akanthoú 22 De
Akapatok Island 31 lb
Akashi 17 Dg
Akbulak 12 Ic
Akçakoca 22 Cb
Akchar (hist. reg.) 24 Abc
Akdağ [Tur.] (mt.) 22 Bd
Akdağ [Tur.] (mt.) 22 Eb
Akdağ [Tur.] (mt.) 22 Ed
Akdağ [Tur.] (mt.) 22 BCc
Aketi 25 Cd
Akhḍar, Al Jabal al– (mts.) 24 Ea
Akhdar, Gebel al– (mt.) 21 Fe
Akheloos (riv.) 11 Dd
Akhisar 22 ABc
Aki 17 CDh
Akimiski Island 31 GHc
Akita 16 IJc
Akjoujt 24 Abc
Akkajaure (l.) 4 Db
Akkeshi 17 Ic
'Akko 22 Ef
Akköy 11 Ge
Aklavik 31 Bb
Akmola (Celinograd) 13 Gd
Akobo 25 Dd
Akola 20 Ed
Akranes 4 map no.1
Akritas, Ákra– 11 De
Akron 32 Ca
Akrotiri 22 De
Akrotíri, Kersónisos– 11 Ff
Aksaj 12 Hc
Aksaray 22 DEc
Akşehir 22 Cc
Akşehir Gölü 22 CDc
Akseki 22 CDd
Aksenovo–Zilovskoje 14 Ed
Aksoran, gora– (mt.) 13 Gde
Aksu [China] 13 He
Aksu [Kaz.] 13 Gd
Aktaš 13 Hd
Aktau (Ševčenko) 13 Ee
Aktjubinsk 13 Ede
Aktogaj 13 Ge
Akureyri 4 map no.1
Akyab → Sittwe 19 Bde
Alabama (riv.) 32 Cb
Alabama (State) 32 Cb
Alaca 22 Eb
Alacahan 22 FGc
Alacrán, Arrecife– (rf.) 34 CDb
Ala Dağ (mt.) 22 Dcd
Ala dağları (mts.) 22 Ed
Alagoas (State) 38 Db
Alagoinhas 38 Dc
Alagón 9 Eb
Alagón (riv.) 9 Bbc
Alajuela 35 Bbc

© ISTITUTO GEOGRAFICO DE AGOSTINI S.p.A. - Novara

Arcos de la Frontera **9** BCd
Arctic Bay **31** Ga
Arda (riv.) **11** Fc
Ardabīl **21** Db
Ardakān **21** Ec
Ardatov **12** Gc
Arderin (mt.) **7** BCe
Ardestān **21** Ec
Ardmore **32** Bb
Ardrossan **7** Dd
Arecibo **35** Db
Areia Branca **38** Db
Arendal **4** Bd
Arequipa **39** Aa
Arévalo **9** Cb
Arezzo **10** Cc
Argens (riv.) **8** Gf
Argentan **8** CDc
Argentat **8** Ee
Argenteuil **8** Ec
Argentina (Ind. St.) **36** Dgh
Argentino, Lago- **40** Abc
Argenton-sur-Creuse **8** Dd
Argeş (riv.) **6** GHd
Arghandab (riv.) **20** Cb
Argolis, Gulf of- **11** Ee
Argonne (mts.) **8** Fc
Árgos **11** Ee
Argostólion **11** Dd
Argun (riv.) **16** Ea
Arhangelsk **3** Ha
Århus **4** Bd
Ariano Irpino **10** Ed
Ari Atoll **20** Dh
Arica [Chile] **39** Aa
Arica [Col.] **37** Bc
Arica, Golfo de- **39** Aa
Arid, Cape- **29** Ce
Ariège (riv.) **8** Df
Arima **37** Ca
Arinos (riv.) **38** Bc
Aripuanã (riv.) **37** CDc
Aripuanã **37** CDc
Ariquemes **37** Ccd
'Arīsh, Al- **25** Da
'Arīsh, Wādī al- (riv.) **22** Dgh
Arizaro, Salar de- (s. m.) **39** Bb
Arizona (State) **33** Bc
Arjeplog **4** Db
Arjona **37** Bab
Arkadak **12** Fc
Arkalyk **13** Fde
Arkansas (riv.) **33** Cc
Arkansas (State) **32** Bb
Arkansas City **32** Bb
Arklow **7** CDe
Arkona, Kap- **5** Da
Arkonam **20** EFf
Arkticeskoga Instituta, ostrova- **13** GHb
Arlberg (p.) **5** Ce
Arles **8** Ff
Arlon **8** Fc
Armagh **7** Cd
Armagnac (hist. reg.) **8** Df
Armavir **13** De
Armenia **37** Bb
Armenia (Ind. St.) **13** Def
Armentières **8** Eb
Armidale **29** Ie
Armu (riv.) **17** DEab
Arnauti, Akra- **22** CDe
Arnedillo **9** DEa
Arnhem **8** FGb
Arnhem, Cape- **29** Fa
Arnhem Land **29** Ea
Arno (riv.) **10** Cc
Arnøy (i.) **4** DEa
Arnsberg **5** Bc
Arnstadt **5** Cc
Aroa **37** Ca
Aroab **26** ABd
Arorae Island **27** Dc
Ar-Rachidiya **24** Ba
Arrah **20** Fc
Arraias **38** Cc
Arraiján **35** map no.1
Arran, Island of- **7** Dd
Arras **8** Eb
Arrée, Monts d'- (mts.) **8** ABc
Arsenjev **14** Ge
Arsenjevka (riv.) **17** Cbc
Arsuk **31** JKb
Art (i.) **28** map no.4
Árta **11** Dd
Artá **9** Gc
Artawiyah, Al- **21** Dd
Artem **14** Ge
Artemisa **35** Ba
Artemovsk [Russia] **14** Cd
Artemovsk [Ukr.] **12** Ed
Artemovski [Russia] **12** Jb
Artemovski [Russia] **14** Ed
Artic Ocean **41** grid square no.4
Artigas **39** Cc
Artois (hist. reg.) **8** DEb
Aru, Kepulauan- **27** Bc
Arua **26** Ca
Aruanã **39** CDa
Aruba (i.) **37** Ca
Arumã **37** Cc
Arunachal Pradesh (State) **19** BCc
Arusha **26** Cb
Aruwimi (riv.) **26** Ba
Arvida **31** Hd
Arvidsjaur **4** Db
Arvika **4** Cd
Arys **13** Fe
Arzamas **13** Dd
Arzgir **12** Fd
Aša **12** Ib
Asadābād **20** CDab
Asahikawa **16** Jb
Asamankese **24** Bd
Asansol **20** Gd
Asbest **13** Fd
Ascension (i.) **23** Af
Aschaffenburg **5** Bd
Ascó **9** Fb
Ascoli Piceno **10** Dc
Aseb **25** Ec
Åsele **4** Db
Asenovgrad **11** Fbc
Ašgabat **15** Bf
Ashburton River **29** Bc
Asheville **32** Cb
Ashibetsu **16** Jb
Ashikaga **16** Ic
Ashington **7** EFd
Ashizuri-Misaki **17** Ch
Ashkharah, Al- **21** FGe
Ashland [Ky.-U.S.] **32** Cb
Ashland [Wi.-U.S.] **32** BCa
Ashmūn **22** Cg
Ashqelon **22** Eg
Ashuanipi **31** Ic
Asinara **10** Bd
Asinara, Golfo dell'- **10** Bd
Asino **13** Hd
'Asīr (hist. reg.) **21** Cef
Asker **4** Bd
Askersund **4** Cd
Askja (mt.) **4** map no.1
Asmara **25** Dc
Asnam, El- **24** BCa
Asosa **25** Dcd
Aso-San (mt.) **17** Bh
Asoteriba, Jabal- (mt.) **25** Db
Aspres-sur-Buëch **8** Fe
Aspromonte (mts.) **10** Ee
Assam (State) **19** BCc
Assen **8** Ga
Assens **5** BCa
Assiniboia **33** Cb
Assiniboine (riv.) **33** Cab
Assis **39** Cb
Assisi **10** Dc
Astakós **11** Dd
Astara **21** Db
Asti **10** Bb
Astipálata (i.) **11** Ge
Astorga **9** BCa
Astoria **33** Ab
Astrahan **13** De
Asturias (phys. reg.) **9** BCa
Asunción **39** Cb
Asunción, La- **37** Ca
Aswān **25** Db
Asyût **25** CDb
Atacama, Desierto de- **39** ABb
Atacama, Salar de- (sal. l.) **39** Bb
Atafu Atoll **28** Ac
Ata Island **28** Ad
Atakpamé **24** Cd
Atalándi **11** Ed
Atalaya **37** Bd
Atami **17** Fg
Ataqa, Jabal- (mt.) **25** map no.1
Atar **24** Abc
Atasu **13** Ge
Atauat, Phou- (mt.) **19** Ee
Atauro, Pulau- (i.) **18** Gf
Atáviros (mt.) **11** GHe
'Aṭbarah **25** Dc
'Aṭbarah (riv.) **25** Dc
Atbasar **13** Fd
Atchinson **32** Bb
Aterau (Gurjev) **13** DEe
Atessa **10** Ec
Athabasca (riv.) **31** Dc
Athabasca **31** Dc
Athabasca, Lake- **31** Ec
Athenry **7** Be
Athens [Ga.-U.S.] **32** Cb
Athens [Grc.] **11** EFe
Atherton **29** GHb
Athi Galana **26** Cb
Athlone **7** BCe
Áthos (mt.) **11** Fc
Ati **25** Bc
Atico **39** Aa
Atikokan **32** Ba
Atiu (i.) **28** Bcd
Atka **14** Ic
Atkarsk **12** FGc
Atlanta **32** Cb
Atlantic City **32** Db
Atlantic Ocean **2**
Atlin, Lake- **31** Bc
Atlixco **34** Cc
Atoyac, Río- (riv.) **34** Cc
Atoyac de Álvarez **34** Bc
Atrato (riv.) **37** Bb
Atrek (riv.) **21** Fb
'Aṭrun, Al- **25** Cc
Atsumi **17** Fe
Attapu **19** Eef
Attawapiskat (riv.) **31** Db
Attica (hist. reg.) **11** Ed
Atuel (riv.) **39** Bc
Aubagne **8** FGf
Aube (riv.) **8** Fc
Aubenas **8** Fe
Aubrac, Monts d'- (mts.) **8** Ee
Aubusson **8** Ee
Aucanquilcha, Cerro- (mt.) **39** Bb
Auch **8** Df
Auckland **27** Dd
Auckland Islands **27** De
Auckland Peninsula **27** Dd
Aude (riv.) **8** Ef
Audincourt **8** Gd
Aue **5** Dc
Augathella **29** Hd
Augila **24** Eb
Augsburg **5** Cd
Augusta [Austl.] **29** ABe
Augusta [Ga.-U.S.] **32** Cb
Augusta [It.] **10** Ef
Augusta [Me.-U.S.] **32** Ea
Augustów **5** Ib
Augustus, Mount- **29** Bc
Auki **27** Dc
Auld, Lake- **29** Cc
Aumale **8** Dc
Aunis (hist. reg.) **8** Cd
Aurangabad **20** DEde
Aur Atoll **27** Db
Aurillac **8** Ee
Aus **26** Ad
Ausangate, Nudo- (mt.) **39** ABa
Austin [Mn.-U.S.] **32** Ba
Austin [Nv.-U.S.] **33** Bc
Austin [Tx.-U.S.] **32** Bb
Austin, Lake- **29** Bd
Australia (Ind. St.) **29** CGd
Australian Alps **29** Hf
Australian Capital Territory (State) **29** Hf
Australian Capital Territory → A.C.T. **29** Hf
Austria (Ind. St.) **3** Ec
Austvågøy (i.) **4** Ca
Autlán de Navarro **34** Bc
Autun **8** EFd
Auvergne (hist. reg.) **8** Ee
Auxerre **8** Ee
Avallon **8** EFd
Avalon Peninsula **31** JKd
Avanos **22** Ec
Avarua **28** Bd
Aveiro **9** Ab
Avellino **10** Ed

© ISTITUTO GEOGRAFICO DE AGOSTINI S.p.A. - Novara

Bandiagara **24** Bc
Bandikui **19** Gi
Bandırma **22** ABb
Bandundu **26** Ab
Bandundu (reg.) **26** ABb
Bandung **15** Dj
Băneasa **6** Hd
Banes **35** Ca
Bañeza, La– **9** BCa
Banff [Can.] **31** Dc
Banff [U.K.] **7** Ec
Bangalore **15** Ch
Bangassou **25** Cd
Banggai (i.) **18** Fe
Banggai, Kepulauan– **18** Fe
Banggi, Pulau– (i.) **18** Ec
Bangil **18** Df
Bangka, Pulau– [Indon.] (i.) **18** FGd
Bangka, Pulau– [Indon.] (i.) **18** Ce
Bangkalan **18** Df
Bangkinang **18** ABd
Bangko **18** Be
Bangkok **15** Dh
Bangladesh (Ind. St.) **15** CDg
Bangor [N. Ire.–U.K.] **7** Dd
Bangor [U.S.] **32** DEa
Bangor [Wales–U.K.] **7** DEe
Bangriposi **19** Ik
Bangued **18** Fa
Bangui [C.A.R.] **25** Bd
Bangui [Phil.] **18** EFa
Bangweulu, Lake– **26** BCc
Banhā **22** Cg
Bani (riv.) **24** Bc
Banī Suwayf **25** Db
Banī Walīd **24** Da
Bāniyās **22** EFe
Banja Luka **6** Cd
Banjarmasin **18** De
Banjul **24** Ac
Banks, Îles– **28** map no.4
Banks Island **31** CDa
Banks Strait **29** map no.1
Bankura **20** Gd
Ban Mae Sariang **19** Ce
Bann (riv.) **7** Cd
Bannu **20** CDb
Banská Bystrica **5** GHd
Banská Stiavnica **5** Gd
Bansko **11** Ec
Bantaeng **18** Ef
Bantry **7** Bf
Bantry Bay **7** ABf
Banyak Islands **18** Ad
Banyuwangi **18** Df
Banzare Coast **42** grid square no.4
Bao'an **16** Df
Baoding **16** DEc
Baoji **15** Df
Baoshan **19** Ccd
Baotou **16** CDb
Baquedano **39** Bb
Bar [Ukr.] **6** Hb
Bar [Yugo.] **11** Cb
Baraawe **25** Ed
Barabinsk **13** GHd
Baracaldo **9** Da
Baracoa **35** Ca
Baradero **39** BCc
Bărăganului, Cîmpia– **6** Hd
Barahona **35** Cb
Baraka (riv.) **25** Dc
Baraki **20** Cb
Baramula **20** DEb
Baranof Island **31** Bc
Baranoviči **13** Bd
Barat Daya, Kepulauan– **18** Gf
Barbacena **39** Db
Barbacoas **37** Bb
Barbados (i.) **35** Db
Barbados (Ind. St.) **30** Lh
Barbar **25** Dc
Barbas, Cabo– **24** Ab
Barbastro **9** Fa
Barbezieux **8** CDe
Barbuda (i.) **35** Db
Barcaldine **29** GHc
Barce → Al Marj **24** DEa
Barcellona **10** Ee
Barcelona [Sp.] **9** Gb
Barcelona [Ven.] **37** Cab
Barcelonnette **8** FGe
Barcelos [Braz.] **37** Cc
Barcelos [Port.] **9** Ab
Barcoo River **29** Gcd
Barcs **6** Ccd
Bardaï **25** Bb
Bardawīl, Sabkhet el–(l.)**22** Dg
Bardejov **5** Hd
Bardiyah **24** Ea
Bareeda **25** Fc
Bareilly **20** EFc
Barentsburg **13** Ab
Barents Sea **41** grid square no.3
Barentù **21** Bfg
Barfleur, Pointe de–(cap.)**8** Cc
Barga **20** Fb
Barhi **20** Gd
Bari **10** Fd
Barīm **25** Ec
Barima (riv.) **37** Db
Barinas **37** BCb
Baripada **19** Ik
Barisal **20** GHd
Barisan, Pegunungan– **18** Be
Barito (riv.) **18** Df
Barka **21** Fe
Barkam **16** Bd
Barkly Tableland **29** Fb
Barkol **14** Cf
Barla dağı (mt.) **22** Ccd
Bar–le–Duc **8** Fc
Barlee, Lake– **29** Bd
Barletta **10** Fd
Barmer **20** Dc
Barnaul **13** Hd
Barnstaple **7** Df
Baro **24** Cd
Barqah al Bahrīyah (phys. reg.) **24** Ea
Barquisimeto **37** BCab
Barra **38** Cc
Barra (is.) **7** BCc
Barrackpur **19** Jk
Barra de Navidad **34** Bc
Barra do Bugres **39** Ca
Barra do Garças **39** Ca
Barra do São Manuel **38** Bb
Barra Head **7** BCc
Barrancabermeja **37** Bb
Barrancas **37** Cb
Barranquilla **36** Cb
Barreiras **38** Cc
Barreiro **9** Ac
Barreiros **38** Db
Barretos **39** Db
Barrie **31** GHd
Barrington Tops (mt.) **29** Ie
Barrow **30** CDb
Barrow (riv.) **7** Ce
Barrow, Point– **41** grid square no.2
Barrow Creek **29** Ec
Barrow–in–Furness **7** Ed
Barrow Island **29** ABc
Barruecopardo **9** Bb
Barry **7** Ef
Barsi **20** Ee
Barstow **33** Bc
Bar–sur–Aube **8** Fc
Barth **5** Da
Bartica **37** Db
Bartin **22** Db
Bartle Frere, Mount– **29** Hb
Bartoszyce **5** Ha
Barun–Urt **14** Ee
Barwon River **29** Hde
Baryš **12** Gc
Basankusu **25** BCd
Bas–Congo (reg.) **26** Ab
Basel **5** Ae
Bashi Haixia (str.) **16** Ff
Bashkir (Aut. Rep.) **13** Ed
Basilan (i.) **18** Fc
Basilan City **18** Fc
Basilicata (reg.) **10** EFde
Basilio **39** Cc
Basoko **25** Cd
Basque Provinces (phys. reg.) **9** Da
Basra **21** Dc
Bass, Îlots de– **28** BCd
Bassano del Grappa **10** Cb
Bassein **15** Dh
Basseterre **35** Db
Bass Strait **29** map no.1
Bastak **21** EFd
Basti **19** Hj
Bastia **8** map no.1
Bastogne **8** FGbc
Basuto **26** Bc
Bata **24** CDd
Batabanó, Golfo de– **35** Ba
Batagaj **14** Gc
Batajsk **12** EFd
Batak **11** Fc
Batala **20** Eb
Batan (i.) **18** Fa
Batang **15** Df
Batanga **24** Ce
Batangafo **25** Bd
Batangas **18** EFb
Batanghari (riv.) **18** Be
Batan Islands **15** Eg
Batanta, Pulau– (i.) **18** GHe
Batapažinsk (Čerkessk) **13** De
Batchelor **29** Ea
Bătdâmbâng **19** Df
Bath **7** Ef
Bathinda **20** DEb
Bathurst [Austl.] **29** He
Bathurst [Can.] **31** Id
Bathurst, Cape– **31** BCa
Bathurst Inlet **31** DEb
Bathurst Island [Austl.] **29** Da
Bathurst Island [Can.] **30** HIb
Bāţin, Wādī al– **21** Dd
Batna **24** Ca
Baton Rouge **32** BCb
Batopilas **34** Bb
Batouri **24** Dd
Batrūn, Al– **22** Ee
Batticaloa **20** Fg
Battle Harbour **30** Md
Battonya **6** Ec
Batu, Kepulauan– **18** Ade
Batudaka, Pulau– (i.) **18** Fe
Batumi **21** Ca
Baturaja **18** BCe
Baturité **38** Db
Bau **18** Dd
Baubau **18** Ff
Bauchi **24** CDcd
Baudh **16** Cf
Bauld, Cape– **31** Jc
Baule–Escoublac, La– **8** Bd
Bauru **39** Db
Bautzen **5** Ec
Bavaria (State) **5** CDd
Bawean, Pulau– (i.) **18** Df
Bawīţī, Al– **25** CDb
Bayamo **35** Ca
Bayamón **35** Db
Bayana **19** Gj
Bayan Har Shan (mts.) **16** ABd
Bayan Obo **16** CDb
Bayawan **18** Fc
Baybay **18** FGb
Bayburt **21** Ca
Bay City [Mi.–U.S.] **32** Ca
Bay City [Tx.–U.S.] **32** Bc
Bayḑā', Al– **24** DEa
Bayerischer Wald (mts.) **5** Dd
Bayeux **8** Cc
Bayındır **22** Ac
Bayombong **18** Fa
Bayonne **8** Cf
Bayreuth **5** Ccd
Baza **9** Dd
Beagle, Canal– **40** Ac
Beal Range **29** Gcd
Beardmore Glacier **42** grid square no.4
Bear Island **41** grid square no.3
Béarn (hist. reg.) **8** Cf
Beas (riv.) **20** DEb
Beatrice **32** Ba
Beatty **33** Bc
Beauce (phys. reg.) **8** DEc
Beaudesert **29** Id
Beaufort **18** Ec
Beaufort Sea **41** grid square no.2
Beaufort West **26** Be
Beaujolais, Monts du– (mts.) **8** Fde
Beaumont **32** Bb
Beaune **8** Fd
Beauvais **8** Ec
Beawar **20** Dc
Bečej **6** DEd
Béchar **24** Ba
Beckley **32** Cb
Bedford **7** FGe

© ISTITUTO GEOGRAFICO DE AGOSTINI S.p.A. - Novara

Bedourie **29** Fc
Be'er Sheva **22** Eg
Beeville **32** Bc
Befale **26** Ba
Bega **29** Hlf
Bègles **8** Ce
Behbahān **21** Ec
Behshahr **21** Eb
Beihai **16** Cf
Beijing (Peking) **16** Ebc
Beira (hist. reg.) **9** ABb
Beira **26** Cc
Beirut **22** Ef
Bei Shan (mts.) **16** Ab
Beitbridge **26** Cd
Beiuş **6** EFc
Beja **9** Bcd
Béjaïa **24** Ca
Béjar **9** Cb
Bejneu **13** Ee
Békés **6** Ec
Békéscsaba **6** Ec
Bekily **26** map no.1
Bela [India] **20** Fc
Bela [Pak.] **20** Cc
Bela Crkva **6** Ed
Belaja (riv.) **13** Ed
Belaja Cerkov **6** IJb
Bel'an **16** Ga
Belarus (Ind. St.) **13** BCd
Bela Vista **39** Cb
Belcher Islands **31** GHc
Belebej **12** Hc
Beledweyne **25** Ed
Belém **38** Cb
Belen **33** Cc
Belén **39** Bb
Belene **11** Fb
Bélep, Iles- **27** Dc
Belev **12** Ec
Belfast **7** Dd
Belfort **8** Gd
Belgaum **20** De
Belgium (Ind. St.) **3** Db
Belgorod **13** Cd
Belgorod-Dnestrovski **6** IJc
Belgrade **6** Ed
Belgrade-Zemun **6** Ed
Bélinga **26** Aa
Belitung, Pulau- (i.) **15** Dj
Belize (Ind. St.) **30** Jh
Belize City **35** Bb
Belkovski, ostrov- **14** Gb
Bellac **8** Dd
Bellary **20** Eef
Bellavista **37** Bc
Bella Vista [Arg.] **39** Cb
Bella Vista [Arg.] **39** Bb
Belle Fourche **33** Cb
Bellegarde-sur-Valserine **8** FGde
Belle-Ile (i.) **8** Bd
Belle Isle (i.) **31** Jc
Belle Isle, Strait of- **31** IJcd
Belleville **31** Hd
Bellin (Payne Bay) **31** HIbc
Bellingham **33** Ab
Bellingshausen **42** grid square no.1
Bellingshausen Sea **42** grid square no.1
Bellinzona **10** Ba
Belluno **10** Da
Bell Ville **39** Bc
Belmonte **38** Dc
Belmopan **35** Bb
Belo **26** map no.1
Belogorsk **14** FGd
Belo Horizonte **39** Dab
Beloje ozero **12** Ea
Belomorsk **13** Cc
Belopolje **12** DEc
Beloreck **13** EFd
Belovo **13** Hd
Belozersk **12** Eab
Belterra **38** Bb
Beluha, gora- (mt.) **13** Hde
Bely, ostrov- **13** FGb
Belyando River **29** Hc
Bely Jar **13** Hd
Bemidji **32** Ba
Benalla **29** Hf
Benares → Varanasi **20** Fcd
Benavente **9** BCab
Benbecula (i.) **7** BCc
Bend **33** Ab
Bender Beyla **25** Fd
Bendery → Tighina **6** Ic
Bendigo **29** GHf
Benešov **5** Ed
Benevento **10** Ed
Bengal (phys. reg.) **20** Gd
Bengal, Bay of- **20** Gef
Bengasi **24** DEa
Bengbu **16** Ed
Bengkulu **18** Be
Benguela **23** Dg
Benguerir **24** Ba
Ben Hope (mt.) **7** Db
Beni (riv.) **37** Cd
Beni-Abbès **24** Bab
Benicarló **9** Fb
Benidorm **9** Fc
Benin (Ind. St.) **23** Cde
Benin, Bight of- **24** Cd
Benin City **24** Cd
Benjamin Constant **37** BCc
Ben Macdhui (mt.) **7** DEc
Ben More Assynt (mt.) **7** Db
Bennet, ostrov- **14** Hb
Ben Nevis (mt.) **7** Dc
Benoni **26** Bd
Bensheim **5** Bd
Benson **33** BCc
Bent **21** Fd
Benteng **18** Ff
Bentinck (i.) **19** Cf
Bentinck Island **29** FGb
Benue (riv.) **24** Cd
Benxi **16** Fb
Beppu **17** Bh
Berati **11** CDc
Berbera **25** Ec
Berberati **25** Bd
Berbice (riv.) **37** Db
Berchtesgaden **5** De
Berck-Plage **8** Db
Berčogur **12** Id
Berdičev **12** Ccd
Berdjansk **12** Ed
Beregomet **6** Gb
Beregovo **5** Id
Berenice (r.) **25** Db
Bereza **5** Jb
Berežany **6** Gb
Berezina (riv.) **12** Cc
Berezniki **13** Ed
Berezovka **12** Dd
Berezovo **13** Fc
Berga **9** Fa
Bergama (Pergamum) **22** Ac
Bergamo **10** Bb
Bergen **4** Ac
Bergen (Rügen) **5** Da
Bergerac **8** De
Berhampur **20** FGe
Beringa, ostrov- **14** Jd
Beringovski **14** Kc
Bering Sea **41** grid square no.2
Bering Strait **41** grid square no.2
Berit dağı (mt.) **22** Fcd
Berja **9** Dd
Berkeley **33** Ac
Berkner Island **42** grid square no.1
Berkovica **11** Eb
Berlengas, Ilhas- **9** Ac
Berlin [Ger.] **5** DEb
Berlin [U.S.] **32** Da
Bermejo **39** Bb
Bermejo, Río- [Arg.] (riv.) **39** Bbc
Bermejo, Río- [Bol.] (riv.) **39** Bb
Bermeo **9** Da
Bermuda Islands **30** Lf
Bern **5** Ae
Bernalda **10** Fd
Bernardo de Irigoyen **39** Cb
Bernay **8** Dc
Bernburg **5** CDc
Berner Alpen **10** ABa
Bernina (mt.) **10** Ba
Beroroha **26** map no.1
Beroun **5** Ed
Berounka (riv.) **5** Dcd
Berre, Étang de- (sw.) **8** Ff
Berre-l'Étang **8** Ff
Berrouaghia **9** Gd
Berry (hist. reg.) **8** DEd
Berry, Canal de- **8** Ed
Bertolínia **38** Cb
Bertoua **24** Dd
Berwick-upon-Tweed **7** EFd
Besalampy **26** map no.1
Besançon **8** Gd
Beskidy Zachodnie (mts.) **5** GHd
Besna Kobila (mt.) **11** Eb
Besni **22** Fd
Bessarabia (phys. reg.) **6** HIbc
Bessarabka **6** Ic
Bessemer **32** Cb
Betanzos [Bol.] **39** Ba
Betanzos [Sp.] **9** ABa
Bétaré Oya **24** Dd
Bethanien **26** Ad
Bethel **30** Bc
Bethlehem [Jor.] **22** Eg
Bethlehem [S. Afr.] **26** Bd
Béthune **8** Eb
Béticos, Sistema- (mts.) **9** CEcd
Betioky **26** map no.1
Betpak-Dala **13** FGe
Betroka **26** map no.1
Bet She'an **22** Ef
Betsiboka (riv.) **26** map no.1
Bettiah **19** HIj
Bettyhill **7** Fe
Betul **20** Ed
Betwa (riv.) **20** Ec
Beverley [Austl.] **29** Be
Beverley [U.K.] **7** FGe
Beycuma **22** CDb
Bey dağı (mt.) **22** EFc
Bey dağları (mts.) **22** BCd
Beyla **24** Bd
Beyoneisu-Retsugan **17** Fi
Beypazarı **22** CDb
Beyşehir **22** CDd
Beyşehir Gölü **22** Cd
Bežeck **12** Eb
Béziers **8** Ef
Bhabua **19** Hj
Bhadgaon **20** Gc
Bhadrak **20** Gd
Bhadravati **20** Ef
Bhagalpur **15** CDg
Bhamo **19** Cd
Bharatpur **20** Ec
Bharuch **20** Dd
Bhatpara **20** Gd
Bhavnagar **20** Dd
Bhawanipatna **20** Fe
Bheri (riv.) **19** Hi
Bhilai **20** Fd
Bhima (riv.) **20** DEe
Bhind **20** Ec
Bhiwani **19** Gi
Bhola (i.) **19** Jk
Bhopal **20** Ed
Bhubaneswar **20** FGde
Bhuj **20** Cd
Bhusawal **20** Ed
Bhutan (Ind. St.) **15** Dg
Biafra (phys. reg.) **24** Cd
Biafra, Bight of- **24** Ccd
Biak, Pulau- **27** Bc
Biała Podlaska **5** Ibc
Białobrzegi **5** Hc
Białogard **5** Fab
Białystok **5** Ib
Biarritz **8** Cf
Bibā **22** Ch
Bibai **17** Gc
Biberach an der Riss **5** BCde
Bicaz **6** GHc
Biçer **22** Cc
Bickerton Island **29** Fa
Bida **24** Cd
Bidar **20** Ee
Bideford **7** Df
Bidon 5 → Poste-Maurice-Cortier **24** Cb
Bié, Planalto do- **26** Ac
Biel **5** Ae
Bielawa **5** Fc
Bielefeld **5** Bbc
Biella **10** Bb
Bielsko-Biała **5** Gd
Bielsk Podlaski **5** Ib
Bien Hoa **19** Ef
Biga **22** Ab
Biğadiç **22** Bc
Biggar **33** Ca
Bighorn (riv.) **33** Cb

© ISTITUTO GEOGRAFICO DE AGOSTINI S.p.A. - Novara

Bighorn Mountains **33** Cb
Big Island **31** Hb
Big River **31** Ec
Big Spring **33** Cc
Bihać **6** Bd
Bihar (State) **20** FGc
Bihar **20** Gcd
Biharamulo **26** Cb
Bihoro **17** Ic
Bija (riv.) **13** Hd
Bijagos Islands **24** Ac
Bijapur **20** Ee
Bijauri **19** Hi
Bijeljina **6** Dd
Bijie **16** Ce
Bijsk **13** Hd
Bikaner **20** Dc
Bikin (riv.) **16** Hla
Bikin **14** Ge
Bikini Atoll **27** Db
Bikljan **12** Hb
Bikoro **26** Ab .
Bilaspur **20** Fd
Bilauktaung Range **19** Cf
Bilbao **9** Da
Bilbays **22** Cg
Bileća **11** Cb
Bilecik **22** BCb
Bilé Karpaty (mts.) **5** FGd
Bilin **19** Ce
Billings **33** Cb
Bill of Portland **7** EFf
Bilma **24** Dc
Biloela **29** Hlc
Bilo gora (mts.) **6** Ccd
Biloxi **32** Cb
Biltine **25** Cc
Bina **20** Ed
Binalud, Kuh– e– (mt.) **21** Fb
Binboğa dağ (mts.) **22** Fcd
Bingen **5** ABcd
Binghamton **32** Da
Bingöl **21** Cb
Binhai **16** EFd
Binjai **18** Ad
Binongko, Pulau– (i.) **18** Ff
Bintuhan **18** Be
Bintulu **18** Dd
Bio Bío, Río– (riv.) **39** Ac
Biograd na Moru **6** Bde
Bioko **24** Cd
Biqâ', Al– (phys. reg.) **22** EFef
Bi'r, Al– **21** Bd
Birāk **24** Db
Bi'r al Wa'r **24** Db
Birao **25** Ccd
Biratnagar **19** Ij
Bîr Damdûm **22** Ag
Birdsville **29** FGd
Birdum **29** Eb
Birecik **22** Gd
Bireuen **18** Ac
Birganj **20** FGc
Birjand **21** FGc
Birjusa (riv.) **14** Cd
Birk, Al– **21** Cf
Birkenhead **7** Ee
Bîrlad **6** Hlc
Bîrlad (riv.) **6** Hcd
Birmingham [U.K.] **7** Fe
Birmingham [U.S.] **32** Cb
Birmitrapur **19** Ik

Birnin Kebbi **24** Cc
Birni Nkonni **24** Cc
Birobidžan **14** Ge
Birpur **19** Ij
Birr **7** BCe
Bi'r Safâjah **25** Db
Birsk **13** Ed
Bîr Tarfâwi **25** Cb
Biržai **4** Fd
Bisa, Pulau– (i.) **18** Ge
Bisbee **33** BCc
Biscay, Bay of– **8** BCef
Bisceglie **10** Fd
Bischofshofen **5** De
Bishah, Wâdî– **21** Cf
Bishnupur **19** Ik
Biškek (Frunze) **13** Ge
Biskra **24** Ca
Bismarck **33** CDb
Bismarck Archipelago **27** Cc
Bissau **24** Ac
Bissett **31** Fc
Bistriţa **6** Gc
Bistriţa (riv.) **6** Gc
Bitam **24** Dd
Bitlis **21** Cb
Bitola **11** Dc
Bitonto **10** Fd
Bitterfontein **23** Di
Bitterroot Range **33** Bb
Biu **24** Dc
Biwa–Ko **16** Ic
Biyad, Al– (phys. reg.) **21** De
Biyalā **22** Cg
Bizerte **24** CDa
Bjala Slatina **11** Eb
Bjargtangar (cap.) **4** map no.1
Bjelovar **6** Ccd
Bjerkreim **4** Ad
Bjuröklubb (cap.) **4** Eb
Blackall **29** Hc
Blackburn **7** Ee
Black Forest (mts.) **5** ABde
Black Hills **33** Cb
Blackpool **7** Ee
Black River **19** Dd
Black Sea **13** Ce
Black Volta (riv.) **24** Bcd
Blackwater (riv.) **7** Be
Blackwood River **29** Be
Blagodarny **12** Fd
Blagojevgrad **11** Ebc
Blagoveščensk [Russia] **14** FGd
Blagoveščensk [Russia] **12** Hlb
Blair Athol **29** Hc
Blaj **6** FGc
Blanc, Cap– [Mtna.] **24** Ab
Blanc, Cap– [Tun.] **24** CDa
Blanc, Le– **8** Dd
Blanc, Mont– **10** Ab
Blanca, Bahía– (b.) **39** BCcd
Blanca, Cordillera– (mts.) **37** Bc
Blanca, Costa– **9** Ec
Blanca Peak **33** Cc
Blanche, Lake– **29** FGd
Blanco, Cape– **33** Ab
Blanc–Sablon **31** IJc
Blanquilla, Isla– (i.) **35** Db
Blantyre **26** Cc
Blåvands Huk (cap.) **5** ABa

Blaye **8** Ce
Bloemfontein **23** Eh
Blois **8** Dd
Błonie **5** Hb
Bluefield **32** Cb
Bluefields **35** Bb
Blue Mountains **33** Bb
Blue Nile **25** Dc
Blue Ridge **32** Cb
Blumenau **39** Db
Blyth **7** Fd
Blythe **33** Bc
Blytheville **32** BCb
Bo **24** Ad
Boac **18** Fb
Bo'ai **16** Dc
Boano, Pulau– (i.) **18** Ge
Boa Vista **37** Cb
Bobbio **10** Bb
Bobo Dioulasso **24** Bc
Bóbr (riv.) **5** Ec
Bobriki (Novomoskovsk) **13** CDd
Bobrka **6** Gb
Bobrujsk **13** BCd
Bôca do Acre **37** Cc
Bôca do Jari **38** Bb
Bôca do Moaco **37** Cc
Boca Grande (riv. m.) **37** CDb
Bocas del Toro **35** Bc
Bochnia **5** Hd
Bocholt **5** Ac
Bochum **5** Ac
Bocşa **6** Ed
Böda **4** Dd
Bodajbo **14** Ed
Bodélé (phys. reg.) **25** Ac
Boden **4** Eb
Bodmin **7** Df
Bodø **4** Cb
Bodrum **22** ABd
Boende **25** Cde
Boffa **24** Acd
Bogalusa **32** BCb
Bogan River **29** He
Bogatynia **5** Ec
Boğazlıyan **22** Ec
Bogdanović **12** Jb
Bogor **18** Cf
Bogorodick **12** Ec
Bogorodsk **12** Fb
Bogra **19** Jj
Bogué **24** Ac
Bo Hai (b.) **16** EFc
Bohemia (phys. reg.) **5** DEcd
Bohemian Forest (mts.) **5** DEd
Bohol (i.) **18** Fbc
Boiaçu **37** Cc
Bois (riv.) **39** CDa
Boise **33** Bb
Bojador, Cabo– **24** Ab
Bojnurd **21** Fb
Boké **24** Ac
Boknafjorden (b.) **4** Ad
Bokspits **26** Bd
Bolama **24** Ac
Bolbec **8** Dc
Bolehov **6** FGb
Bolesławiec **5** Ec
Bolgatanga **24** Bcd
Bolgrad **6** Id
Boli **16** Ha

Boliden **4** DEb
Bolinao **18** Ea
Boliohertu (mt.) **18** Fd
Bolívar, Pico– (mt.) **37** Bb
Bolivia (Ind. St.) **36** De
Bolivia, Altiplano de– **38** Acd
Bolkar dağları (mts.) **22** Ed
Bollnäs **4** Dc
Bollon **29** Hd
Boločanka **14** Cb
Bologna **10** Cb
Bologne **8** Fc
Bologoje **12** Db
Bolšaja Ussurka (riv.) **16** Hla
Bolsena, Lago di– **10** Cc
Bolševik, ostrov– **41** grid square no.4
Bolsõj Anjuj (riv.) **14** Jc
Bolšoj Begičev, ostrov– **14** Eb
Bolsoj Jenisej (riv.) **14** Cd
Bolsoj Ljahovski, ostrov– (i.) **14** Hlb
Bolšoj Uzen (riv.) **12** Gd
Bolton **7** Ee
Bolu **22** Cb
Bolzano **10** Ca
Boma **26** Ab
Bombala **29** Hlf
Bombay → Mumbai **15** Ch
Bom Comércio **37** Cc
Bom Despacho **39** Da
Bomili **26** Ba
Bom Jesus **38** Cb
Bom Jesus da Lapa **38** Cc
Bon, Cape– **24** Da
Bonaire (i.) **35** Db
Bonaparte Archipelago **29** CDa
Bonavista **31** Jd
Bonda **26** Ab
Bondo **25** Cd
Bondowoso **18** Df
Bone → Watampone **18** EFe
Bone, Teluk– **18** Fef
Bongor **25** Bcd
Bonifacio **8** map no.1
Bonifacio, Strait of– **10** Bd
Bonin Islands **27** Ca
Bonn **5** Ac
Bontoc **18** Fa
Bonyhád **6** Dc
Boosaaso **25** EFc
Boothia Gulf **31** FGab
Boothia Peninsula **31** Fa
Booué **26** Aab
Bophuthatswana (hist. reg.) **26** Bd
Bor [Russia] **12** Fb
Bor [Sud.] **25** Dd
Bor [Tur.] **22** Ed
Bor [Yugo.] **6** Fd
Borah Peak **33** Bb
Borås **4** Cd
Borāzjān **21** DEd
Borba **37** CDc
Borcea, Bratul– (riv.) **6** Hd
Bordeaux **8** Cc
Borden Peninsula **31** Ga
Bordertown **29** FGf
Bordj Omar Driss **24** Cb
Borgå **4** Fc
Borgarnes **4** map no.1
Børgefjell (mt.) **4** Cb

© ISTITUTO GEOGRAFICO DE AGOSTINI S.p.A. - Novara

Bunbury **29** ABe
Bundaberg **29** Icd
Bundoran **7** Bd
Bungo-Suidō **17** BCh
Bunguran (i.) **18** Cd
Bunja **25** CDd
Buon Me Thuot **19** Ef
Buqayq **21** DEd
Buraydah **21** Cd
Buraymī, Al- **21** Fe
Burdekin River **29** Hbc
Burdur **22** BCd
Burdur Gölü **22** BCd
Burdwan **20** Gd
Bure **25** Dd
Bureinski Hrebet **14** Gde
Bureja (riv.) **14** Gd
Bureja **14** FGe
Būr Fuad **25** map no.1
Burgas **11** Gb
Burgas, Gulf of- **11** GHb
Burgenland (phys. reg.) **5** Fe
Burghausen **5** Dd
Burgio **10** Df
Burgos **9** Da
Burgsvik **4** Dd
Burgundy (phys. reg.) **8** EFd
Burias (i.) **18** Fb
Burjasot **9** EFc
Burketown **29** Fb
Burkina (Ind. St.) **23** BCd
Burlington [Ia.-U.S.] **32** Ba
Burlington [Vt.-U.S.] **32** Da
Burmah, Al- **24** CDa
Burnie **29** map no.1
Burnley **7** Ee
Burns **33** Bb
Bur'o **25** Ed
Burra **29** Fe
Burravoe **7** Fa
Burriana **9** EFc
Burruyacú **39** Bb
Bursa **22** Bb
Būr Taufiq **25** map no.1
Burton-upon-Trent **7** Fe
Buru, Pulau- (i.) **18** Ge
Burullus, Buḩayrat al- **22** Cg
Burundi (Ind. St.) **26** BCb
Bururi **26** BCb
Buryat (Aut. Rep.) **14** Dd
Bury Saint Edmunds **7** Ge
Būshehr **21** Ed
Businga **26** Ba
Busko Zdrój **5** Hc
Buşrá ash Shām **22** Ff
Busselton **29** ABe
Busto Arsizio **10** Bb
Busuanga (i.) **18** Eb
Buta **25** Cd
Butarirari Islands **27** Db
Butha Qi **16** Fa
Butte **33** Bb
Butuan **18** Gc
Butung (i.) **18** Fef
Buuloberde **25** Ed
Büyük Ağrı dağı → Ararat (mt.) **21** Cb
Büyük Egri dağ (mt.) **22** Dd
Büyük Mahya (mt.) **22** ABb
Büyük Menderes (riv.) **22** ABd
Buzançais **8** Dd
Buzău **6** Hd
Buzuluk **13** Ed
Bydgoszcz **5** FGb
Bygdeå **4** DEb
Byhov **12** Dc
Bylot Island **30** Kb
Byrd Glacier **42** grid square no.4
Byron, Cape- **29** Id
Byrranga Gory **14** CDb
Bytom **5** Gc
Bytów **5** Fa
Bzura (riv.) **5** Gb

C

Ca (riv.) **19** DEe
Caanood, Laas- **25** Ed
Caapiranga **37** Cc
Caatinga **38** Cbc
Cabanatuan **18** Fa
Cabedelo **38** Db
Cabeza del Buey **9** Cc
Cabezón de la Sal **9** Ca
Cabimas **37** Ba
Cabinda **26** Ab
Caborca **34** Aa
Cabot Strait **31** IJd
Cabra **9** Cd
Cabras **10** Be
Cabrera, Isla- (i.) **9** Gc
Cabrera, Sierra de la- (mts.) **9** Ba
Cábriel (riv.) **9** Ec
Cabruta **37** Cb
Caçador **39** Cb
Čačak **6** Ede
Caccia, Capo- **10** Bd
Cacequí **39** Cbc
Cáceres [Braz.] **39** Ca
Cáceres [Sp.] **9** Bc
Cachimbo, Serra do- (mts.) **38** Bb
Cachoeira **38** Dc
Cachoeira do Sul **39** Cbc
Cachoeiro de Itapemirim **39** DEb
Cacolo **26** Abc
Caconda **26** Ac
Cadale **25** Ed
Čadan **14** BCd
Cadillac **32** Ca
Cádiz **9** Bd
Cadiz **18** Fb
Cádiz, Golfo de- **9** Bd
Čadyr-Lunga **6** Ic
Caen **8** CDc
Caernarvon **7** De
Caetité **38** Cc
Cagan-Aman **12** Gd
Cagayan (riv.) **18** Fa
Cagayan de Oro **18** Fc
Cagayan Islands **18** Fc
Cagayan Sulu (i.) **18** Ec
Čagda **14** Gd
Cagliari **10** Be
Cagliari, Golfo di- **10** Be
Caguas **35** Db
Cahama **26** Ac
Cahersiveen **7** Af
Cahora Bassa, Lago de- **26** Cc
Cahors **8** De
Caia **26** Cc
Caiabis, Serra dos- (mts.) **38** Bc
Caicó **38** Db
Caicos Islands **32** Dc
Caimito (riv.) **35** map no.1
Cairns **29** Hb
Cairo [Eg.] **25** Dab
Cairo [Il.-U.S.] **32** Cb
Cajamarca **37** Bc
Cajàzeiras **38** Db
Čajkovski **12** Hlb
Çal **22** Bcd
Calabar **24** Cd
Calabozo **36** Dc
Calabria (reg.) **10** EFef
Calafat **6** Fde
Calafate **40** Ac
Calahorra **9** Ea
Calais [Fr.] **8** Db
Calais [U.S.] **32** Ea
Calama [Braz.] **37** Cc
Calama [Chile] **39** Bb
Calamar **37** Bab
Calamian Group **18** EFb
Calamocha **9** Eb
Călan **6** Fd
Calandula **26** Ab
Calapan **18** Fb
Călăraşi **6** Hd
Calatayud **9** Eb
Calatrava (r.) **9** CDc
Calayan (i.) **18** Fa
Calbayog **18** FGb
Calçoene **38** BCa
Calcutta **15** Cg
Caldas da Rainha **9** Ac
Caldera **39** Ab
Caldwell **33** Bb
Caledon (riv.) **26** Bde
Caledonian Canal **7** Dc
Calera, La- **39** Ac
Caletta **10** Bd
Calgary **30** Gde
Cali **36** Cc
Calicut **20** DEf
Caliente **33** Bc
California (State) **33** ABc
California, Gulf of- **33** Bcd
Călimani, Munţii- **6** Gc
Călimăneşti **6** Gd
Callabonna, Lake- **29** Gde
Callao **36** Ce
Callao, El- **37** Cb
Caloundra **29** Id
Calpe **9** Fc
Caltagirone **10** Ef
Caltanissetta **10** Ef
Caluire-et-Cuire **8** Fe
Caluula **25** EFc
Calvi **8** map no.1
Calvinia **26** ABe
Calw **5** Bd
Camabatela **26** Ab
Camacupa **26** Ac
Camagüey **35** Ca
Camagüey, Archipiélago de- (is.) **35** Ca
Camaná **39** Aa
Camapuã, Sertão de- (steppe) **39** CDa
Camaquã **39** Cc
Camargo **39** Bb
Camargue (phys. reg.) **8** Ff
Camarones **40** Bb
Ca Mau Point **19** Dg
Cambodia (Ind. St.) **15** Dh
Cambrai **8** Eb
Cambrian Mountains **7** DEef
Cambridge [U.K.] **7** FGe
Cambridge [U.S.] **32** DEa
Cambridge Bay **31** Eb
Çam Burun **22** FGb
Camden **32** Db
Cameroon (Ind. St.) **23** CDe
Cameroon Mountains **24** CDd
Cametá **38** BCb
Camiguin (i.) **18** Fa
Camiri **39** Bb
Camocim **38** CDb
Camooweal **29** Fbc
Camorta (i.) **19** Bg
Campagna **10** Ed
Campana, Isla- (i.) **40** Ab
Campanario, Cerro- (mt.) **39** ABc
Campania (reg.) **10** DEd
Campanquiz, Cerros- (mt.) **37** Bc
Campbell Island **27** De
Campbell River **31** Cc
Campbellton **31** Id
Campbell Town **29** map no.1
Campbeltown **7** Dd
Campeche **34** Cc
Campeche, Bahía de- **34** Cc
Campeche Bank **34** CDb
Camperdown **29** Gf
Campina Grande **38** Db
Campinas **39** Db
Campobasso **10** Ed
Campo Formoso **38** Cc
Campo Gallo **39** Bb
Campo Grande **39** Cab
Campo Maior **38** Cb
Campo Mourão **39** Cb
Campos **39** Db
Campos [Braz.] (phys. reg.) **38** Cc
Campos [Braz.] (phys. reg.) **38** Bc
Campos, Tierra de- (phys. reg.) **9** Cab
Cam Ranh **19** Ef
Camrose **31** Ab
Çan **11** Gc
Canada (Ind. St.) **30** GKcd
Cañada de Gómez **39** Bc
Canadian River **32** Bb
Çanakkale **22** Ab
Canal du Centre (can.) **8** Fd
Cananea **33** BCc
Canarreos, Archipiélago de los- (is.) **35** Bb
Canary Islands **24** Aab
Canaveral, Cape- (Kennedy, Cape-) **32** CDc
Canavieiras **38** Dc
Canberra **29** Hlf
Cancún **34** Db
Çandır **22** Db
Canelones **39** Cc
Cangamba **26** ABc
Cangas de Narcea **9** Ba
Cangzhou **16** Ec
Caniapiscau (riv.) **31** Ic

© ISTITUTO GEOGRAFICO DE AGOSTINI S.p.A. - Novara

© ISTITUTO GEOGRAFICO DE AGOSTINI S.p.A. - Novara

© ISTITUTO GEOGRAFICO DE AGOSTINI S.p.A. - Novara

© ISTITUTO GEOGRAFICO DE AGOSTINI S.p.A. - Novara

Dabola **24** Ac
Dąbrowa Górnicza **5** GHc
Dăbuleni **6** FGe
Dachau **5** Cd
Dachstein (mt.) **5** De
Dadanawa **37** Db
Daday **22** Db
Dādra and Nagar Haveli **20** Dd
Dadu **20** Cc
Dadu He (riv.) **16** Be
Daet **18** Fb
Dafir **21** Ee
Dagestan (Aut. Rep.) **13** De
Dagupan **18** Fa
Dahlak (i.) **21** Cf
Dahna', Ad– (phys. reg.) **21** CDde
Dahra **24** Db
Dahra (phys. reg.) **9** Fd
Daimiel **9** Dc
Dai–Sen **17** Cg
Daitō Islands **16** He
Dajarra **29** FGc
Dakar **24** Ac
Dakhla **24** Ab
Dakhla Oasis **25** Cb
Đakovica **11** Db
Dalai Nur (l.) **16** Eb
Dalälven (riv.) **4** Dc
Dalaman (riv.) **22** Bd
Dalan–Dzadagad **14** De
Dalan–Džargalan **16** CDa
Dalap–Uliga–Darrit **27** Db
Da Lat **19** Ef
Dalbandin **20** Bc
Dalby **29** Id
Dale **4** Ac
Dalhart **33** Cc
Dali [China] **19** CDc
Dali [China] **16** CDcd
Dalian (Lüda) **16** Fc
Dalías **9** Dd
Dallas **32** Bb
Dalles, The– **33** Ab
Dalmatia (phys. reg.) **6** BDde
Dalmatovo **12** Jb
Dalnegorsk **14** Ge
Dalnerečensk **14** Ge
Daloa **24** Bd
Dalrymple, Mount– **29** Hc
Daltonganj **20** Fd
Dalupiri (i.) **18** Fa
Dalwallinu **29** Be
Daly River **29** Ea
Daly Waters **29** Eb
Daman **20** Dd
Damanhûr **25** CDa
Damar, Pulau– (i.) **18** Gf
Damaraland (hist. reg.) **26** Ad
Damâs **22** Cg
Damascus **22** Ff
Damāvand (mt.) **21** Eb
Dāmghān **21** EFb
Damietta **25** Da
Daming **16** DEc
'Dāmir, Ad– **25** Dc
Dammām, Ad– **21** Ed
Damme **5** ABb
Damodar (riv.) **19** Ik
Damoh **20** EFd
Dampier **29** Bc
Dampier Archipelago **29** ABbc
Dampier Strait **18** He
Damqawt **21** Ef
Danakil Plain (phys. reg.) **25** DEc
Da Nang **19** Ee
Dandong **16** Fbc
Daneborg **31** Ma
Dangjin Shankou **16** Ec
Dangriga **35** Bb
Danilov **12** Fb
Dankov **12** Ec
Danmark Havn **30** PQb
Danube (riv.) **6** Fd
Danube, Mouths of the– **6** Id
Danville [Il.–U.S.] **32** Ca
Danville [Va.–U.S.] **32** CDb
Danxian **16** Cg
Danzig → Gdańsk **5** Ga
Dar' ā **22** Ff
Dārāb **21** EFd
Darabani **6** Hb
Đaravica (mt.) **11** Db
Darb, Ad– **21** Cf
Darbhanga **20** Gc
Dardanelles (str.) **11** Gcd
Darende **22** Fc
Dar es Salaam **23** FGf
Dārfūr (State) **25** Cc
Darhan **15** De
Darién, Golfo de– **37** Bb
Dariyah **21** Ce
Darjeeling **20** Gc
Darlag **16** Ad
Darling Range **29** Be
Darling River **29** Ge
Darlington **7** EFd
Darłowo **5** EFa
Darmstadt **5** Bd
Darnah **24** Ea
Daroca **9** Eb
Dart, Cape– **42** grid square no.3
Dartmoor (mt.) **7** DEf
Dartmouth [Can.] **31** Id
Dartmouth [U.K.] **7** Ef
Daru **27** Cc
Daruvar **6** Cd
Darwin **29** Ea
Das (i.) **21** Ede
Dašhovuz (Tašauz) **13** Ee
Dasht (riv.) **20** Bc
Dasht–e–Kavir (des.) **21** EFc
Dasht–e–Lut (des.) **21** Fc
Datca **22** Ad
Date **17** Gc
Datia **19** Gj
Datong **16** Dbc
Datu Piang (Dulawan) **18** Fc
Daugavpils **13** Bd
Dauphin **33** CDa
Dauphiné (hist. reg.) **8** FGe
Davangere **20** DEf
Davao **15** Ei
Davao Gulf **18** Gc
Davenport **32** BCa
David **35** Bc
Davis **42** grid square no.2
Davis, Fort– **35** map no.1
Davis Sea **42** grid square no.2
Davis Strait **31** Jb
Davlekanovo **12** HIc
Davos **5** BCe
Dawadmi, Ad– **21** Ce
Dawāsir, Wādī ad– **21** Ce
Dawei **18** Ab
Dawson **30** Ec
Dawson, Isla– (i.) **40** ABc
Dawson Creek **31** Cc
Dawson River **29** HIcd
Dawu **16** Bd
Dax **8** Cf
Daxian **16** Cd
Daxinggou **17** ABc
Daym Zubayr **25** Cd
Dayr az Zawr **21** BCb
Dayton **32** Cb
Daytona Beach **32** CDc
Dayu **16** De
De Aar **23** Ei
Dead Sea **22** EFg
Deán Funes **39** Bc
Dease Strait **31** Eb
Death Valley **33** Bc
Deauville **8** CDc
Debao **16** Cf
Debar **11** Dc
Debica **5** Hc
Dęblin **5** Hc
Dębno **5** Eb
Debrecen **6** EFc
Debre Markos **25** Dcd
Debre Tabor **25** Dc
Decatur [Il.–U.S.] **32** Cab
Decatur [U.S.] **32** Cb
Decazeville **8** Ee
Deccan **20** Eef
Děčín **5** Ec
Decize **8** Ed
Deda **6** Gc
Dedegül dağ (mt.) **22** Cd
Dédougou **24** Bc
Dee [Scot.–U.K.] (riv.) **7** Ec
Dee [Wales–U.K.] (riv.) **7** Ee
Deer Lake **31** Jd
Degeh Bur **25** Ed
Deggendorf **5** Dd
De Grey River **29** BCc
Dehiwala–Mount Lavinia **20** Eg
Dehra Dun **20** Ebc
Dehri **19** HIj
Dej **6** Fc
Dekese **26** Bb
Delano Peak **33** Bc
Delaware **32** Ca
Delaware Bay **32** Db
Delft **8** Fab
Delfzijl **8** Ga
Delgado, Cape– **26** Dc
Delhi **20** Ec
Delice (riv.) **22** Ec
Delingha **16** Ac
Deljatin **12** Bd
Delmenhorst **5** ABb
Delmiro Gouveia **38** Db
De Long Islands **14** HIb
De Long Strait **41** grid square no.4
Delphi (r.) **11** Ed
Del Rio **33** CDd
Delvina **11** CDd
Demanda, Sierra de la– (mts.) **9** Da
Demerara → Georgetown **37** Db
Deming **33** Cc
Deminí (riv.) **37** Cbc
Demirci **11** Hd
Demirköy **11** GHc
Demjanskoje **13** FGd
Demmin **5** Db
Democratic Republic of Congo (Ind. St.) **23** DEf
Dempo, Gunung– (mt.) **18** Be
Denain **8** Eb
Dengkou **16** Cb
Denham **29** Ad
Den Helder **8** EFa
Denia **9** Fc
Deniliquin **29** GHf
Denizli **22** Bd
Denmark (Ind. St.) **3** DEb
Denmark **29** Bef
Denmark Strait **30** OPc
Denpasar **18** Ef
Denton **32** Bb
D'Entrecasteaux Islands **27** Cc
Denver **33** Cc
Deoghar **19** Ij
Deo Mu Gia (p.) **19** Ee
Deoria **19** Hj
Deputatski **14** GHc
Dera Ghazi Khan **20** CDbc
Dera Ismail Khan **20** CDb
Deražnja **6** Hb
Derbent **13** De
Derby [Austl.] **29** Cb
Derby [U.K.] **7** Fe
Derecske **6** Ec
Dereköy **22** Ab
Derg, Lake– **7** Be
Dermatás, Ákra– **11** Ed
De Rose Hill **29** Ed
Derudeb **25** Dc
Derventa **6** CDd
Derwent (riv.) **7** Fde
Desaguadero [Arg.] (riv.) **39** Bc
Desaguadero [Bol.] (riv.) **39** Ba
Dese **25** DEc
Deseado (riv.) **40** Bb
Desemboque, El– **34** Aa
Desenzano del Garda **10** Cb
Desertas, Ilhas– (is.) **24** Aa
Des Moines (riv.) **32** Ba
Des Moines **32** Ba
Desna (riv.) **12** Dc
Desolación, Isla– (i.) **40** Ac
Desroches (i.) **15** Bi
Dessau **5** Dc
Detroit **32** Ca
Deutsche Bucht (b.) **5** Aa
Deva **6** Fd
Develi **22** Ec
Deventer **8** FGa
Devil's Island **37** Db
Devils Lake **32** Ba
Devin **11** Fc
Devolli (riv.) **11** Dc
Devoluy (mt.) **8** Fe
Devon (co.) **7** DEf
Devon Island **41** grid square no.1
Devonport **29** map no.1
Devrek **22** CDb
Devrez (riv.) **22** Db
Dewa (riv.) **25** Dd
Dewas **20** Ed

© ISTITUTO GEOGRAFICO DE AGOSTINI S.p.A. - Novara

Dulovo **11** Gb
Duluth **32** Ba
Dūmā **22** Ff
Dumaguete **18** Fc
Dumaran (i.) **18** EFb
Dumbarton **7** Dcd
Dumfries **7** Ed
Dumka **19** Ij
Dumond d'Urville **42** grid square no.4
Dumont D'Urville Sea **42** grid square no.4
Dunaföldvár **6** Dc
Dunaharaszti **6** Dc
Dunajevcy **6** Hb
Dunántúl (phys. reg.) **6** CDc
Dunaújváros **6** Dc
Duncansby Head **7** Eb
Dundalk **7** Cde
Dundalk Bay **7** CDe
Dundas, Lake– **29** Ce
Dundas Strait **29** Ea
Dundee **7** Ec
Dunedin **27** De
Dunfermline **7** DEc
Dungarpur **20** Dd
Dungarvan **7** Cef
Dungeness (cap.) **7** Gf
Dunhua **16** Gb
Dunkerque **8** Eb
Dunkwa **24** Bd
Dún Laoghaire / Dunleary **7** CDe
Dunleary / Dún Laoghaire **7** CDe
Dunqulah **25** CDc
Duns **7** Ed
Duolun **16** Eb
Durance (riv.) **8** Ge
Durango **33** Cc
Durazno **39** Cc
Durazzo **11** Cc
Durban **23** Fhi
Durg **20** Fd
Durgapur **19** IJk
Durham [U.K.] **7** EFd
Durham [U.S.] **32** Db
Durmitor (mt.) **11** Cb
Durness **7** Db
Dursunbey **11** Hd
Durūz, Jabal al– (mt.) **22** Ff
Dušanbe **13** Ff
Dushan **16** Ce
Düsseldorf **5** CDc
Dutch Harbor **31** Bc
Duwaym, Ad– **25** Dc
Duyun **16** Ce
Düzce **22** Cb
Dyer Plateau (plat.) **42** grid square no.1
Dymer **6** IJa
Dyrhólaey (cap.) **4** map no.1
Džalal-Abad **13** Ge
Džalinda **14** Fd
Džambul → Taraz **13** Ge
Dzamyn-Ud **16** Db
Džankoj **12** Dd
Džardžan **14** Fc
Džargalant, Ar– **16** DEa
Dzeržinsk **12** Fb
Džetygara **13** Fd
Džezkazgan → Żezkazgan **13** Fe
Dzhugdzhur Range **14** Gd
Działdowo **5** Hb
Dzierżoniów **5** Fc
Dzun-Bajan **16** CDb
Dzungarian Basin (phys. reg.) **14** Be
Džungarski Alatau, Hrebet– (mts.) **13** GHe
Dzun-Mod **14** De
Džusaly **13** Fe

E

Eagle **31** Ab
Eagle Pass **33** CDd
Eastbourne **7** Gf
East Cape **27** Dd
East China Sea **16** FGde
Easter Island **2**
Eastern Carpathians (mts.) **6** FHbc
Eastern Ghats (mts.) **20** EFef
Eastern Malaysia **18** DEcd
Eastern Prussia (hist. reg.) **5** GIab
East Falkland (i.) **40** Cc
East London **26** Be
Eastmain (riv.) **31** Eb
Eastmain **31** Hc
East Point **32** Cb
East Saint Louis **32** BCb
East Sea / Japan, Sea of– **16** HIbc
East Siberian Sea **41** grid square no.4
Eau Claire **32** BCa
Eau Gallie **32** CDc
Eauripik Atoll **27** Cb
Ebensee **5** DEe
Eber Gölü **22** Cc
Eberswalde **5** Db
Ebla (r.) **21** Bb
Eboli **10** Ed
Ebro (riv.) **9** Da
Eceabat **22** Ab
Echigo-Sanmyaku (mts.) **17** FGef
Echo Bay **30** GHc
Echuca **29** GHf
Écija **9** Cd
Ecuador (Ind. St.) **36** BCd
Ed **25** Ec
Edéa **24** CDd
Edefors **4** Eb
Eden **29** HIf
Edgeøya **13** Bb
Edhessa **11** DEc
Edinburgh **7** Ed
Edirne **11** Gc
Edith Ronne Ice Shelf **42** grid square no.1
Edith Ronne Land **42** grid square no.1
Edjeleh **24** Cb
Edmonton **30** Gd
Edmundston **31** Id
Edremit **22** Ac
Edremit Körfezi **22** Ac
Edsel Ford Ranges **42** grid square no.3
Edward, Lake– **25** Ce
Edwards Creek **29** Ee
Edwards Plateau **33** CDcd
Edward VII Peninsula **42** grid square no.3
Efaté, Île– (i.) **28** map no.4
Effingham **32** Cb
Eforie **6** Id
Egadi, Isole– **10** Df
Egan Range **33** Bbc
Egedesminde / Aasiaat **31** JKb
Eger **6** Ec
Egersund **4** Ad
Eğnar **22** Ed
Eğridir **22** Cd
Eğridir Gölü **22** Ccd
Eğrigöz dağı (mt.) **22** Bc
Egvekinot **14** KLc
Egypt (Ind. St.) **23** EFc
Ehingen **5** Bd
Eiao, Île– (i.) **28** Bc
Eibar **9** Da
Eichstätt **5** Cd
Eifel (mt.) **5** Ac
Eigg (i.) **7** Cc
Eight Degree Channel **20** Dg
Eights **42** grid square no.1
Eights Coast **42** grid square no.1
Eighty Mile Beach **29** Cb
Eindhoven **8** Fb
Eiriksjökull (gl.) **4** map no.1
Eirunepé **37** BCc
Eisenach **5** BCc
Eisenerz **5** Ee
Eisenhüttenstadt **5** Eb
Eisenstadt **5** Fe
Eisleben **5** Cc
Ejin Qi **16** Bb
Ekecek dağı (mt.) **22** DEc
Ekenäs **4** EFcd
Ekibastuz **13** Gd
Ekonda **14** Dc
El Affroun **9** Gd
Elafonísou, Stenón– (str.) **11** Ee
Elassŏn **11** Ed
Elat **22** Eh
Elâziğ **21** BCb
Elba (i.) **10** Cc
Elbasani **11** CDc
El-Bayadh **24** Ca
Elbe (riv.) **5** Cb
Elbert, Mount– **33** Cc
Elbeuf **8** Dc
Elbistan **22** Fc
Elbląg **5** Ga
El Boulaïda **24** Ca
Elbrus (mt.) **21** Ca
Elburz Mountains **21** DEb
Elche **9** Ec
Elda **9** Ec
Eldoret **25** Dde
Elektrostal **12** EFb
Eleusís **11** Ed
Eleuthera Island **32** Dc
Elgin **7** Ec
Elgon (mt.) **25** Dd
Elhovo **11** Gb
Elista **13** De
Elizabeth City **32** Db
Elizabeth Island **28** map no.3
Ełk **5** Ib
Elk City **33** CDc
Elko **33** Bb
Ellesmere Island **41** grid square no.1
Elliston **29** EFe
Ellora (r.) **20** Ed
Ellsworth Highland **42** grid square no.3
Ellsworth Mountains **42** grid square no.1
Elmalı **22** BCd
Elmira **32** Da
Elmshorn **5** BCb
Elne **8** Ef
Elorza **37** BCb
El Salvador (Ind. St.) **30** IJh
Eluru **20** Fe
Elvas **9** Bc
Elverum **4** BCc
Ely **33** Bc
Emaé (i.) **28** map no.4
Emāmshahr **21** Fb
Emba **13** Ee
Emba (riv.) **13** Ee
Embarcación **39** Bb
Embetsu **17** Gb
Embu **26** Cb
Emden **5** Ab
Emerald **29** Hc
Emerson **31** Fd
Emet **22** Bc
Emi Koussi (mt.) **25** Bbc
Emilia-Romagna (reg.) **10** BCb
Emine, Nos– **22** ABa
Emirdağ **22** Cc
Emir dağları (mts.) **22** Cc
Emmen **8** Ga
Emmendingen **5** ABd
Emmet **29** Gc
Empalme **34** ABb
Émpoli **10** Cc
Emporia **32** Bb
Ems (riv.) **5** Ab
Encantada, Cerro de la– (mt. **34** Aa
Encarnación **39** Cb
Ende **18** Ff
Endeavour Strait **29** Ga
Enderbury Atoll **28** Ac
Enderby Land **42** grid square no.2
Enewetak Atoll **27** Db
Enez **11** Gc
Enez Körfezi **11** Fc
Engaru **17** Hb
Engels **13** Dd
Enggano, Pulau– (i.) **18** Bf
England (reg.) **7** EFde
Englewood **33** Cc
English Channel **8** ACbc
Enid **32** Bb
Enkhuizen **8** Fa
Enköping **4** Dd
Enna **10** Ef
Ennadai **31** Eb
Ennedi (plat.) **25** Cc
Ennis **7** Be
Enniscorthy **7** CDe
Enniskillen **7** Cd
Enns (riv.) **5** DEe
Enontekiö **4** EFa
Enschede **8** Ga

© ISTITUTO GEOGRAFICO DE AGOSTINI S.p.A. - Novara

© ISTITUTO GEOGRAFICO DE AGOSTINI S.p.A. - Novara

© ISTITUTO GEOGRAFICO DE AGOSTINI S.p.A. - Novara

Habban **21** Dg
Haboro **17** Gb
Habost **7** Cb
Hachijō-Jima (i.) **16** IJd
Hachinohe **16** Jb
Hachiōji **17** Fg
Ḥadāribah, Ra's al- **25** Db
Hadd, Al- **21** FGe
Ḥadd, Ra's al- **21** FGe
Haddington **7** Ecd
Hadejia **24** CDc
Hadera **22** Ef
Haderslev **5** Ba
Hadīboh **21** Eg
Haditha **21** Cc
Hadiyah **21** Bd
Ḥaḍramawt (phys. reg.) **21** Dfg
Hadseløya (i.) **4** Ca
Haeju **16** FGc
Hafar al Batin **21** CDd
Hafnarfjörður **4** map no.1
Hafun **23** Hd
Hafun, Ras- **25** Ec
Hagen **5** Ab
Hagerstown **32** Db
Hagfors **4** Cc
Hagi **17** Bg
Ha Giang **19** DEd
Hague, Cap de la- (cap.) **8** BCc
Haguenau **8** Gc
Hahajima-Rettō (i.) **27** Ca
Haicheng **16** Fb
Haifa **22** Ef
Haig **29** De
Haikou **15** Dgh
Ḥā'il **21** Cd
Hailar **16** EFa
Hailar He (riv.) **14** EFe
Hailin **17** Ab
Hailong **16** Gb
Hailun **16** Ga
Hailuoto (i.) **4** EFb
Haimen [China] **16** Fe
Haimen [China] **16** Fd
Hainan (prov.) **15** Dh
Haines **31** Bc
Haines Junction **31** Bb
Hai Phong **15** Dg
Haiti (Ind. St.) **30** Kh
Haiti → Hispaniola (i.) **35** Cb
Haizhou **16** EFd
Hajdúböszörmény **6** Ec
Hajdúnánás **6** EFc
Hajipur **20** Gc
Hajnówka **5** IJb
Hakken-Zan (mt.) **17** Dgh
Hakodate **16** IJb
Ḥalā'ib **25** Db
Halawa **28** map no.1
Halberstadt **5** Cc
Halcon, Mount- **18** Fb
Halden **4** BCd
Haleakala Crater (mt.) **28** map no.1
Hali **21** Cf
Halicarnassus (r.) **22** ABd
Halifax [Can.] **31** Id
Halifax [U.K.] **7** EFe
Halifax Bay **29** Hb
Hālil (riv.) **21** Fd
Halland (hist. reg.) **4** Cd
Ḥallat 'Ammār **22** EFh
Hall Beach **31** GHb
Halle / Saale **5** CDc
Hallein **5** De
Halley Bay **42** grid square no.1
Hall in Tirol **5** Ce
Hall Islands **27** Cb
Hall Peninsula **31** Ib
Halls Creek **29** Db
Halmahera (i.) **18** Gd
Halmahera, Laut- **18** GHe
Halmer-Ju **13** Fc
Halmstad **4** Cd
Haltiatunturi (mt.) **4** Ea
Halturin **12** Gb
Hamada **17** BCg
Hamadān **21** Dbc
Hamāh **21** Bbc
Hamamatsu **16** Id
Hamar **4** Bc
Hamburg **5** Cb
Ḥamd, Wādī al- **21** Bd
Hämeenlinna **4** EFc
Hameln **5** Bb
Hamersley Range **29** Bc
Hamhŭng **14** FGe
Hami **15** De
Hamilton [Austl.] **29** Gf
Hamilton [Can.] **31** GHd
Hamilton [N.Z.] **27** Dd
Hamilton [U.K.] **7** DEd
Hamilton [U.S.] **32** Cb
Hamilton Inlet **31** Jc
Hamina **4** FGc
Hamirpur **19** GHj
Hamm **5** ABc
Ḥammāmāt **10** Cf
Ḥammāmāt, Khalīj- (g.) **10** Cf
Ḥammān, Al- **22** Bg
Ḥammār, Hawr al- **21** Dc
Hammerfest **4** Ea
Hammond **32** Ca
Hampshire (co.) **7** Ff
Ḥamrā', Al Ḥamādah- (des.) **24** Dab
Hāmūn-e Hīrmand, Daryācheh- ye- (sw.) **21** Gc
Hāmun-e-Jāz-Muryān (sw.) **21** FGd
Hāmūn-e Sāberi (l.) **21** Gc
Hamun-i-Mashkel (sw.) **21** Gd
Hana **28** map no.1
Hanak **21** Bd
Hancock **32** BCa
Handa **17** Eg
Handan **16** Dc
Handyga **14** Gc
Hānegev (phys. reg.) **22** Eg
Hanford **33** ABc
Hangaj, Hrebet- **14** CDe
Hanggin Houqi **16** Cb
Hanggin Qi **16** Cbc
Hangö **4** Ed
Hangu **16** Ec
Hangzhou **15** DEf
Hanka, ozero- **16** Hab
Hankendi **21** Dab
Hanmon-Kaikyō **17** ABg
Hann, Mount- **29** CDb
Hanna **31** DEc
Hannamaki **16** Jc
Hannover **5** BCb
Hanöbukten **4** Ce
Hanoi **15** Dg
Hanover, Isla- (i.) **40** Ac
Han Shui (riv.) **16** Dd
Hanty-Mansijsk **13** Fc
Hanyuan **16** Be
Hanzhong **16** Cd
Hao Atoll **28** BCc
Hāora **20** Gd
Haparanda **4** EFb
Hapčeranga **14** Ede
Hapur **20** Ec
Haql **21** ABd
Ḥaraḍ **21** DEe
Harare (Salisbury) **26** Cc
Harbin **16** Ga
Harboi Hill (mt.) **20** Cc
Hardangerfjord **4** Ac
Hardangeriøkulen **4** Ac
Hardangervidda (mts.) **4** Acd
Hardoi **19** GHj
Hardwar **20** Ebc
Harer **25** Ed
Harfleur **8** CDc
Hargeysa **25** Ed
Harghita, Munţi- **6** Gc
Har Hu (l.) **16** Ac
Harib **21** CDfg
Hariq, Al- **21** De
Hari Rud **20** Bb
Harjavalta **4** Ec
Harkov **13** Cde
Harlingen [Neth.] **8** Fa
Harlingen [U.S.] **32** Bc
Harmanli **11** FGc
Härnösand **4** Dc
Haro **9** Da
Harovsk **12** Fab
Harper **24** Bd
Harrach **9** Gd
Harrach-Algeri, El- **9** Gd
Harrah **21** Efg
Harricanaw (riv.) **32** Da
Harris (phys. reg.) **7** Cc
Harrisburg **32** Dab
Harrismith **26** BCd
Harrogate **7** Fde
Harstad **4** Da
Hartford **32** Da
Hartlepool **7** Fd
Harut rud (riv.) **20** Bb
Harwich **7** Gf
Haryana (State) **20** DEc
Harz (mts.) **5** Cc
Ḥasā, Al- **22** EFg
Hasa, Al- (phys. reg.) **21** DEde
Hasan dağı (mt.) **22** Ec
Hasavjurt **12** Ge
Haskovo **11** Fc
Hassan **20** Ef
Hasselt **8** Fb
Hässleholm **4** Cd
Hastings [U.K.] **7** Gf
Hastings [U.S.] **32** Ba
Hašuri **12** Fe
Ḥasy al Qaṭṭār **22** Ag
Hatanga **14** Db
Hatanga (riv.) **14** Db
Hatangski zaliv **14** DEb
Hatches Creek **29** EFc
Haţeg **6** Fd
Hatgal **14** CDd
Hathras **20** Ec
Hatia Islands **19** Jk
Ḥaṭībah, Ra's- **21** Be
Ha Tien **19** Dfg
Ha Tinh **19** Ee
Hatteras, Cape- **32** Db
Hattiesburg **32** Cb
Hatvan **6** DEc
Hat Yai **19** CDg
Hatyrka **14** Kc
Haugesund **4** Ad
Haukipudas **4** Fb
Haukivesi **4** FGc
Hausruck (mt.) **5** Dd
Hautmont **8** EFb
Hauts Plateaux **24** BCb
Havana **35** Ba
Havast **13** Fe
Havel (riv.) **5** Db
Haverfordwest **7** Df
Havířov **5** FGd
Havlíčkův Brod **5** Ed
Havre **33** BCb
Havre, Le- **8** CDc
Havza **22** Eb
Hawaii (i.) **28** map no.1
Hawaiian Islands **28** map no.1
Ḥawātah, Al- **25** Dc
Hawd (phys. reg.) **25** Ed
Hawi **28** map no.1
Hawick **7** Ed
Hawkes, Mount- **42** grid square no.1
Hay (riv.) **31** Dbc
Hay **29** GHe
Haynin **21** Df
Hay River **30** Gcd
Hay River (riv.) **29** Fc
Hays **32** Bb
Hayy, Al- **21** Dc
Hayyā **25** Dc
Hazārān, Kūh- e- **21** Fd
Hazaribagh **19** Ijk
Hazelton **31** Cc
Hearst **31** Gcd
Hebei (prov.) **16** DEc
Hebrides **7** Cbc
Hebrides, Sea of the- **7** Cc
Hebron [Can.] **31** Ic
Hebron [Jor.] **22** Eg
Hecate Strait **31** Bc
Hechuan **16** Cde
Hede **4** Cc
Hedemora **4** Cc
Heerenveen **8** FGa
Heerlen-Kerkrade **8** FGb
Hefei **16** Ed
Hegang **16** GHa
Hegura-Jima (i.) **17** Ef
Heide **5** Ba
Heidelberg [Ger.] **5** Bd
Heidelberg [S. Afr.] **26** Be
Heidenheim an der Brenz **5** Cd
Heilbronn **5** Bd
Heilong Jiang (riv.) **14** Fd
Heilongjiang (prov.) **16** FHa
Heinola **4** Fc
Hekimhan **22** FGc
Hekla (mt.) **4** map no.1

© ISTITUTO GEOGRAFICO DE AGOSTINI S.p.A. - Novara

Hel **5** Ga
Helagsfjället (gl.) **4** BCc
Helan Shan (mts.) **16** Cc
Helena [Ar.-U.S.] **32** BCb
Helena [Mt.-U.S.] **33** Bb
Helen Reef (i.) **27** Bb
Helgeland (phys. reg.) **4** Cb
Helgoland (i.) **5** Aa
Hellín **9** Ec
Hell Ville **23** GHg
Helmand (riv.) **20** Bb
Helmsdale **7** Eb
Helmstedt **5** Cb
Helsingborg **4** BCde
Helsingfors / Helsinki **4** Fcd
Helsingør **5** CDa
Helsinki / Helsingfors **4** Fcd
Henan (prov.) **16** Dd
Henares (riv.) **9** Db
Henbury **29** Ec
Henderson **33** Bc
Henderson Island **28** Cd
Hengchun **16** EFf
Hengelo **8** Ga
Hengxian **16** Cf
Hengyang **15** Dg
Hénin-Liétard **8** Eb
Hennebont **8** Bd
Henzada **19** BCe
Hepu **16** Cf
Heras, Colonia de- **36** CDh
Herāt **15** Cf
Hercegnovi **11** Cb
Heredia **35** Bbc
Hereford **7** Ee
Hereheretule Atoll **28** Bc
Hereke **22** BCb
Herford **5** Bb
Herma Ness (cap.) **7** Fa
Hermanus **26** Ae
Hermōn (mt.) **22** Ef
Hermosillo **34** Ab
Hernandarias **39** Cb
Herning **4** Bd
Herrera del Duque **9** Cc
Herson **13** Ce
Hertford **7** FGf
Hertogenbosch, 's- **8** FGb
Hervás **9** BCb
Hervey Bay **29** Icd
Hervey Bay (g.) **29** Icd
Herzegovina (phys. reg.) **11** BCb
Hessen (State) **5** Bc
Heta (riv.) **14** Cb
Heves **6** Ec
Hexian **16** Df
Heyuan **16** Df
Hibbing **32** Ba
Hida (mts.) **17** Efg
Hidaka-Sanmyaku (mts.) **17** Hc
Hidalgo del Parral **34** Bb
Hierro (i.) **24** Ab
Higashine **17** FGe
High River **31** Dc
Highs Atlas (mts.) **24** Ba
Hiiumaa (i.) **4** Ed
Híjar **9** Eb
Ḥijāz, Al- (hist. reg.) **21** BCde
Hikone **17** DEg
Hildesheim **5** BCb
Hilla, El- **25** Cc
Ḥillah, Al- **21** CDc
Hillsboro **32** Bb
Hilo **28** map no.1
Hilok (riv.) **16** Da
Hilok **14** Ed
Hilversum **8** Fa
Himachal Pradesh (State) **20** Eb
Himalayas (mts.) **20** EHbc
Himara **11** CDc
Himeji **16** Hcd
Himi **17** Ef
Himki **12** Eb
Ḥinākīyah, Al- **21** Ce
Hînçeşti (Kotovsk) **6** Ic
Hinche **35** Cb
Hinchinbrook Island **29** Hb
Hindukush (mts.) **20** CDa
Hindustan (phys. reg.) **20** DGc
Hingol (riv.) **20** Cc
Hinnøya (i.) **4** CDa
Hınzır Burun **22** Ed
Hiou (i.) **28** map no.4
Hirado **17** Ah
Hīrākud **16** Cf
Hiratsuka **17** Fg
Hirfanlı Barajı **22** DEc
Hirgis-Nur (l.) **14** Ce
Hiroo **17** Hc
Hirosaki **16** Jb
Hiroshima **16** Hd
Hirson **8** Fc
Hîrşova **6** Hld
Hisār **20** DEc
Hispaniola (Haiti) (i.) **35** CDb
Hita **17** Bh
Hitachi **16** Jc
Hitiaa **28** map no.2
Hitoyoshi **17** Bh
Hitra (i.) **4** ABc
Hiva **13** Fe
Hiva Oa, Île- (i.) **28** Cc
Hjälmaren (l.) **4** CDd
Hjørring **4** Bd
Hkakabo Razi (mt.) **19** Cc
Hmelnicki **6** Hb
Hmelnik **6** Hlb
Ho **24** Cd
Hoa Binh **19** DEd
Hobart **29** map no.1
Hobbs **33** Cc
Hobbs Coast **42** grid square no.3
Hobyo **25** Ed
Hochgolling (mt.) **5** DEe
Ho Chi Minh **15** Dhi
Hodaka-Dake (mt.) **17** Ef
Hodh (phys. reg.) **24** Bc
Hódmezővásárhely **6** Ec
Hodonín **5** Fd
Hodorov **6** Gb
Hodžejli **13** Ee
Hodžent (Leninabad) **13** Fe
Hoek van Holland, Rotterdam- **8** EFb
Hof **5** CDc
Höfn **4** map no.1
Hofrat en Nahas **25** Cd
Hofsjökull (gl.) **4** map no.1
Hōfu **17** Bgh
Hohe Tavern (mts.) **5** De
Hohhot **16** Db
Hoi An **19** Ee
Hojniki **12** CDc
Hokitika **27** De
Hokkaidō (i.) **16** JKb
Holbæk **5** Ca
Holguín **35** Ca
Hollywood, Los Angeles- **33** ABc
Holm **12** Db
Holman Island **31** CDa
Holmsk **14** He
Holmsund **4** Ec
Holon **22** Efg
Holstebro **4** ABd
Holsteinsborg / Sisimiut **31** Jb
Holyhead **7** De
Homalin **19** BCcd
Hombori **24** Bc
Home Bay **31** Ib
Home Hill **29** Hbc
Homestead **32** Cc
Homoljske planina (mts.)**6** EFd
Homs **21** Bc
Honaz dağı **22** Bd
Honbetsu **17** Hc
Hondo (riv.) **34** Dc
Honduras (Ind. St.) **30** Jh
Honduras, Golfo de- **34** Dc
Honghu **16** De
Hong Kong → Xianggang **15** Dg
Hongshui He **16** Cef
Honguedo, Détroit d'- **32** Ea
Hongze Hu (l.) **16** Ed
Honiara **27** CDc
Honjō **17** FGe
Honningsvag **4** EFa
Honokaa **28** map no.1
Honolulu **28** map no.1
Honshū (i.) **16** HIbc
Honuu **14** Hc
Hood, Mount- **33** Ab
Hoogeveen **8** Ga
Hooker, Bîr- **22** BCg
Hoolehua **28** map no.1
Hoover Dam (dam) **33** Bc
Hopedale **31** IJc
Hopen (i.) **13** Bb
Hopër (riv.) **12** Fc
Hopetoun **29** Ce
Hopkins, Lake- **29** Dc
Hor (riv.) **16** Ia
Hor **14** Ge
Horlick Mountains **42** grid square no.3
Hormigas **34** Bb
Hormuz, Strait of- **21** Fd
Horn (cap.) **4** map no.1
Horn **5** Ed
Horn, Cabo- **40** Bc
Horn, Cape- **36** Di
Hornavan (l.) **4** Db
Horn Islands **27** DEc
Horog **13** Gf
Horqin Youyi Qianqi **16** EFa
Horqueta **39** Cb
Horsens **4** Bde
Horsham **29** Gf
Horten **4** Bd
Hospet **20** Fe
Hospitalet de Llobregat **9** Gb
Hoste, Isla- (i.) **40** ABc
Hotan **20** EFa
Hotin **6** Hb
Hot Springs [Ar.-U.S.] **32** Bb
Hot Springs [S.D.-U.S.] **33** Cb
Houaïlou **28** map no.4
Houei Sai **19** Dd
Houlton **32** Ea
Houma **32** Bc
Houston **32** Bc
Houtman Abrolhos (is.) **29** Ad
Hovran Gölü **22** Cc
Howar **25** Cc
Howe, Cape- **29** HIf
Howe, West Cape- (cap.) **29** Bf
Howland Island **28** Ab
Hoy (i.) **7** Eb
Høyanger **4** Ac
Hoyos **9** Bb
Hradec Králové **5** EFc
Hristinovka **6** IJb
Hromtau **12** Ic
Hron (riv.) **5** Gd
Hrubieszów **5** Ic
Ḥsakah **21** BCb
Hsinchu **16** Ff
Huachacalla **39** Ba
Huacho **37** Bd
Huai He (riv.) **16** Ed
Huailai **16** Eb
Huainan **16** Ed
Hualien **16** Ff
Huallaga (riv.) **37** Bc
Huambo **26** Ac
Huanan **17** Ba
Huancane **39** ABa
Huancavelica **37** Bd
Huancayo **36** Ce
Huang Hai → Yellow Sea **16** Fc
Huang He **16** Ed
Huang He (riv.) **16** DEc
Huangshi **16** DEde
Huang Shui (riv.) **16** Bc
Huangyan **16** Fe
Huangyuan **16** Bc
Huánuco **37** Bc
Huaráz **37** Bc
Huascarán, Nevado- (mt.) **37** Bc
Hubei **16** Dd
Hubli **15** Ch
Hubsugul (l.) **14** Dd
Ḥudaydah, Al- **21** Cfg
Huddersfield **7** Fe
Hudiksvall **4** Dc
Hudson (riv.) **32** Da
Hudson Bay **31** Gbc
Hudson Strait **31** HIb
Hue **15** Dh
Huedin **6** Fc
Huehuetenango **35** Ab
Huelma **9** Dd
Huelva **9** Bd
Huércal-Overa **9** DEd
Huesca **9** Ea
Huéscar **9** Dd
Huete **9** Db
Hufūf, Al- **21** DEd
Hughenden **29** Gc
Huila, Nevado del- (mt.) **37** Bb
Huili **16** Be
Huinan **16** Gb

© ISTITUTO GEOGRAFICO DE AGOSTINI S.p.A. - Novara

Huinca Renancó **39** Bc
Huixian **16** Cd
Huize **16** Be
Huizhou **16** DEf
Hukuntsi **26** Bd
Hulan **16** Ga
Hulga (riv.) **12** Ja
Hulin **16** Ha
Hull **31** Hd
Hull (i.) **28** Ac
Hulun Nur (l.) **16** Ea
Ḥulwān **22** Ch
Humacao **35** Db
Humaitá **37** Cc
Humansdorp **26** Be
Humber (riv.) **7** FGe
Humberto de Campos **38** Cb
Humboldt (riv.) **33** Bb
Humenné **5** Hld
Hün **24** Db
Húnaflói (g.) **4** map no.1
Hunan (prov.) **16** De
Hunchun **17** Bc
Hunedoara **6** Fd
Hungary (Ind. St.) **3** EFc
Hüngnam **16** Gbc
Hungtao Yu → Lan Hsu (is.)
 16 Ff
Hunsrück **5** Ad
Hunter Island **29** map no.1
Huntingdon **7** FGe
Huntington **32** Cb
Huntsville [Al.–U.S.] **32** Cb
Huntsville [Tx.–U.S.] **32** Bb
Hunyuan **16** DEc
Huon, Île– (is.) **27** Dc
Huraymila **21** Dd
Huron **32** Bc
Huron, Lake– **32** Ca
Húsavík **4** map no.1
Huşi **6** Ic
Huskvarna **4** Cd
Hust **6** Fb
Husum **5** Ba
Hutchinson **32** Bb
Huzhou → Wuxing **16** EFd
Hvalynsk **12** Gc
Hvammstangi **4** map no.1
Hvannadalshnúkur (mt.) **4**
 map no.1
Hvar (i.) **11** Bb
Hwange **26** Bc
Hyderabad [India] **15** Ch
Hyderabad [Pak.] **15** Cg
Hyères **8** Gf
Hyères, Iles d'– **8** Gf
Hyesan **16** Gb
Hyūga **17** BCh
Hyvinkää **4** EFc

I

Iaco (riv.) **37** BCcd
Iaçu **38** Cc
Ialomiţa (riv.) **6** Hd
Iaşi **6** Hc
Iauareté **37** Cb
Ibadan **24** Cd
Ibague **37** Bb
Ibar (riv.) **11** Db
Ibarra **37** Bb

Ibb **21** Cg
Iberia **37** Cd
Ibérico, Sistema– (mts.) **9**
 DEab
Ibi **24** CDd
Ibiá **39** Da
Ibiapaba, Serra da– (mts.) **38**
 Cb
Ibicuy **39** Cc
Ibiza (i.) **9** Fc
Ibiza **9** Fc
Iblei, Monti– **10** Ef
Ibn Hāni', Ra's– **22** Ee
Ibo **26** Dc
Ibra **21** Fe
Ibradi **22** Cd
'Ibri **21** Fe
Ibshawäy **22** Ch
Ibusuki **17** Bi
Ica **37** Bd
Içá (riv.) **37** Cc
Içana **37** Cb
Içana (riv.) **37** Cb
Iceland (Ind. St.) **3** ABa
Ichalkaranji **20** De
Ichinomiya **17** Eg
Ichinoseki **17** Ge
Icó **38** Db
Idah **24** Cd
Idaho (State) **33** Bb
Idaho Falls **33** Bb
Iddan **25** Ed
Idfu **25** Db
Idhi Óros **11** Ff
Ídhra (i.) **11** Ee
Idlib **22** Fe
Idre **4** Cc
Idrija **6** Bcd
Ieper **8** Eb
Ierápetra **11** FGf
Ierisós **11** EFc
Ifakara **26** Cb
Ifalik Atoll **27** Cb
Ife **24** Cd
Iferouâne **24** Cc
Iforas, Adrar des– (mt.) **24**
 Cbc
Igarka **13** Hc
Iğdir **22** Eb
Ighil–Izane **24** Ca
Iglesias **10** Be
Igli **24** Ba
Igloolik **31** GHb
Iğneada **22** ABab
Igoumenítsa **11** Dd
Igra **12** Hb
Igreja, Morro da– (mts.) **39**
 CDb
Iguaçu (riv.) **39** Cb
Igualada **9** Fb
Iguala de la Independencia
 34 BCc
Iguape **39** Db
Iguassu Falls **39** Cb
Iguatu **38** CDb
Iharagna **26** map no.1
Iheya–Jima **16** Ga
Ihosy **26** map no.1
Ihtiman **11** Eb
Ii **4** Fb
Ii (riv.) **4** Fb
Iida **17** Eg
Iisalmi **4** FGc

Iizuka **17** Bh
IJsselmeer **8** Fa
Ijuw **27** map no.2
Ikaría (i.) **11** FGe
Ikeda [Jap.] **17** CDgh
Ikeda [Jap.] **17** Hc
Ikela **26** Bb
Iki (i.) **17** Ah
Ilagan (i.) **18** Fa
Ilan **16** Ff
Iława **5** Gb
Ilebo **23** Ef
Ile–de–France (hist. reg.) **8**
 DEc
Ilek (riv.) **12** Ic
Ilesha **24** Cd
Ilfracombe **7** Df
Ilgaz dağları (mts.) **22** DEb
Ilgın **22** Cc
Ilha Grande **37** Cc
Ilhavo **9** Ab
Ilhéus **38** Dc
Ili (riv.) **13** Ge
Iličevsk **12** Dd
Iligan (i.) **18** Fc
Ilinski **14** He
Illampu, Nevado de– **39** Ba
Illapel **39** Ac
Illéla **24** Cc
Iller (riv.) **5** Cd
Illimani, Nevado– (mt.) **39** Ba
Illinois (State) **32** BCab
Illizi **24** Cb
Ilmen, ozero– **12** Db
Ilo **39** Aa
Iloilo **18** Fb
Ilomantsi **4** Gc
Ilorin **24** Cd
Imabari **17** Cg
Imandra, ozero– **4** GHb
Imari **17** ABh
Imatra **4** Gc
Imbābah **22** Cg
Imbituba **39** Db
Imola **10** Cb
Imotski **6** Ce
Imperatriz **38** Cb
Imperia **10** ABc
Impfondo **25** Bd
Imphal **15** Dg
Ïmrali Adası (i.) **22** Bb
Iñapari **37** Bcd
Inarajan **27** map no.1
Inari **4** Fa
Inarijärvi **4** FGa
Inca **9** Gc
Ince Burun **22** Ea
Inch'ŏn **16** FGc
Incudine, Monte– **8** map no.1
Indals (riv.) **4** Dc
Independence **32** Bb
Inderagiri (riv.) **18** Be
Inderborski **13** Ee
India (Ind. St.) **15** Cg
Indiana (State) **32** Ca
Indianapolis **32** Cab
Indian Ocean **2**
Indiga **13** DEc
Indigirka (riv.) **14** Hbc
Indonesia (Ind. St.) **15** DEj
Indore **20** DEd
Indramayu **18** Cf
Indravati (riv.) **20** Fe

Indre (riv.) **8** Dd
Indus (riv.) **20** CDc
Indus, Mouths of the– **20** Cd
Inebolu **22** DEb
Inegöl **22** Bb
Ineu, Vîrful– (mt.) **6** Gc
Infiernillo, Presa del–(l.) **34** Bc
Inga **26** Ab
I–n–Gall **24** Cc
Ingeniero Guillermo Nuño
 Juárez **39** Bb
Ingeniero Jacobacci **40** ABb
Ingham (l.) **29** Hb
Ingolstadt **5** CDd
Ingräj Bäzär **20** Gcd
Ingrid Christensen Kyst **42**
 grid square no.2
Ingush (Aut. Rep.) **13** De
Inhambane **23** Fh
Inini (riv.) **38** Ba
Inírida (riv.) **37** Cb
Inja **14** Hd
Injune **29** Hd
Inland Sea **16** Hd
Inn / En (riv.) **5** Dd
Innamincka **29** FGd
Inner Mongolia (Aut. Reg.) **15**
 DEe
Innisfail **29** Hb
Innsbruck **5** Ce
Inongo **26** Ab
Inoucdjouac **31** Hc
Inowrocław **5** FGb
Inquisivi **39** Ba
In–Salah **24** Cb
Inscription, Cape– **29** Ad
Inta **13** EFc
Intanagar **19** Bc
Interlaken **10** ABa
International Falls **32** Ba
Interview (i.) **19** Bf
Invercargill **27** De
Inverell **29** Ide
Invergordon **7** Dc
Inverness **7** DEc
Investigator Group **29** Ee
Investigator Strait **29** Ff
Inyanga, Mountains– **26** Cc
Inza **12** Gc
Inžavino **12** Fc
Ioánnina **11** Dd
Iolotan **21** Gb
Ionian Islands **11** CDde
Iony, ostrov– (i.) **14** Hd
Ios (i.) **11** Fe
Iô–Shima (i.) **17** Bi
Iowa (State) **32** Ba
Iowa City **32** Ba
Ipameri **39** Da
Ipiales **37** Bb
Ipiranga **37** Cc
Ipiros (phys. reg.) **11** Dcd
Ipixuna **37** Bc
Ipoh **19** Dh
Iporá **39** Ca
Ipsala **22** Ab
Ipswich [Austl.] **29** Id
Ipswich [U.K.] **7** Ge
Ipu **38** Cb
Iquique **39** ABab
Iquiri → Ituxi (riv.) **37** Cc
Iquitos **36** Cd
Iracoubo **37** Db

© ISTITUTO GEOGRAFICO DE AGOSTINI S.p.A. - Novara

Irafshān **21** Gd
Iráklia (i.) **11** Fe
Íráklion **11** Ff
Iran (Ind. St.) **15** Bf
Iran, Penunungan- **18** Dd
Irānshahr **21** Gd
Irapuato **34** Bb
Iraq (Ind. St.) **15** Bf
Irati **39** Cb
Irazú, Volcán- (mt.) **35** Bc
Irbid **22** Ef
Irbit **12** Jb
Ireland (Ind. St.) **3** BCb
Irgiz **13** Fe
Irian Jaya (prov.) **27** Bc
Irian Jaya **27** Bc
Iringa **26** Cb
Iriomote-Jima (i.) **16** Ff
Iriri (riv.) **38** Bb
Irish Sea **7** De
Irkutsk **14** Dd
Iroise (b.) **8** Ac
Iron Gate (p.) **6** Fd
Iron Knob **29** Fe
Iron Mountain **32** BCa
Ironwood **32** BCa
Irpen **6** Ja
'Irqah, Al- **21** Dg
Irrawaddv, Mouths of the- **19** BCe
Irrawaddy (riv.) **19** Ccd
Irtyš (riv.) **13** Gd
Irún **9** DEa
Isabela, Isla- (i.) **36** Ad
Isafjörđur **4** map no.1
Isahaya **17** ABh
Isar (riv.) **5** Dd
Ischia (i.) **10** Dd
Ise **17** Eg
Iseo **10** Cb
Iseo, Lago d'- (l.) **10** Cb
Isère (riv.) **8** Fe
Iserlohn **5** Ac
Isernia **10** Ed
Ise-Wan **17** Eg
Iseyin **24** Cd
İsfendiyar → Küre dağları (mts.) **22** DEb
Ishigaki-Jima (i.) **16** FGf
Ishikari-Gawa (riv.) **17** Hc
Ishikari-Wan **17** Gc
Ishinomaki **16** Jc
Ishizuchi-Yama (mt.) **17** Ch
Ishurdi **20** Gd
Işik dāg (mt.) **22** Db
Isilkul **13** Gd
Išim (riv.) **13** Fd
Išim **13** Fd
Isimbaj **12** Ic
Isiro **26** Ba
Iskar (riv.) **11** EFb
İskenderun **22** Fd
İskenderun Körfezi **22** EFd
Iskilip **22** DEb
Iskitim **13** Hd
Isla-Cristina **9** Bd
Islâhiye **22** Fd
Islamabad **15** Cf
Island Lagoon **29** Fe
Islay (i.) **7** Cd
Isle (riv.) **8** De
Ismailia **25** Da
Isna **25** Db
Isoka **26** Cc
Isola del Liri **10** Dd
Isparta **22** Cd
Isperih **11** Gb
Israel (Ind. St.) **15** Bf
Issoire **8** Ee
Issoudun **8** DEd
Issyk-Kul (Rybačje) **13** Ge
Issyk-Kul, ozero- (l.) **13** Ge
İstanbul (Constantinople) **22** Bb
Istanbul-Üsküdar **22** Bb
Istiaía **11** Ed
Istmina **37** Bb
Istra **6** ABd
Itabaiana **38** Dc
Itaberaba **38** Cc
Itabira **39** Da
Itabuna **38** Dc
Itacaiúnas (riv.) **38** BCb
Itacoatiara **38** Bb
Itagüí **37** Bb
Itaituba **38** Bb
Itajaí **39** Db
Itajubá **39** Db
Italia, Cerro- **40** Bc
Italy (Ind. St.) **3** Ec
Itambé, Pico de- (mt.) **39** Da
Itaperuna **39** Db
Itapetinga **38** CDc
Itapeva **39** Db
Itapicuru [Braz.] (riv.) **38** Cb
Itapicuru [Braz.] (riv.) **38** Dc
Itapipoca **38** Db
Itaqui **39** Cb
Itararé **39** Db
Itarsi **20** Ed
Itea **11** Ed
Ithaca **32** Da
Ithaca (i.) **11** Dd
Itoigawa **17** Ef
Itseqqortoormit / Scoresbysund **30** PQb
Ituí (riv.) **37** Bc
Itumbiara **39** Da
Iturup, ostrov- / Etorofu Tō (i.) **14** He
Ituxi (Iquiri) (riv.) **37** Cc
Itzehoe **5** Bb
Iultin **14** KLc
Ival (riv.) **39** Cb
Ivalo **4** FGa
Ivalojoki (riv.) **4** Fa
Ivangorod **4** Gd
Ivanhoe **29** GHe
Ivankov **6** Ia
Ivano-Frankovsk **6** Gb
Ivanovo **3** GHb
Ivdel **13** EFc
Ivittuut **31** Kb
Ivory Coast (Ind. St.) **23** Be
Ivory Coast (phys. reg.) **24** Bd
Ivrea **10** Ab
Ivujvik **31** Hb
Iwaki **16** Jc
Iwakuni **17** BCg
Iwamisawa **17** Gc
Iwanai **17** FGc
Iwanuma **17** Gef
Iwate-San (mt.) **17** Gde
Iwo **24** Cd
Ixtlán del Río **34** Bb
Iyadh **21** Dfg
Izamal **34** Db
Izberbaš **21** Da
Iževsk **13** Ed
Izjaslav **6** Ha
Izjum **12** Ed
Izki **21** Fe
Izmail **6** Id
İzmir **22** Ac
Izmir Bay **22** Ac
Izmit **22** BCb
Iznalloz **9** Dd
Iznik **22** BCb
İznik Gölü **22** Bb
Izozog, Bañados del- **39** Ba
Izúcar de Matamoros **34** Cc
Izu-Hantō **17** Fg
Izumo **17** Cg
Izu-Shotō **16** IJd
Izvesti C.I.K., ostrova- **13** GHb

J

Jabal Iweibid **25** map no.1
Jabalón (riv.) **9** Dc
Jabalpur **15** Cg
Jablah **22** Ee
Jablanica (mt.) **11** Dc
Jablanica **10** Fc
Jablonec-nad-Nisou **5** Ec
Jablonicki, pereval- **6** FGb
Jablunkovsky prusmyk **5** Gd
Jaboatão **38** Db
Jabor **28** map no.3
Jaburu **37** Cc
Jaca **9** Ea
Jacarézinho **39** CDb
Jaciparaná **37** Cc
Jackson [Mi.-U.S.] **32** Ca
Jackson [Ms.-U.S.] **32** BCb
Jackson [Tn.-U.S.] **32** Cb
Jacksonville **32** CDb
Jacobabad **20** Cc
Jacobina **38** Cc
Jacques Cartier, Détroit de- (str.) **32** Eab
Jacuí **39** Cbc
Jadida, El- **24** ABa
Jaén [Peru] **37** Bc
Jaén [Sp.] **9** Dd
Jaffna **15** Chi
Jafr, Al- **22** Fg
Jagdalpur **20** Fe
Jaghbūb, Al- **24** Eab
Jaguarão **39** Cc
Jaguariaíva **39** CDb
Jaguaribe (riv.) **38** Db
Jahrom **21** Ed
Jaipur **15** Cg
Jaisalmer **20** Dc
Jajce **6** Cd
Jajva **12** Ib
Jakarta **18** Cf
Jakobstad **4** Ec
Jakutsk **14** Fc
Jakuvlevca (mt.) **17** Cb
Jalalabad **20** CDb
Jalālah al Baḩrāyah, Jabal- (mt.) **22** CDh
Jalālah al Qibliah, Jabal- (mt.) **22** CDh
Jalandhar **20** Eb
Jalapa Enriquez **34** Cbc
Jalgaon **20** DEd
Jalingo **24** Dd
Jalna **20** Ee
Jalón (riv.) **9** Eb
Jalpaiguri **19** Jj
Jalta **13** Ce
Jālū, Wāḩāt- **24** Eb
Jaluit Atoll **27** Db
Jaluit Atoll (at.) **28** map no.3
Jalutorovsk **13** Fd
Jamaame **25** Ee
Jamaica (Ind. St.) **30** JKh
Jamaica Channel **35** Cb
Jamalpur [Bngl.] **20** GHcd
Jamalpur [India] **19** Ij
Jamantau, gora- (mt.) **13** Ed
Jamanxim (riv.) **38** Bb
Jambol **11** Gb
Jambongan, Pulau- (i.) **18** Ec
James (riv.) **32** Ba
James Bay **30** JKd
James Ross Island **42** grid square no.1
Jamestown [N.D.-U.S.] **33** CDb
Jamestown [N.Y.-U.S.] **32** Da
Jammu **20** DEb
Jammu e Kashmir (State) **20** DEab
Jamnagar **15** Cg
Jampol [Ukr.] **6** GHb
Jampol [Ukr.] **6** Ib
Jämsä **4** Fc
Jamshedpur **20** FGd
Jamsk **14** Id
Jana (riv.) **14** Gc
Janaúba **39** Da
Janesville **32** Ca
Janghai **19** Hj
Janīn **22** Ef
Janisjärvi, ozero- **4** Gc
Jan Mayen (i.) **30** Rbc
Jánoshalma **6** Dc
Janski **14** Gc
Jantra (riv.) **11** FGb
Januária **39** Da
Japan (Ind. St.) **15** Ef
Japan, Sea of- / East Sea **16** HIbc
Japurá (riv.) **37** Cc
Japurá **37** Cc
Jar **12** Hb
Jarābulus **22** FGd
Jaramillo **40** Bb
Jaransk **12** Gb
Jarcevo [Russia] **14** BCcd
Jarcevo [Russia] **12** Db
Jardines de la Reina (i.) **35** BCa
Jari (riv.) **38** Bab
Jarīd, Shaţţ al- (l.) **24** Ca
Jarocin **5** FGbc
Jaroslavl **13** Cd
Jarosław **5** Icd
Järpen **4** Cc
Jarub **21** Ef
Järvenpää **4** Fc
Jarvis Island **28** Abc
Jāsk **21** Fd
Jasło **5** Hd

© ISTITUTO GEOGRAFICO DE AGOSTINI S.p.A. - Novara

© ISTITUTO GEOGRAFICO DE AGOSTINI S.p.A. - Novara

Kahovka 12 Dd
Kahovskoje vodohranilišče 12 DEd
Kahramanmaras 21 Bb
Kahuku Point 28 map no.1
Kai, Kepulauan– 27 Bc
Kaiama 24 Cd
Kaieteur Falls 37 Db
Kaifeng 16 DEcd
Kaikoura 27 De
Kailua 28 map no.1
Kainji Reservoir 24 Ccd
Kaiserslautern 5 ABd
Kaishantun 17 ABc
Kaiwi Channel 28 map no.1
Kaiyuan [China] 16 Fb
Kaiyuan [China] 16 Bf
Kajaani 4 Fb
Kajabbi 29 FGbc
Kakamas 26 ABd
Kakegawa 17 EFg
Kakinada 20 Fe
Kala, El– 10 Bf
Kalabáka 11 DEd
Kalabo 26 Bc
Kalač 12 Fc
Kalač–na–Donu 12 Fd
Ka Lae (cap.) 28 map no.1
Kalahari Desert 26 Bd
Kalakan 14 Ed
Kalámai 11 DEe
Kalamazoo 32 Ca
Kalamunda 29 ABe
Kalannie 29 Be
Kalao, Pulau– (i.) 18 EFf
Kalaotoa, Pulau– (is.) 18 Ff
Kalapana 28 map no.1
Kalaraš 6 Hlc
Kalat 20 Cc
Kalaus (riv.) 12 Fd
Kalavarda 22 ABd
Kalávrita 11 Ed
Kale [Tur.] 22 BCd
Kale [Tur.] 22 Bd
Kalecik 22 Db
Kalemie 26 Bb
Kalevala 4 Gb
Kalewa 19 BCd
Kalgoorlie 29 Ce
Kaliakra, Nos– 11 Hb
Kalibo 18 Fb
Kalimantan → Borneo (i.) 18 DEd
Kálimnos (i.) 11 Ge
Kalimpong 19 Jj
Kalinin → Tver 13 Cd
Kaliningrad 13 ABd
Kalininsk 12 FGc
Kalinkoviči 3 FGb
Kalinovka 6 Ib
Kalispell 33 Bb
Kalisz 5 Gc
Kalixälven (riv.) 4 Eb
Kaljazin 12 Eb
Kalkfontein 26 Bd
Kallavesi (l.) 4 Fc
Kallsjön (l.) 4 Cc
Kalmar 4 CDd
Kalmyk (Aut. Rep.) 13 De
Kalmykovo 12 Hd
Kalocsa 6 Dc
Kalpa 20 Eb
Kalpeni Island 20 Dfg

Kalpi 20 EFc
Kaluga 13 Cd
Kalumburu 29 Da
Kalundborg 5 Ca
Kaluš 6 Gb
Kalvarija 5 Ia
Kalyan 20 De
Kama (riv.) 12 Hb
Kamaishi 17 GHe
Kamarän 21 Cf
Kambalda 29 Ce
Kambarka 12 Hlb
Kambove 26 Bc
Kamčatka (riv.) 14 Id
Kamchatka Peninsula 14 Id
Kamčija (riv.) 6 He
Kamenec–Podolski 6 Hb
Kamenjak, Rt– 6 Ad
Kamenka [Russia] 17 DEb
Kamenka [Russia] 12 Fc
Kamenka–Bugskaja 6 Ga
Kamen Kaširski 12 BCc
Kamen–na–Obi 13 GHd
Kamen–Rybolov 17 BCb
Kamenskoje 14 Jc
Kamenskoje vodohranilišče 12 Ib
Kamensk–Šahtinski 12 Fd
Kamensk–Uralski 13 Fd
Kamenz 5 Ec
Kamień Pomorski 5 Eab
Kamina 23 Ef
Kamino–Shima (i.) 17 Ag
Kamloops 33 Aa
Kampala 25 Dde
Kampar (riv.) 18 Bde
Kampar 19 Dh
Kampen 8 Fa
Kâmpóng Chhnãng 19 Df
Kâmpóng Saôm →
Sihanoukville 19 Df
Kampot 19 Df
Kamyšin 13 Dde
Kananga 26 Bb
Kanaš 12 Gb
Kanazawa 16 Ic
Kanchanaburi 19 Cf
Kanchenjunga (mt.) 19 IJj
Kānchipuram 20 EFf
Kandalakša 13 BCc
Kandangan 18 Ee
Kandavu Island 27 Dc
Kandavu Passage (str.) 28 map no.6
Kandi 24 Cc
Kandıra 22 Cb
Kandla 20 CDd
Kandy 20 EFg
Kanem (phys. reg.) 25 Bc
Kaneohe 28 map no.1
Kang 20 Bb
Kangaatsiaq / Kangâtsiaq 31 Jb
Kangaba 24 Bc
Kangâmiut 31 Jb
Kangän 21 Ed
Kangar 19 Dg
Kangaroo Island 29 Ff
Kangaruma 37 Db
Kangâtsiq / Kangaatsiaq 31 Jb
Kangding 16 Bde

Kangean, Kepulauan– 18 Ef
Kangean, Pulau– (i.) 18 Ef
Kanggye 16 Gb
Kangmar 19 Ji
Kangnŭng 16 Gc
Kangto (mt.) 19 Bc
Kaniama 26 Bb
Kanin, Poluostrov– 13 Dc
Kanin Nos, mys– 13 Dc
Kanjiža 6 Ec
Kankan 24 Bc
Kankossa 24 ABc
Kannauj 19 GHj
Kano 24 Cc
Kanoya 17 Bi
Kanpur 15 Cg
Kansas (riv.) 32 Bb
Kansas (State) 32 Bb
Kansas City 32 Bb
Kansk 14 Cd
Känthi 19 Ik
Kantō–Heiya (phys. reg.) 17 FGf
Kanton Atoll 28 Ac
Kanye 26 Bd
Kaohsiung 16 EFf
Kaolack 24 Ac
Kaoma 26 Bc
Kapaa 28 map no.1
Kapanga 26 Bb
Kapčagaj 13 Ge
Kapela (mt.) 6 Bd
Kapfenberg 5 Ee
Kapidaği, Yarimadasi– 11 GHc
Kapingamarangi, Atoll– 27 CDb
Kapisigdlit / Kapisillit 31 JKb
Kapisillit / Kapisigdlit 31 JKb
Kapit 18 Dd
Kaposvár 6 Cc
Kapsukas → Marijampolė 5 Ia
Kapuas (riv.) 18 Def
Kapuas Hulu, Pegunungan– 18 Dd
Kapuskasing 31 GHd
Kapuvár 6 Cc
Kara 24 BCd
Karaağaç 11 Gc
Karababa daği (riv.) 22 EFc
Karabaš 12 IJb
Karabiga 11 Gc
Kara–Bogaz–Gol, zaliv– (b.) 13 Ee
Karabük 22 Db
Karacabey 22 Bb
Karacaköy 11 Hc
Karačev 12 Ec
Karachi 15 Cg
Kara Dağ (mt.) 22 Dd
Karagajly 13 Ge
Karaganda 13 Ge
Karaginski, ostrov– (i.) 14 Jd
Karagöl daği (mt.) 22 Gb
Karaisalı 22 Ed
Karaj 21 Eb
Karak, Al– 22 Eg
Kara–Kolpak (Aut. Rep.) 13 Ee
Karakoram (mts.) 20 Eab
Karakoram Pass 20 Ea
Karaköse–Ağri 21 Cab

Karakumski Kanal 13 EFf
Karakumy (phys. reg.) 13 EFef
Karaman 22 Dd
Karamay 15 Ce
Karamiran Shankou 20 Ga
Karapınar 22 Dd
Karasburg 26 Ad
Kara Sea 41 grid square no.3
Karasjok 4 Fa
Kara Strait 41 grid square no.3
Karasu 22 Cb
Karasuk 13 Gd
Karatas 22 Ed
Karatau, Hrebet– (mts.) 13 FGe
Karatsu 17 ABh
Karaul 13 Hb
Karauli 19 Gj
Karáva (mt.) 11 Dd
Karažal 13 FGe
Karbalâ′ 21 Cc
Karcag 6 Ec
Kardhítsa 11 DEd
Kärdla 4 Ed
Kärdžali 11 Fc
Karekelong, Pulau– (i.) 18 Gd
Karelia (phys. reg.) 13 Cc
Karelia (Aut. Rep.) 13 Cc
Karen (State) 19 Ce
Kargopol 12 Ea
Karhula 4 Fc
Kariai 11 EFc
Kariba 26 Bc
Kariba, Lake– 26 Bc
Karibib 26 Ad
Karimata Islands 18 Ce
Karimata Strait 18 Ce
Karimnagar 20 EFe
Karimunjawa Islands 18 CDf
Karin 25 Ec
Karis 4 Fc
Karisimbi (mt.) 26 Bb
Karkheh (riv.) 21 Dc
Karkinitski zaliv 12 Dd
Karlobag 6 Bd
Karlovac 6 Bd
Karlovo 11 Fb
Karlovy Vary 5 Dc
Karlshamn 4 Cd
Karlskoga 4 Cd
Karlskrona 4 CDd
Karlsruhe 5 ABd
Karlstad 4 Cd
Karmah 25 Dc
Karnali (riv.) 20 Fc
Karnataka (State) 20 DEf
Karnobat 11 Gb
Karonga 26 Cbc
Karoo (phys. reg.) 26 Be
Karora 25 Dc
Káros (i.) 11 Fe
Kárpathos (i.) 11 Gf
Kárpathos 11 Gf
Karpaty (mts.) 12 BCd
Karpenision 11 DEd
Karpinsk 12 IJab
Karpuzlu 22 ABd
Kars 21 Ca
Karsakpaj 13 Fe
Karši 13 Ff
Kartal 22 Bb

© ISTITUTO GEOGRAFICO DE AGOSTINI S.p.A. - Novara

Kartaly 13 Fd
Karumba 29 Gb
Kārun (riv.) 21 Dc
Karviná 5 Gd
Karwar 20 Df
Karymskoje 14 Ed
Kaş 22 Bd
Kasai (riv.) 26 ABb
Kasai Occidental (reg.) 26 Bb
Kasai Oriental (reg.) 26 Bb
Kasama 26 Cbc
Kasane 26 Bc
Kasba Lake 31 Eb
Kasempa 26 Bc
Kasenga 26 Bc
Kasese 25 CDde
Kasganj 19 Gj
Kāshān 21 Ec
Kashi 15 Cf
Kashipur 19 Gi
Kashiwazaki 17 EFf
Kāshmar 21 Fb
Kashmir 20 Eb
Kasimov 12 Fc
Kašira 12 Ec
Kasiruta, Pulau– (i.) 18 Ge
Kaskö 4 Ec
Káson, Stenón– 11 Gf
Kasongo 26 Bb
Kásos (i.) 11 Gf
Kaspijski 12 Gd
Kasr, Ra's– 25 Dc
Kassala 25 Dc
Kassándra (pen.) 11 Ecd
Kassándra, Gulf of– 11 Ecd
Kassel 5 Bc
Kasserine 24 Ca
Kassubia (hist. reg.) 5 FGab
Kastamonu 22 DEb
Kastéllion 11 Ef
Kastoría 11 Dc
Kastornoje 12 Ec
Kasur 20 Db
Katanga (hist. reg.) 26 Bb
Katangli 14 Hd
Katanning 29 Be
Katarnian Ghat 19 Hi
Katav–Ivanovsk 12 Ic
Katchall (i.) 19 Bg
Katerini 11 Ec
Katha 19 Cd
Katherine 29 Ea
Kathgodam 19 Gi
Kathiawar (phys. reg.) 20 CDd
Kathmandu 15 Cg
Katihar 19 Ij
Katingan (riv.) 18 De
Katiola 24 Bd
Káto Akhaïa 11 Dde
Katoomba 29 Ie
Katowice 5 Gc
Kätrīnā, Jabal– (mt.) 25 Db
Katrineholm 4 CDd
Katsina 24 Cc
Kattakurgan 13 Ff
Kattegat (str.) 4 BCd
Katun (riv.) 13 Hd
Kau 18 Gd
Kauai (i.) 28 Ba
Kauai Channel 28 map no.1
Kaufbeuren 5 Ce
Kauhajoki 4 Ec

Kaula (i.) 28 map no.1
Kaulakahi Channel 28 map no.1
Kauliranta 4 EFb
Kaunas 4 EFe
Kaura Namoda 24 Cc
Kautokeino 4 EFa
Kavacık 22 Bc
Kavaja 11 Cc
Kavála 11 Fc
Kavalerovo 17 Db
Kavaratti (i.) 20 Df
Kavarna 11 Hb
Kawagoe 17 Ffg
Kawaguchi 17 FGfg
Kawaikini (mt.) 28 map no.1
Kawasaki 16 IJc
Kawio, Kepulauan– 18 FGd
Kawm 25 Db
Kawthaung 19 Cfg
Kaya 24 Bc
Kayah (State) 19 Ce
Kayan (riv.) 18 Ed
Kayes 24 Ac
Kayoa, Pulau– (i.) 18 Gde
Kayseri (Cesarea Mazaca) 22 EFc
Kazačje 14 Gb
Kazakhstan (Ind. St.) 13 EGe
Kazalinsk 13 EFe
Kazan 13 Dd
Kazan (riv.) 31 Eb
Kazanlák 11 Fb
Kazatin 6 Ib
Kaz daği (mt.) 22 Ac
Kāzerun 21 Ed
Kažim 12 Ha
Käẓimīyah, Al– 21 Cc
Kazincbarcika 6 Eb
Kéa (i.) 11 Ff
Kearney 33 CDb
Kebir (riv.) 22 Fe
Kebnekaise (mt.) 4 Dab
Kecskemét 6 Dc
Kédainiai 4 Ee
Kediri 18 Df
Kédougou 24 Ac
Keele Peak 31 Bb
Keelung 16 Fef
Keetmanshoop 23 DEh
Keewatin, District of– 31 Fb
Kefa (phys. reg.) 25 Cd
Keflavík 4 map no.1
Kehl 5 ABd
Keitele (l.) 4 Fc
Keith 29 Gf
Kelang 18 Bd
Kelang, Pulau– (i.) 18 Ge
Kelasa, Selat– 18 Ce
Kelkit (riv.) 22 Fb
Kéllé 26 Ab
Kelloselkä 4 FGb
Kelowna 31 Dcd
Keltepe (mt.) 22 Db
Keluang 18 Bd
Kem 13 Cc
Kemerovo 13 Hd
Kemi 4 Fb
Kemijärvi (l.) 4 Fb
Kemijärvi 4 Fb
Kemijoki (riv.) 4 Gb
Kempsey 29 Ie
Kempten im Allgäu 5 Ce

Ken (riv.) 20 Ed
Kendal 7 Ed
Kendari 18 Fe
Kenema 24 Ad
Kenge 26 Ab
Kengtung 19 Cd
Kenhardt 26 Bd
Kéniéba 24 ABc
Kénitra 24 Ba
Kenmare 7 Bf
Kenmare River 7 ABf
Kennedy, Cape– →
  Canaveral, Cape– 32 CDc
Keno Hill 31 Bb
Kenora 31 Fcd
Kent (co.) 7 Gf
Kent 24 Ad
Kentau 13 FGe
Kent Peninsula 31 Eb
Kentucky (State) 32 Cb
Kenya (Ind. St.) 23 Fe
Kenya (mt.) 25 De
Keokuk 32 Ba
Keonjhargarh 20 Gd
Kerala (State) 20 Efg
Kerama–Rettō 16 Ge
Kerč 13 Ce
Kerčensky Poluostrov 12 Ed
Kerempe Burun 22 Da
Keren 25 Dc
Kerguelen, Îles– (is.) 2
Kerinci, Gunung– (mt.) 18 Be
Kerkennah Islands 24 Da
Kerki 13 Ff
Kerkíras, Stenón– (str.) 11 CDd
Kermadec Islands 27 Ed
Kermān 21 Fc
Kermānshāh 21 Dc
Kerme Körfezi 11 GHe
Kérouané 24 ABd
Kerulen (riv.) 14 Ee
Keşan 11 Gc
Keşap 22 Gb
Kesennuma 17 GHe
Keshan 16 FGa
Kestenga 4 Gb
Kestep 22 Bd
Keszthely 6 Cc
Kéta 24 Cd
Ketapang 18 CDe
Ketchikan 31 BCc
Ketoj, ostrov– (i.) 14 Ie
Ketrzyn 5 Ha
Kettering 7 Fe
Keuruu 4 Fc
Keweenaw Peninsula 32 Ca
Key West 32 Cc
Kezel Owzan (riv.) 21 Db
Kežma 14 CDd
Khābūra, Al– 21 Fe
Khairpur 20 Cc
Khalīg el Tina (g.) 25 map no.1
Khálki (i.) 11 Hf
Khalkís 11 EFd
Khalūf 21 Fe
Khamasin, Al– 21 CDe
Khambhāt 20 Dd
Khambhāt, Gulf of– 20 Dd
Khamir 21 Cf
Khamis Mushayt 21 Cf
Khamsa 25 map no.1

Khanabad 20 CDa
Khanaqin 21 Dc
Khandaq, Al– (str.) 25 CDc
Khandwa 20 Ed
Khanewal 20 Db
Khanh Hung 19 Eg
Khánia 11 EFf
Khaníon, Kólpos– 11 EFf
Khanpur 20 Dc
Khān Yūnus 22 DEg
Kharagpur 15 Cg
Kharga Oasis 25 CDb
Khárijah, Al– 25 CDb
Khârk, Jazireh– ye– (i.) 21 DEd
Khartoum 25 Dc
Khartoum North 25 Dc
Khâsh 21 Gd
Khashm al Qirbah 25 Dc
Khasi–Jaintia Hill 16 Fe
Khawr al Fakkān 21 Fd
Khaybar 21 BCd
Khíos 22 Ac
Kholm 20 Ca
Khong 19 Ef
Khong Sedon 19 Ee
Khon Kaen 19 De
Khorāsān (phys. reg.) 21 Fbc
Khóra Sfakíon 11 Ff
Khorat → Nakhon
  Ratchasima 19 Def
Khorixas 26 Ad
Khorramābād 21 Dc
Khorramshahr 21 DEc
Khouribga 24 Ba
Khrisí (i.) 11 Ff
Khufrah, Al– 24 Eb
Khulna 20 GHd
Khums, Al– 24 Da
Khuriyā Muriya, Jazā'ir– 21 Ff
Khurmah, Al– 21 Ce
Khuzdar 20 Cc
Khvoy 21 CDb
Khyber Pass 20 Db
Kiantajärvi 4 Gb
Kibombo 26 Bb
Kibondo 26 Cb
Kičevo 11 Dc
Kidal 24 Cc
Kidderminster 7 Ee
Kidira 24 Ac
Kiel 4 Be
Kiel Canal 5 Bab
Kielce 5 Hc
Kieler Bucht 5 Ca
Kieta 27 Cc
Kiev 13 Cd
Kiffa 24 Ac
Kifisiá 11 EFd
Kigali 26 BCb
Kigoma 23 EFf
Kii–Hantō 17 Fh
Kii–Suidō 17 Dh
Kijevskoje vodohranilišče 12 CDc
Kikai–Jima (i.) 16 GHe
Kikinda 6 Ed
Kikonai 17 FGd
Kikori 27 Cc
Kikwit 26 Ab
Kil 4 Cd
Kilambé, Cerro– (mt.) 35 Bb

© ISTITUTO GEOGRAFICO DE AGOSTINI S.p.A. - Novara

© ISTITUTO GEOGRAFICO DE AGOSTINI S.p.A. - Novara

Leer in Ostfriesland **5** Ab
Leeuwarden **8** FGa
Leeuwin, Cape– **29** ABe
Leeward Islands **28** Bc
Lefke **22** De
Legazpi **18** Fb
Legges Tor (mt.) **29** map no.1
Legionowo **5** Hb
Legnago **10** Cb
Legnica **5** Fc
Leh **20** Eb
Lehua (i.) **28** map no.1
Leibnitz **5** Ee
Leibo **16** Be
Leicester **7** Fe
Leichhardt River **29** Fb
Leiden **8** Fa
Leie (riv.) **8** Eb
Leigh Creek **29** Fe
Leine (riv.) **5** Bbc
Leinster (prov.) **7** Ce
Leipzig **5** Dc
Leiria **9** Ac
Leirvik **4** Ad
Leitha (riv.) **5** Fe
Leiyang **16** De
Leizhou Bandao **16** Cf
Leman, Lac– → Geneva,
  Lake– **10** Aa
Lemdiyya **24** Ca
Lempa, Río– (riv.) **35** Bb
Lena (riv.) **14** Fc
Lendery **4** Gc
Lenina, pik– **13** Gf
Leninabad → Hodžent **13** Fe
Leningrad → Saint
  Petersburg **13** Cd
Leningradskaja **42** grid
  square no.4
Leninkan → Kumayri **13** De
Leninogorsk [Kaz.] **13** Hd
Leninogorsk [Russia] **12** Hc
Leninsk Kuznecki **13** Hld
Leninskoje **12** Gb
Lenkoran **13** DEf
Lennox, Isla– **40** Bc
Lens **8** Eb
Lensk **14** Ec
Lentini **10** Ef
Léo **24** Bc
Leoben **5** Ee
León (mt.) **34** Cc
León [Mex.] **34** Bb
León [Sp.] **9** Ca
Leonidhion **11** Ee
Leonora **29** Cd
Leopold and Astrid Coast **42**
  grid square no.2
Lepel **12** Cc
Leping **16** Ee
Lepontine Alps **10** Ba
Leppävirta **4** FGc
Lepsy **13** GHe
Leptis Magna (r.) **24** Da
Lérida **9** Dab
Lerma **9** Dab
Léros (i.) **11** Ge
Lerwick **7** Fa
Lesbos (i.) **11** FGd
Leshan **16** Be
Leskovac **11** DEb
Lesnoj **13** Ecd
Lesotho (Ind. St.) **23** Ehi

Lesozavodsk **14** Ge
Lesparre–Médoc **8** Ce
Lesser Antilles (is.) **36** Db
Lesser Kingan Range **14** Fde
Lesser Slave Lake **31** Dc
Leszno **5** Fc
Letha Range **19** Bd
Lethbridge **33** Bb
Lethem **37** CDb
Leticia **36** Dd
Leti Island **18** Gf
Letterkenny **7** BCd
Leucas **11** Dd
Leucas (i.) **11** Dd
Leuna **5** CDc
Leuser, Gunong– (mt.) **18** Ad
Leuven **8** Fb
Levádhia **11** Ed
Levanger **4** BCc
Lévanzo (i.) **10** Def
Lévêque, Cape– **29** Cb
Leverkusen **5** Ac
Levice **5** Gd
Lévis **32** Da
Lévitha (i.) **11** Ge
Levká Óri (mts.) **11** EFf
Levski **11** Fb
Lewis, Butt of– (cap.) **7** Cb
Lewis, Isle of– **7** Cbc
Lewiston [Id.–U.S.] **33** Bb
Lewiston [Me.–U.S.] **32** DEa
Lewistown **33** Cb
Lexington **32** Cb
Leyre (riv.) **8** Ce
Leyte (i.) **18** FGb
Ležajsk **5** Ic
Lezha **11** Cc
Lgov **12** DEc
Lhasa **15** CDfg
Lhazê **20** Gc
Lhokseumawe **18** Acd
Lianxian **16** Def
Lianyungang **16** EFcd
Lianyungang (Xinpu) **16** EFd
Liaodong Bandao (pen.) **16**
  Fbc
Liao He (riv.) **16** Fb
Liaoning (prov.) **16** Fb
Liaoyang **16** Fb
Liaoyuan **16** FGb
Liard (riv.) **31** Cbc
Libenge **25** Bd
Liberal **33** CDc
Liberec **5** Fc
Liberia (Ind. St.) **23** ABe
Liberia **35** Bb
Libertad, La– **35** ABb
Libertador General San
  Martín **39** Bb
Libertador General San
  Martín, Cumbre del– (mt.)
  39 Bb
Libourne **8** CDe
Libreville **24** CDde
Libya (Ind. St.) **23** DEc
Libyan Desert **24** Eb
Licata **10** Df
Lichinga **26** Cc
Lida **12** Cc
Lidköping **4** Cd
Lido di Ostia **10** Dd
Lidzbark Warminski **5** Ha
Liechtenstein (Ind. St.) **5** Be

Liège **8** Fb
Lieksa **4** Gc
Lielupe (riv.) **4** EFd
Lienz **5** De
Liepäja **4** Ed
Lier **8** Fb
Liestal **5** Ae
Liévin **8** Eb
Liezen **5** Ee
Lifford **7** Cd
Lifou, Île– (i.) **27** Dd
Liguria (reg.) **10** ABbc
Ligurian Sea **10** Bc
Lihou Reefs and Cays (is.) **29**
  Ib
Lihue **28** map no.1
Liimaa **4** Ec
Lijiang **16** Be
Lika (mts.) **6** Bd
Likasi **26** Bc
Likiep Atoll **27** Db
Lille **8** Eb
Lille Bælt (str.) **4** Be
Lillehammer **4** BCc
Lillesand **4** Bd
Lilongwe **26** Cc
Lim (riv.) **11** Cb
Lima (riv.) **9** Ab
Lima [Mt.–U.S.] **33** Bb
Lima [Oh.–U.S.] **32** Ca
Lima [Peru] **36** Ce
Limasol **22** De
Limay (riv.) **39** Bcd
Limay Mahuida **39** Bc
Limbe **24** Cd
Limburg an der Lahn **5** Bc
Limeira **39** Db
Limerick **7** BCe
Limfjorden (b.) **4** ABd
Límni **11** Ed
Límnos (i.) **11** Fcd
Limoges **8** De
Limon **33** Cc
Limón **35** Bbc
Limón, El– **35** map no.1
Limón Bay **35** map no.1
Limousin (hist. reg.) **8** Dde
Limousin, Plateaux du– **8** De
Limoux **8** Ef
Limpopo **26** Cd
Linapacan (i.) **18** EFb
Linares [Chile] **39** Ac
Linares [Sp.] **9** Dc
Linares [Ven.] **34** Cb
Lincang **16** CDd
Lincoln [Arg.] **39** Bc
Lincoln [U.K.] **7** Fe
Lincoln [U.S.] **32** Ba
Lindau (Bodensee) **5** BCe
Linden **37** Db
Lindesnes (cap.) **4** Ad
Lindhos **11** Hef
Lindi **26** CDbc
Línea, La– **9** Cd
Line Islands **28** ABbc
Linfen **16** Dc
Lingayen **18** EFa
Lingayen Gulf **18** EFa
Lingen an der Ems **5** Ab
Lingga, Kepulauan– **18** BCe
Lingga, Pulau– (i.) **18** BCde
Lingling **16** De
Linguère **24** Ac

Linhai **16** Fe
Linhares **39** DEa
Linjiang **16** Gb
Linköping **4** CDd
Linkou **16** GHa
Linosa (i.) **10** Dg
Linqing **16** DEc
Linru **16** Dd
Lins **39** Db
Lintao **16** Bc
Linxi **16** Eb
Linxia **16** Bc
Linyi **16** Ecd
Linz **5** Ed
Lion, Golfe du– **8** EFf
Lipari (i.) **10** Ee
Lipari, Isole– → Eolie, Isole–
  10 Ee
Lipeck **13** CDd
Lipno **5** Gb
Lipova **6** EFcd
Lipovec **6** Ib
Lippe (riv.) **5** Ac
Lira **25** Dd
Liria **9** Ec
Lisala **25** Cd
Lisbon **9** Ac
Lisburn **7** CDd
Lisburne, Cape– **41** grid
  square no.2
Lishi **16** Dc
Lishui **16** EFe
Lisianski Island **28** Aa
Lisičansk **12** Ed
Lisieux **8** Dc
Lismore **29** Id
Listowel **7** Be
Litang [China] **16** Bde
Litang [China] **16** Cf
Litani [Leb.] (riv.) **22** Ef
Litani [S. Amer.] (riv.) **38** Ba
Lith, Al– **21** BCef
Lithgow **29** Hle
Lithinon, Ákra– **11** Ff
Lithuania (Ind. St.) **4** EFe
Litin **6** Ib
Litókhoron **11** Ecd
Litomĕřice **5** Ec
Litovko **14** Ge
Little Aden **21** CDg
Little Andaman (i.) **19** Bf
Little Bitter Lake **25** map no.1
Little Cayman (i.) **35** BCab
Little Colorado (riv.) **33** BCc
Little Falls **32** Ba
Little Inagua Island **35** Ca
Little Missouri (riv.) **33** Cb
Little Nicobar (i.) **19** BCg
Little Poland (hist. reg.) **5**
  GHc
Little Rock **32** Bb
Liuzhou **16** Cf
Livermore, Mount– **33** Cc
Liverpool [Can.] **32** Ea
Liverpool [U.K.] **7** Ee
Liverpool Bay **7** Ee
Livingston **33** BCb
Livingstone → Maramba **26**
  Bc
Livingstone Falls **26** Ab
Livno **6** Ce
Livny **12** Ec

© ISTITUTO GEOGRAFICO DE AGOSTINI S.p.A. - Novara

Livonia (phys. reg.) **4** Fd
Livorno **10** Cc
Lixian **16** De
Lizard Point **7** Dg
Ljubar **6** Hb
Ljubercy **12** Eb
Ljubljana **6** Bc
Ljuboml **5** IJc
Ljubotin **12** DEcd
Ljudinovo **12** DEc
Ljungan (riv.) **4** CDc
Ljungby **4** Cd
Ljusdal **4** Dc
Ljusnan (riv.) **4** Cc
Llandrindod Wells **7** Ee
Llanelli **7** DEf
Llanes **9** Ca
Llano Estacado (plat.) **33** Cc
Llanos (phys. reg.) **37** BCb
Llanquihue, Lago- **40** Ab
Llobregat (riv.) **9** Fab
Lluchmayor **9** Gc
Llullaillaco, Volcán- (mt.) **39** Bb
Loa (riv.) **39** ABb
Loange (riv.) **26** Bb
Lobatse **26** Bd
Lobería **39** Cc
Lobito **23** Dg
Lobos **39** Cc
Lobos, Islas- **37** Ac
Lobva **12** Jb
Lochboisdale **7** BCc
Loches **8** Dd
Lochgilphead **7** CDc
Loc Ninh **19** Ef
Locri **10** Fe
Lod **22** Efg
Lodejnoje-Pole **13** Cc
Lodève **8** Ef
Lodi [It.] **10** Bb
Lodi [U.S.] **33** Ac
Lodja **26** Bb
Lodwar **25** Dd
Łódź **5** Gc
Loei **19** De
Lofoten (is.) **4** Cab
Logan **33** Bb
Logan, Mount- **31** ABb
Logone (riv.) **24** Dcd
Logroño **9** Da
Logrosán **9** Cc
Lohardaga **19** Hlk
Loikaw **19** Ce
Loir (riv.) **8** Dd
Loire (riv.) **8** Cd
Loja [Ec.] **37** Bc
Loja [Sp.] **9** Cd
Lokeren **8** Eb
Lokoja **24** Cd
Lokomo **24** Dd
Lol (riv.) **25** Cd
Lolland (i.) **4** Be
Lom (riv.) **11** FGb
Lom **11** Eb
Lomami (riv.) **26** Bb
Loma Mountains **24** ABd
Lombardia (reg.) **10** BCab
Lomblen, Pulau- (i.) **18** Ff
Lombok, Pulau- (i.) **15** Djk
Lomé **24** Cd
Lomela **26** Bb
Lomela (riv.) **26** Bb
Lomié **24** Dd
Lomitas, Las- **39** BCb
Lomonosov **4** Gcd
Łomża **5** Hlb
London [Can.] **31** GHd
London [U.K.] **7** FGf
Londonderry **7** Cd
Londonderry, Cape- **29** Da
Londonderry, Isla- (i.) **40** Ac
Londrina **39** Cb
Long Beach **33** Bc
Longford **7** Ce
Long Island [Bah.] **35** Ca
Long Island [U.S.] **32** Da
Longjiang **16** Fa
Longkou **16** EFc
Longreach **29** Gc
Longview [Tx.-U.S.] **32** Bb
Longview [Wa.-U.S.] **33** Ab
Longwy **8** Fc
Longxi **16** BCcd
Long Xuyen **15** Dhi
Longyan **16** Eef
Longyearbyen **13** ABb
Lonja (riv.) **6** Cd
Lons-le-Saunier **8** Fd
Loop Head **7** ABe
Lopatka, mys- **14** Id
Lop Buri **19** Def
Lopez, Cap- **24** Ce
Lop Nur (l.) **15** Def
Lopori (riv.) **25** Cd
Lopphavet (str.) **4** Ea
Lora del Río **9** Cd
Lorain **32** Ca
Lorca **9** Ed
Lord Howe Island **27** CDd
Lordsburg **33** BCc
Lorestān **21** Dc
Loreto [Bol.] **39** Ba
Loreto [Mex.] **34** Ab
Loreto [Par.] **39** Cb
Lorica **37** Bb
Lorient **8** Bd
Lorne, Firth of- (str.) **7** CDc
Lörrach **5** ABe
Lorraine (hist. reg.) **8** FGc
Lošinj (i.) **6** Bd
Los Islands **24** Ad
Lot (riv.) **8** De
Lota **39** Ac
Lotofaga **28** map no.5
Lotta (riv.) **4** Ga
Loubomo **26** Ab
Loudéac **8** Bc
Loudima **26** Ab
Louga **24** Ac
Louisiade Archipelago **27** Cc
Louisiana (State) **32** Bbc
Louis Trichardt **26** BCd
Louisville **32** Cb
Louis XIV, Point- **31** GHc
Louny **5** DEc
Lourdes **8** Cf
Lourenço Marques → Maputo **26** Cd
Louth [Austl.] **29** He
Louth [U.K.] **7** FGe
Louviers **8** Dc
Lovat (riv.) **12** Db
Loveč **11** Fb
Lovisa **4** Fc
Lowell **32** DEa
Lower Lough Erne **7** BCd
Lower Tunguska (riv.) **14** CDc
Lowestoft **7** GHe
Łowicz **5** Gb
Loxton **29** FGe
Loyalty Islands **27** Dcd
Lozère (mt.) **8** Ee
Loznica **6** Dd
Lozovaja **12** Ed
Lozva (riv.) **12** Ja
Lualaba (Zaïre) (riv.) **26** Bb
Luama (riv.) **26** Bb
Lu'an **16** Ed
Luanda **26** Ab
Luanda (prov.) **26** Ab
Luang Prabang **15** Dgh
Luangwa **26** Cc
Luangwa (riv.) **26** Cc
Luan He (riv.) **16** Eb
Luanshya **23** Eg
Luapula (riv.) **26** Bbc
Luarca **9** Ba
Luau **26** Bc
Lubań **5** Ec
Lubango **26** Ac
Lubbock **33** Cc
Lübeck **5** Cb
Lübecker Bucht **5** Ca
Lubefu **26** Bb
Lubin **5** Fc
Lublin **5** Ic
Lubliniec **5** Gc
Lubny **12** Dc
Luboń **5** Fb
Lubuklinggau **18** Be
Lubumbashi **26** Bc
Lubutu **25** Ce
Lucca **10** Cc
Lucena [Phil.] **18** Fb
Lucena [Sp.] **9** Cd
Lučenec **5** Gd
Lucera **10** Ed
Luciara **38** Bc
Lucipara, Kepulauan- **18** Gf
Luck **13** Bd
Luckeesarai **19** Ij
Luckenwalde **5** Db
Lucknow **15** Cg
Luçon **8** Cd
Lüderitz **23** Dh
Ludhiana **20** Eb
Ludogorije (mts.) **11** Gb
Luduş **6** Gc
Ludvika **4** Ccd
Ludwigsburg **5** BCd
Ludwigshafen am Rhein **5** ABd
Ludwigslust **5** Cb
Ludza **4** FGd
Luebo **26** Bb
Luena **26** ABc
Lüeyang **16** BCd
Lufeng **16** Ef
Lufkin **32** Bb
Luga **13** BCd
Luga (riv.) **4** Gd
Lugano **10** Ba
Lugansk (Vorošilovgrad) **13** CDe
Lugenda (riv.) **26** Cc
Lugnaquillia Mountain **7** Ce
Lugo [It.] **10** Cb
Lugo [Sp.] **9** Ba
Lugoj **6** EFd
Lugovoj **13** Ge
Luhayyah, Al- **21** Cf
Luiana **26** Bc
Luiro (riv.) **4** Fb
Luishia **26** Bc
Luitpold Coast **42** grid square no.1
Lukenie (riv.) **26** Bb
Lukojanov **12** FGb
Łuków **5** Ic
Lukuga (riv.) **26** Bb
Luleå **4** Eb
Luleälven (riv.) **4** Eb
Lüleburgaz **11** Gc
Lulonga (riv.) **26** Aa
Lulua (riv.) **26** Bb
Lumajang **18** Df
Lumbala **26** Bc
Lumbo **26** CDc
Lumding **19** Bc
Lumphăt **19** Ef
Lund [Nor.] **4** Ad
Lund [Swe.] **4** Ce
Lunda **26** ABb
Lundy (i.) **7** Df
Lüneburg **5** BCb
Lüneburger Heide **5** Cb
Lunenburg **32** Ea
Lunéville **8** Gc
Lungué-Bungo (riv.) **26** ABc
Luni (riv.) **20** Dcd
Luo He (riv.) **16** Cc
Luohe **16** Dd
Luoyang **16** Dd
Lupeni **6** Fd
Lure **8** Gd
Lúrio **26** Dc
Lúrio (riv.) **26** Cc
Lusaka **23** Eg
Lusambo **26** Bb
Lushnja **11** Cc
Lushoto **26** Cb
Luton **7** Fef
Lutong **18** Dd
Lützow-Holm Bay **42** grid square no.2
Luuq **25** Ed
Luvua (riv.) **26** Bb
Luwegu (riv.) **26** Cb
Luwuk **18** Fe
Luxembourg (Ind. St.) **3** Dbc
Luxembourg **5** CDd
Luxor **25** Db
Luza **12** Ga
Luzern **5** ABe
Luzhou **16** BCe
Luzilândia **38** Cb
Luzon (i.) **18** Fa
Luzon Strait **16** Ffg
Lvov **13** Bde
Lyakhov Islands **14** HIb
Lycksele **4** Db
Lyme Bay **7** Ef
Łyna (riv.) **5** Ha
Lynchburg **32** CDb
Lyngen (b.) **4** Ea
Lynn Lake **30** HId
Lyon **8** Fe
Lys (riv.) **8** Eb
Lysva **12** Ib

© ISTITUTO GEOGRAFICO DE AGOSTINI S.p.A. - Novara

M

© ISTITUTO GEOGRAFICO DE AGOSTINI S.p.A. - Novara

Marx 12 Gc
Mary 13 Ff
Maryborough 29 Id
Maryland (State) 32 Db
Masaka 25 De
Masan 16 Gcd
Masasi 23 Fg
Masaya 35 Bb
Masbate 18 Fb
Masbate (i.) 18 Fb
Mascara 24 Ca
Mascarene Islands 23 map no.1
Masela (i.) 17 Hlg
Maseru 23 Eh
Mashhad 21 FGb
Mashike 17 Gc
Mashkel (riv.) 20 Bc
Mashra'ar Raqq 25 CDd
Masīlah, Wādī al– 21 DEf
Masindi 25 Dd
Maşīrah, Jazīrat– (i.) 21 FGe
Maşīrah, Khalīj– 21 Fef
Masjed–Soleymān 21 DEc
Mask, Lake– 7 Be
Masoala, Cap– 26 map no.1
Mason City 32 Ba
Massa 10 Cbc
Massachusetts (State) 32 Da
Massa Marittima 10 Cc
Massangena 26 Cd
Massapê 38 CDb
Massat 8 Df
Massawa 25 DEc
Massena 32 Da
Massénya 25 Bc
Masset 31 Bc
Massif Central (mts.) 8 EFe
Massinga 26 Cd
Mastouta 10 Bf
Masuda 17 BCg
Masuku 26 Ab
Masvingo 26 Ccd
Maşyāf 22 Fe
Matadi 26 Ab
Matagalpa 35 Bb
Matagorda Bay 32 Bc
Mataiea 28 map no.2
Matak, Pulau– (i.) 18 Cd
Matala 26 Ac
Matam 24 Ac
Matamoros 30 Ig
Matanzas 35 Ba
Matão, Serra do– (mts.) 38 Bbc
Matapán, Cape– 11 Ee
Mataporquera → Valdeolea 9 CDa
Matara 20 EFg
Mataram 18 Ef
Mataranka 29 Eab
Matariya, El– 25 map no.1
Mataró 9 Gb
Matehuala 34 BCb
Matera 10 Fd
Matese (mts.) 10 Ed
Mátészalka 6 Fc
Mathura 20 Ec
Mati 18 Gc
Mâtir 10 Bf
Matočkin Šar 13 EFb
Matočkin Šar, proliv– 13 EFb
Mato Grosso (State) 38 Bc

Mato Grosso 39 BCa
Mato Grosso, Plateau of– 38 Bc
Mato Grosso do Sul (State) 39 Cab
Matopo Hills 26 Bcd
Matosinhos 9 Ab
Mátra 6 DEc
Matrah 21 Fe
Maţrūḩ 25 Ca
Matsue 16 Hc
Matsu Liehtao 16 Fe
Matsumae 17 FGd
Matsumoto 16 Ic
Matsusaka 17 Egh
Matsuyama 16 Hd
Matua, ostrov– (i.) 14 Ie
Matuku Island 28 map no.6
Maturin 37 Cb
Mau 19 Hj
Maubeuge 8 EFb
Maui 28 Ba
Maumere 18 Ff
Maun 26 Bc
Mauna Kea (mt.) 28 map no.1
Mauna Loa (mt.) 28 map no.1
Maungdaw 19 Bd
Maupihaa Atoll 28 Bc
Mau Ranipur 19 Gj
Mauriac 8 Ee
Mauritania (Ind. St.) 23 ABcd
Mauritius (Ind. St.) 23 map no.1
Mawchi 19 Ce
Mawlaik 19 BCd
Mawson 42 grid square no.2
Mayaguana Island 32 Dc
Mayagüez 35 Db
Maydh 25 Ec
Mayenne 8 Cd
Mayenne (riv.) 8 Cd
Maynas (phys. reg.) 37 Bc
Mayo 31 Bb
Mayor, Puig– (mt.) 9 Gc
Mayotte (i.) 23 Gg
May Pen 35 Cb
Mayumba 26 Ab
Mayum La (p.) 20 Fb
Mazabuka 26 Bc
Mazagão 38 Bb
Mazamet 8 Ef
Mazara del Vallo 10 Df
Mazār–e Sharīf 15 Cf
Mazarrón 9 Ed
Mazaruni (riv.) 37 CDb
Mazatlán 30 Hg
Mažeikiai 12 Bb
Mazirbe 12 Bb
Mazovia (phys. reg.) 5 GHb
Mbabane 26 Cd
Mbaïki 25 Bd
Mbala (Abercorn) 26 Cb
Mbale 26 Ca
Mbalmayo 24 Dd
Mbandaka 26 Aab
M'banza Congo 26 Ab
Mbanza–Ngungu 26 Ab
Mbeya 23 Ff
Mbinda 26 Ab
Mbini (phys. reg.) 24 CDd
Mbomou (riv.) 26 Ba
Mbout 24 Ac

M'Bridge (riv.) 26 Ab
Mbuji–Mayi 26 Bb
Mbulu 26 Cb
Mburucuya 39 Cb
Mead, Lake– 33 Bc
Meadow Lake 31 DEc
Mealháda 9 ABb
Mearim (riv.) 38 Cb
Meaux 8 Ec
Mecca 21 BCe
Mechelen 8 Fb
Mecklenburg (hist. reg.) 5 CDb
Mecklenburger Bucht 5 Ca
Mecsek (mt.) 6 Dc
Medan 15 Di
Medellín 36 Cc
Mederdra 24 Ac
Medford 33 Ab
Medgidia 6 Id
Media Agua 39 Bc
Mediaş 6 Gc
Medicine Hat 33 BCab
Medina 21 BCe
Medinaceli 9 Db
Medina del Campo 9 Cb
Medina del Rioseco 9 Cb
Medina–Sidonia 9 Cd
Medinīpur 20 Gd
Mediterranean Sea 23 CEb
Medjerda, Montes de la– 10 ABf
Medjez el–Bab 10 Bf
Mednogorsk 12 Ic
Medny, ostrov– 14 Jd
Médoc (phys. reg.) 8 Ce
Medvedica (riv.) 12 Fc
Medveži, ostrova– 14 Jb
Medvežjegorsk 13 Cc
Medyado Atoll 28 map no.3
Medyai Atoll 28 map no.3
Medžibož 6 Hb
Meekatharra 29 Bd
Meerut 20 Ec
Mega 25 Dd
Mega, Pulau– (i.) 18 Be
Megara 11 Ede
Meghalaya (State) 19 Bc
Meghna (riv.) 19 Jjk
Meia Ponte (riv.) 39 Da
Meiganga 24 Dd
Meiktila 19 Cd
Meiningen 5 Cc
Meissen 5 Dc
Meixian 16 Ef
Mejillones 39 Ab
Mékambo 24 Dd
Mekele 25 DEc
Meknès 24 Ba
Mekong (riv.) 19 Eef
Mekong Delta 19 Efg
Mekongga, Gunung– (mt.) 18 Fe
Melaka (Malacca) 18 Bd
Melalap 18 Ec
Melanesia (is.) 27 BDbc
Melawi (riv.) 18 Dde
Melbourne 29 GHf
Melchor Ocampo 34 Bc
Melenki 12 Fb
Meleuz 12 Hic
Melfi [Chad] 25 Bc
Melfi [It.] 10 Ed

Melilla 24 Ba
Mèlito di Porto Salvo 10 Ef
Melitopol 12 DEd
Mêlnik 5 Ec
Melo 39 Cc
Melrhir, Chott– (l.) 24 Ca
Melun 8 Ec
Melville 33 Ca
Melville, Cape– 29 GHa
Melville Bay 29 Fa
Melville Island [Austl.] 29 Ea
Melville Island [Can.] 41 grid square no.2
Melville Peninsula 31 Gb
Memmingen 5 Cde
Mempawah 18 Cd
Memphis 32 Cb
Menai Strait 7 De
Ménaka 24 Cc
Mende 8 Ee
Mendocino, Cape– 33 Ab
Mendoza 39 Bc
Menemen 22 Ac
Meneng Point 27 map no.2
Mengdingjie 19 CDd
Menggala 18 Cd
Menglian 19 CDd
Mengzi 16 Bf
Menindee 29 Ge
Meningie 29 Ff
Menongue 26 Ac
Menphis (r.) 22 Ch
Mentakab 18 Bd
Mentawai, Selat– 18 ABde
Mentawai Islands 18 Ae
Mentok 18 BCe
Menzies 29 Cde
Menzies, Mount– 42 grid square no.1
Meppel 8 FGa
Meppen 5 Ab
Mequinenza, Embalse de– (l.) 9 EFb
Merabéllou, Kólpos– 11 FGf
Merak 18 Cf
Méralab (i.) 28 map no.4
Merano 10 Ca
Meratus, Pegunungan– 18 Ee
Merauke 27 BCc
Merced 33 ABc
Mercedes [Arg.] 39 Cc
Mercedes [Arg.] 39 Cb
Mercedes [Arg.] 39 Bc
Mercedes [Ur.] 39 Cc
Merceg 25 Ed
Merefa 12 Ed
Mergenevo 12 Hd
Mergui 19 Cf
Mergui Archipelago 19 Cf
Meriç (riv.) 11 Gc
Mérida [Mex.] 30 IJg
Mérida [Sp.] 9 Bc
Mérida [Ven.] 37 Bb
Mérida, Cordillera de– (mts.) 37 BCb
Meridian 32 Cb
Mérignac 8 Ce
Merir (i.) 27 Bb
Merksen 5 Cc
Merredin 29 Be
Merrick (mt.) 7 Dd
Merritt 31 CDc

© ISTITUTO GEOGRAFICO DE AGOSTINI S.p.A. - Novara

Merriwa **29** Ie
Mersa Fatma **21** Cg
Merseburg **5** CDc
Mersey (riv.) **7** Ee
Mersin **22** Ed
Merta Road **20** Dc
Merthyr Tydfil **7** Ef
Merzifon **22** Eb
Mesa **33** Bc
Mesagne **10** Fd
Mesola **10** Db
Mesolóngion **11** Dd
Mesopotamia [Arg.] (phys. reg.) **39** Cbc
Mesopotamia [Iraq] (phys. reg.) **21** CDbc
Messalo (riv.) **26** Cc
Messaoud, Hassi– **24** Ca
Messina [It.] **10** Ee
Messina [S. Afr.] **23** EFh
Messina, Gulf of– **11** Ee
Messina, Stretto di– **10** Ee
Messíni **11** DEe
Mesta (Néstos) (riv.) **11** Fc
Mestghanem **24** BCa
Meta (riv.) **37** Bb
Meta, La– (mt.) **10** DEd
Metán **39** Bb
Metauro (riv.) **10** Dc
Metković **11** BCb
Metrz Glacier **42** grid square no.4
Métsovon **11** Dd
Metz **8** Gc
Meulaboh **18** ABd
Meurthe (riv.) **8** Gc
Meuse (riv.) **8** Fc
Mexiana, Ilha– **38** Cab
Mexicali **34** Aa
Mexico (Ind. St.) **30** HIgh
Mexico, Gulf of– **34** CDb
Mexico City **30** Igh
Meyísti (i.) **22** Bd
Meymaneh **20** BCa
Mezdra **11** EFb
Mezen (riv.) **13** Dc
Mezen **13** Dc
Mézenc, Mont– (mt.) **8** Fe
Mezőkövesd **6** Ec
Mezőtúr **6** Ec
Mhow **20** Ed
Miami **32** Cc
Miandrivazo **26** map no.1
Miáneh **21** Db
Miangas, Pulau– (is.) **18** Gc
Mianwali **20** Db
Mianyang **16** BCd
Miaodao Qundao **16** EFc
Miarinarivo **26** map no.1
Miass **13** EFd
Miastko **5** Fab
Micenae (r.) **11** Ee
Michalovce **5** HId
Michigan (State) **32** Ca
Michigan, Lake– **32** Ca
Michigan City **32** Ca
Michipicoten **31** Gd
Micronesia (is.) **27** BDbc
Mičurin **11** GHb
Mičurinsk **12** Fc
Midar **24** Ba
Middelburg [S. Afr.] **26** BCd
Middelburg [S. Afr.] **26** Be

Middelfart **5** BCa
Middle Andaman (i.) **19** BCf
Middle Atlas (mts.) **24** Ba
Middlesbrough **7** FGd
Midi, Canal du– **8** DEf
Midi d'Ossau, Pic du– (mt.) **8** Cf
Midland **33** Ca
Midway Islands **28** Aa
Midžor (mt.) **11** Fe
Miechów **5** GHc
Międzyrzec Podlaski **5** Ibc
Międzyrzecz **5** EFb
Mielec **5** Hc
Miercurea Ciuc **6** GHc
Mieres **9** BCa
Miguel Alves **38** Cb
Mihajlovgrad **11** Fe
Mihajlovka **13** Dd
Mikkeli **4** FGc
Mikonos (i.) **11** Fe
Mikun **13** DEc
Mikuni–Sanmyaku (mts.) **17** Ff
Mikura–Jima (i.) **17** FGh
Miladummadulu Atoll **20** DEg
Milagro, El– **39** Bc
Milan **10** Bb
Milás **22** ABd
Milazzo **10** Ee
Mildura **29** Ge
Miles **29** HId
Miles City **33** Cb
Miletus (r.) **22** Ad
Milfort Haven **7** Df
Miliana **9** FGd
Milikapiti **29** Ea
Miling **29** Bde
Milk (riv.) **33** Cb
Millau **8** Ee
Millerovo **12** Fd
Millevaches, Plateau de– (plat.) **8** DEe
Millicent **29** FGf
Milos (i.) **11** Fe
Milparinka **29** Gde
Milwaukee **32** Ca
Milwaukee Depth **35** Dab
Mimizan **8** Ce
Mimmaya **17** FGd
Mînâ' al 'Aḥmadî **21** Dd
Minahassa **18** Fd
Minamata **17** ABh
Minami–Daitō–Jima (i.) **16** He
Minami–Iō–Jima **27** BCa
Minas **39** Cc
Minas–cué **39** Cb
Minas de Riotinto **9** BCd
Minas de São Domingos **9** ABd
Minas Gerais (State) **39** Da
Minatitlán **34** Cc
Minbu **19** Bde
Minbya **19** Bd
Minchinmávida, Volcán– (mt.) **40** Ab
Mindanao (i.) **15** Ei
Minden **5** Bb
Mindoro (i.) **15** DEh
Mindoro Strait **18** EFb
Mineiros **39** Da
Mineralnyje Vody **12** Fe
Minervino Murge **10** Fd

Minfeng **20** Fa
Mingan **31** Ic
Minhe **16** Bc
Minho (riv.) **9** Aab
Minho (hist. reg.) **9** Ab
Minicoy Island **20** Dg
Minigwal, Lake– **29** Cd
Minilya **29** Ac
Minjar **12** Ib
Min Jiang (riv.) **16** Ee
Minna **24** Cd
Minneapolis **32** Ba
Minnesota (State) **32** Ba
Minnipa **29** EFe
Miño (riv.) **9** Ba
Minorca (i.) **9** GHc
Minot **33** Cb
Minqin **16** Bc
Min Shan (mts.) **16** Bd
Minsk **13** Bd
Mińsk Mazowiecki **5** HIb
Minto, Lac– **31** Hc
Minusinsk **14** Cd
Minxian **16** Bd
Minyä, Al– **25** CDb
Miquelon (i.) **31** Jd
Mira (riv.) **9** Ad
Miracema do Tocantins **38** Cbc
Miraflores **37** Bb
Miraflores Locks **35** map no.1
Miraj **20** DEe
Miramar **39** Cc
Miranda **39** Cb
Miranda de Ebro **9** Da
Miranda do Douro **9** Bb
Mirande **8** CDf
Mirandela **9** Bb
Mirandola **10** Cb
Mirbat **21** EFf
Mirecourt **8** FGc
Mirgorod **12** Dd
Miri **18** Dd
Mirim, Lagoa– (lag.) **39** Cc
Mírina **11** Fd
Mirny [Ant.] **42** grid square no.4
Mirny [Russia] **14** Ec
Mirpur Khas **20** CDc
Miryang **17** Ag
Mirzapur **20** Fcd
Mishan **16** Ha
Mi–Shima (i.) **17** Bg
Misiones, Sierra de– (mts.) **39** Cb
Miskitos, Cayos– (is.) **35** Bb
Miskolc **6** Eb
Mismär **21** Bf
Mismîyah, Al– **22** Ff
Misool, Pulau– (i.) **18** He
Mississauga **31** GHd
Mississippi (riv.) **32** Bb
Mississippi (State) **32** BCb
Missoula **33** Bb
Missouri (State) **32** Bb
Missouri (riv.) **32** Ba
Mistassini, Lac– **31** Eb
Mistelbach an der Zaya **5** Fd
Misti, Volcán– (volc.) **39** Aa
Misurata **24** Da
Mitchell [Austl.] **29** Hd
Mitchell [U.S.] **32** Ba
Mitchell, Mount– **32** Cb

Mitchell River **29** Gb
Mitchell River (riv.) **29** Gb
Mit Ghamr **22** Cg
Mithimna **11** FGd
Mitiaro Island **28** Bc
Mitilíni **22** Ac
Mitilinis, Stenón– **11** Gd
Mitla Pass **25** map no.2
Mito **17** Gf
Mittellandkanal (can.) **5** ABb
Mitú **37** BCb
Mitumba, Monts– **26** Bbc
Mitwaba **26** Bb
Mitzic **24** Dd
Miyake–Jima (i.) **17** FGg
Miyako **16** Jc
Miyako–Jima (i.) **16** Gef
Miyakonojō **16** Hd
Miyanoura–Dake (mt.) **17** Bi
Miyazaki **16** Hd
Miyun **16** Eb
Mizdah **24** Da
Mizen Head **7** ABf
Mizil **6** Hd
Mizoč **6** GHa
Mizoram (State) **19** Bd
Mizuho **42** grid square no.2
Mizusawa **17** Ge
Mjølby **4** Cd
Mjøsa (l.) **4** Bc
Mkuze **26** Cd
Mladá Boleslav **5** Ec
Mladenovac **6** Cd
Mława **5** GHb
Mljet (i.) **11** Bb
Mo **4** Cb
Moa (riv.) **24** Ad
Moa, Pulau– (i.) **18** Gf
Moala (i.) **28** map no.6
Moanda **26** Ab
Moba **26** Bb
Mobaye **26** Ba
Mobayi–Mbongo **26** Ba
Mobile **32** Cb
Mobridge **33** Cb
Moçambique **23** FGg
Mocha, Isla– (i.) **39** Ac
Mochis, Los– **34** ABb
Mochudi **26** Bd
Mocímboa da Praia **26** Dc
Môco, Serra– (mts.) **26** Ac
Mocoa **37** Bb
Mocuba **23** Fg
Modane **8** Ge
Módena **10** Cb
Modica **10** Ef
Modřany **5** Ecd
Moe **29** Hf
Mogadishu **25** Ed
Mogaung **19** Cc
Mogi das Cruzes **39** Db
Mogilev **13** Cd
Mogilev–Podolski **6** Hb
Mogoča **14** EFd
Mogok **19** Cd
Mogrein **24** ABb
Moguer **9** Bd
Mohács **6** Cd
Mohanganj **19** Jj
Mohenjo Daro (r.) **20** Cc
Moinești **6** Hc
Moissac **8** De
Mojave **33** Bc

Mojave Desert **33** Bc
Mojynty **13** Ge
Mokolo **24** Dc
Mokp'o **14** Ff
Mola di Bari **10** Fd
Moldav (riv.) **5** Ed
Moldavia (phys. reg.) **6** Hcd
Molde **4** Ac
Moldefjorden (b.) **4** Ac
Moldova (Ind. St.) **6** Ic
Moldova Nouă **6** Ed
Moldoveanu, Vîrful- (mt.) **6** Gd
Molepolole **26** Bd
Molfetta **10** Fd
Molise (reg.) **10** Ed
Mollendo **39** Aa
Mölndal **4** BCd
Molodečno **12** Cc
Molodežnaja **42** grid square no.2
Mologa (riv.) **12** Eb
Molokai (i.) **28** Ba
Molopo (w.) **26** Bd
Moluccas (is.) **18** GHde
Molucca Sea **18** Gef
Moma **26** CDc
Mombasa **23** FGf
Mombetsu **16** Jb
Momboyo (riv.) **25** BCe
Momčilgrad **11** Fc
Møn (i.) **5** Da
Mona, Isla- (i.) **35** Db
Monaco (Ind. St.) **10** Ac
Monaghan **7** Cd
Mona Passage (str.) **35** Db
Moncayo, Sierra del- (mts.) **9** DEb
Mončegorsk **13** Cc
Mönchengladbach **5** CDc
Monclova **34** Bb
Moncton **31** Id
Mondego (riv.) **9** ABb
Mondego, Cape- **9** Ab
Mondello **10** De
Mondovi **10** Ab
Monemvasía **11** Ee
Moneron, ostrov- (i.) **17** Ga
Monfalcone **10** Db
Monforte de Lemos **9** Ba
Monga **26** Ba
Mongalla **25** Dd
Mong Cai **19** Ed
Monger, Lake- **29** Bd
Monghpayak **19** CDd
Mongnai **16** Af
Mongo **25** BCc
Mongolia (Ind. St.) **15** De
Mongolski Altaj (mts.) **14** Ce
Mongororo **25** Cc
Mongu **26** Bc
Monkoto **25** BCe
Monmouth **7** Ef
Monopoli **10** Fd
Monor **6** Dc
Monreale **10** De
Monroe **32** Bb
Monrovia **24** Ad
Mons **8** EFb
Monselice **10** Cb
Montagne Noire (mt.) **8** Ef
Montalbán **9** Eb
Montana (State) **33** BCb
Montaña, La- (phys. reg.) **37** Bcd
Montánchez **9** Bc
Montargis **8** Ed
Montauban **8** DEef
Montbard **8** Fd
Montbéliard **8** Gd
Montceau-les-Mines **8** EFd
Mont-de-Marsan **8** CDef
Montdidier **8** Ec
Mont Dore **8** Ee
Monteagudo **39** Ba
Monte Albán (r.) **34** Cc
Monte Alegre **38** Bb
Monte Azul **39** Da
Monte Bello Islands **29** ABc
Monte Caseros **39** Cbc
Montecatini Terme **10** Cc
Monte Comán **39** Bc
Montecristo (i.) **10** Cc
Montefiascone **10** Dc
Montego Bay **35** Cb
Monteiro **38** Db
Montélimar **8** Fe
Monte Lindo (riv.) **39** BCb
Monte Lirio **35** map no.1
Montemorelos **34** Cb
Montenegro **11** Cb
Montepuez **26** Cc
Montepulciano **10** Cc
Montereau-Faut-Yonne **8** Ec
Monterey **33** Ac
Montería **37** Bb
Monterós **39** Bb
Monterrey **34** BCb
Monte Sant'Angelo **10** Ed
Montes Claros **39** Da
Montevideo **39** Cc
Montgenèvre (p.) **10** Ab
Montgomery [U.K.] **7** Ee
Montgomery [U.S.] **32** Cb
Montigny-lès-Metz **8** Gc
Montijo [Port.] **9** Ac
Montijo [Sp.] **9** Bc
Montilla **9** Cd
Mont-Joli **32** Ea
Mont-Laurier **32** Da
Montluçon **8** Ed
Montmagny **31** Hd
Montmorillon **8** Dd
Monto **29** Icd
Montoro **9** Ccd
Montpelier **32** Da
Montpellier **8** EFf
Montréal **31** Hd
Montreux **10** Aa
Montrose [U.K.] **7** EFc
Montrose [U.S.] **33** Cc
Mont-Saint-Michel, Le- **8** Cc
Montserrat (i.) **35** Db
Monywa **19** BCd
Monza **10** Bb
Monzón **9** Fb
Moonie **29** Id
Moonta **29** Fe
Moora **29** Be
Moore, Lake- **29** Bde
Moorea (i.) **28** map no.2
Moorhead **32** Ba
Moose (riv.) **32** Ca
Moose Jaw **33** Cab
Moosonee **31** Db
Mopti **24** Bc
Moquegua **39** ABa
Mora [Port.] **9** Ac
Mora [Sp.] **9** CDc
Mora [Swe.] **4** Cc
Moradabad **15** Cg
Mora de Rubielos **9** Eb
Moratalla **9** DEc
Morava **5** Fd
Morava, Južna- **11** DEb
Moravia (phys. reg.) **5** Fd
Morawa **29** Bd
Morawhanna **37** Db
Moray Firth (b.) **7** Ec
Morcenx **8** Cef
Mordvinia (Aut. Rep.) **13** Dd
Morecambe Bay **7** Ede
Moree **29** HId
Morelia **34** Bc
Morella **9** EFb
Morena **19** Gj
Morena, Sierra- (mts.) **9** BDc
Morenci **33** Cc
Moresby Island **31** Bc
Moreton **29** Ga
Moreton Bay **29** Id
Moreton Island **29** Id
Mórfou **22** De
Morgan **29** FGe
Mori **17** Gc
Morioka **16** Jc
Morlaix **8** ABc
Mornington Island **29** FGb
Morocco (Ind. St.) **23** Bbc
Morogoro **23** Ff
Moro Gulf **18** Fc
Morombe **26** map no.1
Morón **35** Ca
Morondava **23** Gh
Morón de la Frontera **9** Cd
Moroni **26** Dc
Morotai, Pulau- **18** Gd
Morotai, Selat- **18** Gd
Moroto **26** Ca
Morozovsk **12** Fd
Morphou Bay **22** De
Morris Jesup, Kap- **41** grid square no.1
Morrumbene **26** Cd
Moršansk **12** Fc
Mortara **10** Bb
Mortes, Rio das- (riv.) **38** Bc
Mortlock Islands **27** Cb
Morvan, Monts du- **8** EFd
Morven (mt.) **7** Eb
Morven **29** Hd
Morvi **20** Dd
Morwell **29** Hf
Moscow **13** Cd
Mosel (riv.) **5** Acd
Moselle (riv.) **5** Acd
Moshi **26** Cb
Mosjøen **4** Cb
Moskenesøya (i.) **4** BCb
Moskva (riv.) **12** Eb
Mosonmagyaróvár **5** Fe
Mosqueiro **38** Cb
Mosquitia (phys. reg.) **35** Bb
Mosquitos, Costa de- **35** Bb
Mosquitos, Golfo de los- **35** Bbc
Moss **4** Bd
Mossaka **24** De
Mosselbaai **23** Ei
Mossendjo **26** Ab
Mossman **29** Hb
Mossoró **38** Db
Moss Vale **29** HIe
Most **5** Dc
Mostar **11** BCb
Mostiska **5** Id
Mosty **12** Bc
Mosul **21** Cb
Motagua (riv.) **35** ABb
Motala **4** Cd
Motherwell **7** Ed
Motihari **20** FGc
Motril **9** Dd
Motu One Atoll **28** Bc
Moudjéria **24** Ac
Moúdros **11** Fd
Mouila **26** Ab
Mould Bay **41** grid square no.2
Moulins **8** Ed
Moulmein **15** Dh
Moulouya (riv.) **24** Ba
Moultrie **32** Cb
Moundou **25** Bd
Mountain Nile (riv.) **25** Dd
Mount Barker **29** Bef
Mount Douglas **29** Hc
Mount Gambier **29** FGf
Mount Garnet **29** GHb
Mount Isa **29** Fc
Mount Magnet **29** Bd
Mount Morgan **29** HIc
Mount Vernon **32** Cb
Moura [Austl.] **29** Hc
Moura [Braz.] **37** Cc
Moura [Port.] **9** Bc
Mourne Mountains **7** CDd
Mouscron **8** Eb
Moussoro **25** Bc
Moyale **25** Dd
Moyo, Pulau- (i.) **18** Ef
Moyobamba **37** Bc
Mozambique (Ind. St.) **23** Fgh
Mozambique Channel **26** CDcd
Možga **12** Hb
Mozyr **12** Cc
Mpanda **26** Cb
Mpika **26** Cc
Mragowo **5** Hb
Mreïti, El- **24** Bb
Mreyyé, El- (phys. reg.) **24** Bc
Mtwara **23** FGfg
Muang Pakxan **19** De
Muang Sing **19** Dd
Muang Xaignabouri **19** De
Muang Xépôn **19** Ee
Muar **18** Bd
Muarasiberut **18** Ae
Muaratebo **18** Be
Muaratewe **18** De
Mubarraz, Al- **21** Dd
Mubi **24** Dc
Muchinga Mountains **26** Cc
Mudan Jiang (riv.) **17** Ab
Mudanjiang **16** GHb
Mudanya **22** Bb
Mudawwarah, Al- **22** Fh
Mueda **26** Cc
Muende **26** Cc
Mufulira **26** Bc
Mugi **17** Dh
Muğla **22** Bd

© ISTITUTO GEOGRAFICO DE AGOSTINI S.p.A. - Novara

Muglad, Al- **25** Cc
Mugodžary (mts.) **13** Ee
Muḩammad Qawl **25** Db
Mühldorf am Inn **5** CDd
Mühlhausen **5** Cc
Mühlig-Hofmann Gebirge **42** grid square no.1
Muhu (i.) **4** Ed
Muisne **37** ABb
Mujnak **13** Ee
Mukačevo **5** Id
Mukalla, Al- **21** Dg
Mukhā, Al- **21** Cg
Mukinbudin **29** Be
Mula **9** Ec
Mulhacén (mt.) **9** Dd
Mulhouse **8** Gd
Muling **17** Bb
Muling He (riv.) **17** Bbc
Mull, Island of- **7** CDc
Mullewa **29** Bd
Mullingar **7** Ce
Mulobezi **26** Bc
Mulock Glacier **42** grid square no.4
Multan **15** Cfg
Mumbai (Bombay) **15** Ch
Mumbwa **26** Bc
Mun (riv.) **19** De
Muna, Pulau- (i.) **18** Fef
Münden **5** Bc
Mundiwindi **29** BCc
Mundo Novo **38** Cc
Mundubbera **29** HId
Mungbere **25** Cd
Munger **20** Gcd
Mungindi **29** Hd
Munich **5** CDd
Munku-Sardyk, gora- (mt.) **14** CDd
Muñoz Gamero, Península- **40** Ac
Munster (prov.) **7** BCe
Münster **5** ABbc
Muntele Mare, Vîrful-(mt.) **6** Fc
Muntenia (phys. reg.) **6** GHd
Muong Sen **19** DEe
Muonio **4** EFb
Muonioälven (riv.) **4** Ea
Mur (riv.) **5** Ee
Mura (riv.) **6** Cc
Murakami **17** Fe
Murallón, Cerro- (mt.) **40** Ab
Muraši **13** Dd
Murat (riv.) **21** Cb
Murat dağı (mt.) **22** Bc
Muratlı **22** Ab
Murchison River **29** Bd
Murcia **9** Ed
Murcia (phys. reg.) **9** Ec
Muren **14** CDe
Mureş (riv.) **6** FGc
Muret **8** Df
Murgab **16** Ac
Murge, Le- (mts.) **10** Fd
Murghab (riv.) **20** BCa
Murgon **29** Id
Müritz (l.) **5** Db
Murmansk **13** Cc
Murmaši **4** GHa
Muro Lucano **10** Ed
Murom **12** Fb
Muroran **16** Jb
Muros **9** Aa
Muroto **17** Dh
Muroto-Zaki **17** Dh
Murray Bridge **29** FGf
Murray River **29** Hf
Murrumbidgee River **29** GHe
Murud, Gunong- (mt.) **18** Ed
Mururoa Atoll **28** BCd
Murwara **20** Fd
Murwillumbah **29** IJd
Murzuq **24** Db
Mürzzuschlag **5** EFe
Muş **21** Cb
Musala (mt.) **11** Eb
Musan **16** Gb
Muscat (phys. reg.) **21** Fe
Muscat **21** Fe
Musgrave **29** Ga
Musgrave Ranges **29** Ed
Mus-Haja, gora- (mt.) **14** Hc
Mushie **26** Ab
Musi (riv.) **18** Be
Muskegon **32** Ca
Muskogee **32** Bb
Musoma **25** De
Mussende **26** Ac
Mustafa-Kemalpaşa **22** Bbc
Mustang **19** Hli
Mustvee **4** Fd
Muswellbrook **29** Hle
Mut **25** Cb
Mutarara **26** Cc
Mutare **26** Cc
Mutatá **37** Bb
Mutsu **16** Jb
Mutsu-Wan **17** Gd
Muwayh, Al- **21** Ce
Muxima **26** Ab
Muyinga **26** BCb
Muzaffarpur **20** Gc
Muztag (mt.) **20** Fa
Mvolo **25** Cd
Mwali (i.) **26** Dc
Mwanza **26** Cb
Mweelrea (mt.) **7** Be
Mwene Ditu **26** Bb
Mweru, Lake- **26** Bb
Mwinilunga **26** Bc
Myanmar (Burma) (Ind. St.) **15** Dg
Myaungmya **19** Be
Myingyan **19** Cd
Myitkyina **15** Dg
Mymensingh **20** Hd
Myoshi **17** Cg
Mýrdalsjökl (gl.) **4** map no.1
Mysore **15** Ch
Mys Šmidta **14** KLc
My Tho **19** Efg
Mytišči **12** Eb
Mzimba **26** Cc
Mzuzu **26** Cc

N

Naab (riv.) **5** Dd
Naalehu **28** map no.1
Naantali **4** Ec
Naas **7** Ce
Nabadwip **19** Jk
Naberežnyje Čelny **13** DEd
Nabesna **31** Ab
Nabire **27** Bc
Nabk, An- **22** Fef
Nablus **22** Ef
Nābul **10** Cf
Nacala **26** Dc
Nacala-a-Velha **26** CDc
Nacaome **35** Bb
Nachingwea **26** Cbc
Náchod **5** EFc
Nacozari de García **34** Bab
Nadiad **20** Dd
Nádusa **11** DEc
Nadvornaja **6** Gb
Næstved **4** BCe
Nafīdah, An- **10** Cf
Nafūd, Al- (phys. reg.) **21** BCd
Naga **18** Fb
Nagaland (State) **19** Bc
Nagano **16** Ic
Nagaoka **16** Ic
Nagappattinam **20** EFf
Nagasaki **16** Gd
Nagato **17** Bg
Nagda **20** Ed
Nagercoil **20** Eg
Nagorny **14** Fd
Nagoya **16** Ic
Nagpur **15** Cg
Nagqu **19** Bb
Nagyatád **6** Cc
Nagykanizsa **6** Cc
Nagykörös **6** DEc
Naha **16** Ge
Nahodka **14** Ge
Nahuel Huapi, Lago- **40** Ab
Nain **31** Ic
Nā'īn **21** Ec
Nairn **7** Ec
Nairobi **25** De
Naivasha **26** Cb
Najafābād **21** Ec
Najd (hist. reg.) **21** CDe
Najin **16** Hb
Najran **21** CDf
Nakadōri-Jima (i.) **17** Ah
Naka-lō-Jima (i.) **27** BCa
Nakaminato **17** Gf
Naka-no-Shima (i.) **17** ABj
Nakashibetsu **17** Ic
Nakatsu **17** Bh
Nakhichevan (Aut. Rep.) **13** De
Nakhl, An- **22** DEh
Nakhon Pathom **19** CDf
Nakhon Phanom **19** De
Nakhon Ratchasima (Khorat) **19** Def
Nakhon Sawan **19** CDe
Nakhon Si Thammarat **19** CDg
Nakina **31** Gc
Nakło nad Notećią **5** Fb
Nakonde **26** Cb
Nakskov **5** Ca
Naktong-gang (riv.) **17** Ag
Nakuru **25** De
Nal (riv.) **20** Cc
Nalčik **13** De
Nalut **24** Da
Namak, Daryācheh- ye- **21** Ec
Namakzār (l.) **20** Bb
Namakzar-e-Shandād **21** Fcd
Namangan **13** Ge
Namapa **26** CDc
Nambour **29** Id
Nambucca Heads **29** IJe
Namcha Barwa (mt.) **19** BCc
Namche Bazar **19** Ij
Nam Co (l.) **19** Bb
Namdalen (phys. reg.) **4** Cb
Nam Dinh **19** Ed
Namib Desert **26** Acd
Namibe **23** CDg
Namibia (Ind. St.) **23** Dh
Naminga **14** EFd
Namlea **18** Ge
Namoi River **29** Hle
Namonuito Atoll **27** Cb
Namorik Atoll **27** Db
Nampa **33** Bb
Nampala **24** Bc
Namp'o **16** FGc
Nampula **26** CDc
Namsos **4** Bb
Nam Tha **19** Dd
Namtu **19** Cd
Namur **8** Fb
Namuruputh **26** Ca
Namwala **26** Bc
Nan (riv.) **19** De
Nan **19** De
Nanaimo **33** Ab
Nanao **17** Ef
Nanatsu-Shima **17** Ef
Nancha **16** Ga
Nanchang **15** DEg
Nancheng **16** Ee
Nanchong **16** Cd
Nancy **8** Gc
Nanda Devi (mt.) **20** EFb
Nānded **20** Ee
Nandi [Fiji] **28** map no.6
Nandi [Zimb.] **26** Cd
Nanga Parbat (mt.) **20** Dab
Nangapinoh **18** De
Nangatayap **18** De
Nanjing (Nanking) **16** Ed
Nanking → Nanjing **16** Ed
Nan Ling (mts.) **16** Def
Nanning **15** Dg
Nanortalik **31** Kbc
Nanping **16** Ee
Nansei-Shotō → Ryukyu Islands **16** FGef
Nanshan Islands **18** Dcd
Nanterre **8** DEc
Nantes **8** Cd
Nantes-Brest, Canal- **8** Bcd
Nantong **16** Fd
Nanumea Atoll **27** Dc
Nanuque **39** DEa
Nanusa, Pulau- Pulau- **18** Gd
Nanxiong **16** DEef
Nanyang **16** Dd
Nanyuki **25** Dde
Nanzhang **16** Dd
Não, Cabo de la- (cap.) **9** Fc
Napier **27** Dd
Napier Mountains **42** grid square no.2
Naples **10** Ed

© ISTITUTO GEOGRAFICO DE AGOSTINI S.p.A. - Novara

Naples, Gulf of– **10** Ed
Napo (riv.) **37** Bc
Napuka, Île– (is.) **28** BCc
Nara [Jap.] **17** DEg
Nara [Mali] **24** Bc
Naracoorte **29** FGf
Narayanganj **20** GHd
Narbonne **8** Ef
Nardò **10** Gd
Nares Strait **41** grid square no.1
Narew (riv.) **5** Hb
Narjan-Mar **13** Ec
Narlı **22** Fd
Narmada (riv.) **20** Ed
Narnaul **19** Gij
Narodnaja, gora– (mt.) **13** EFc
Naro-Fominsk **12** DEb
Narrabri **29** HIe
Narrandera **29** Hef
Narrogin **29** Be
Narsaq / Narssaq **31** Kb
Narsimhapur **20** EFd
Narssaq / Narsaq **31** Kb
Narva **4** Gd
Narva (riv.) **4** Fd
Narvik **4** Da
Naryn **13** Ge
Naryn (riv.) **16** ABb
Năsăud **6** FGc
Nashville **32** Cb
Našice **6** Dd
Näsijärvi (l.) **4** EFc
Nāsik **20** Dde
Nassau **32** Dc
Nassau Island **28** Ac
Nasser, Lake– **25** Db
Nässjö **4** Cd
Nata **26** Bcd
Natal [Braz.] **36** Gd
Natal [Indon.] **18** Ad
Natchez **32** Bb
Natividade **38** Cc
Natuna Islands **18** Cd
Naturaliste, Cape– **29** Ae
Naturaliste Channel **29** Acd
Nauâdbhibou, Dakhlet– **24** Abc
Nauâdhibou **24** Ab
Náuplion **11** Ee
Nauru (Ind. St.) **27** Dc
Nautanwa **19** HIj
Nautla **34** Cb
Navan / An Uaimh **7** CDe
Navarin, mys– **14** KLc
Navarino, Isla– (i.) **40** Bc
Navarra (phys. reg.) **9** DEa
Navassa Island **35** Cb
Navaya Sibir, ostrov– (i.) **41** grid square no.4
Navoi **13** Fe
Navojoa **34** ABb
Návpaktos **11** DEd
Navsari **20** Dd
Nawabganj [Bngl.] **19** Jj
Nawabganj [India] **19** Hj
Nawabshah **20** CDc
Nawakot **19** Iij
Náxos (i.) **11** Fe
Náxos **11** Fe
Nāyband **21** Ed
Nayoro **16** Jb
Nazaré [Braz.] **38** Dc
Nazaré [Port.] **9** Ac
Nazareth **22** Ef
Nazarovo **13** HId
Nazca **39** Aa
Naze **16** Ge
Nazilli **22** Bcd
Nazwa **21** Fe
Nazyvajevsk **13** Gd
Ndalatando **26** Ab
Ndélé **25** Cd
N'djamena **25** Bc
Ndjolé **24** CDde
Ndola **23** EFg
Neagh, Lake– **7** Cd
Neale, Lake– **29** DEc
Neales, The– (riv.) **29** EFd
Neápolis [Grc.] **11** Dc
Neápolis [Grc.] **11** Ee
Nebit-Dag **13** Ef
Neblina, Pico da– (mt.) **37** Cb
Nebraska (State) **33** CDb
Nebrodi (mts.) **10** Ef
Neckar (riv.) **5** Bd
Necker Island **28** Aa
Necochea **39** Cc
Nêdong **19** Bc
Needles **33** Bc
Neftekamsk **12** HIb
Negelli **25** DEd
Negola **26** Ac
Negombo **20** Eg
Negonego Atoll **28** Bc
Negotin **6** Fd
Negra, Cordillera– (mts.) **37** Bc
Negreşti **6** Hc
Negro, Río– (riv.) **39** Bcd
Negro, Rio– [Braz.] (riv.) **37** Cbc
Negro, Río– [Ur.] (riv.) **40** Bab
Negros (i.) **18** Fbc
Negru Vodă **6** Ie
Nehbandān **21** FGc
Neijiang **14** Fe
Neisse (riv.) **5** Ec
Neiva **37** Bb
Neja **12** Fb
Nekemt **25** Dd
Neksø **5** Ea
Nelidovo **12** Db
Nelkan **14** Gd
Nellore **20** EFf
Nelma **14** Ge
Nelson (riv.) **31** Fc
Nelson [Can.] **33** Bb
Nelson [N.Z.] **27** De
Nelspruit **26** Cd
Néma **24** Bc
Neman **4** Ee
Nemira, Vîrful– (mt.) **6** GHc
Nemirov **6** Ib
Nemuna, Bjeshkët e– **11** CDb
Nemunas / Neman (riv.) **13** Bd
Nemuro **16** Ic
Nemuro-Kaikyō **17** Ib
Nenagh **7** BCe
Nendo Island **27** Dc
Nene (riv.) **7** Ge
Nen Jiang (Nun Kiang) (riv.) **16** Fa
Nepal (Ind. St.) **15** Cg
Nepalganj **19** Hij
Nephin (mt.) **7** Bde
Nérac **8** CDe
Nerčinsk **14** Ed
Nerehta **12** Fb
Neretva (riv.) **6** De
Neringa **4** Ee
Neriquinha **26** ABc
Neris (riv.) **4** Fe
Nerva **9** Bd
Nesebăr **11** GHb
Neskaupstadur **4** map no.1
Ness, Loch– (l.) **7** Dc
Nesterov [Russia] **5** Ia
Nesterov → Zovkva [Ukr.] **5** Ic
Néstos → Mesta (riv.) **11** Fc
Netanya **22** Ef
Netherdale **29** Hc
Netherlands (Ind. St.) **3** Db
Neubrandenburg **5** Db
Neuchâtel **5** Ae
Neuchâtel, Lac de– **10** Aa
Neufchâteau [Bel.] **8** Fc
Neufchâteau [Fr.] **8** Fc
Neumünster **5** BCa
Neunkirchen [Aus.] **5** EFe
Neunkirchen [Ger.] **5** Ad
Neuquén **39** Bc
Neuquén (riv.) **39** ABc
Neusiedler See **5** Fe
Neustrelitz **5** Db
Neu Ulm **5** BCd
Neuwied **5** Ac
Neva (riv.) **12** Db
Nevada (State) **33** Bc
Nevada, Sierra– [Sp.] (mts.) **9** Dd
Nevada, Sierra– [U.S.] (mts.) **33** ABbc
Nevada del Cocuy, Sierra– (mt.) **37** Bb
Nevada de Santa Marta, Sierra– (mts.) **37** Ba
Nevel **12** CDb
Nevelsk **17** Ga
Never **14** Fd
Nevers **8** Ed
Nevis (i.) **35** Db
Nevjansk **12** Jb
Nevşehir **22** Ec
New Albany **32** Cb
New Amsterdam **38** Ba
Newark **32** Da
Newark-on-Trent **7** FGe
New Bedford **32** DEa
New Bern **32** Db
New Britain **27** Cc
New Byrd **42** grid square no.3
New Caledonia (i.) **27** Dd
Newcastle [Austl.] **29** Ie
Newcastle [Can.] **32** Ea
Newcastle [S. Afr.] **26** BCd
Newcastle [U.S.] **33** Cb
Newcastle upon Tyne **7** EFd
Newcastle Waters **29** Eb
Newdegate **29** BCe
New Delhi **19** Gi
New England Range **29** Ide
Newfoundland (prov.) **31** IJcd
Newfoundland (i.) **30** Me
New Georgia Island **27** CDc
New Glasgow **32** Ea
New Guinea (i.) **27** BCc
New Hampshire (State) **32** Da
New Hanover Island **27** Cc
Newhaven **7** FGf
New Haven **32** Da
New Hebrides (is.) **27** Dc
New Iberia **32** Bbc
New Ireland Island **27** Cc
New Jersey (State) **32** Da
New Liskeard **31** Hd
New London **32** Da
Newman **29** BCc
New Mexico (State) **33** Cc
New Norfolk **29** map no.1
New Orleans **32** BCc
New Plymouth **27** Dd
Newport [Eng.-U.K.] **7** Ff
Newport [Wales-U.K.] **7** Ef
Newport News **32** Db
New Providence **32** Dc
New Ross **7** Ce
Newry **7** Cd
New Schwabenland **42** grid square no.1
New Siberian Island **41** grid square no.4
New South Wales (State) **29** GHe
Newton **32** Bb
Newtownabbey **7** Dd
New Westminster **33** Ab
New York **32** Dab
New York (State) **32** Da
New Zealand (Ind. St.) **27** DEe
Neyriz **21** Ed
Neyshābūr **21** Fb
Nežin **13** Cd
Ngain Atoll **28** map no.3
Ngaliema, Chutes– (Stanley Falls) **26** Ba
Ngami, Lake– **26** Bd
Ngangla Ringco (l.) **20** Fb
Nganglong Kangri (mt.) **16** Cd
Ngaoundéré **24** Dd
Ngau Island **28** map no.6
Ngoc Linh (mt.) **19** Eef
Ngoring Hu (l.) **16** Acd
Ngourti **24** Dc
Nguigmi **24** Dc
Ngulu Atoll **27** BCb
Nguru **24** CDc
Nhamundá (riv.) **38** Bb
Nha Trang **19** EFf
Nhill **29** Gf
Nhulunbuy **29** Fa
Niagara Falls (wf.) **32** Da
Niagara Falls [Can.] **32** CDa
Niagara Falls [U.S.] **32** Da
Niamey **24** Cc
Niangara **25** Cd
Nias, Pulau– (i.) **15** Di
Nicaragua (Ind. St.) **30** Jh
Nicaragua, Lago de– **35** Ba
Nice **8** Gf
Nichinan **17** BCi
Nicholson River **29** Fb
Nicobar Islands **19** Bg
Nicosia [Cyp.] **22** De
Nicosia [It.] **10** Ef
Nicoya, Golfo de– **35** Bc
Nicoya, Peninsula de– (pen.) **35** Bbc

© ISTITUTO GEOGRAFICO DE AGOSTINI S.p.A. - Novara

© ISTITUTO GEOGRAFICO DE AGOSTINI S.p.A. - Novara

Nowshera **20** Db
Nowy Dwór Mazowiecki **5** Hb
Nowy Sącz **5** Hd
Nowy Targ **5** Hd
Noya **9** Aa
Nsanje **26** Cc
Nsukka **24** Cd
Nuayriyah, An– **21** Dd
Nubian Desert (phys. reg.) **25** Dbc
Nueltin Lake **31** Fbc
Nueva Casas Grandes **34** Ba
Nueva Gerona **35** Ba
Nueva Rosita **34** Bb
Nueve de Julio **39** Bc
Nuevitas **35** Ca
Nuevo, Golfo– **40** Bb
Nuevo Arraiján **35** map no.1
Nuevo Chagres **35** map no.1
Nuevo Laredo **34** BCb
Nuevo Rocafuerte **37** Bc
Nuhūd, An– **25** Cc
Nui Atoll **27** Dc
Nukhayb **21** Cc
Nuku'alofa **28** Ad
Nukufetau Atoll **27** DEc
Nuku Hiva, Île– (i.) **28** BCc
Nukunonu Atoll **28** Ac
Nukuoro Atoll **27** Cb
Nukus **13** EFe
Nules **9** EFc
Nullagine **29** BCc
Nullarbor Plain **29** DEe
Numancia (r.) **9** Db
Numata **17** Ff
Numazu **17** Fg
Nunivak Island **41** grid square no.2
Nunkun (mt.) **20** Eb
Nuoro **10** Bd
Nurmes **4** Gc
Nürnberg **5** Cd
Nuruhak dağ (mt.) **22** Fcd
Nutak **31** IJc
Nutrias, Ciudad de– **37** Cb
Nuuk / Godthåb **30** MNc
Nuwaybi' al Muzayyinah **22** Eh
Nuyts Archipelago **29** Ee
Nyainqêntanglha Shan **20** GHbc
Nyala **25** Cc
Nyasa, Lake– → Malawi, Lake– **26** Cc
Nyborg **5** Ca
Nybro **4** CDd
Nyda **13** Gc
Nyingchi **19** Bc
Nyíregyháza **6** EFbc
Nykarleby **4** Ec
Nykøbing **4** Be
Nyköping **4** CDd
Nymburk **5** Ec
Nynäshamn **4** Dd
Nyngan **29** He
Nyong (riv.) **24** CDd
Nysa **5** Fc
Nysa (riv.) **5** Ec
Nytva **12** Hlb
Nzega **26** Cb
Nzérékoré **24** Bd
Nzeto **26** Ab
Nzwani (i.) **26** Dc

O

Oahe, Lake– **33** CDd
Oahu (i.) **28** Eb
Oakham **7** Fe
Oakland **33** Ac
Oak Ridge **32** Cb
Oamaru **27** De
Oaxaca de Juarez **34** Cc
Ob (riv.) **13** Gc
Oba **31** Gd
Obama **17** Dg
Oban **7** Dc
Oberá **39** Cb
Oberhausen **5** Ac
Ober–Österreich (phys. reg.) **5** DFd
Ob Gulf **13** Gc
Obi, Pulau– (i.) **18** Ge
Óbidos **38** Bb
Obihiro **16** Jb
Oblačnaja (mt.) **17** Dc
Obluče **14** Ge
Obninsk **12** Ebc
Obo **26** Ba
Obojan **12** Ec
Obozerski **13** Dc
Obrenovac **6** DEd
Obšči Syrt (mts.) **12** Hc
Ocakbaşı **12** EFf
Ocala **32** Cc
Ocaña **37** Bb
Ocean → Kure Island **27** DEa
Ocean Falls **31** Cc
Ocean Island **27** Dc
Ōda **17** Cg
Oda, Jabal– (mt.) **25** Dbc
Odate **17** Gd
Odawara **16** IJcd
Odda **4** Ac
Odemira **9** Ad
Ödemiş **22** ABc
Odense **4** Be
Odenwald (mt.) **5** Bd
Oder (riv.) **5** Eb
Odessa [Ukr.] **13** Ce
Odessa [U.S.] **33** Cc
Odienné **24** Bcd
Odorheiu Secuiesc **6** Gc
Odra (riv.) **5** Eb
Oeiras **38** Cb
Oeno Island **28** Cd
Offenbach am Main **5** Bcd
Offenburg **5** ABd
Ofotfjord (g.) **4** CDa
Ofu (i.) **28** map no.5
Ōfunato **17** GHe
Oga **17** Fe
Ogadèn (phys. reg.) **25** Ed
Oga–Hantō **17** Fde
Ōgaki **17** DEg
Ogallala **33** Cb
Ogbomosho **24** Cd
Ogden **33** Bb
Oglio (riv.) **10** Cb
Ogooué (riv.) **26** Ab
Ogre **4** Fd
Ogulin **6** Bd
Oha **14** Hd
Ohanet **24** CDb
Ohansk **12** Hlb
Ōhata **17** Gd

Ohio (riv.) **32** Cb
Ohio (State) **32** Cab
Ohotsk **14** Hd
Ohře (riv.) **5** DEc
Ohrid **11** Dc
Ohrid, Lake– **11** Dc
Oi (riv.) **17** Fg
Oiapoque (riv.) **38** Ba
Oiapoque **38** Ba
Oil City **32** Da
Oise (riv.) **8** Ec
Ōita **16** Hd
Ojinaga **34** Bb
Ojmjakon **14** Hc
Ojos del Salado, Nevado– (mt.) **39** Bb
Oka [Russia] (riv.) **14** Dd
Oka [Russia] (riv.) **13** Cd
Okahandja **26** Ad
Okara **20** Db
Okavango (riv.) **26** ABc
Okavango Swamp **26** Bc
Okaya **17** EFfg
Okayama **16** Hcd
Okazaki **17** Eg
Okeechobee, Lake– **32** Cc
Okha **15** Cg
Okhaldhunga **19** Ij
Okhostk, Sea of– **41** grid square no.4
Oki–Daitō–Jima (i.) **16** Hef
Okinawa–Jima (i.) **16** Ge
Okinoerabu–Jima (i.) **16** Ge
Okino–Shima **17** Ch
Okino–Tori–Shima (i.) **27** BCab
Oki–Shotō **17** Cf
Oklahoma (State) **32** Bb
Oklahoma City **32** Bb
Oknica **6** Hb
Øksfjord **4** Ea
Okstindane (mt.) **4** Cb
Oktjabrsk **13** Ee
Oktjabrski [Bela.] **12** Cc
Oktjabrski [Russia] **12** Hc
Oktjabrski [Russia] **14** Id
Oktjabrskoje **13** Fc
Oktjabrskoj Revoljuci, ostrov– **41** grid square no.4
Okulovka **12** Db
Okushiri–Tō (i.) **16** Ib
Okusi **18** Ff
Olafsfjördur **4** map no.1
Olanchito **35** Bb
Öland (i.) **4** Dd
Olanga **4** Gb
Olavarría **39** Bc
Oława **5** Fc
Olbia **10** Bd
Old Crow **31** ABb
Olden **4** Ac
Oldenburg in Holstein **5** Ca
Oldenburg in Oldenburg **5** ABb
Oldham **7** EFe
Oldman (riv.) **33** Bab
Olëkma (riv.) **14** Fd
Olëkminsk **14** EFc
Olenegorsk **4** GHa
Olenëk **14** Ec
Olenëk (riv.) **14** Fb
Oleni, ostrov– **13** Gb
Oléron, Ile d'– (i.) **8** BCe

Oleśnica **5** Fc
Olevsk **6** Ha
Olga **14** Ge
Olhão **9** Bd
Olib **10** Eb
Olimarao Atoll **27** Cb
Olimbía (r.) **11** De
Ólimbos **11** Gf
Olinda **38** Db
Olivenza **9** Bc
Oljutorski **14** Kc
Oljutorski, mys– **14** Kd
Olkusz **5** Gc
Ollagüe **39** Bb
Olmedo **9** Cb
Olomouc **5** Fd
Olonec **12** Da
Olongapo **18** Fb
Oloron–Sainte–Marie **8** Cf
Olot **9** Ga
Olovjannaja **14** Ed
Olsztyn **5** Hb
Olt (riv.) **6** Gcd
Olten **5** ABe
Oltenia (phys. reg.) **6** FGd
Oltenita **6** Hd
Oltetul **6** FGd
Oluanpi (cap.) **16** Ff
Olvera **9** Cd
Olympia **33** Ab
Olympus → Troödos, Mount– **22** De
Olympus, Mount– [Grc.] **11** Ec
Olympus, Mount– [U.S.] **33** Ab
Omagh **7** Cd
Omaha **32** Ba
Ōma–Kaki **17** Gd
'Oman (phys. reg.) **21** Fe
'Oman (Ind. St.) **21** EFef
Oman, Gulf of– **21** FGe
Omaruru **26** Ad
Omboué **24** Ce
Ombrone (riv.) **10** Cc
Ombu **20** Gb
Omdurman **25** Dc
Omiš **10** Fc
Omo (riv.) **25** Dd
Omolon (riv.) **14** Jc
Omsk **13** Gd
Ōmu **17** Hb
Omu, Vîrful– (mt.) **6** Gd
Ōmuta **17** Bh
Omutninsk **12** Hb
Ondangwa **26** Ac
Ondjiva **26** Ac
Ondo **24** Cd
Onega **13** Cc
Onega (riv.) **13** Cc
Onega, Lake– **13** Cc
Onekotan (i.) **14** Ie
Ongjin **16** FGc
Ongole **20** EFe
Onitsha **24** Cd
Ōno **17** Efg
Ono–i–Lau Islands **27** DEd
Onomichi **17** Cg
Onon (riv.) **14** Ed
Onslow **29** Bc
Ontario (prov.) **31** FGcd
Ontario **33** Bb
Ontario, Lake– **32** Da

Paistunturit (mt.) **4** FGa
Paita **37** Ac
Pajala **4** Eb
Pajaros, Farallon de– (i.) **27** Ca
Pakanbaru **18** Bd
Pakistan (Ind. St.) **15** Cg
Pakokku **19** Bd
Pak Phanang **19** Dg
Paks **6** Dc
Pakxé **19** Ee
Pala **25** Bd
Palagruža **11** Bb
Palana **14** IJd
Palangkaraya **18** De
Palanpur **20** Dd
Palapye **26** Bd
Palau **10** Bd
Palau Islands **27** Bb
Palauli **28** map no.5
Palaw **19** Cf
Palawan (i.) **15** Dhi
Palayankottai **20** Eg
Paldiski **4** EFd
Paleleh **18** Fd
Palembang **15** Dj
Palencia **9** CDab
Palermo **10** De
Palestina **39** ABb
Palestine (phys. reg.) **22** Efg
Paletwa **19** Bd
Palghat **20** Ef
Pali **20** Dc
Palikir **27** Cb
Palinuro, Capo– **10** Ed
Palk Strait **20** EFfg
Pallasovka **12** Gc
Pallastunturi (mt.) **4** EFa
Palles, Bisthi i– **11** Cc
Palma **9** Gc
Palma, La– **35** Cc
Palma, La– (i.) **24** Ab
Palmas, Cape– **24** Bd
Palmas, Las– **24** Ab
Palma Soriano **35** Cab
Palmeira dos Indios **38** Db
Palmer Land **42** grid square no.1
Palmer Station (sc. stat.) **42** grid square no.1
Palmerston Atoll **28** Ac
Palmi **10** Ee
Palmira **37** Bb
Palm Springs **33** Bc
Palmyra **21** Bc
Palmyra Atoll **28** Ab
Paloma, La– **39** Cc
Palomani, Nevado– (mt.) **39** Ba
Palomar Mountain (mt.) **33** Bc
Palopo **18** EFe
Palos, Cabo de– (cap.) **9** Ed
Palu **18** EFe
Pamekasan **18** Df
Pamiers **8** DEf
Pamir (plat.) **13** Gf
Pamlico Sound **32** Db
Pampa **33** CDc
Pampas (phys. reg.) **39** Bc
Pamplona [Col.] **37** Bb
Pamplona [Sp.] **9** DEa
Panagjurište **11** Fb
Panaitan, Pulau– (i.) **18** BCf
Panaji (Nova Goa) **20** De
Panamá (Ind. St.) **30** JKi
Panamá **36** Cbc
Panama, Gulf of– **35** Cc
Panama City **32** Cbc
Panaro (riv.) **10** Cb
Panay (i.) **15** Eh
Pančevo **6** Ed
Panciu **6** Hd
Panevėžys **4** Fe
Panfilov **13** GHe
Pangaíon Óros (mts.) **11** EFc
Pangi **26** Bb
Pangkalanberandan **18** Ad
Pangkalpinang **18** Ce
Pangnirtung **31** Ib
Pangutaran Group **18** EFc
Panié, Mont– (mt.) **28** map no.4
Panjgur **20** Bc
Panna **19** Hj
Pannawonica **29** Bc
Panorama **39** Cb
Pantanal (sw.) **39** Ca
Pantar, Pulau– (i.) **18** Ff
Pantelleria (i.) **10** CDf
Pánuco (riv.) **34** Cb
Pao, El– **37** Cb
Pão de Açúcar **38** Db
Paola **10** Fe
Papa **28** map no.3
Pápa **6** Cc
Papaikou **28** map no.1
Papeete **28** map no.2
Papenoo **28** map no.2
Papetoai **28** map no.2
Papua, Gulf of– **27** Cc
Papua New Guinea (Ind. St.) **27** Cc
Papuk (mts.) **6** Cd
Papun **19** Ce
Pará (State) **38** Bb
Pará (riv.) **38** BCb
Paraburdoo **29** Bc
Paracatu (riv.) **39** Da
Paracatu **39** Da
Paracel Islands **15** Dh
Paraguá (riv.) **39** Ba
Paragua (riv.) **37** Cb
Paragua, La– **37** Cb
Paraguai (riv.) **38** Bc
Paraguaipoa **37** Ba
Paraguaná, Peninsula de– (pen.) **37** Ca
Paraguay (riv.) **39** Cb
Paraguay (Ind. St.) **36** DEf
Paraíba (State) **38** Db
Paraíba do Sul (riv.) **39** Db
Paraíso **35** map no.1
Parakou **24** Cd
Paramaribo **36** Ec
Paramonga **37** Bd
Paramušir, ostrov– (i.) **14** Id
Paraná **39** BCc
Paranã **38** Cc
Paranã (riv.) **38** Cc
Paraná (riv.) **39** Cb
Paraná (State) **39** Cb
Paranaguá **39** Db
Paranaíba **39** Cab
Paranaíba (riv.) **39** Da
Paranapanema (riv.) **39** Cb
Paranapiacaba, Serra do– (mts.) **39** CDb
Paranavaí **39** Cb
Parapetí (riv.) **39** Bab
Paray-le-Monial **8** Fd
Parbati (riv.) **20** Ed
Parbhani **20** Ee
Parchim **5** Cb
Parczew **5** Ic
Pardo [Braz.] (riv.) **38** CDc
Pardo [Braz.] (riv.) **39** Db
Pardubice **5** EFcd
Parecis, Chapada dos– (mts.) **38** ABc
Parepare **18** Ee
Párga **11** Dd
Paria, Golfo de– **37** Ca
Pariaman **18** ABe
Parika **37** Db
Parima, Sierra– (mts.) **37** Cb
Pariñas, Punta– (cap.) **37** Ac
Parîngul Mare, Vîrful– (mt.) **6** FGd
Parintins **38** Bb
Paris [Fr.] **8** Ec
Paris [U.S.] **32** Bb
Parkersburg **32** CDb
Parkes **29** He
Park Range **33** Cbc
Parma **10** Cb
Parnaguá **38** Cbc
Parnaíba **36** FGd
Parnaíba (riv.) **38** Cb
Parnassós Óros (mt.) **11** Ed
Párnon Óros (mts.) **11** Ee
Pärnu **13** Bd
Paroo Channel (riv.) **29** Gde
Paroo River **29** GHd
Paropamisus (mts.) **20** BCab
Páros (i.) **11** Fe
Parral **39** Ac
Parras **34** Bb
Parry, Cape– **31** Cab
Parry Islands **41** grid square no.2
Parry Sound **31** GHd
Parşeta (riv.) **5** Fb
Parsons **32** Bb
Parthenay **8** CDd
Partinico **10** De
Partizansk **14** Ge
Paru (riv.) **38** Ba
Părvomaj **11** Fb
Pas, The– **31** Bb
Pasadena [Ca.-U.S.] **33** Bc
Pasadena [Tx.-U.S.] **32** Bc
Pa Sak (riv.) **19** Def
Paşcani **6** Hc
Pasco **33** Bb
Pascoal, Monte– **38** CDc
Pasewalk **5** DEb
Pasir Mas **19** Dg
Pasni **20** Bc
Paso, El– **33** Cc
Paso de Indios **40** Bb
Paso de los Libres **39** Cb
Paso de los Toros **39** Cc
Passau **5** Dd
Passero, Capo– **10** Ef
Passo Fundo **39** Cb
Passos **39** Db
Pastaza (riv.) **37** Bc
Pasto **36** Cc
Pastos Bons **38** Cb
Pasvik (riv.) **4** Ga
Patagonia (phys. reg.) **40** ABbc
Patagonica, Cordillera– (mts.) **40** Aab
Patan [India] **20** Dd
Patan [Nep.] **20** Gc
Paternò **10** Ef
Paterson **32** Da
Pathankot **20** Eb
Pati **18** Df
Patía **37** Bb
Patía (riv.) **37** Bb
Patiala **20** Ebc
Pátmos (i.) **11** Ge
Patna **15** Cg
Patomskoje Negorje **14** Ed
Patos **38** Db
Patos, Lagoa dos– (lag.) **39** Cc
Patos de Minas **39** Da
Patquía **39** Bbc
Pátrai **11** DEd
Patraïkós Kólpos **11** Dd
Patrocínio **39** Da
Pattani **19** Dg
Patti **10** Ee
Patuakhali **19** Jk
Patuca (riv.) **35** Bb
Patuca, Punta– (cap.) **35** Bb
Pau **8** Cf
Pau d'Arco **38** Cb
Pau dos Ferros **38** Db
Pauillac **8** Ce
Pauini **37** Cc
Pauini (riv.) **37** Cc
Paulatuk **31** Cb
Paulista **38** Db
Paulistana **38** Cb
Paulo Alfonso, Cachoeira de– **38** Db
Pavia **10** Bb
Pavlodar **13** Gd
Pavlovo **12** Fb
Pavlovsk **12** EFc
Pavlovskaja **12** EFd
Paxoí (i.) **11** CDd
Payne Bay → Bellin **31** HIbc
Payne's Find **29** Bd
Paysandú **39** Cc
Pays de Caux (phys. reg.) **8** Dc
Paz, La– [Arg.] **39** Cc
Paz, La– [Arg.] **39** Bc
Paz, La– [Bol.] **39** Ba
Paz, La– [Mex.] **34** Ab
Pazardžik **11** EFb
Peace River (riv.) **31** Dc
Peace River **31** Dc
Peak Hill **29** Bd
Pearl Harbor **28** map no.1
Peary Land **41** grid square no.1
Pebane **26** Cc
Pebas **37** Bc
Peć **11** Db
Peçanha **39** Da
Pečenga **13** Cbc
Pečora (riv.) **13** Ec
Pečora **13** Ec
Pecoraro, Monte– **10** Fe
Pečory **4** Fd
Pecos (riv.) **33** Cc

© ISTITUTO GEOGRAFICO DE AGOSTINI S.p.A. - Novara

Q

© ISTITUTO GEOGRAFICO DE AGOSTINI S.p.A. - Novara

Ros - Sai

Roşiori de Vede **6** Gd
Roskilde **5** Da
Roslavl **13** Cd
Rossano **10** Fe
Ross Ice Shelf (gl.) **42** grid square no.3
Ross Island **42** grid square no.4
Rosslare **7** CDe
Rosso **24** Ac
Rossoš **12** Ec
Ross River **31** Bb
Ross Sea **42** grid square no.3
Røssvatnet (l.) **4** Cb
Røst (i.) **4** Bb
Rostock **5** Da
Rostock–Warnemünde **5** CDa
Rostov **12** Eb
Rostov–na–Donu **13** CDe
Roswell **33** Cc
Rota Island **27** Cb
Rothaar–Gebirge (mts.) **5** Bc
Rothera (i.) **42** grid square no.1
Rothesay **7** Dd
Roti, Pulau– (i.) **18** Fg
Rotidian Point **27** map no.1
Roto **29** GHe
Rotondo, Monte– **8** map no.1
Rotterdam **8** EFb
Rotterdam–Hoek van Holland **8** EFb
Rottweil **5** Bd
Rotuma Island **27** Dc
Roubaix **8** Eb
Rouen **8** Dc
Round Mountain, The– (mt.) **29** le
Rousay (i.) **7** Eb
Roussillon (phys. reg.) **8** Ef
Rouyn **31** Hd
Rov (riv.) **6** Hb
Rovaniemi **4** Fb
Rovereto **10** Cb
Rovigo **10** Cb
Rovno **13** Bd
Rovuma (riv.) **26** Cc
Rowley Shoals (is.) **29** Bb
Roxas **18** Fb
Royal Canal **7** Ce
Royale, Isle– **32** Ca
Royal Tunbridge Wells **7** Gf
Royan **8** Ce
Roy Hill **29** BCc
Rozewie, Przylądek– (cap.) **4** De
Rožňava **5** Hd
Roztocze (mts.) **5** lcd
Rtanj (mt.) **6** EFe
Rtiščevo **13** Dd
Ruafa, El– **22** Eg
Ruapehu, Mount– **27** Dd
Rub'al Khali **21** DEef
Rub'al Khali (Ar Rimal) **21** DEef
Rubcovsk **13** Hd
Rubežnoje **12** Ed
Rubinéia **39** CDab
Rubio **37** Bb
Ruda Śląska **5** Gc
Rūdbār **20** Bbc
Rudkøbing **5** Ca
Rudnaja–Pristan **14** Ge
Rudnica **6** Ib
Rudničny **12** Hb

Rudny [Kaz.] **13** Fd
Rudny [Russia] **17** Db
Rudolf, Lake– **25** Dd
Rueil–Malmaison **8** DEc
Rufiji (riv.) **26** Cb
Rufino **39** Bc
Rufisque **24** Ac
Rugby **7** Fe
Rügen (i.) **4** Ce
Rügen → Bergen **5** Da
Ruhea **19** Jj
Ruhr (riv.) **5** Bc
Rui'an **16** Fe
Ruijin **16** Ee
Rujen (mt.) **11** Eb
Ruki (riv.) **26** Aab
Rukwa, Lake– **26** Cb
Ruma **6** Dd
Rumbek **25** Cd
Rum Cay (i.) **32** Dc
Rumia **5** Ga
Rum Jungle **29** DEa
Rummah, Wādī ar– **21** Cd
Rumoi **17** Gbc
Rungwa (riv.) **26** Cb
Rungwa **26** Cb
Ruo Shui (riv.) **16** Bb
Rupununi (riv.) **37** Db
Rurrenabaque **39** Ba
Rurutu, Île– (i.) **28** Bd
Ruşayris, Ar– **25** Dc
Ruse **11** FGb
Russas **38** Db
Russia (Ind. St.) **15** BDc
Russki, Ostrov– **17** BCc
Rustavi **13** De
Ruţbah, Ar– **21** Cc
Ruteng **18** Ff
Ruthenia (phys. reg.) **6** FGb
Rutland **32** Da
Rutland (i.) **19** Bf
Rutog **15** Cf
Ruvuma (riv.) **26** Cc
Ruwenzori (mt.) **25** CDde
Ruzajevka **12** Fc
Ružomberok **5** Gd
Rwanda (Ind. St.) **26** BCb
Rybačje → Issyk–Kul **13** Ge
Rybinsk **13** CDd
Rybinskoje vodohranilišče **13** Cd
Rybnica **6** Ic
Rybnik **5** Gc
Rylsk **12** DEc
Ryōtsu **17** EFef
Ryukyu Islands (Nansei–Shotō) **16** FGef
Rzeszów **5** Hlc
Ržev **13** Cd

S

Saale (riv.) **5** Cc
Saalfeld **5** Cc
Saar (riv.) **5** Ad
Saarbrücken **5** Ad
Saaremaa (i.) **4** Ed
Saarlouis **5** Ad
Šabac **6** Dd
Sabadell **9** FGb
Sabah (State) **15** Di

Sabalän, Kūhhā– ye– (mt.) **21** Db
Sabanalarga **37** Ba
Sab'Bi' Ār **22** Ff
Sabhā **24** Db
Šabia, Nos– **11** Hb
Sabinas **34** Bb
Sabinas Hidalgo **34** BCb
Sabine (riv.) **32** Bb
Sabini, Monti– **10** Dc
Sable, Cape– [Can.] **31** Id
Sable, Cape– [U.S.] **32** Cc
Sable Island **30** LMe
Sables–d'Olonne, Les– **8** BCd
Sabor (riv.) **9** Bb
Şabrātah **24** Da
Sabrina Coast **42** grid square no.4
Sabya **21** Cf
Sabzevār **21** Fb
Sabzevārān **21** Fd
Sacajawea Peak **33** Bb
Sacedón **9** Db
Sachs Harbour **31** Ca
Sacramento (riv.) **33** Ac
Sacramento **33** ABc
Sacramento, Pampas del– (phys. reg.) **37** Bc
Sádaba **9** Ea
Sa' dah **21** Cf
Saddle Island **28** map no.4
Sadiya **15** Dg
Sado (riv.) **9** Ac
Sado–Shima (i.) **16** Ic
Šadrinsk **13** Fd
Şafāqis **24** CDa
Säffle **4** Cd
Safi **24** ABa
Şāfī, Aş– **22** Eg
Safīd (riv.) **21** Db
Safonovo **12** Db
Saga [China] **20** FGc
Saga [Jap.] **16** GHd
Sagaing **19** BCd
Sagar **20** Ed
Sagauli **19** Ij
Saginaw **32** Ca
Sagiz (riv.) **12** Hd
Sagiz **12** Hld
Sagra, La– (mt.) **9** Dd
Sagres **9** Ad
Sagua La Grande **35** BCa
Sagunto **9** EFc
Sahagún **9** Ca
Sahara (des.) **24** CDbc
Saharan Atlas (mts.) **24** BCa
Saharanpur **20** Ebc
Saharsa **19** Ij
Sahibganj **19** IJj
Sahiwal **20** Db
Şahty **13** De
Šahunja **12** Gb
Sai (riv.) **19** Hj
Sa'īdābād **21** EFd
Saidpur [Bngl.] **19** Jj
Saidpur [India] **19** Hj
Saiki **17** BCh
Saimaa **4** FGc
Saimaan Canal **4** FGc
Saint Affrique **8** Ef
Saint Albans **7** Ff

Saint Amand–Mont–Rond **8** Ed
Saint André, Cap– (cap.) **26** map no.1
Saint Andrews **7** Ec
Saint Anthony **31** Jc
Saint Augustine **32** CDbc
Saint Austell **7** Df
Saint Bernard Paß (p.) **10** Ba
Saint Boniface **31** Fcd
Saint Brieuc **8** Bc
Saint Catharines **32** CDa
Saint Céré **8** DEe
Saint Chamond **8** EFe
Saint Charles **32** Bb
Saint Christopher / Saint Kitts **35** Db
Saint–Claude **8** FGd
Saint Cloud **32** Ba
Saint Croix (i.) **35** Db
Saint David's Head (cap.) **7** Df
Saint Denis [Fr.] **8** Ec
Saint Denis [Reu.] **23** map no.1
Saint Dié **8** Gc
Saint Dizier **8** Fc
Saint Elias, Mount– **31** ABbc
Saint Elias Mountains **31** ABbc
Saint Elie **37** Db
Sainte Marie, Cap– (cap.) **26** map no.1
Saintes **8** Ce
Sainte Savine **8** EFc
Saint Étienne **8** EFe
Saint Étienne–du–Rouvray **8** Dc
Saint Florent, Golfe de– **8** map no.1
Saint Flour **8** Ee
Saint Gaudens **8** Df
Saint George [Austl.] **29** Hd
Saint George [U.S.] **33** Bc
Saint Georges (i.) **35** Db
Saint George's **37** Ca
Saint Georges **38** Ba
Saint George's Channel **7** CDef
Saint Girons **8** Df
Saint Helena (i.) **23** Bg
Saint Helena Bay **26** Bd
Saint Helens **7** Ee
Saint Helier **8** Bc
Saint Hyacinthe **31** Hd
Saint Jean, Lac– (l.) **31** Hd
Saint Jean–d'Angély **8** Cde
Saint Jean–de–Luz **8** Cf
Saint Jean–Pied–de–Port **8** Cf
Saint John **31** Id
Saint John (riv.) **32** Ea
Saint John's [Atg.] **35** Db
Saint John's [Can.] **31** JKd
Saint Joseph **32** Bab
Saint Jurien **8** De
Saint Kilda (i.) **7** Bc
Saint Kitts / Saint Christopher (i.) **35** Db
Saint Kitts–Nevis (Ind. St.) **30** Lh
Saint Laurent **37** Db
Saint Lawrence (riv.) **31** Id

San Gallan, Isla– **37** Bd
Sangar **14** FGc
Sangeang, Pulau– (i.) **18** Ef
Sanggau **18** CDde
Sangha (riv.) **24** Dd
Sangihe, Pulau– (i.) **18** FGd
Sangi Islands **18** Gd
San Gil **37** Bb
San Giovanni in Fiore **10** Fe
Sangkulirang **18** Ed
Sangli **20** DEe
San Gottardo (p.) **10** Ba
Sangre de Cristo Mounts **33** Cc
Sangue, Rio do– (riv.) **38** Bc
San Ignacio **39** Ba
San Javier **39** Ba
Sanjō **17** Ff
San Joaquin (riv.) **33** Ac
San Jorge, Golfo– **40** Bb
San José [Bol.] **39** Ba
San José [C.R.] **35** Bc
San José [Guat.] **35** Ab
San Jose [Phil.] **18** Fa
San Jose [Phil.] **18** Fb
San José [U.S.] **33** Ac
San Jose de Buenavista **18** Fb
San José de Jáchal **39** Bbc
San José del Cabo **34** Bb
San José del Guaviare **37** Bb
San José de Mayo **39** Cc
San José de Ocune **37** BCb
San Juan (i.) **30** Lh
San Juan (riv.) **33** BCc
San Juan [Arg.] **39** ABc
San Juan [Peru] **39** Aa
San Juan, Río– **35** Bb
San Juan Bautista **39** Bb
San Juan de la Maguana **35** Cb
San Juan del Norte **35** Bb
San Juan de los Cayos **37** Ca
San Juan de los Morros **37** Cb
San Julián **36** Dh
San Justo **39** BCc
Sankh (riv.) **19** Ik
Sankosh (riv.) **15** Pj
Sankt Gallen **5** Be
Sankt Moritz **10** Ba
Sankt Pölten **5** Ed
Sankt Veit an der Glan **5** DEe
Sankuru (riv.) **26** Bb
San Lázaro, Cabo– **34** Ab
San Lorenzo **37** Bb
San Lorenzo de El Escorial **9** CDb
Sanlúcar de Barrameda **9** Bd
San Luis [Arg.] **39** Bc
San Luis [Mex.] **33** Cd
San Luis Obispo **33** Ac
San Luis Potosí **30** Hlg
San Marco, Capo– **10** Be
San Marcos **32** Bbc
San Marino **10** Dbc
San Marino (Ind. St.) **10** Dbc
San Martín (sc. stat.) **42** grid square no.1
San Martín **37** Bb
San Martin (riv.) **39** Ba
San Martín, Lago– **40** Ab
San Martin de los Andes **40** ABab

San Martín de Valdeiglesias **9** Cb
San Mateo **33** Ac
San Matías **39** Ca
San Matías, Golfo– **40** Bb
San Miguel (riv.) **39** Ba
San Miguel **35** Bb
San Miguel de Tucumán **39** Bb
San Miguel Islands **18** Ec
Sanmyaku (mts.) **17** EFg
Sannär **25** Dc
Sannicandro Garganico **10** Ed
San Nicolás de los Arroyos **39** Bc
Sanok **5** Hld
San Pablo **18** Fb
San Pedro [Arg.] **39** Bb
San Pedro [I.C.] **24** Bd
San Pedro [Par.] **39** Cb
San Pedro de Arimena **37** Bb
San Pedro de las Bocas **37** Cb
San Pedro de las Colonias **34** Bb
San Pedro Sula **35** Bb
San Pietro **10** Be
Sanquhar **7** DEd
San Quintín **34** Aa
San Rafael [Arg.] **39** Bc
San Rafael [Ven.] **37** Ba
San Ramón de la Nueva Orán **39** Bb
San Remo **10** Ac
San Roque **9** Cd
San Salvador **35** Bb
San Salvador (i.) **32** Dc
San Salvador de Jujuy **39** Bb
Sansanné–Mango **24** Cc
San Sebastián **9** DEa
San Severo **10** Ed
Santa, Río– (riv.) **37** Bc
Santa Ana [Bol.] **39** Ba
Santa Ana [El Sal.] **35** ABb
Santa Ana [U.S.] **33** Bc
Santa Bárbara **34** Bb
Santa Barbara **33** ABc
Santa Catarina (State) **39** CDb
Santa Clara **35** BCa
Santa Coloma de Gramanet **9** Gb
Santa Cruz (riv.) **40** ABc
Santa Cruz [Phil.] **18** Fb
Santa Cruz [U.S.] **33** Ac
Santa Cruz de la Sierra **39** Ba
Santa Cruz del Sur **35** Ca
Santa Cruz de Moya **9** Ec
Santa Cruz de Tenerife **24** Ab
Santa Cruz do Sul **39** Cb
Santa Cruz Islands **27** Dc
Santa Elena de Uairén **37** CDb
Santa Eugenia (Ribeira) **9** Aa
Santa Eulalia del Río **9** FGc
Santafé **9** Dd
Santa Fe **30** Hf
Santa Fe **36** DEg
Santa Fe de Bogotá **36** Cc
Santa Genoveva (mt.) **34** Ab
Santahar **19** Jj

Santa Inés, Isla– (i.) **40** Ac
Santa Isabel [Arg.] **39** Bc
Santa Isabel [Braz.] **39** Ba
Santa Isabel Island **27** CDc
Santa Maria [Braz.] **39** Cb
Santa Maria [U.S.] **33** Ac
Santa Maria da Vitória **38** Cc
Santa Maria di Leuca, Capo– **10** Ge
Santa María Island **28** map no.4
Santa Marta **37** Ba
Santa Maura → Leucade (i.) **11** Dd
Santa Monica **33** ABc
Santana do Livramento **39** Cc
Santander **9** Da
Sant'Antioco (i.) **10** Be
Santañy **9** Gc
Santarém [Braz.] **36** Ed
Santarém [Port.] **9** Ac
Santa Rosa [Arg.] **39** Bc
Santa Rosa [Braz.] **39** Cb
Santa Rosa [Ca.–U.S.] **33** Ac
Santa Rosa [Hond.] **35** Bb
Santa Rosa [N.M.–U.S.] **33** Cc
Santa Rosalía **34** Ab
Santa Vitória do Palmar **39** Cc
Sant'Eufemia, Golfo di– **10** Fe
Sant Feliu de Guíxols **9** Gb
Santiago (riv.) **37** Bc
Santiago [Chile] **39** ABc
Santiago [Pan.] **35** Bc
Santiago [Sp.] **9** Aa
Santiago, Rio Grande de– (riv.) **34** Bb
Santiago de Cuba **35** Cab
Santiago de la Ribera **9** EFd
Santiago del Estero **39** Bb
Santiago Papasquiaro **34** Bb
Santo Amaro **38** Dc
Santo André **39** Db
Santo Ângelo **39** Cb
Santo Antonio Abad **9** Fc
Santo Antônio de Jesus **38** CDc
Santo Antônio do Içá **37** Cc
Santo Antônio do Leverger **39** Ca
Santo Domingo [Dom. Rep.] **30** KLh
Santo Domingo [Mex.] **34** Bb
Santo Domingo del Pacífico **34** Ab
Santoña **9** Da
Santos **39** Db
Santo Tomé **39** Cb
San Valentin, Cerro– (mt.) **40** Ab
San Vicente **35** Bb
San Vicente de Cañete **37** Bd
San Vicente de la Barquera **9** CDa
San Vito, Capo– **10** De
São Borja **39** Cb
São Félix **38** Bc
São Félix do Xingu **38** Bb
São Francisco (riv.) **38** Cc
São Francisco do Sul **39** Db
São João del Rei **39** Db

São José do Rio Prêto **39** CDb
São Leopoldo **39** CDb
São Lourenço (riv.) **39** Ca
São Luís **38** Cb
São Luís Gonzaga **39** Cb
São Marcos, Baía de– (b.) **38** Cb
São Mateus **39** Ea
Saône (riv.) **8** Fd
São Paulo (State) **39** CDb
São Paulo **39** Db
São Paulo de Olivença **37** Cc
São Pedro e São Paulo, Penedos de– (is.) **36** GHc
São Raimundo Nonato **38** Cb
São Roque, Cabo– **38** Db
São Sebastião, Ilha de– (i.) **39** Db
São Sebastião, Ponta– (cap.) **26** Cd
São Simão **39** CDa
São Tomé (i.) **24** Cde
Sao Tome and Principe (Ind. St.) **23** Ce
Saoura (riv.) **24** Bb
São Vicente, Cabo de– (cap.) **9** Ad
Sapiéntza (i.) **11** De
Sapporo **16** Jb
Sapudi, Pulau– (i.) **18** Df
Saqqez **21** Db
Saraburi **19** Df
Saragossa **9** Eb
Sarajevo **6** DEe
Saraji Mine **29** Hc
Sarakhs **21** Gb
Saraktaš **12** Ic
Saramati (mt.) **19** BCc
Saran **13** Ge
Saranda **11** CDd
Sarangani Islands **18** Gc
Saransk **13** Dd
Sarapul **13** Ed
Sarasota **32** Cc
Saratov **13** Dd
Saratovskoje vodohranilišče **12** Gc
Saravan **19** Ee
Sarawak (State) **15** Di
Sarāyā **22** Ee
Sarbisheh **21** Fc
Sardinia (reg.) **10** Bde
Sarektjåkkå (mt.) **4** Db
Sargodha **20** Db
Šargorod **6** Hlb
Sarh **25** BCd
Sārī **21** Eb
Saría (i.) **11** Gf
Sarikei **18** Dd
Sarina **29** Hlc
Sariñena **9** Eb
Sarir **24** Bb
Sariwon **16** Gc
Šarja **13** Dd
Sark (i.) **8** Bc
Şarkişla **22** Fc
Şarköy **22** Ab
Sarlat–la–Canéda **8** De
Sarmiento **40** Bb
Särna **4** Cc
Sarnen **5** ABe
Sarnia **31** Gd

Sarny 13 Bd
Saroako 18 Fe
Saroma–Ko 17 Hlb
Saronikos Kólpos 11 Ee
Saros, Gulf of– 22 Ab
Sárospatak 6 Eb
Šar planina (mts.) 11 Dbc
Sarpsborg 4 BCd
Sarrebourg 8 Gc
Sarreguemines 8 Gc
Sarria 9 Ba
Sars, As– 10 Bf
Sartène 8 map no.1
Sarthe (riv.) 8 Cd
Sárvár 6 Cc
Saryč, mys– 12 De
Saryg–Sep 14 Cd
Sarysu (riv.) 13 Fe
Sary–Taš 13 Gef
Saryžaz 13 GHe
Sasaram 19 Ij
Sasebo 16 Gd
Saskatchewan (prov.) 31 Ec
Saskatchewan (riv.) 31 Bb
Saskatoon 33 Ca
Saskylah 14 Eb
Sasovo 12 Fc
Sassandra (riv.) 24 Bd
Sassandra 24 Bd
Sassari 10 Bd
Sassnitz 4 Ce
Sata–Misaki 17 Bi
Satara 20 De
Satawal Island 27 Cb
Säter 4 CDc
Satka 12 Ibc
Satna 20 Fcd
Sátoraljaújhely 6 Eb
Sätpura Range 20 Ed
Satsuma–Hantō 17 ABi
Sattahip 19 CDf
Satu Mare 6 Fc
Satun 19 Cg
Sauda 4 Ad
Saudárkrókur 4 map no.1
Saudi Arabia (Ind. St.) 15 Bgh
Sauldre (riv.) 8 Ed
Sault Sainte Marie [Can.] 31 Gd
Sault Sainte Marie [U.S.] 32 Ca
Saumur 8 Cd
Saurimo 26 Bbc
Sava (riv.) 6 Dd
Savai'i Island 28 Ac
Savannah (riv.) 32 Cb
Savannah 32 CDb
Savannakhet 19 DEe
Savanna–la–Mar 35 Cb
Savaştepe 22 ABc
Savé 24 Cd
Save [Fr.] (riv.) 8 Df
Save [Moz.] (riv.) 26 Cd
Saveh 21 DEb
Savigliano 10 Ab
Savona 10 Bb
Savonlinna 4 Gc
Savoy (hist. reg.) 8 Gde
Savran 6 IJb
Savusavu 28 map no.6
Savu Sea 18 Ffg
Sawahlunto 18 Be

Sawai Madhopur 20 Ec
Sawākin 25 Dc
Sawhāj 25 Db
Sawqirah 21 Ff
Şawqirah, Ghubbat– 21 Ff
Sawu, Pulau– (i.) 18 Fg
Saxony (phys. reg.) 5 DEc
Say 24 Cc
Sayhut 21 Efg
Sazanit, Ishull i– (i.) 11 Cc
Sázava (riv.) 5 Ed
Scapa Flow (g.) 7 Eb
Scarborough 7 FGd
Scarborough Reef (i.) 18 Ea
Šćekino 12 Ec
Schaffhausen 5 Be
Schefferville 31 Ld
Schelde (riv.) 8 EFb
Schenectady 32 Da
Schleswig 5 Ba
Schleswig–Holstein (State) 5 BCab
Schlüchtern 5 Bc
Schmidta, ostrov– 14 BCa
Schouwen (i.) 8 Eb
Schwaben (phys. reg.) 5 BCde
Schwäbische Alb (mts.) 5 BCd
Schwäbisch Hall 5 BCd
Schwandorf in Bayern 5 Dd
Schwaner, Pegunungan– 18 De
Schwarze Elster (riv.) 5 Dc
Schwedt 5 Eb
Schweinfurt 5 Cc
Schwerin 5 Cb
Sciacca 10 Df
Scicli 10 Ef
Šćigry 12 Ec
Scilly, Isles of– 7 Cg
Scoresby Land 41 grid square no.1
Scoresbysund / Itseqqortoormit 30 PQb
Šćors 12 Dc
Scotland (reg.) 7 DEcd
Scott 42 grid square no.4
Scott, Cape– 31 Cb
Scott, Mount– 33 Ab
Scott Island 42 grid square no.3
Scott Reef (i.) 29 Ca
Scottsbluff 33 Cb
Scottsdale [Austl.] 29 map no.1
Scottsdale [U.S.] 33 Bc
Scranton 32 Da
Šćučinsk 13 Gd
Scunthorpe 7 FGe
Scutari, Lake– 11 Cb
Seabra 38 Cc
Seal, Cape– 26 Be
Seattle 33 Ab
Sebastián Vizcaíno, Bahía– (g.) 34 Ab
Šebekino 12 Ec
Seben 22 Cb
Sebeş 6 Fd
Sebuku, Pulau– (i.) 18 Ee
Secchia (riv.) 10 Cb
Sechura, Bahía de– 37 Ac
Sechura, Desierto de– (des.) 37 ABc

Second Cataract 25 CDb
Sedan 8 Fc
Sederot 22 Eg
Sédhiou 24 Ac
Seeheim 26 Ad
Sefidar, Kūh– e– (mt.) 21 Ed
Segeza 13 Cc
Ségou 24 Bc
Segovia 9 Cb
Segré 8 Cd
Segre (riv.) 9 Fb
Seguédine 24 Dbc
Séguéla 24 Bd
Seguin 32 Bc
Segura (riv.) 9 DEc
Segura, Sierra de– (mts.) 9 Dcd
Sehwan 20 Cc
Seinäjoki 4 EFc
Seine (riv.) 8 Dc
Seine, Baie de la– 8 Cc
Sejm (riv.) 12 Dc
Sejmčan 14 Ic
Sekondi–Takoradi 24 Bd
Sekota 25 DEc
Šeksna 12 Eb
Šelagski, mys– 14 Kb
Selajar, Pulau– (i.) 18 EFf
Selajar, Selat– 18 EFf
Selatan, Cape– 18 De
Selçuk 11 Gde
Selemdža (riv.) 14 Gd
Selenga (riv.) 14 De
Sélestat 8 Gc
Sélibabi 24 Ac
Selinunte (r.) 10 Df
Selkirk 7 Ed
Selkirk Mountains 33 Bab
Selma 32 Cb
Selvagens, Ilhas– 24 Aab
Selvas (phys. reg.) 37 CDc
Selwyn 29 Gc
Selwyn Range 29 FGc
Semani (riv.) 11 Cc
Semara 24 ABb
Semarang 15 Dj
Semenovka 12 Dc
Semeru, Gunung– (mt.) 18 Df
Semiluki 12 Ec
Semipalatinsk 13 GHd
Semmering (p.) 5 Ee
Semnän 21 Eb
Šemonaiha 13 GHd
Semur–en–Auxois 8 Fd
Senador Pompeu 38 Db
Sena Madureira 37 Cc
Senanga 26 Bc
Sendai [Jap.] 17 ABhi
Sendai [Jap.] 16 Jc
Senegal (riv.) 24 Ac
Senegal (Ind. St.) 23 Ad
Senftenberg 5 Ec
Sengilej 12 Gc
Senhor do Bonfim 38 CDc
Senigallia 10 Dc
Senj 6 Bd
Senja (i.) 4 Da
Senkaku–Shotō 16 Fe
Šenkursk 12 Fa
Senmonorom 19 Ef
Senneterre 31 Hd
Sens 8 Ec

Senta 6 Ecd
Sento Sé 38 Cbc
Senyavin Islands 27 CDb
Seo de Urgel 9 Fa
Seoni 20 Ed
Seoul (Sŏul) 14 Ff
Sepanjang, Pulau– (i.) 18 Ef
Šepetkovo 14 IJc
Šepetovka 6 Ha
Sept–Îles 31 Ic
Serafimovič 12 Fd
Seraing 8 Fb
Serang 18 Cf
Serbia 6 Ede
Serdobsk 12 FGc
Şereflikochisar 22 Dc
Seremban 18 Bd
Serena, La– 39 Ab
Serengeti Plain 26 Cb
Seret (riv.) 6 Gb
Sergeja Kirova, ostrova– 14 BCb
Sergiev Posad (Zagorsk) 13 Cd
Sergino 13 Fc
Sergipe (State) 38 Dc
Seria 18 Dd
Seribu Kepulauan 18 Cf
Sérifos (i.) 11 Fe
Sernyje Vody 12 Hc
Serov 13 Fd
Serowe 26 Bd
Serpa 9 Bd
Serpentine Lakes 29 DEd
Serpuhov 3 Gb
Sérrai 11 Ec
Serrana, Banco de– (is.) 35 BCb
Serranilla, Banco de– (is.) 35 BCb
Serrat, Cap– 10 Bf
Serra Talhada 38 Db
Serrezuela 39 Bc
Serrinha 38 Dc
Sertão (phys. reg.) 38 CDbc
Serua, Pulau– (i.) 18 Hf
Sesfontein 26 Ac
Sesheke 26 Bc
Sesimbra 9 Ac
Sestao 9 Da
Sestroreck 4 Gc
Setana 17 Fc
Sète 8 Ef
Sete Lagoas 39 Da
Sete Quedas, Saltos das– 39 Cb
Sétif 24 Ca
Settat 24 Ba
Setté Cama 26 Ab
Setúbal 9 Ac
Seul, Lac– 31 Fc
Sevan, Lake– 21 Da
Sevastopol 13 Ce
Ševčenko → Aktau 13 Ee
Severn [Can.] (riv.) 31 FGc
Severn [U.K.] (riv.) 7 Eef
Severnaja Zemlja (i.) 41 grid square no.4
Severnyje Uraly (mts.) 12 GHab
Severodvinsk 13 CDe

© ISTITUTO GEOGRAFICO DE AGOSTINI S.p.A. - Novara

Sinnūris **22** Ch
Sinop **22** Eab
Sîntana **6** Ec
Sintang **18** Dde
Sint Maarten / Saint Martin **35** Db
Sint Niklaas **8** EFb
Sintra **9** Ac
Sinŭiju **14** Ff
Siófok **6** CDc
Sion **10** Aa
Sioux City **32** Ba
Sioux Falls **32** Ba
Sioux Lookout **31** Fcd
Siping **16** Fb
Siple, Mount- **42** grid square no.3
Siple Station **42** grid square no.3
Sipora, Pulau- (i.) **18** Ae
Siquijor **18** Fc
Siracusa **10** Ef
Sirajganj **20** Gd
Sir Edward Pellew Group **29** Fb
Siret (riv.) **6** Hc
Siret **6** GHc
Sirḥān, Wādī as- (w.) **21** Bc
Sirina (i.) **11** Ge
Sirino, Monte- **10** Ed
Siros (i.) **11** Fe
Sirsa **20** DEc
Sirtica (phys. reg.) **24** Da
Sisak **6** Cd
Si Sa Khet **19** DEef
Sisimiut / Holsteinsborg **31** Jb
Sistan (phys. reg.) **20** Bb
Sisteron **8** Fe
Sitapur **20** Fc
Sithonia (pen.) **11** Ec
Sitia **11** Gf
Sitio da Abadia **39** Da
Sitka **31** Bc
Sittang (riv.) **19** Ce
Sittwe (Akyab) **19** Bde
Sivaki **14** Fd
Sıvas **22** Fc
Sivaš, ozero- **12** Dd
Siverek **21** Bb
Sivrihisar **22** CDc
Sīwah **25** Cb
Siwālik Range **19** HIij
Siwan **19** Ij
Siwa Oasis **25** Cb
Sixth Cataract **25** Dc
Sjælland **4** BCe
Sjöbo **5** Da
Skadovsk **12** Dd
Skagerrak (str.) **4** ABd
Skagway **30** EFd
Skåne (phys. reg.) **4** Ce
Skanör-Falsterbo **5** Da
Skara **4** Cd
Skardu **20** Eab
Skarżysko-Kamienna **5** Hc
Skawina **5** GHcd
Skegness **7** Ge
Skellefteå **4** Eb
Skellefteälven (riv.) **4** Db
Skelleftehamn **4** Eb
Skhíza (i.) **11** De
Skhoinoúsa (i.) **11** Fe
Skíatos (i.) **11** Ed
Skibbereen **7** Bf
Skien **4** Bd
Skierniewice **5** Hc
Skikda **24** Ca
Skirakawa **17** Gf
Skíro (i.) **11** Fd
Skive **4** Bd
Skjoldungen **31** KLb
Skole **5** Id
Skópelos **11** Ed
Skopin **12** EFc
Skopje **11** Dbc
Škotovo **17** Cc
Skövde **4** Cd
Skovorodino **14** Fd
Skvira **6** Ib
Skye, Island of- **7** Cc
Slagesle **5** Ca
Slamet, Gunung- (mt.) **18** Cf
Slancy **4** Gd
Slatina **6** Gd
Slautnoje **14** JKc
Slave Coast **24** Cd
Slave River **31** Dbc
Slavgorod **13** Gd
Slavjanka **17** Bc
Slavjansk **13** Cd
Slavjansk na-Kubani **12** Ed
Slavonia (phys. reg.) **6** CDd
Slavonska Požega **6** CDd
Slavonski Brod **6** Dd
Slavuta **6** Ha
Sławno **5** Fa
Sleaford **7** Fe
Sliema **10** Efg
Sligo **7** Bd
Slite **4** Dd
Sliven **11** Gb
Slivnica **11** Eb
Sljudjanka **14** Dd
Slobodka **6** Ic
Slobodskoj **12** Hb
Slobodzeja **6** IJc
Slobozia **6** Hd
Słonie **5** Hb
Slonim **12** Cc
Slough **7** Ff
Slovakia (Ind. St.) **3** EFc
Slovakia (phys. reg.) **5** GHd
Slovenia (Ind. St.) **6** Bcd
Slovenské Rudohorie **5** GHd
Słubice **5** Eb
Sluč (riv.) **6** Ha
Sluck **12** Cc
Slunj **6** Bd
Słupsk **5** Fa
Småland (phys. reg.) **4** Cd
Smederevo **6** Ed
Smederevska Palanka **6** Ed
Smela **12** Dd
Smith Strait **41** grid square no.1
Smithton **29** map no.1
Smøla (i.) **4** Ac
Smolensk **13** Cd
Smólicas (mt.) **11** Dc
Smoljan **11** Fc
Smorgon **4** Fe
Snæfellsjökull (gl.) **4** map no.1
Snag **31** ABb
Snake River **33** Bb
Snake River Plain **33** Bb
Sneek **8** Fa
Sniardwy, Jezioro- **5** HIb
Sniežka (mt.) **5** EFc
Snigirevka **12** Dd
Snøhetta (mt.) **4** Bc
Snowdon (mt.) **7** DEe
Snowdrift **31** DEb
Snowy River **29** Hf
Snyder **33** Cc
Soalala **26** map no.1
Soasiu **18** Gd
Sobat (riv.) **25** Dd
Sobral **38** CDb
Sochaczew **5** GHb
Soči **13** Ce
Society Islands **28** Bc
Socna **24** Db
Socompa, Paso de- (p.) **39** Bb
Socorro [Col.] **37** Bb
Socorro [U.S.] **33** Cc
Socorro, Isla- (i.) **34** ABc
Socotra (i.) **25** Fc
Socuéllamos **9** Dc
Sodankyla **4** Fb
Soddu **25** Dd
Söderala **4** Dc
Söderhamn **4** Dc
Söderköping **4** Dd
Södertälje **4** Dd
Soest **5** Bc
Sofala, Baía de- **26** Cd
Sofia **11** Eb
Sofijsk **14** Gd
Sōfu Gan (i.) **27** BCa
Sogamoso **37** Bb
Soğanlı (riv.) **22** Db
Sognefjorden (b.) **4** Ac
Sögüt Gölü **22** Bd
Soissons **8** Ec
Soitué **39** Bc
Sokal **5** Jc
Söke **22** Ad
Sokodé **24** BCd
Sokol **13** Dd
Sokółka **5** Ib
Sokolo **24** Bc
Sokolov **5** Dc
Sokoto (riv.) **24** Cc
Sokoto **24** Cc
Sol, Costa del- **9** CDd
Solāpur **15** Ch
Soledade **37** Cc
Soligalič **12** Fb
Soligorsk **12** Cc
Solikamsk **13** Ecd
Sol-Ileck **13** Ed
Solingen **5** Ac
Sollefteå **4** Dc
Sóller **9** Gc
Solling (mts.) **5** Bc
Solnečnogorsk **12** Eb
Solo → Surakarta **18** Df
Sologne (phys. reg.) **8** DEd
Solomon Islands **27** CDc
Solomon Islands (Ind. St.) **27** Dc
Solomon Sea **27** Cc
Solothurn **5** Ae
Solta (i.) **11** Bb
Soltau **5** Bb
Solvyčegodsk **12** Ga
Solway Firth (b.) **7** DEd
Solwezi **26** Bc
Soma **22** Ac
Somalia (Ind. St.) **23** Ge
Sombor **6** Dd
Sombrerete **34** Bb
Sombrero, El- **37** Cb
Somcuța Mare **6** FGc
Somerset **29** Ga
Somerset (co.) **7** Ef
Somerset Island **31** Fa
Someş (riv.) **6** Fc
Somme (riv.) **8** Ec
Somport, Puerto de- (p.) **9** Ea
Son (riv.) **20** Fd
Sønderborg **4** Be
Søndre Strømfjord **31** JKb
Sondrio **10** Ba
Songea **26** Cc
Songhua Hu **16** Gb
Songhua Jiang → Sungari **17** Aab
Songjiang **16** Fd
Songkhla **15** Di
Songnim **16** Gc
Songo **26** Cc
Sonhat **19** Hk
Sonid Youqi **16** Db
Son La **19** Dd
Sonneberg **5** Cc
Sonora (riv.) **34** Ab
Sonoyta **34** Aa
Sonsón **37** Bb
Sonsonate **35** ABb
Sonsorol Islands **27** Bb
Son Tay **19** Ed
Sopot **5** Ga
Sopron **6** Cc
Sorbas **9** Dd
Sorel **32** Da
Sorgues **8** Fef
Soria **9** Db
Sorø **5** Ca
Sorocaba **39** Db
Soročinsk **12** Hc
Soroki **6** HIb
Sorol Atoll (i.) **18** IJc
Sorong **18** He
Soroti **25** Dd
Sørøya (i.) **4** Ea
Sorraia (riv.) **9** Ac
Sorrento **10** Ed
Sør Rondane **42** grid square no.2
Sorsatunturi (mt.) **4** Gb
Sorsele **4** Db
Sorsogon **18** FGb
Sort **9** Fa
Sortavala **4** Gc
Sortland **4** Ca
Sosnovka **12** Hb
Sosnowiec **5** Gc
Šostka **12** Dc
Sosva **12** Jb
Sotteville-lès-Rouen **8** Dc
Souanké **26** Aa
Soudan **29** Fbc
Souflíon **11** FGc
Souk-Ahras **10** ABf
Sŏul → Seoul **14** Ff
Soure **38** Cb
Sousel **38** Bb
Sousse **24** Da

© ISTITUTO GEOGRAFICO DE AGOSTINI S.p.A. - Novara

© ISTITUTO GEOGRAFICO DE AGOSTINI S.p.A. - Novara

Sumbawa Besar **18** Ef
Sumbawanga **26** Cb
Sumbe **26** Ac
Sumburgh Head **7** Fb
Šumen **11** Gb
Šumerlja **12** Gb
Sumgait **13** DEe
Sumisu-Jima (i.) **17** FGi
Summerside **32** Ea
Summit **35** map no.1
Šumperk **5** Fcd
Sumprabum **19** Cc
Sumter **32** CDb
Sumy **13** Cd
Sundarbans (phys. reg.) **20** GHd
Sunda Strait **18** Cf
Sunderland **7** Fd
Sundiken dağı (mt.) **22** Cbc
Sundsvall **4** Dc
Sungai Petani **19** Dg
Sungari (Songhua Jiang) (riv.) **16** Gb
Sungurlu **22** Eb
Sun Kosi (riv.) **19** Ij
Sunndalsöra **4** Bc
Sunne **4** Cd
Suntar **14** Ec
Suntar-Hajata, Hrebet- **14** GHc
Sunyani **24** Bd
Suojarvi **12** Da
Suolahti **4** Fc
Suomenselkä (mts.) **4** EGc
Suomussalmi **4** Gb
Suonenjoki **4** Fc
Superior **32** Ba
Superior, Lake- **32** Ca
Süphan dağ (mt.) **21** Cb
Suqian **16** Ed
Sur **21** Fe
Sur, Submeseta- (phys. reg.) **9** CDbc
Sura (riv.) **12** Gbc
Surabaya **15** Djk
Surakarta (Solo) **18** Df
Surat [Austl.] **29** Hd
Surat [India] **15** Cg
Surat Thani **15** Di
Surgut **13** Gc
Suri **19** Ijk
Surigao **18** Gc
Surin **19** Def
Suriname (Ind. St.) **36** Ec
Suriname (riv.) **37** Db
Surkhab (riv.) **20** Ca
Surprise, Île- (i.) **28** map no.4
Surrey (co.) **7** Ff
Surt **24** Da
Surtsey (i.) **4** map no.1
Suruga-Wan **17** Fg
Surulangun **18** Be
Susa **10** Ab
Susa (r.) **21** Dc
Susaki **17** Ch
Suşehri **22** Gb
Susong **16** Ed
Susques **39** Bb
Sussex (co.) **7** FGf
Susuman **14** Hc
Susurluk **22** ABc
Sutlej (riv.) **20** Eb
Suttor River **29** Hc
Suva **28** map no.6
Suvorovo **6** Id
Suwałki **5** Ia
Suwarrow Atoll **28** Ac
Suwaydā, As- **22** Ff
Suwŏn **16** Gc
Suxian [China] **16** Dd
Suxian [China] **16** Ed
Suzhou **16** Fd
Suzu **17** Ef
Suzu-Misaki **17** Ef
Svålbard **41** grid square no.3
Svartisen (mt.) **4** Cb
Svealand (phys. reg.) **4** CDd
Svedala **5** Da
Sveg **4** Cc
Švenčionėlia **12** Cbc
Svendborg **4** Be
Sverdlovsk → Jekaterinburg **13** EFd
Sverdrup, ostrov- **13** Gb
Sverdrup Islands **41** grid square no.2
Svetlaja **14** Ge
Svetlogorsk **12** Cc
Svetlograd **12** Fd
Svetlovodsk **12** Dd
Svetly **13** Fd
Svetogorsk **4** Gc
Svetozarevo **6** Ede
Svilengrad **11** FGc
Svir (riv.) **12** Da
Svištov **11** Fb
Svitavy **5** Fd
Svobodny **14** FGd
Svolvær **4** Ca
Swain Reefs (is.) **29** Ic
Swains Atoll **28** Ac
Swakop (riv.) **26** Ad
Swakopmund **23** Dh
Swale (riv.) **7** Fd
Swan Hill **29** Gf
Swan River **33** Ca
Swansea **7** DEf
Swarzędz **5** Fb
Swaziland (Ind. St.) **23** Fh
Sweden (Ind. St.) **3** Ea
Sweetwater **33** Cc
Swellendam **26** Be
Świdnica **5** Fc
Świdnik **5** Ic
Świdwin **5** EFb
Świebodzin **5** Eb
Świecie **5** FGb
Swift Current **33** Cab
Swindon **7** Ff
Swinoujście **5** Eab
Switzerland (Ind. St.) **3** Dc
Syčevka **12** DEb
Sydney [Austl.] **29** Ie
Sydney [Can.] **31** IJd
Sydprøven / Alluitsup Paa **31** Kb
Syktyvkar **13** Ec
Sylarna (mt.) **4** BCc
Sylhet **20** Hcd
Sylt **5** Ba
Syowa **42** grid square no.2
Syracuse **32** Da
Syrdarja (riv.) **13** Fe
Syria (Ind. St.) **15** Bf
Syriam **19** Ce
Syrian Desert **21** BCc
Sysert **12** Jb
Sysmä **4** Fc
Syvulja (mt.) **5** IJd
Syzran **13** Dd
Szamos (riv.) **5** Ide
Szamotuły **5** Fb
Szczecinek **5** Fb
Szczytno **5** Hb
Szeged **6** DEc
Székesfehérvár **6** Dc
Szekszárd **6** Dc
Szentes **6** Ec
Szolnok **6** Ec
Szombathely **6** Cc

T

Tabajara **37** Cc
Ţabarqah **10** Bf
Ţabas **21** Fc
Tabašino **12** Gb
Tabelbala **24** Bb
Taberg (mt.) **5** DEa
Tabernas **9** DEd
Tablas (i.) **18** Fb
Tablas, Las- **35** BCc
Tábor **5** Ed
Tabor **14** HIb
Tabora **26** Cb
Tabory **12** Jb
Tabou **24** Bd
Tabrīz **21** Db
Tabuaeran (Fanning) **28** Bb
Tabuk **21** Bd
Tacazzè (riv.) **25** Dc
Tacheng **13** He
Tacloban **18** FGb
Tacna **39** Aa
Tacoma **33** Ab
Tacora (mt.) **39** ABa
Tacuarembó **39** Cc
Tacutu (riv.) **37** CDb
Tademaït, Plateau du- **24** Cb
Taegu **14** FGf
Taejŏn **14** Ff
Tafalla **9** Ea
Ţafīlah, Aţ- **22** Eg
Tafí Viejo **39** Bb
Taftān, Kuh- e- (mt.) **21** Gd
Taga **28** map no.5
Taga Dzong **20** GHc
Taganrog **13** CDe
Taganrogski zaliv **12** Ed
Tagaytay City **18** EFb
Tagbilaran **18** Fc
Tagula Island **27** Cc
Tahan, Gunong- (mt.) **19** Dgh
Tahat (mt.) **24** Cb
Tahiti, Île- **28** Bc
Tahlab (riv.) **21** Gd
Tahoua **24** Cc
Tahtalı dağ (mt.) **22** Fc
Tahulandang, Pulau- (i.) **18** FGd
Tai'an **16** Ec
Taiarapu, Presqu'île de- **28** map no.2
Taichung **16** Ff
Tā'if, Aţ- **21** BCe
Tai Hu (l.) **16** Fd
Tailai **16** Fa
Tain **7** DEc
Tainan **16** EFf
Taipei **15** Eg
Taiping **19** CDgh
Taisetsu-Zan (mt.) **16** Jb
Taitao, Península de- **40** Ab
Taitao, Peninsula de- **36** Ch
Taitung **16** Ff
Taivalkoski **4** FGb
Taiwan (Formosa) (Ind. St.) **15** Eg
Taiwan Strait **15** DEg
Taíyetos Óros (mts.) **11** Ee
Taiyuan **15** Df
Taizhou **16** EFd
Ta'izz **21** Cg
Tajga **13** Hd
Tajgonos, Poluostrov- **14** Jc
Tajikistan (Ind. St.) **13** FGf
Tajimi **17** Eg
Tajmyr, Ozero- **14** Db
Tajmyr, Poluostrov- **14** CDb
Tajmyra (riv.) **14** Cb
Tajo (riv.) **9** Db
Tajrish **21** Eb
Tajšet **14** Cd
Tajumulco, Volcán- (mt.) **34** Cc
Tajuña (riv.) **9** Db
Tak **19** Ce
Takada **17** EFf
Takahe, Mount- **42** grid square no.3
Takamatsu **16** HId
Takaoka **17** Ef
Takaroa Atoll **28** Bc
Takasaki **17** Ff
Takayama **17** Ef
Takefu **17** DEfg
Takengon **18** Ad
Take-Shima / Tok-Do (i.) **17** Bf
Takikawa **17** Gc
Tako-Bana **17** Cg
Talak (phys. reg.) **24** Cc
Talara **37** Ac
Talas **13** Ge
Talâta **25** map no.1
Talaud, Kepulauan- **18** Gd
Talavera de la Reina **9** Cbc
Talca **39** Ac
Talcahuano **39** Ac
Talcher **20** Gd
Taldy-Kurgan **13** Ge
Talence **8** Ce
Talgar **16** Bb
Taliabu, Pulau- (i.) **18** FGe
Talica **12** Jb
Tall 'Afar **21** Cb
Tallahassee **32** Cbc
Tallinn **4** Fd
Tall Kalakh **22** Fe
Tāloqān **20** CDa
Talsi **4** Ed
Taltal **39** Ab
Tamale **24** BCd
Tamanrasset **24** Cb
Tamar River **29** map no.1
Tamarugal, Pampa del- **39** Bab
Tamazunchale **34** Cb
Tambacounda **24** Ac
Tambao **24** BCc

© ISTITUTO GEOGRAFICO DE AGOSTINI S.p.A. - Novara

Tam - Tep

© ISTITUTO GEOGRAFICO DE AGOSTINI S.p.A. - Novara

Tol - Tub

Tolmezzo **10** Da
Tolo, Gulf of– **18** Fe
Tolosa **9** DEa
Tolstoje **6** Gb
Toltén **39** Ac
Tolú **37** Bb
Toluca de Lerdo **34** BCc
Tom (riv.) **13** Hd
Toma, La– **39** Bc
Tomakomai **17** GHc
Tomari **14** He
Tomaševka **5** IJc
Tomašpol **6** Ib
Tomaszów Lubelski **5** IJc
Tomaszów Mazowiecki **5** Hc
Tombador, Serra do– (mts.) **38** Bc
Tomb–e Bozorg **21** EFd
Tombôco **26** Ab
Tombouctou **24** Bc
Tombua **26** Ac
Tomé **39** Ac
Tomelilla **5** Ea
Tomelloso **9** Dc
Tomini **18** Fd
Tomini, Teluk– **18** Fde
Tommot **14** Fd
Tomorit (mt.) **11** Dc
Tom Price **29** Bc
Tomsk **13** Hd
Tomtabacken (mt.) **4** Cd
Tonalá **34** Cc
Tondano **18** FGd
Tønder **5** Ba
Tone (riv.) **17** Gg
Tonekábon **21** Eb
Tonga Islands (Ind. St.) **28** Acd
Tongatapu Group **28** Ad
Tongchuan **16** CDc
Tonghe **16** Ga
Tonghua **16** FGb
Tongjiang **16** Ha
Tongliao **16** Fb
Tongoa (i.) **28** map no.4
Tongsa Dzong **19** Jj
Tongzi **16** Ce
Tónichi **34** Bb
Tonk **20** Ec
Tonkin (phys. reg.) **19** DEd
Tonkin, Gulf of– **19** Ede
Tonle Sap (l.) **19** Df
Tonneins **8** CDe
Tonopah **33** Bc
Tonota **26** Bd
Tons (riv.) **19** Hj
Tønsberg **4** Bd
Toora–Hem **14** Cd
Toowoomba **29** Id
Topaklı **22** Ec
Topeka **32** Bb
Topki **13** Hd
Toplița **6** Gc
Topol'čany **5** FGd
Topolovgrad **11** Gbc
Topozero, ozero– **4** Gb
Torat–e–Heydariyeh **21** FGbc
Torbalı **11** Gd
Torbay **7** Ef
Toréz **12** Ed
Torgau **5** Dc
Tori–Shima (i.) **17** Gi
Tormes (riv.) **9** Bb

Torneälven (riv.) **4** EFb
Torneträsk (l.) **4** DEa
Torngat Mountains **31** Ic
Tornio **4** Fb
Tornionjoki (riv.) **4** EFb
Toro **9** Cb
Toro, Cerro del– (mt.) **39** ABb
Toro, Punta– (cap.) **35** map no.1
Törökszentmiklós **6** Ec
Toronto **31** GHd
Toropec **12** Db
Tororo **25** Dd
Torre del Greco **10** Ed
Torrelavega **9** CDa
Torremolinos **9** Cd
Torrens, Lake– **29** Fe
Torrens Creek **29** GHc
Torrente **9** Ec
Torreón **30** Hg
Torrés, Îles– **28** map no.4
Torres Strait **27** Cc
Torrijos **9** Cc
Torrington **33** Cb
Torsby **4** Cc
Tortona **10** Bb
Tortosa **9** Fb
Tortosa, Cabo de– (cap.) **9** Fb
Tortue, Ile de la– (i.) **35** Cab
Tortuga, Isla la– (i.) **37** Ca
Toruń **5** Gb
Torżok **12** DEb
Tosashimizu **17** Ch
Tosa–Wan **17** Ch
Toscana (reg.) **10** BCbc
Toscano, Arcipelago– **10** BCc
Tossa **9** Gb
Tostado **39** Bb
Tosya **22** Eb
Totana **9** Ed
Totma **12** Fab
Totness **37** Db
Totoya (i.) **28** map no.6
Tottori **16** Hc
Toubkal, Jebel– (mt.) **24** Ba
Touggourt **24** Ca
Touho **28** map no.4
Toul **8** FGc
Toulon **8** FGf
Toulouse **8** DEf
Toungoo **19** Ce
Touraine (phys. reg.) **8** Dd
Tourcoing **8** Eb
Touriñan, Cabo– (cap.) **9** Aa
Tournon **8** Fe
Tours **8** Dd
Towada **17** Gd
Townshend, Cape– **29** Ic
Townsville **29** Hb
Towuti, Danau– **18** Fe
Toyama **16** Ic
Toyama–Wan **17** Ef
Toyohashi **16** Id
Toyooka **17** Dg
Toyota **17** Eg
Tozanlı (riv.) **22** Fb
Trabzon **21** BCa
Trafalgar, Cabo– (cap.) **9** Bd
Trail **33** Bb
Trajan's wall **6** Hld
Tralee **7** ABe

Tranås **4** Cd
Trang **19** Cg
Trani **10** Fd
Transantarctic Mountains **42** grid square no.4
Transcona **33** Da
Transkei (hist. reg.) **26** Be
Transylvania (phys. reg.) **6** FGc
Transylvanian Alps (Southern Carpathians) **6** FGd
Trapani **10** Df
Trasimeno, Lago– **10** Dc
Tras–os–Montes (phys. reg.) **9** Bb
Trat **19** Df
Traunstein **5** Dde
Traverse City **32** Ca
Travnik **6** Cd
Trbovlje **6** Bc
Trebbia (riv.) **10** Bb
Třebíč **5** Ed
Trebinje **11** Cb
Trebišov **5** Hd
Třebová **5** Fd
Tree Pagodas Pass **19** Cef
Treinta y Tres **39** Cc
Trélazé **8** Cd
Trelew **40** Bb
Trelleborg **4** Ce
Tremiti, Isole– **10** Ec
Tremp **9** Fa
Trenčín **5** Gd
Trenque Lauquen **39** Bc
Trent (riv.) **7** Fe
Trentino–Alto Adige (reg.) **10** Ca
Trento **10** Ca
Trenton **32** Dab
Tréport, Le– **8** Dbc
Tres Arroyos **39** BCc
Três Casas **37** Cc
Tres Esquinas **37** Bb
Três Lagoas **39** Cb
Tres Lagos **40** ABb
Tres Picos, Cerro– (mt.) **39** Bc
Tres Puntas, Cabo– **40** Bb
Três Rios **39** Db
Tres Virgenes, Las– (mt.) **34** Ab
Treungen **4** ABd
Treviso **10** Db
Tricase **10** Ge
Trichur **20** Ef
Tridentine Alps **10** Ca
Trier **5** Ad
Trieste **10** Db
Trikala **11** Dd
Trikhonis, Limni– **11** Dd
Trincomalee **15** Ci
Trindade, Ilha da– (i.) **36** Gef
Třinec **5** Gd
Trinidad (i.) **37** CDa
Trinidad [Bol.] **39** Ba
Trinidad [U.S.] **33** Cc
Trinidad, Rio– (riv.) **35** map no.1
Trinidad and Tobago (Ind. St.) **36** DEbc
Trinity (riv.) **32** Bb

Tripoli [Leb.] **22** Ee
Tripoli [Lib.] **24** Da
Trípolis **11** Ee
Tripura (State) **19** Bd
Tristan da Cunha (is.) **23** ABi
Trivandrum **15** Ci
Trnava **5** FGd
Trogir **10** Fc
Troglav (mt.) **6** Ce
Troia **10** Ed
Troick **13** Fd
Troicko–Pečorsk **13** EFc
Trois–Rivières **31** HId
Trojan **11** Fb
Trojansky prohod **11** Fb
Trollhättan **4** BCd
Trollheimen (mt.) **4** Bc
Trombetas (riv.) **38** Ba
Tromelin (i.) **23** map no.1
Tromsø **4** DEa
Tronador (mt.) **40** Ab
Trondheim **4** Bc
Trondheimsfjorden (b.) **4** Bc
Troödos, Mount– (Olympus) **22** De
Trotus (riv.) **6** Hc
Trouville–sur–Mer **8** CDc
Trowbridge **7** EFf
Troy (r.) **22** Ac
Troy [Al.–U.S.] **32** Cb
Troy [N.Y.–U.S.] **32** Da
Troyes **8** Fc
Trucial Coast **21** EFe
Trudovoje [Kaz.] **13** Fd
Trudovoje [Russia] **17** Cc
Trujillo [Hond.] **35** Bb
Trujillo [Peru] **36** BCd
Trujillo [Sp.] **9** BCc
Trujillo [Ven.] **37** BCb
Truk Islands **27** Cb
Truro [Can.] **31** Id
Truro [U.K.] **7** Df
Truskavec **6** FGb
Trutnov **5** Ec
Trysil (riv.) **4** Cc
Trzcianka **5** EFb
Tsaratanana (mt.) **26** map no.1
Tsau **26** Bcd
Tshabong **26** Bd
Tshela **26** Ab
Tshikapa **26** Bb
Tshuapa (riv.) **26** Bb
Tsinan (Jinan) **15** Df
Tsingtao (Qingdao) **16** Fc
Tsu **16** Id
Tsugaro–Kaikyō **16** IJb
Tsumeb **23** Dg
Tsuruga **16** Ic
Tsuruoka **17** Fe
Tsushima **17** Ag
Tsushima (is.) **16** Gd
Tsushima–Kaikyō **17** Agh
Tsuyama **16** Hcd
Tual **18** Hf
Tuamoto Archipelago **28** BCcd
Tuapse **13** Ce
Tuban **18** Df
Tubarão **39** Db
Tübingen **5** Bd
Ţubruq **24** Ea
Tubuaï, Île– (i.) **28** Bd

Tubuai Islands **28** Bd
Tucson **33** Bc
Tucumcari **33** Cc
Tucupita **37** Cb
Tucuruí **38** Cb
Tudela **9** Ea
Tufi **27** Cc
Tuguegarao **18** Fa
Tugur **14** Gd
Tujmazy **12** Hc
Tukangbesi, Kepulauan- **18** FGf
Tūkrah **24** DEa
Tuktoyaktuk **31** BCb
Tukums **4** Ed
Tula **13** Cd
Tulancingo **34** Cb
Tulcán **37** Bb
Tulcea **6** Id
Tulčin **6** Ib
Tuli **26** BCd
Tullamore **7** Ce
Tulle **8** De
Tully **29** Hb
Tuloma (riv.) **4** GHa
Tulsa **32** Bb
Tuluá **37** Bb
Tulun **14** Dd
Tumaco **37** Bb
Tuman-gang **17** Ac
Tumbes **37** ABc
Tumd Youqi **16** Db
Tumen (riv.) **16** Gb
Tumkur **20** Ef
Tumpat **19** Dg
Tumucumaque, Serra- (mts.) **37** Db
Tumut **29** Hf
Tunduru **26** Cc
Tundža (riv.) **11** Gb
Tungabhadra (riv.) **20** Ee
Tungsten **31** Cb
Tūnis **24** CDa
Tunis, Gulf of- **10** Cf
Tunisia (Ind. St.) **23** CDb
Tunja **37** Bb
Tunuyán **39** Bc
Tunxi **16** Ede
Tupelo **32** Cb
Tupiza **39** Bb
Tuque, La- **31** Hd
Tura (riv.) **12** Jb
Tura [India] **19** Jj
Tura [Russia] **14** Dc
Turabah **21** Ce
Turan **14** Cd
Turayf, Aţ- **21** Bc
Turbah, At- **21** Cg
Turbat **20** Bc
Turbo **37** Bb
Turda **6** Fc
Tureia Atoll **28** Cd
Turek **5** Gbc
Turgaj (riv.) **13** Fe
Turgaj **13** Fe
Turgutlu **22** Ac
Türi **4** Fd
Turia → Guadalaviar (riv.) **9** Ebc
Turiaçu **38** Cb
Turin **10** Ab
Turinsk **12** Jb
Turi Rog **17** Bb
Turka **5** Id
Turkana, Lake- **25** Dd
Turkestan **13** Fe
Turkey (Ind. St.) **15** ABf
Türkmenbaši (Krasnovodsk) **21** Ea
Turkmenistan (Ind. St.) **13** EFf
Turks Islands **32** Dc
Turku **4** Ec
Turneffe Islands **35** Bb
Turnhout **8** Fb
Turnov **5** Ec
Turnu-Măgurele **6** Ge
Turnu Roşu, Pasul- **6** FGd
Turnu-Severin **6** Fd
Turpan **15** Ce
Turuhansk **14** BCc
Tuscaloosa **32** Cb
Tutajev **12** Eb
Tuticorin **20** Eg
Tutóia **38** Cb
Tutrakan **11** Gab
Tuttlingen **5** Bde
Tutuila Island **28** map no.5
Tuva (Aut. Rep.) **14** Cd
Tuvalu Islands (Ind. St.) **27** Dc
Tuwayq, Jabal- **21** Def
Túxpan **34** Bb
Tuxpan de Rodríguez Cano **34** Cb
Tuxtla Gutiérrez **34** Cc
Túy **9** Aab
Tuy Hoa **19** Ef
Tuz, Lake- **22** Dc
Tūz Khurmātū **21** Cc
Tuzla **6** Dd
Tvedestrand **4** ABd
Tver (Kalinin) **13** Cd
Tweed (riv.) **7** Ed
Twillingate **31** Jcd
Twin Falls **33** Bb
Tychy **5** Gc
Tyler **32** Bb
Tympákion **11** Ff
Tynda **14** Fd
Tynemouth **7** Fd
Tynset **4** Bc
Tyre **22** Ef
Tyrrhenian Sea **10** De

U

Uaboe **27** map no.2
Ua Huka, Île- (i.) **28** Cc
Ualdia **21** BCg
Uaroo **29** Bc
Uatumã (riv.) **37** Dc
Uaupés **37** Cbc
Uaupés (riv.) **37** Cb
Ubá **39** Db
Ubaitaba **38** Dc
Ubangi (riv.) **26** Aa
'Ubaylah, Al- **21** DEe
Ubayyid, Al- **25** CDc
Ube **17** Bgh
Ubeda **9** Dcd
Uberaba **39** Da
Uberlândia **39** Da
Ubon Ratchathani **15** Dh
Ubsu-Nur (l.) **14** Cd
Ubundu **26** Bab
Učaly **12** Ic
Ucayali (riv.) **37** Bcd
Uchiura-Wan **17** Gc
Učur (riv.) **14** Gd
Uda [Russia] (riv.) **14** Gd
Udaipur **20** Dd
Uddevalla **4** Bd
Uddjaur **4** Db
Udhampur **20** Eb
Udine **10** Da
Udipi **20** Df
Udmurt (Aut. Rep.) **13** Ed
Udon Thani **19** De
Ueda **17** Ff
Uele (riv.) **25** Cd
Uelen **14** Lc
Uelzen **5** Cb
Ufa **13** Ed
Ufa (riv.) **12** Ib
Uganda (Ind. St.) **23** Fef
Uglegorsk **14** He
Uglekamensk **17** CDc
Uglič **12** Eb
Uherské Hradiště **5** Fd
Uhta **13** Ec
Uige **26** Ab
Uil (riv.) **12** Hd
Uil **12** Hd
Uinta Mountains **33** BCb
Ŭisŏng **17** Af
Uitenhage **26** Be
Ujae Atoll **27** Db
Ujelang Atoll **27** CDb
Uji-Guntō (i.) **17** Ai
Ujiji **26** Bb
Ujjain **20** Ed
Ujung Pandang (Makasar) **18** Eef
Ukiah **33** Ac
Ukmergė **4** Fe
Ukraine (Ind. St.) **13** BCe
Uku-Jima (i.) **17** Ah
Ula **11** He
Ula, Al- **21** Bd
Ulahe **17** CDb
Ulan-Bator **14** De
Ulangom **14** Ce
Ulan-Ude **14** DEd
Ulaş **22** Fc
Ulchin **17** Af
Ulcinj **11** Cc
Ulegej **14** BCe
Ulhasnagar **20** De
Ulithi Atoll **27** Cb
Uljanovsk → Simbirsk **13** DEd
Uljasutaj **14** Ce
Ullapool **7** Dc
Ullŭng-Do (i.) **16** Hc
Ulm **5** BCd
Ulsan **16** GHc
Ulster (prov.) **7** BCd
Ulubat Gölü **22** Bb
Uludağ (mt.) **22** Bbc
Ulukişla **22** DEd
Ulungur He (riv.) **14** BCe
Uman **12** CDd
Umanak / Uummannaq **30** MNb
Umatac **27** map no.1
Umbria (reg.) **10** CDc
Umbro-Marchigiano, Appennino- **10** Dc
Umeå **4** Ec
Umeälven (riv.) **4** Db
Umm al Hayt, Wādī- **21** Ef
Umm Lajj **21** Bd
Umm Qaşr, Khawr- **21** Dcd
Umm Ruwābah **25** Dc
Umtata **26** Be
Una (riv.) **6** Cd
'Unayzah **21** Cd
Under-Han **16** Da
Uneča **12** Dc
Ungava, Péninsula d'- **31** Hb
Ungava Bay **31** Ic
Ungeny **6** HIc
Unggi **17** ABc
União da Vitória **39** Cb
Unimak Island **30** BCd
Unión, La- [Col.] **37** Bb
Unión, La- [El Sal.] **35** Bb
Unión, La- [Sp.] **9** Ed
Uniondale **26** Be
Union Islands / Tokelau **28** Ac
United Arab Emirates (Ind. St.) **21** EFe
United Kingdom (Ind. St.) **3** CDb
United States (Ind. St.) **30** GJef
Unnao **19** Hj
Unst (i.) **7** Fa
Unstrut (riv.) **5** Cc
Unter, Île- **27** Dd
Ünye **22** Fb
Unža (riv.) **12** Fb
Upata **37** Cb
Upernavik **30** MNb
Upi **27** map no.1
Upington **23** DEh
Upolu Island **28** map no.5
Upolu Point **28** map no.1
Upper Lough Erne **7** Cd
Uppsala **4** Dcd
'Uqaylah, Al- **24** DEab
Ur (r.) **21** Dc
Urakawa **17** Hc
Ural (riv.) **13** Ee
Ural Mountains **13** EFcd
Uralsk **13** Ed
Urandangi **29** Fc
Urandí **39** Da
Uranium City **30** Hcd
Uraricoera **37** Cb
Uraricoera (riv.) **37** Cb
Urawa **17** FGfg
Urbett Atoll **28** map no.3
Urbino **10** Dc
Urbión, Picos de- (mts.) **9** Dab
Urdoma **12** Ga
Ure (riv.) **7** Fd
Uren **12** Gb
Urfa **21** Bb
Urgenč **13** Fe
Uribia **37** Ba
Urjupinsk **12** Fc
Urla **11** Gd
Urmia, Lake- **21** CDb
Uroševac **11** Db
Uruaçu **38** BCc
Uruapan del Progreso **34** Bc
Urubamba (riv.) **37** Bd

© ISTITUTO GEOGRAFICO DE AGOSTINI S.p.A. - Novara

Vetlanda **4** Cd
Vetluga (riv.) **12** Gb
Vetta d'Italia (mt.) **10** CDa
Vézère (riv.) **8** De
Viacha **39** Ba
Viana **38** Cb
Viana do Castelo **9** Ab
Viareggio **10** Cc
Viborg **4** Bd
Vibo Valentia **10** Fe
Vic **9** Gb
Vicecomodoro Morambio **42** grid square no.1
Vicenza **10** Cb
Vichada (riv.) **37** BCb
Vichy **8** Ed
Vicksburg **32** BCb
Victor Harbour **29** Ff
Victoria (State) **29** Gf
Victoria [Can.] **33** Ab
Victoria [Chile] **39** Ac
Victoria [Mala.] **18** Ecd
Victoria [Malta] **10** Ef
Victoria [U.S.] **32** Bc
Victoria, Lake- **26** Cb
Victoria, Mount- **19** Bd
Victoria de Durango **34** Bb
Victoria de las Tunas **35** Ca
Victoria Falls **26** Bc
Victoria Falls (wf.) **26** Bc
Victoria Island **31** DEa
Victoria Land **42** grid square no.4
Victoria River **29** Eb
Victoria River Downs **29** DEb
Victoria West **26** Be
Victorica **39** Bc
Vičuga **12** Fb
Videle **6** Gd
Vidim **14** Dd
Vidin **11** Eab
Vidisha **20** Ed
Vidzy **4** Fe
Viedma **40** Bb
Viedma, Lago- **40** Ab
Vienna **5** Fd
Vienne (riv.) **8** Dd
Vienne **8** Fe
Vientiane **15** Dh
Vieques, Isla de- (i.) **35** Db
Vierwaldstätter See **5** Be
Vierzon **8** Ed
Vieste **10** Fd
Vietnam (Ind. St.) **15** Dh
Vigan **18** EFa
Vigan, Le- **8** Ef
Vigia **38** Cb
Vigía Chico **34** Dc
Vignemale, Pic de- (mt.) **8** CDf
Vigo **9** Aa
Vihren (mt.) **11** Ec
Viitasaari **4** Fc
Vijayawada **15** Ch
Vijkitski Strait **14** CDb
Vikna (i.) **4** Bb
Viktorija, ostrov- **13** CDab
Vila Franca de Xira **9** Ac
Vilaine (riv.) **8** Cd
Vila Murtinho **37** Cd
Vilanculos **26** Cd
Vila Nova de Gaia **9** Ab
Vilanova i la Geltrú **9** FGb
Vila Real **9** Bb
Vila Real de Santo Antonio **9** ABd
Vila Velha [Braz.] **38** Ba
Vila Velha [Braz.] **38** CDd
Vila Viçosa **9** Bc
Vilejka **12** Cc
Vilhelmina **4** CDb
Vilhena **39** BCa
Viljandi **12** Cb
Viljuj (riv.) **14** Fc
Viljujsk **14** Fc
Villa Angela **39** Bb
Villablino **9** Ba
Villacañas **9** Dc
Villacarrillo **9** Dc
Villacidro **10** Be
Villaco **5** De
Villa Colón **39** Bc
Villa Dolores **39** Bc
Villafranca del Bierzo **9** Ba
Villafranca de los Barros **9** BCc
Villafranca del Panadés **9** Fb
Villagarcía de Arosa **9** ABa
Villaguay **39** Cc
Villa Hayes **39** Cb
Villahermosa **34** Cc
Villajoyosa **9** EFc
Villalba **9** Ba
Villa Maria **39** Bc
Villa Montes **39** Bb
Villanueva de la Serena **9** Cc
Villanueva de los Infantes **9** Dc
Villarreal de los Infantes **9** Ec
Villarrica **39** Cb
Villarrobledo **9** DEc
Villaverde, Madrid- **9** Db
Villavicencio **37** Bb
Villaviciosa **9** Ca
Villazón **39** Bb
Villefranche-de-Rouergue **8** DEe
Villefranche-sur-Saône **8** Fde
Villena **9** Ec
Villeneuve-sur-Lot **8** De
Villeurbanne **8** Fe
Vilnius **4** Fe
Viña del Mar **39** Ac
Vinaroz **9** Fb
Vincennes **32** Cb
Vincennes Bay **42** grid square no.4
Vinchina **39** Bb
Vindelälven (riv.) **4** Db
Vindhya Range **20** DFd
Vinh **15** Dh
Vinh Loi **19** Eg
Vinita **32** Bb
Vinkovci **6** Dd
Vinnica **13** Be
Vinogradov **5** Id
Vinogradovka **17** Cc
Vinson Massif (mt.) **42** grid square no.1
Vir **10** Eb
Virac **18** Fb
Virden **33** Cab
Vire **8** Cc
Virgenes, Cabo- **40** Bc
Virginia **32** Ba
Virginia (State) **32** Db
Virgin Islands **36** Db
Virovitica **6** Cd
Virrat **4** Ec
Virtsu **12** Bb
Vis (i.) **11** ABb
Visalia **33** Bc
Visby **4** Dd
Viscount Melville Sound **31** DEa
Višegrad **6** De
Višera (riv.) **12** Ia
Viseu [Braz.] **38** Cb
Viseu [Port.] **9** ABb
Vişeu de Sus **6** Gc
Vishakhapatnam **15** Ch
Viso, Mont- (mt.) **10** Ab
Vistula (riv.) **5** Gb
Vit (riv.) **11** Fb
Vitebsk **13** Cd
Viterbo **10** Dc
Viti Levu (i.) **27** Dc
Vitim (riv.) **14** Ed
Vitória **39** DEb
Vitoria **9** Da
Vitória da Conquista **39** Da
Vitoša (mt.) **11** Eb
Vitré **8** Cc
Vitry-le-François **8** EFc
Vittel **8** FGc
Vittorio Veneto **10** Dab
Vityaz I Depth **27** Cb
Vityaz II Depth **28** Ad
Vityaz III Depth **28** Ad
Vivero **9** Ba
Vize **11** GHc
Vizianagaram **20** FGe
Vižnica **6** Gb
Vjatka (Kirov) **13** Dd
Vjatskije Poljany **12** GHb
Vjazemski **14** Ge
Vjazma **12** Db
Vjazniki **12** Fb
Vjedinenija, ostrov- **13** GHb
Vjosa (riv.) **11** CDc
Vladikavkaz (Ordžonikidze) **13** De
Vladimir **13** CDd
Vladimirski Tupik **12** Db
Vladimir-Volynski **5** Jc
Vladivostok **14** Ge
Vlašić (mt.) **6** Cd
Vlissingen **5** Bc
Vltava → Moldau (riv.) **5** Ed
Vogelsberg (mt.) **5** Bc
Voghera **10** Bb
Voi **26** Cb
Voinijama **24** ABd
Vóïon (mts.) **11** Dc
Voiron **8** Fe
Vóïviís, Limni- **11** Ed
Vojvodina (phys. reg.) **6** DEd
Volcano Islands **27** Ca
Volčansk **12** IJab
Volda **4** Ac
Volga (riv.) **13** Dd
Volgo-Baltijski vodny put imeni V.I. Lenina **12** Eab
Volgodonsk **12** Fd
Volgo-Donskoj sudohodny kanal imeni V.I. Lenin **12** Fd
Volgograd **3** Hc
Volgogradskoje vodohranilišče **12** Gcd
Volhov (riv.) **12** Db
Volhov **13** Gd
Volinskaja vozvyšennost (phys. reg.) **6** GHa
Volissós **11** Fd
Völkermarkt **10** Ea
Völklingen **5** Ad
Volkovysk **12** Bc
Volnovaha **12** Ed
Vologda **13** CDd
Vólos **11** Ed
Volsk **13** Dd
Volta, Lake- **24** Bd
Volta Redonda **39** Db
Volterra **10** Cc
Volturino, Monte- **10** Ed
Volturno (riv.) **10** Ed
Vólvi, Limni- **11** Ec
Volžsk **12** Gb
Volžski **13** De
Vopnafjördur **4** map no.1
Vorarlberg (reg.) **5** BCe
Vordingborg **5** Ca
Vórios Evvoïkós, Kólpos- **11** Ed
Vorkuta **13** EFc
Vorogovo **14** BCc
Voronež **13** CDd
Vorošilovgrad → Lugansk **13** CDe
Vörts järv **4** Fd
Võru **4** Fd
Vosges (mts.) **8** Gcd
Voss **4** Ac
Vostok **42** grid square no.4
Vostok Island **28** Bc
Votkinsk **13** Ed
Voúxa, Ákra- **11** Ef
Vouziers **8** Fc
Voznesensk **12** Dd
Vraca **11** Eb
Vranica (mt.) **6** CDde
Vranje **11** Db
Vrbas **6** DEd
Vrbas (riv.) **6** Cd
Vršac **6** Ed
Vryburg **26** Bd
Vsetín **5** FGd
Vukovar **6** Dd
Vulcan **6** Fd
Vulcano (i.) **10** Ee
Vúlture, Monte- **10** Ed
Vung Tau **19** Ef
Vuotso **4** FGa
Vyborg **13** BCc
Vyčegda (riv.) **13** Ec
Vyksa **12** Fb
Vyšni Voloček **13** Cd
Vysokogorny **14** GHde
Vysokoje **5** Ib
Vytegra **3** Ga

W

Wāāt Salīmah **25** Db
Wabe Shebele (riv.) **25** Ed
Wabowden **31** Fc
Wąbrzeżno **5** Gb
Wachussett Seamount **28** Bd

© ISTITUTO GEOGRAFICO DE AGOSTINI S.p.A. - Novara

© ISTITUTO GEOGRAFICO DE AGOSTINI S.p.A. - Novara

Wooramel River **29** ABd
Worcester [S. Afr.] **26** ABe
Worcester [U.K.] **7** Ee
Worcester [U.S.] **32** Da
Workington **7** DEd
Worland **33** Cb
Worms **5** ABd
Worthing **7** FGf
Wotje Atoll **27** Db
Wowoni, Pulau– (i.) **18** Fe
Woy Woy **29** Ie
Wrangel Island **41** grid
  square no.2
Wrangell **31** BCc
Wrangell Mountains **31** Ab
Wrath, Cape– **7** Db
Wreck Reef (i.) **29** Jc
Wrigley **31** Cb
Wrocław → Breslau **5** Fc
Września **5** FGb
Wuchuan **16** Df
Wugang **16** De
Wuhan **15** Df
Wuhu **16** Ed
Wu Jiang (riv.) **16** Ce
Wunstorf **5** Bb
Wuntho **19** Cd
Wuppertal **5** ABc
Wurno **24** Cc
Würzburg **5** BCd
Wurzen **5** Dc
Wushi **16** Bb
Wusuli Jiang → Ussuri **16** Ha
Wuwei [China] **15** Df
Wuwei [China] **16** Ed
Wuxi **16** EFd
Wuxing (Huzhou) **16** EFd
Wuyuan **14** De
Wuzhong **16** Cc
Wuzhou **16** Df
Wyandra **29** Hd
Wyndham **29** Db
Wyoming (State) **33** Cb
Wysoke Tatry (mts.) **5** GHd

X

Xainxa **19** Ab
Xai Xai **26** Cd
Xam Nua **19** Dd
Xianggang (Hong Kong) **15** Dg
Xangongo **26** Ac
Xánthi **11** Fc
Xapuri **37** Cc
Xar Moron He (riv.) **16** Eb
Xiamen **16** Ef
Xi'an **15** Df
Xiangfan **16** Dd
Xiang Jiang (riv.) **16** De
Xiangkhoang, Plateau de– **19** Dde
Xiangtan **16** De
Xiangyin **16** De
Xianyang **16** Cd
Xiaogan **16** DEd
Xichang **16** Be
Xieng Khouang **19** De
Xigazê **15** Cg
Xi Jiang (riv.) **16** Df
Xinghai **16** Ac

Xingren **16** Ce
Xingtai **16** Dc
Xingu (riv.) **38** Bb
Xining **15** Df
Xinjiulong **16** DEf
Xinkai He (riv.) **16** Fb
Xinmin **16** Fb
Xinpu → Lianyungang **16** EFd
Xinxian **16** Dc
Xinxiang **16** DEc
Xinyang **16** DEd
Xique–Xique **38** Cc
Xixabangma Feng (mt.) **20** FGc
Xuancheng **16** Ed
Xuanhua **16** DEb
Xuanwei **16** Be
Xuchang **16** DEd
Xuguit Qi **14** Fe
Xuwen **16** Df
Xuyong **16** BCe
Xuzhou **15** Df

Y

Ya'an **16** Bde
Yablonovy Range **14** Ed
Yabrin **21** De
Yacuiba **39** Bb
Yafran **24** Da
Yagishiri–Tō (i.) **17** Gb
Yagoua **24** Dcd
Yakima **33** ABb
Yako **24** Bc
Yakumo **17** FGc
Yakupica (mt.) **11** Dc
Yaku–Shima (i.) **16** Hd
Yakutat **31** ABc
Yakutsk (Aut. Rep.) **14** Fc
Yala **19** Dg
Yalgoo **29** Bd
Yalıköy **22** Bb
Yalinga **25** Cd
Yalong Jiang (riv.) **16** Be
Yalova **22** Bb
Yalu Jiang (riv.) **16** FGb
Yamagata **16** IJc
Yamaguchi **17** Bg
Yamal, Peninsula– **13** FGb
Yambí, Mesa de– (plat.) **37** Bb
Yambio **25** Cd
Yamdena, Pulau– (i.) **27** Bc
Yamethin **19** Cd
Yamma Yamma, Lake– **29** Gd
Yampi Sound **29** Cb
Yamuna (riv.) **20** Ec
Yamzho Yumco (l.) **19** ABc
Yanbu' **21** Be
Yanchang **16** CDc
Yancheng **16** Fd
Yangchun **16** Df
Yangjiang **16** Df
Yangon (Rangoon) **19** BCe
Yangor **27** map no.2
Yangquan **16** DEc
Yangtze River **16** Ede
Yangzhou **16** Ed

Yanji **16** Gb
Yankton **32** Ba
Yantai **16** Fc
Yanzhou **16** Ec
Yaoundé **24** Dd
Yao Yai, Ko– (i.) **19** Cg
Yapen, Pulau– (i.) **27** Bc
Yap Islands **27** Bb
Yapu **19** Cf
Yaqui (riv.) **34** Bb
Yaraka **29** Gcd
Yarí (riv.) **37** Bb
Yarim **21** Cg
Yarkant He (riv.) **13** GHf
Yarlung Zangbo Jiang →
  Brahmaputra (riv.) **19** Bc
Yarmouth **31** Id
Yarram **29** Hf
Yarumal **37** Bb
Yasawa (i.) **28** map no.6
Yasawa Group **28** map no.6
Yass **29** Hef
Yata **39** Ba
Yathkyed Lake **31** Fb
Yatsushiro **17** Bh
Yauca **39** Aa
Yavari (riv.) **37** Bc
Yavi **22** Fc
Yaví, Cerro– (mt.) **37** Cb
Yawatahama **17** Ch
Yaxian **16** Cg
Yayapura **27** Cc
Yayladağı **22** EFde
Yazd **21** EFc
Ye **19** Ce
Yecla **9** Ec
Yei **25** Dd
Yell (i.) **7** Fa
Yellowknife **30** GHc
Yellow River **16** Cb
Yellow Sea (Huang Hai) **16** Fc
Yellowstone **33** Cb
Yellowstone National Park **33** Bb
Yemen (Ind. St.) **15** Bh
Yen Bai **19** DEd
Yenice **22** Ac
Yenice [Tur.] (riv.) **22** CDb
Yenice [Tur.] (riv.) **22** Ecd
Yenki **16** Gb
Yeo, Lake– **29** CDd
Yeovil **7** Ef
Yeppoon **29** Ic
Yerköy **22** Ec
Yeşilhisar **22** Ec
Yesilırmak (riv.) **22** Fb
Yeste **9** Dc
Ye–u **19** BCd
Yeu, Ile d'– (i.) **8** Bd
Yexian **16** EFc
Yiannitsá **11** Ec
Yíaros (i.) **11** Fe
Yibin **16** BCe
Yichang **16** Dd
Yichun [China] **16** De
Yichun [China] **16** Ga
Yilan **16** Cc
Yıldız dağı (mt.) **22** Fbc
Yildiz dağları (mts.) **22** Aab
Yiliang **16** Be
Yinchuan **16** BCc
Yingde **16** Df
Ying He (riv.) **16** DEd

Yingkou **16** Fb
Yining **15** Ce
Yioúra (i.) **11** EFd
Yirga Alem **25** Dd
Yirshi **16** EFa
Yithion **11** Ee
Yixian **16** Fb
Yiyang **16** De
Ylikitka **4** Eb
Ylivieska **4** EFb
Yogyakarta **18** CDf
Yokadouma **24** Dd
Yokkaichi **16** Icd
Yoko **24** Dd
Yokohama **16** IJc
Yokosuka **16** IJcd
Yokote **16** IJc
Yola **24** Dd
Yom (riv.) **19** Ce
Yona **27** map no.1
Yonago **17** Cg
Yona–Guni–Jima (i.) **16** Ff
Yonezawa **16** Jc
Yŏngan **17** Ad
Yŏngch'on **17** Afg
Yŏngdok **17** ABf
Yongxiu **16** DEe
Yonkers **32** Da
Yonne **8** Ecd
York (riv.) **7** Fe
York, Cape– **29** Ga
Yorke Peninsula **29** Fef
York Factory **31** Fc
Yorkton **31** Bb
Yoron–Jima (i.) **16** GHe
Yoshino–Gawa (riv.) **17** Dg
Yoshiwara **17** Fg
Yōsu **16** Gcd
Yōtei–Zan (mt.) **17** Gc
Yotvata **22** Eh
Youghal **7** Cf
You Jiang (riv.) **16** Cf
Youngstown **32** CDa
Yozgat **22** Ec
Ypacaraí **39** Cb
Yssingeaux **8** EFe
Ystad **4** Ce
Yu 'Allîq, Jabal– (mt.) **22** Dg
Yuan Jiang (riv.) **16** De
Yuanling **16** CDe
Yuba City **33** Ac
Yūbari **16** Jb
Yucatán (pen.) **34** CDbc
Yucatán Channel **34** Db
Yuci **16** Dc
Yuendumu **29** Ec
Yueyang **16** De
Yugoslavia (Ind. St.) **3** EFc
Yukon (riv.) **30** Cc
Yukon Territory **31** Bb
Yulin [China] **16** Cc
Yulin [China] **16** Df
Yulin Jiao **16** Cg
Yuma **33** Bc
Yumen **16** Abc
Yumenzhen **16** Ab
Yunak **22** Cc
Yuncheng **16** Dcd
Yungas (phys. reg.) **39** Ba
Yunnan (prov.) **16** ABe
Yunxian **16** Dd
Yurimaguas **37** Bd
Yushan **16** Ee

© ISTITUTO GEOGRAFICO DE AGOSTINI S.p.A. - Novara